Foundations
for
Independence

second edition

Foundations for Independence

second edition

by

Sally Featherstone and Ros Bayley

Foundations for Independence

Developing independent learning in the Foundation Stage

by Sally Featherstone and Ros Bayley

2nd edition, 2006

ISBN 1 905019 48 3

©Sally Featherstone and Ros Bayley, 2001, 2006

British Library Cataloguing in Publication Data

Featherstone, Sally
    Foundations for independence. - 2nd ed.
    1.Early childhood education - Great Britain 2.Effective
    teaching - Great Britain
    I.Title II.Bayley, Ros, 1949-
    372.2'1'0941

    ISBN-10: 1905019483

First published in the UK, 2001, by Featherstone Education.
This edition published in the UK, 2006, by Featherstone Education.

Printed in the UK on paper produced in the European Union from managed, sustainable forests

Featherstone Education Ltd
PO Box 6350, Lutterworth LE17 6ZA, United Kingdom

Introduction

Foundations for Independence is intended as a practical handbook. Although it can be read from cover to cover, there are many other ways in which it may be approached. Some users will want to read the book in its entirety. Some will start with the contents page and dip into the chapters that interest them. Some will flick through the pages and stop at images or words that catch their eye or their interests.

Individual practitioners may be interested in refreshing their view of their setting by starting at Chapter 6 and moving on to the rest of the book from there. Many will turn first to the chapters dealing with aspects of learning, to reinforce existing good practice or to look for ideas for fostering independence in all activities offered. Managers of settings may focus first on the section which addresses their role, or in learning more about the examples of excellence from our own and other countries. Some will wish to concentrate on the history, philosophy and psychology of approaches to fostering independence, which are covered in the opening chapters.

We have tried to write the book with all these uses in mind. We hope that it will provoke discussions about the nature of early learning, giving practitioners and administrators confidence to recognise their successes and to change and adapt practice in the interests of the children and their learning.

Foundations for Independence is divided into four sections and nine chapters.

Section 1: Setting the Scene

Chapter 1 introduces the notion of independence in young children and establishes the context for what follows. Chapter 2 looks at the development of views of the education of young children. It traces the theories which dominate present-day approaches, locating the sources of our continuing emphasis on play, first hand experiences, the outdoor curriculum, socialisation, language and working together. Chapter 3 reviews recent research into how the brain develops and relates this to the education of young children. It also explores contemporary pressures on early years practitioners and settings, and suggests ways of responding to them.

Section 2: Developing Independent Learners

Chapter 4 defines independence, what it is and how it develops, and discusses the essential skills and attributes which support independent learning. Chapter 5 looks at the role of adults in promoting and supporting independent learning, and Chapter 6 examines the influence of the setting and the environment, and describes the conditions children need to become independent learners.

Section 3: Promoting Independent Learning

This section consists of a single chapter, Chapter 7, and is intended mainly for practitioners and managers. It takes key features of the early years curriculum, relates them to Early Learning Goals and, with the help of case studies, gives advice and guidance on providing them in settings.

Section 4: Managing the Learning

Chapter 8 describes two important and influential approaches to the early years, that of the schools in Reggio Emilia and the High/Scope programme. It describes both in action and examines how and why they are so successful in developing independence in children. It identifies common features and suggests what can be learned and adapted to UK settings. Chapter 9 explores some of the issues for managers in promoting independence as a principle of their setting, and discusses involving parents and those outside the setting in developing independence in early learning.

The Bibliography lists most of the works we have used and relied on in writing this book. At the end we provide a quality checklist, Ten Essential Elements of a Successful Foundation Stage. Throughout the book you will find quotations from other works, which support and amplify our approach to the independent learning, and sometimes offer examples, illustrations or further information.

After the first edition of *Foundations for Independence* was published in 2001 we were approached by a number of practitioners who were particularly interested in Chapter 7, which deals with practical strategies for fostering independent learning in the setting. As a result of this we augmented and re-presented the material in Chapter 7 in a highly illustrated follow-up book, *We Can Do It*, which appeared in 2004. Readers who wish for amplification of Chapter 7 are referred to *We Can Do It*.

We are always delighted to hear from practitioners, with their reactions to *Foundations for Independence* and *We Can Do It*, and with their experiences of promoting and supporting independent learning in their settings.

Sally Featherstone and Ros Bayley
January 2006

Contents

Section 1
Setting the Scene

... the promotion and development of independence (is) a key feature of practitioners' work   p14

photo by Ros Bayley

Chapter 1:

independent learning in the Foundation Stage

The independence of the individual is at the heart of a free and democratic society. The capacity to become involved in one's own learning, to take responsibility for it and to manage it are keys to success in school and beyond. So the independent learner is sought, not only by teachers and parents, but by employers and in society at large. What is not so universally agreed is the precise nature of independent learning and the skills needed for it.

> *New research reveals that schools and employers have quite different priorities. Skills which are regarded as 'softer skills' by schools are considered by employers to be far more valuable than the three main key skills (IT, communication and the application of number). Employers listed leadership, organisational skills, confidence and the ability to negotiate as key to success at work. Employers were concerned that school leavers lacked initiative and often had unrealistic ideas about work and poor social skills.   TES 25/05/01*

What, then, is an independent learner? What are the skills needed for independent learning? Why are they important, and how do we encourage their development in an education system which, in the recent past, has emphasised content and cognitive ability, with vital skills for learning following in a very slow second place? Happily, there has recently been some reinforcement and reshaping of the view of learning and social skills. This has featured notably in the guidance from the QCA for the promotion of personal and social education within the statutory curriculum, and the defining and recognition of key skills for older learners. This has

> The National Curriculum Key Skills are communication, application of number, ICT, working with others, problem solving, improving own learning & performance.
>
> *DfEE*

given us, albeit loosely, for the first time a national framework for the development of key learning skills from three to 18. At the heart of these lies the independent learner.

Although we all from time to time refer to 'the children' as an amorphous and characterless mass, we cannot do so for long. The personalities and qualities of each member of a group will so force themselves into our consciousness and our conversation. For the most part, when teachers talk about children, they inevitably talk about individuals, with skills, attributes and attitudes to learning. However, discussion among professionals who work with children won't go on for long before referring to the weight of a multitude of content-laden initiatives, the heavy burden of paperwork and the pressures of increased accountability in performance management, target setting and inspection, all of which can easily focus on 'measuring the easily measurable'. Any programme for developing the skills of individuals will have to compete with such pressures, now extended to settings for children from three years old.

We believe that encouraging and enabling children from an early age to think for themselves, take responsibility for what they do and play a major part in managing their own learning is vital if they are to be successful adults, workers and citizens in the 21st century. To illustrate our point, here are three short studies of children at work in the Foundation Stage. They are all based on real people that we knew well. No doubt readers will recognise some of these characteristics in children they know.

Recognising independent learning

DALBIR

Dalbir walks with great purpose towards her nursery. She urges her mother to walk more quickly. Over breakfast she has been busy outlining to interested members of her family her intentions for the morning, and is extremely clear about how she wants to spend her time.

Obligingly, her mother quickens her pace, conscious that Dalbir is anxious to share her plans with her best friend Adam, and enthuse him with the idea of building a house in the large construction area.

As soon as they arrive at the setting, Dalbir finds her name card and hangs it on the board to register herself. She spots Adam coming through the door and hurries to find his name card for him. As she hands it to him she talks excitedly about her ideas for building a house and they begin to share their plans for the morning. Dalbir listens carefully to what Adam has to say. She realises that he has come to school bearing a selection of boxes which he wants to use to make a model of a dinosaur.

She makes a suggestion. 'I've got an idea,' she says, 'I'll help you with your model and then we could build a house!'

'That would be good,' replies Adam, who seems to like the idea. 'The dinosaur can guard the house! I'll put the newspaper on the table and you get the glue and sellotape.'

There is no hesitation. Dalbir and Adam begin to make preparations for their joint project. They proceed to work with concentration and perseverance, seeking assistance from the adults in the room only when they have repeated difficulty in joining one part of the dinosaur to another. On completion of the model making they carefully carry the dinosaur to the painting area, where they paint it with green and purple paint.

'He can't guard the house 'til he's dry,' declares Adam, who is writing his own and Dalbir's name on a white sticky label. As Adam proudly sticks the label on the model, Dalbir suggests that they should come back for the dinosaur when the house is ready. They hurry away to the large construction area.

GEORGE

George stands in the cloakroom beside his peg, waiting patiently as his mother unbuttons his coat and hangs it up. He seems reluctant to say goodbye to her but eventually he gives her a kiss and lets her go. He stands by the window, waving until she is out of sight.

His keyworker, conscious that he has not yet joined the group, calls him over to sit on the carpet with the other children but George appears not to hear her. Lost in his own thoughts he stays rooted to the spot. His keyworker leaves the group, and taking him by the hand brings him over to sit on the carpet for registration.

Once the register is marked the children take their places at tables ready for a focused teaching session. The adults explain the task and give out materials. Some of the children get started but George sits quietly at the art table, showing little interest in any of the materials. His keyworker asks him what he would like to paint, but he says he doesn't know. She makes several suggestions but

George doesn't respond to any of them. Eventually he picks up the paintbrush and tentatively makes some marks on his paper.

He seems happy to do this and continues until most of the paper is covered. He puts down his brush and waits patiently until an adult helper writes his name in a corner of the paper and helps him take his painting to the drying rack. As they are doing this, another child, rushing to put her painting to dry, trips over and bumps into George, spreading paint on his sweatshirt. George doesn't say anything, he just bursts into a flood of tears. In an attempt to console him his keyworker tells him that they can easily sponge the paint from his sweatshirt. She urges him to take it off but George makes no response. He continues to stand still, crying with renewed vigour. Not wanting him to be further distressed, she peels off his sweatshirt and wipes his eyes with a tissue. In no time at all, his sweatshirt is returned with the paint removed and an adult helper puts it back on for him.

The children are given access to a wide range of activities and, while most of them are keen to get started, George stays close to his base. Eventually he picks up a car and begins to push it backwards and forwards over the playmat. He continues to do this until it is time for snack.

KEVIN

Kevin runs into his reception class. He is pretending to be an aeroplane! His teacher politely asks him to sit down with the rest of the children. Kevin ignores her request and continues to hurtle around the carpet area, bumping into children as he goes. Anxious that the other children should not be hurt, his teacher reiterates her request more firmly. Kevin complies, and sits on the carpet.

As soon as everyone is settled and the register has been called, they begin a shared reading session. The children join in, really enjoying the story of 'Mrs Wishy Washy,' although Kevin's attempts to dominate the proceedings detract from the other children's pleasure. He persistently stands up, waves his arms and shouts out, demanding a great deal of the practitioner's attention.

Following this session, the children are told which groups will do what. While some of the children continue to work with adults on adult initiated activities, others are engaged in child initiated activities, supported by another practitioner. Kevin, who is in this second group, hurtles off towards the sand tray and begins furiously digging in the sand. After only a few moments he has scraped all the sand and most of the toys to one end of the sand tray. The other children at the sandpit have nothing to play with.

'We need some sand too,' says Rosie, as she begins to drag some of the sand back with her cupped hands.

'Get off,' shouts Kevin. 'I need all of it!'

'That's not fair,' persists Rosie, snatching back some of the toys.

Kevin grabs the other end of the sand rake and begins to tug at it. 'GIVE IT ME!' he shouts, but Rosie is not to be beaten. She pulls and twists until she finally manages to wrench the rake from Kevin's hands. Kevin, angered by his defeat, throws handfuls of sand into Rosie's face. With her eyes, hair and mouth full of sand, Rosie begins to howl loudly. An adult hurries over to intervene.

There is probably not much doubt which of these behaviours most practitioners would prefer to see in the children in their groups, or which of these children would be the most rewarding to teach. But what is it that accounts for these three very different attitudes? The home? The setting? Different personalities? You may like to ask yourself these questions:

- What do Dalbir, George and Kevin tell us about the emergence of independence in young children?

- What is the difference between independence and self will? Are they both equally desirable?

- Which of the three children is likely to be the most successful long-term learner, and to make best use of the opportunities of school and adult life?

- Is it at all significant that Dalbir is female and the other two children are male?

- What are the essential skills and attributes that support independent learning?

- Is it nature, nurture or something else that enables children to manage their own learning?

- Is independence something we can affect, something we can identify and provide for?

- How does independence develop? What are the key stages in its development, and what can parents, practitioners and other adults do at the early stages of learning to help children to become more independent?

- Where does independence flourish? What is the best environment for its development?

- Where has the emphasis on independence come from? Is it new?

- Why has independent learning become such a subject of interest in the past few years? What is happening in the education and care of children under 6 to give us cause for concern, and what should we be doing to ensure that independence is enabled, not extinguished?

- Are there schools or school programmes where independence is encouraged and children demonstrate all the skills we value?

We shall return to these questions throughout this book, and try to suggest some answers. Our work in researching and writing has led us to revisit and incorporate the thoughts of some of the people who have most influenced practice in early years education.

specialists (theoreticians, philosophers, child psychologists, researchers, policy makers and practitioners from the 17th century to the present day, including those who enquire into how the human brain works and develops)

current practitioners in internationally recognised schools and systems where the principles of independent learning are valued and promoted

We have also drawn on the thoughts, practice and experience of a wide range of practitioners in the many settings we have been privileged to visit and work with as teachers, consultants and trainers.

In the best practice we have seen, the promotion and development of independence in the Foundation Stage has been a key feature of the practitioner's work. All of them agree that the most valuable tools we can give to children are the abilities to choose, to think for themselves, to negotiate, to work collaboratively, to question, reflect, find out, concentrate and persevere. These are also the abilities which will give children a sound basis for lifelong learning and develop in them the enquiring mind that has always been at the heart of our intentions for them.

The capacity to think and act independently, to assume control of and responsibility for one's own behaviour, require support and good models, particularly from the adults who are closest to the children.

Chapter 1: independent learning in the Foundation Stage

We have identified, both in our research and in this book, elements of good practice in adult roles and interactions with children. We have also included some guidance on involving parents in the discussion of the characteristics of independent learners.

The environment in which children learn is a potent force for helping them develop their independence. We have selected a range of activities and for each we have suggested what can be done to help children manage their own work and learning. We have also linked each with the relevant parts of the QCA Guidance for the Foundation Curriculum.

> Children are strong, rich and capable.
> All children have preparedness, potential, curiosity and interest in constructing their learning, negotiating with everything their environment brings to them.
>
> *Lella Gandini, Reggio Emilia*

Chiefly, however, it is the children themselves whose enthusiasm, energy, wonder and spirit of enquiry must be harnessed and guided in directions that enable them to flex and then confidently fly on the wings of independence. Harnessed and guided, not directed. As John Holt has written:

> *Children are born passionately eager to make as much sense as they can of things around them. The process by which children turn experience into knowledge is exactly the same, point for point, as the process by which those we call scientists make scientific knowledge. Children observe, they wonder, they speculate, and they ask themselves questions. They think up possible answers, they make theories, they hypothesise, and then they test theories by asking questions or by further observations or experiments or reading. Then they modify the theories as needed or reject them and the process continues. If we attempt to control, manipulate, or divert this process, we disturb it. If we continue this long enough, the process stops. The independent scientist in the child disappears.*

John Holt, Learning All The Time. 1989

Supporting the 'emerging scientist' is hard work. It is a sensitive, thoughtful activity, involving us in observation, listening, open questioning, taking risks and trusting judgement. Independence does not come cheap, in any sense. It requires patience, dedication, good planning and preparation and a high quality environment. It also takes strength of mind and purpose if the pressures and prescriptions that society sometimes forces on educators care to be managed in the best interests of the children with whom we work.

... the essential nature of hands-on experience   p24

photo by Ros Bayley

Chapter 2:

the story of pre-five education and the child as independent thinker

It has been said that those who know no history are condemned to relive it. It therefore seemed sensible to the authors in planning this book to start by looking at how we got to where we are today. What are the factors, and particularly who are the thinkers, that have contributed to the context in which we work? And what have some of these thinkers concluded about the questions we posed in the last chapter: is it nature, nurture or something else that enables children to manage their own learning? Where has the emphasis on independence come from? Is it new?

Our visit to some of these great minds is necessarily cursory and brief, and because of this we make generalisations and simplifications. Those who wish to go deeper and to find out more are encouraged to go directly to the works we used, many of which are listed in the bibliography.

In the beginning

Until fairly recently the traditional view of children was that they were miniature adults. As such they possessed most of an adult's characteristics and joined in adult activities. For the lower social classes there was an expectation that children would work, and virtually every family in these groups depended on the contribution of children to the family income. Children had no 'innocence that needed to be protected.' As soon as they were weaned they ate, drank and dressed like adults. They worked alongside their parents, and play was considered a pointless activity, something from which children should be discouraged.

Sturdy carts, small gardening tools, printing presses, looms and furniture which takes to pieces and reassemble ... pencils, scissors, paste, tools and workbenches.

Maria Edgeworth setting out in 1789 the requirements for educating a young learner

Around the turn of the 18th century there began to grow a view that childhood was a stage in its own right: not just a preparation for adulthood but a phase of human development that had a place and a purpose all of its own. Those involved in observing the ways in which children learn became fascinated by the place of play in helping thinking, learning and independence.

A landmark in the emergence of this new view of childhood was the work of the French philosopher and writer, Jean Jacques Rousseau. Rousseau's controversial book on upbringing, *Emile*, was written in 1762. It placed a high value on the freedom of action of the child by promoting 'self or free activity' in an education rooted in the natural world. In Emile's education there were no books, no schools, and all lessons were based on direct experience of and interaction with the outside world Emile learnt by doing, with the help of supportive adults. This philosophy, which has been described as emphasising 'the personal experience of the child, supported by loving encouragement' will be familiar to readers as not being too far removed from what is generally considered good practice today. Its principles were:

that childhood is a sacred period

that a child's first hand explorations are the engine of the expanding mind

that education should be provided through action, with direct and first hand observation

that adults should provide support and guidance rather than the mere teaching of facts.

These views were radical when first written and they aroused much opposition. Today many subscribe to their essence and spirit. We may not realise it, but the principles Rousseau set out in *Emile* still affect the way we work with children. The child-centred approach he promoted forms the foundation of the modern approach to education in the early years. P.D.Jimack, in his introduction to *Emile*, rightly points out that '…many of Rousseau's principles, in particular on the psychology of learning, anticipate uncannily the findings of modern scientific investigators.'

The impact of *Emile* was widespread. It was criticised by many but had a profound influence on the future of both child rearing and education across the world. It was taken up and built upon by the great educational thinkers of the late 18th and early 19th centuries. For example, Pestalozzi promoted the essential foundation of learning within the home in a loving relationship with parents. He founded schools promoting 'natural' education, 'where the innate desire to learn is nourished and curiosity is unfettered.' These schools were characterised by their commitment to hands-on experiences and direct observation,

> A child's explorations are the engine of the expanding mind. It matters little what he learns, provided he understands it and knows how to use it.
>
> *Rousseau, Emile. 1762*

natural equality and personal freedom. The children who attended them were not exclusively the children of the upper or middle classes. Pestalozzi's first school in Switzerland opened its doors to orphans and the children of peasants and helped to promote the principle of education for all.

One of Rousseau's most ardent admirers and eminent followers was Friedrich Froebel. Froebel also emphasised the importance of an early start to education. He gave precise advice to parents in a seminal book for mothers of children from four months old, *Mother Play and Nursery Songs*. Froebel's philosophy and methods were explored and expanded in the kindergarten movement of which he was the founder and which became a worldwide influence, spreading from Germany to Scandinavia and the rest of Northern Europe, the USA, the Far East and beyond.

> Our first teachers of philosophy are our feet, our hands and our eyes.
>
> *Pestalozzi*

Froebel's emphasis on practical experience and play embraced the views of both Rousseau and Pestalozzi. He described the child's needs as being

physical movement

self or free activity and choice

object work with real things (e.g. shells, cones, acorns)

action and direct observation

Chapter 2: the story of pre-five education and the child as independent thinker

creativity through song, dance, drawing and three dimensional crafts

nature study, gardening, cultivation and caring for living things.

And, most importantly, his aims were for the child to learn to live in society (of which the kindergarten provided a model) and to have teachers and parents as guides and helpers to learning

To support his methods, and to make the link between 'free' and 'natural' activities, Froebel created a series of specific, structured materials. He called these 'Gifts and Occupations'. They are described in detail in *Inventing Kindergarten*. These 'gifts', in natural materials of wood, wool, clay and paper, were intended to work together with a series of free and adult-directed activities to expand and confirm children's sense of the pattern, order and beauty experienced in nature. The activities included building, weaving, sewing, cutting, folding, drawing and modelling. All of these remain part of our early years curriculum today, both in child-initiated and adult-directed activities.

> In short sessions of directed play, the gifts were used to create pictures, or structures that fit loosely into three fundamental categories – forms of nature (or life), forms of knowledge (or science), and forms of beauty (or art).
>
> *Norman Brosterman, Inventing Kindergarten. 1997*

The influence of Froebel has been crucial to the emergence of the child-centred approach to early education, now general throughout the western world and in many other countries. Froebel's ideas can be seen in action in, for example, the celebrated child-centred, play-based approaches of schools in Reggio Emilia in Italy, in the High/Scope movement in the USA and in quality nursery school practice in the UK. The best contemporary practitioners uphold the value of involvement, first hand experience, play and talk; and of the adult as co-worker with the child, supporting independence, curiosity and self motivation through sensitive and knowledgeable intervention. There are detailed descriptions of the Reggio and High/Scope approaches in Chapter 8.

> Play produces joy, freedom, satisfaction, repose both within and without, peace with the world. The springs of all good rest within it and go out from it. Exuberant curiosity is the most important learning asset.
>
> *Freidrich Froebel*

Into the 20th century

During the early part of the 20th century two important but conflicting influences on early education became apparent. On the one hand there was the rising and continuing emphasis on child development and a developmental view, the notion of children as having clearly defined needs and interests which develop in a definable sequence; on the other, continuing support for an academic approach, emphasising curriculum content, standards of achievement and improvements in teaching. Readers will recognise that this tension still exists today, in some cases to the detriment of the experiences provided for children. We shall return to this later in the book.

The emergence of psychology as a science in its own right, separate and distinct from its parent, philosophy, led to changes in focus. Psychologists recognised that the characteristics and behaviour of adults are rooted in their experiences as children. Child development, therefore, became a consuming interest of this new science. With this the emphasis changed from 'What is the right thing to do?', the question posed by philosophers, to 'What do people do?' And particularly, what do children do, why and at what stage?

The developmental approach

Among the chief proponents of the developmental approach in the first part of the 20th Century were Freud and Piaget, and later Vygotsky and Bruner. These thinkers and theorists were all interested in how children learn, how they build on early learning and at what stage children become independent in their learning and skills. They based their work on extensive and painstaking observations of young children at play and interacting with adults and each other. The outcome was a range of suggested ways of structuring and referring to the processes of learning.

Sigmund Freud is best known as the founder of modern psychoanalysis. However, the more he explored the problems of adults, the greater became his interest in childhood and the formative influences on young children. He investigated links between gender, family relationships and the ability to learn. He was a pioneer in recognising stages of development, although he maintained that the influence of family is so strong that the progress through the stages of learning and the development of different parts of the personality are affected most of all by the quality of these early relationships. He held that the tension between the unconscious mind (which he termed the id), the conscious rational mind (the ego) and the moral mind (the superego) continues throughout life, and governs the development of conscious and unconscious thought, decision and action and, particularly relevant to our purposes, independence.

Jean Piaget constructed an account of the stages of development of children, which he proposed were common to everyone, universal and invariable. The child learns, he suggested, by continually constructing 'schemas'. A schema is a piece of knowledge about things themselves or, significantly, knowledge of how to do things. Schemas have been described by Cathy Nutbrown as 'repeatable patterns of behaviour, representation, speech and thought' with 'threads of thinking running through them'. Later stages revisit, re-work, test and extend the schemas developed in earlier ones. Piaget linked the developmental stages to broad age bands:

> The newborn acts as if the world is centred about himself and must learn to behave in a more adaptive way. Similarly the young child thinks from a limited perspective and must widen it. Both infant and young child must de-centre (i.e. move away from a view of the world that is exclusively egocentric.
>
> *Jean Piaget*

> the Sensory Motor Stage from birth to 18 months or so

> the Concrete Operations Stage from around two to about 11, divided into the pre operational stage (from two to seven) and the operational period from seven to 11

> the Formal Operations Stage from 12 onwards.

Piaget's observations led him to believe that children under seven, although learning fast about the social world, are unable to think or operate in a theoretical or independent way, or to work with abstract concepts such as space and time. However, more recent work in developmental psychology and investigation into brain function and development appear to question some of these assumptions.

Chapter 2: the story of pre-five education and the child as independent thinker

'Schemas', first described by Piaget, are now accepted as a way of understanding and describing the way children make sense of their experiences and turn experience and action into thought. Thought consists of internalised and co-ordinated action schemas. Cathy Nutbrown, in her book *Threads of Thinking*, explains that schemas, or patterns of behaviour, speech, representation and thought can extend learning as they become fitted into children's patterns of thought.'

We have all observed children becoming interested in and then often obsessed with particular conditions, objects or activities; for example, with enclosure, with circles, with verticals, with trajectory, as experienced in dropping something or throwing it. The unconscious thought is, 'Last time I did this, such and such happened. If I do it again, will it happen again?' Children are constantly hypothesising and testing in this way. Repetition reinforces the learning and makes paths for thinking.

Lev Vygotsky, working in Russia at the turn of the last century (but not translated into English until the 1930's), and **Jerome Bruner**, working in the USA in the 1950s and 1960s, both explored the crucial relationship between language and learning, and the importance of sensitive intervention in the learning process by adults, both practitioners and parents. They argued that it is through the acquisition of language that children's understanding of their environment is transformed. The reports of their research emphasise the three aspects of interaction which are most important in the rapport between adult and child:

> sensitivity to the children
>
> stimulation of the children
>
> the ability to give children some degree of autonomy.

Readers will recognise these as principles adopted by the Effective Early Learning Project (1996).

Vygotsky describes the point of learning where the adult can be most effective as 'the zone of proximal or potential development' or ZPD. The ZPD is the gap that exists for an individual child between what she is capable of doing alone and what she can achieve with help from one more knowledgeable and skilled than herself. It is a point 'within the child's extended grasp', one that is almost beyond reach but not quite. The role of the adult (or a more competent peer) is to provide the support the child needs to reach out, stretch and seize this new element of knowledge or understanding. It is the stretching, the extending to the limits of one's capabilities, which for Vygotsky makes for the most effective learning.

> What a child can do with assistance today she will be able to do herself tomorrow.
>
> *Lev Vygotsky*

Bruner added to this notion the view that any subject can be taught effectively in a sane, intellectual and honest form to any child at any stage of development. He conceived the curriculum as a spiral, containing points to be visited again and again at increasing levels of conceptual difficulty. This, he argued, enables a competent and informed practitioner to present any material in a context within the child's current level of understanding.

Bruner describes the role of the adult or peer in such learning as 'scaffolding' which he defines as making it possible 'for the child to internalise external knowledge and convert it into a tool for conscious control.' He warned against the assumption that the most effective scaffolding would be that provided by an adult; he was particularly impressed by the ability of children to co-teach each other through conversation and demonstration. It is in situations like this, he felt, when children are working alongside and with the help of their peers, that the most powerful learning took place.

Learning should not only take us somewhere; it should allow us later to go further more easily. The most sustained, productive conversations come from a pair of children working or playing together.

Jerome Bruner

Four more 20th century practitioners and their philosophies

An indication of the importance with which the education of young children is generally regarded is the fact that almost everyone has an opinion on how it should be done! Many early years practitioners, building on the work of Pestalozzi, Froebel and their contemporaries, developed views that reflected the continuing interest in how children learn and how best to help them. A range of differing approaches emerged, but when we look for references to independent learning some remarkable similarities can be seen. We have selected four of the most influential to discuss here.

Maria Montessori represents the point of view where children are seen as passive recipients of a rich, stimulating, formally organised setting. **Margaret McMillan** illustrates the Frobellian or 'nativist' view of the child in nature, exploring his environment, supported by a sensitive adult. **Susan Isaacs** took from Freud, Froebel and Montessori and evolved a mixed culture, somewhere between freedom and structure. **AS Neill**, founder and leader of Summerhill School, epitomises the extreme in freedom. Building on Freud and Rousseau, he developed a purist view of the child as developing by taking responsibility for his or her own actions, learning and behaviour. Provided here is simply a taste of the style of each of these key figures, and a few words from each relating to independent learning. It cannot do more than cursory justice to the power of their own writing, to which the reader is referred.

Maria Montessori (1869-1952) trained as a doctor and specialised in working with socially and mentally handicapped children in Rome. She believed that the early stages of learning are the inevitable unfolding of a biological programme, and that within this programme there are special periods when the child is particularly receptive to the development of specific skills and activities. The nurseries that bear her name use a structured approach, employing a methodology where children learn from their own spontaneous actions but in a planned and structured environment, and often through a formal, pre-determined series of activities. Montessori placed an emphasis on real-life objects (furniture, crockery, tools) rather than toys and, unlike most practitioners, she saw no place for imaginative or free play, except within a planned and controlled environment as part of the child's progress towards autonomy.

Take certain objects and present them in a certain fashion, then leave the child alone with them and do not interfere.

Maria Montessori

Margaret McMillan (1860-1931) applied and built on the work of Frederick Froebel. Her approach was characterised by a continuing commitment to developing care and education side by side, with parents as partners and strong links between home and school. In her writings and practice she declared her view that play is a vehicle for education, emphasising free access to a setting which offered both indoor and outdoor environments. She emphasised the value of imaginative play, and the importance of language, story and rhyme. Children should be free to choose their own activities and apparatus, learning to exercise responsible choice. The role of adults was to intervene in order to extend learning. She recognised and articulated the links between learning in the nursery garden and the more formal subjects of the school curriculum (e.g. in science, geography), and stressed the place of song, talk and story in developing literacy and music.

Recognise the teachable moment and intervene at the appropriate time.

Margaret McMillan

Play with other children gives the child confidence in himself ...helping him discover the way in which he can carry out his own practical and imaginative pursuits with others, laying down the foundation for a co-operative social life in the later school years.

Susan Isaacs

Susan Isaacs (1885-1948), who worked mainly in the independent sector, was influenced by Freud. She saw the promotion of the free expression of emotion as the way to support children's development. She combined the methodologies of Montessori and Froebel in an approach that balanced freedom with security, observing and recording what children did, and recognising the ability of young children to solve problems and think and reason in a logical way. Her methods and research directly challenged Piaget's view that very young children were egocentric and unable to reason. Making use of observations and examples from her own work and experience, she argued that even very young children are able to understand and to rationalise in ways that often surprise.

AS Neill (1883-1973) was an ardent follower of Freud. A controversial figure throughout his life, he was seen by some as the high priest of freedom, which he promoted as the key to all educational growth. Many of his critics misunderstood the freedom enjoyed by children at Summerhill, his school, mistaking it for licence and seeing its practice as anarchy. In fact the approach at Summerhill emphasised control, but self control rather than control imposed from without. Neill believed that children could develop only if they were able to make decisions and choices, and that it was the job of educators to put them in situations which required this. Their decisions and choices would inevitably sometimes be immature, and would be seen by some adults as 'wrong'. However, he had faith in the child as 'innately

By and large, parents should bestow as much responsibility as they can upon a child, with due regard for his physical safety. Only in this way will a parent develop the child's self assurance.

AS Neill

wise and realistic', and developed Summerhill as a place where a child was free to do 'anything which affects only him'. His opponents thought that he carried the notion of the child as a free agent too far, but Sir Herbert Read described AS Neill as 'bringing light and love into places where there was once tyranny and fear'.

These four thinkers and practitioners, so different in the detail of their approaches, nevertheless held significant principles in common, and these relate clearly to the child's developing independence.

They can be summarised as:

respect for the child

the importance of observing children before intervening

the development of independence through practical activities and play

the centrality of choice

the essential nature of hands-on experience

the capacity of children to learn from each other and from sensitive adult interaction

the requirement for practitioners to be knowledgeable and thoughtful about child development.

These principles offer a framework, an outline for creating a setting in which children can practice and learn independence. Later chapters will return to this framework and suggest ways in which it may be employed to create a rich and rewarding environment for learning. In concluding we invite readers to consider these questions.

What are the pressures today that distract practitioners from the child-centred approach and principles promoted by the thinkers we have discussed in this chapter?

How well are these principles upheld in your setting (or settings that you know)? Are they as obvious in the documents (e.g. aims, evaluation criteria) as they are in practice? What evidence would you look for in monitoring these aspects?

Summary

The principles of independent learning have occupied the thoughts of early years educators and philosophers since the days of Rousseau in the early 18th century. Their aim has been 'developing the individual into a self disciplined adult'.

Early years pioneers with different views and approaches agree on key principles.

These are that—

- children learn best from hands-on experience and by using natural materials in a stimulating environment where work and play are all one

- learning should take place both indoors and out of doors

- the role of the adult is crucial

- we should always observe before intervening in children's learning

- children go through particular stages, and their learning will be affected by their current stage of development.

Chapter 2: the story of pre-five education and the child as independent thinker

Chapter 3:

recent knowledge and recent pressures

The context of education today is dominated by four important influences which hardly featured at all in earlier times. They are research, increased understanding, comparison and accountability

When Rousseau devised an education for Emile the world was a very different place. Although the industrial revolution was under way, the pace of life and the expectations of the population were not very different from what they had been for centuries. By contrast, the 20th century was a time of great change, the pace of which accelerated in the years following the second world war. Technological development, changes in patterns of employment and the working environment,

The past is less and less a guide to the future. Success in the 21st century will depend on the extent to which we and our children develop the appropriate skills to master each of the interconnected forces of speed, complexity and uncertainty.

Rose & Nicholl,
Accelerated Learning
for the 21st Century. 1997

increased mobility, the growth in the material wealth of many people living in the more affluent countries, the widespread instability of family and personal relationships were characteristics of the closing decades of the last century and have continued as features of the present one. These changes in our working and personal lives have had a profound effect. Some of those which have had the greatest impact on families and children are listed below.

- The increasing number of children whose parents go out to work. Many children are now cared for in settings outside their own homes for part or all of the day. Working parents are often too busy or too tired to play, cook or read with their children.

- The rise in divorce rates. One in three marriages or relationships with a partner turns out not to be permanent. This results in more children living in mixed and multiple families, moving from parent to parent, group to group during the day and week.

- The rise in teenage pregnancies. One baby in ten in Britain is born to a teenage mother. This results in many inexperienced mothers who are thrust into the responsibilities of parenthood before they have yet had time to reach maturity themselves.

- A sedentary lifestyle is increasingly the norm for adults and children alike. Children watch TO, use computers, play in their own rooms or in the rooms of other children.

- Toys and games are increasingly made from man-made materials, giving less experience of the natural world. Natural light and night-time darkness are unfamiliar.

- An increasingly protected environment, where children live safe from all sorts of real or perceived dangers. Many young children never go out alone, even in their own gardens. Children are not encouraged to play in the street or the local parks and fields. Many children are now frightened to be alone. If children are involved in activities or friendships outside their own home they are taken and fetched by adults, even over a very short distance.

- The increasingly protective environment is often a response to living in a more overtly violent society. Of course, the history of humankind is stained with violence and always has been. The appalling atrocities of the 21st century are greater in scale but certainly not in degree from what has gone before. But violence is now much more public. Real life and simulated violence invades everyone's home through television, newspapers, radio and computer games. The emergence of terrorism as a fact of modern life underlines this new threat to young children. Violence is commonplace, and many children, even very young ones, will have watched, over and over again, manifestations of anger, violence and hatred, daily brought into their homes by the most powerful media of communication ever developed. Much film and television drama is built on personal conflict. This is a particular feature of the 'soaps' which regularly head the lists of most popular programmes and are screened well before the watershed. Even in homes where such behaviour rarely occurs, children from an early age see adults being angry and violent towards each other; outbursts described by Daniel Goleman as resulting from 'increased emotional ineptitude, desperation and recklessness in our families, our communities and our collective lives.'

> The ability to control impulse is the base of will and character. The root of altruism lies in empathy, the ability to read emotions in others. And if there are any two moral stances that our times call for, they are precisely these: self restraint and compassion.
>
> *Goleman, Emotional Intelligence. 1996*

> The richer the sensory environment and the greater our freedom to explore it, the more intricate the patterns for learning, thought and creativity.
>
> *Carla Hannaford, Smart Moves. 1995*

- Children's health is increasingly affected by our environment. More children have allergies. Asthma and eczema have increased significantly over the past decade and continue to do so. Reactions to foods, drugs and the environment have been shown to have a striking affect on behaviour. We also live in a society where processed and ready-prepared food is easily available and cheap; where eating is more a fuelling operation and less of a social occasion; and where many of the 'junk foods' that children so love contain artificial colourings and additives, some of which can have dramatic and alarming affects.

- We have lively media which apparently revel in bad news. We have also developed a culture where the consumer is king – or queen – and complaint is encouraged. Out of this has grown a public delight in seeing professionals get it wrong. We live in an era of public service accountability, and the education services have not escaped. On the whole this is an excellent thing. Those who work with other people's children and who

> ... during the period from 2 to 6, children develop the intention to regulate their own behaviour
>
> *Brewer and Campbell, Rhythms of Learning. 1991*

provide an essential service for which those people are paying, whether in the public or the private sector, should rightly be accountable. However, there is a down side. The curriculum for the early years has become more clearly described and outcomes and targets identified. The features of effective teaching are examined and reported in public documents. Practitioners are scrutinised, observed and inspected in a way that has never happened before. All this can inhibit the scrapping of what has been planned and prepared in favour of pursuing a spontaneous idea from a child, which has always been a feature of good teaching and is important in helping to develop independent learning.

While we all recognise the reasons for such changes, and let us not forget that many of them have also a beneficial side, the effect on children's independence and autonomy is profound. Often the only place where children are safe and free to experiment and plan their own activities is in their early years setting. The responsibility for practitioners is to provide opportunities for this; the responsibility for parents is to recognise and support the practitioners' commitment to active and autonomous learning.

Virtually the only predictable trend is continuing change.

L Tsantis, Creating the Future.

In the 2001 RSA Jigsaw Lecture, Professor Colin Blakemore of Oxford University said: 'Whatever is the cause, there is an escalating, self-reinforcing problem of a breakdown of society, a lack of understanding of the needs of others, of the benefits of collaboration, of responsibility, of social conscience, and I think that those are things that children are normally programmed to learn between the ages of two, three, four and five. If it's not happening in the home — and I'm afraid we have to admit that increasingly it is not — then we have to see, and I think formally acknowledge that it is the responsibility of our school system to substitute for what homes are no longer giving adequately to a large fraction of our kids, and to seize the opportunity of these extra two years (the Foundation Stage) to design a curriculum which will build kids who have a better sense of self in relation to others and who know the value of altruism, co-operation, collaboration and social duty.'

All children should be given the opportunity to experience the best possible start to their education.

Margaret Hodge,
Under Secretary of State,
DfEE. 2000

However, we are all under pressure to work faster, do better, meet targets for improvement and test our effectiveness. The result can be a restricted curriculum, narrowed opportunities, and children who, like George, our third example in Chapter 1, learn helplessness at an early stage.

A way of coping with this maze of demands and expectations is to stand back from the day-to-day pressures of our jobs and try to do two things:

1. Find out what we now know about **how children learn**, the way their brains develop and the best ways to help them, and

2. Use this information to strengthen our resolve to **do what we know is right** for the children in our care.

In the remainder of this chapter we explore the most recent findings on the working of the human brain and how it develops, and suggest how best to use this knowledge to help children's learning.

We also look at the implications of the age of accountability; the effect of a National Curriculum, with measurable indicators, where settings, schools, regions and nations can be compared.

> Nearly everything we know about the brain we've learned in the last 25 years.
>
> *Dryden & Voss,*
> *The Learning Revolution. 1994*

And we look at how the discussion of methodologies, practices and principles has re-kindled interest in the way young children learn, and the best way to support them.

What we now know about how the brain works

During the second half of the 20th century there was an unprecedented increase in research and information about brain development – how the brain physically develops and, as importantly, how thinking develops. Most of what we know about the brain has been discovered in the last 25 years.

> We learn 10% of what we read, 15% of what we hear, but 80% of what we experience. Neural connections that don't develop in the first five years of life may never develop at all.
>
> *Dryden & Voss*
> *Ibid.*

The outcomes of this research are staggering in their implications. Let us offer you some of them, taken from books identified in our bibliography. They are generalisations, but are no less arresting for that.

We now know that children who have experienced a rich range of sensory experiences in their first year will have laid down more complex neural networks than children who have not been so stimulated.

We now know that children who watch TO for more than six hours a day are more likely to have a lower IQ than those who watch for less than two hours per day. However, we also know that children who watch for up to two hours a day are better informed, have livelier imaginations and are likely to be more literate.

We now know that there is a measurable connection between active learning (physical play, make believe, word play) and brain growth.

We now know that within the first four years children:

> learn two thousand words
>
> double their brain size from birth
>
> develop 50% of their eventual intelligence
>
> develop preferences for activity and learning which are physically based and gender related.

We now know that young boys are more likely to be competitive, physical, active and independent, to like numbers, constructions and objects, and tend to move frequently from activity to activity, because from birth they are dominated by the right half of their brains. Young girls are more likely to be verbal, co-operative, to have a preference for books, drawing, paint, and to be able to concentrate, because they are dominated by the left half of their brains. We were aware of these behaviours before. Now we are beginning to understand the reasons for them.

We now know that the complex skills of reading and writing (concentration, hand/eye co-ordination, an interest in language, etc.) rely on the development of links between the left and the right sides of the brain. These links develop in girls at around the age of four, and in boys rather later, often as late as six. We also know that five times as many boys as girls have significant reading problems at eight. The question we must ask is — are we pushing boys into failure situations by trying to teach them to read and write when the physical development of their brains and bodies is not yet prepared?

During the recent period of extensive research into the way the brain works, there have been some significant landmarks which can help us in our thinking and our practice.

There is a fundamental human urge to be effective, competent and independent, to understand the world and act with skill.

Margaret Donaldson,
Children's Minds. 1978

Margaret Donaldson's influential work *Children's Minds* was published in Britain in 1978. Her radical propositions concerning the way children think challenged the findings of Piaget. Donaldson asserted that children are already skilled thinkers and users of language by the time they go to school. Far from being those egocentric thinkers in Piaget's observations, children as young as three can appreciate other points of view if problems are carefully explained to them and placed in a familiar context. She also explored children's ability to reason, and the crucial relationship between language development and all the other features of the child's mental growth.

In an echo of Vygotsky's ZPD, explained in the last chapter, the research studied by Donaldson indicated that a crucial task for the practitioner in the early years is to guide the child towards things he can do well, but not too easily, assessing his skills, understanding his confidence and responding to his errors in helpful ways.

If a child is going to control and direct his own thinking ... he must become conscious of it.

Margaret Donaldson
Ibid

She includes a quotation from the poet Gerard Manley Hopkins: 'There is a point within me in matters of any size, when I must absolutely have encouragement as much as crops rain ... Afterwards I am independent.' She also discusses the tension for teachers between freedom and control. Schools and settings are social organisations which require rules and order to function properly. However, one of the ways children develop independence of mind is by experimenting with rules and order. They need a structured environment for learning, where they are respected, where they are not afraid of failure, are 'offered opportunities to learn, to ask their own questions, to express themselves spontaneously and be unconstrained.'

Education should try to preserve the most remarkable features of the young mind – its adventurousness, its generativity, its resourcefulness, and its flashes of flexibility and creativity.

Howard Gardner,
The Unschooled Mind. 1982

At about the same time Donaldson was developing her ideas, **Howard Gardner** was working in America to identify various forms of intelligence and to challenge traditional approaches to schooling. Many teachers and parents have observed the ways in which children might achieve highly in one area but badly in others. Gardner postulated that there are different types of learners and thinkers, and that these are linked to different types of intelligence. In doing so he fuelled a worldwide debate about the nature of learning. This debate links what we have discovered about the brain in the last 25 years with features of early years education accepted by practitioners since the days of Froebel and Pestalozzi.

Accelerated Learning links the new knowledge and understanding of the brain and how it develops with techniques for successful learning. Some of the methods suggested may be seen as common sense and have been known and used by good teachers for many years. They have been popularised by, among others, Tony Buzan, and promoted in schools by Alistair Smith. The proponents of Accelerated Learning promote a curriculum that, as well as building specific basic academic, physical and artistic abilities, stresses:

- enjoyment in learning

- high self esteem

- the importance of training in life skills

- the importance of children 'learning how to learn'.

The Accelerated Learning approach offers the view that 'our homes, beaches, forests, playgrounds, zoos, museums and adventure areas are the world's best schools' (Dryden & Voss).

The echoes of Rousseau and all those who followed him still resound, and the schools where these principles survive against the odds of current pressures are those which we now hold up as examples of quality practice.

The importance of the research is that the brain is plastic. What we have here is an opportunity with children to make a huge difference by being systematic in the way that we provide stimulation. The brain is growing faster at that point than it ever will again in the child's lifetime. We can boost that growth curve by increasing the amount of stimulation by light, sound, touch, movement and the contents.

Daniel Goleman,
Emotional Intelligence. 1996

In 1996 **Daniel Goleman** published the now best-selling work on this topic. He called it *Emotional Intelligence*, meaning by that title to make the point that learning how to manage and direct the emotions is as important as learning how to use the intellect or motor skills. This advanced Howard Gardner's work by presenting a new view of the intelligences he had identified in Frames of Mind.

Goleman argued that the growth of all the intelligences is rooted in the emotions. He suggested that emotional intelligence is the most important key to adult success and happiness. Emotional Intelligence, he maintains, is vital, more important than any of the other intelligences and the factor which has been most neglected in recent years. It's lack, he says, results in 'surging rage and despair, whether in the quiet loneliness of latchkey kids left with the TO for a babysitter, or in the pain of children abandoned, neglected or abused, or in the ugly intimacy of marital violence.'

As well as exploring brain structure and development, Goleman addresses what it means to be emotionally intelligent. He discusses the way a child deficient in emotional intelligence is at risk as he or she grows up. He points out how many of the dysfunctions of contemporary society can be linked to immature and undernourished emotions. He also suggests what schools can do to 'educate the

Chapter 3: recent knowledge and recent pressures

whole student, bringing together mind and heart in the classroom.' He includes examples of school programmes for encouraging emotional intelligence, and the results of research into their effectiveness.

Goleman concludes that effective programmes for developing emotional intelligence in children aged five to 11 need to include certain key elements which cover emotional, cognitive and behavioural skills.

Emotional Skills	Cognitive Skills	Behavioural Skills
identifying and labelling feelings expressing feelings assessing the intensity of feelings managing feelings delaying gratification controlling impulses reducing stress knowing the difference between feelings and actions	self talk reading and interpreting social cues problem solving and decision making understanding the perspectives of others understanding behavioural norms positive attitudes to life self awareness	non verbal (eye contact, facial expression, tone of voice, gesture) verbal (clear requests, responding to criticism, resisting negative influences, listening to others, helping others, participating in positive peer groups)

Goleman's research showed that in comparison with control schools, children who have experienced such programmes demonstrate impressive improvements. The children are:

- more responsible
- more assertive
- more popular and outgoing
- more pro-social and helpful
- better understanding of others
- more considerate and concerned
- more pro-social strategies for interpersonal problem solving
- more harmonious
- more democratic
- better able to resolve conflict.

What are the implications of this research for the way practitioners teach and support the children they work with? How should they recognise and provide for the different ways of learning and differences in gender in their groups? How do they counteract the less desirable influences of modern life on the children they work with?

A massive survey of parents and teachers shows a worldwide trend for the present generation of children to be more troubled emotionally than the last; more lonely and depressed, more angry and unruly, more nervous and prone to worry, more impulsive and aggressive.

Daniel Goleman,
Emotional Intelligence. 1996

Each of the people whose contributions we have discussed has worked with principles developed from a passionate interest in children and the way they learn, and with a conviction that childhood is a special period with its own needs and rights, and not just a preparation for the next stage of the person's development. Their conviction is now supported by the research into the human brain. All the evidence confirms that first hand experience in a context of play, talk and the presence of high quality adult support are still the keys to successful learning, and that what is experienced in the first few years of life will determine not only what we learn, but how we learn, how much we learn and how we can use what we learn.

So why are we all still debating the methodology for nurturing the emerging skills of independent thinking and learning, which are at the heart of educational history? Why are we not doing what has been shown to be correct and what we know is right?

The pressures of innovation

For much of the last quarter of the 20th century, education experienced unprecedented upheaval and turmoil. We saw initiatives from successive governments, the introduction of national systems for accountability and a high level of public interest. National programmes often produced mixed messages, creating stress and confusion. Practitioners have been bombarded with a plethora of guidance on the nature and purposes of the early years curriculum – The Rumbold Report, *Starting with Quality* (1990), *First Class* (1993), The Dearing report (1993), *Quality in Diversity* (1998) and the QCA *Guidance on the Foundation Curriculum* (2000). Each of these documents, while containing some valuable ideas and upholding the accepted principles of early years education, proposed different ways of structuring experiences and different ways of characterising excellence.

> The hardest part of this (increasing autonomy) is standing back and not completing the activity for them.
>
> *Pascal & Bertram,*
> *Effective Early Learning. 1997*

Practitioners, writers and researchers have added their voices to the debate about approaches. Tina Bruce, Audrey Curtis, Janet Moyles, Chris Pascall, Kathy Sylva and many others have observed and interpreted learning in the early years, identifying and recording the curriculum in action, promoting the view that play is the best way to 'learn how to learn'. They also present a unified voice in talking about independent learning as 'the source of technological innovation so necessary for our economic survival', while emphasising the need to protect early childhood as 'a stage in its own right, not just as a preparation for adulthood'.

> Practitioners should plan to encourage children to make choices and develop independence by having equipment and materials readily available and well organised.
>
> *QCA, Curriculum Guidance for the Foundation Stage. 2000*

Both the National Curriculum and the QCA Guidance for the Foundation Stage contain explicit recommendations on the promotion of independent learning as an essential element of personal and social education.

> Children's independence and autonomy need to be promoted. Children should be encouraged to take responsibility for their learning.
>
> *The Rumbold Report,*
> *Starting with Quality. 1990*

The guidance on the Foundation Curriculum has stimulated a debate about planning. Conscientious practitioners in all sectors of early years provision have always planned the environment and the experiences offered, and some have involved the children in this planning. However, the message practitioners have received (from their own observation of teachers in schools, as well as from some OFSTED inspectors and LEA advisers) is this: planning means writing, and writing means deciding well before the event what children will do. The danger then is that the needs and preferences of children become overridden by the plan. The plan becomes the focus, rather than the learning. Practitioners may well feel, 'If I have written this plan in my own spare time, the children will have those experiences, whatever emerges as their real preference or need!' We are not against planning. Planning is essential to ensure that children experience range and balance. But over-rigid planning leads to too much emphasis on adult-directed and adult-led tasks, and too little emphasis on independent, child-initiated learning. This is despite the fact that the QCA/DfES guidance explicitly advocates a good balance between adult-directed and child-initiated activities.

Each of the new reforms has brought its own structures, regulatory bodies and systems for quality assurance and accountability - Early Years Partnerships, SureStart, Early Excellence Centres and so on. Practitioners are encouraged to review, monitor and account for the quality of their settings, using a range of instruments. Performance Management and Effective Early Learning (EEL), and new guidance from OFSTED inspection offer valuable and first hand opportunities for practitioners to carry out extensive evaluation of their own practice in order to recognise success and identify targets for improvement. They do, however, add to the paperwork and the growing discussion about workload.

Belonging and connecting – learning about their membership of groups and the possibility of being, at times, dependent and independent, acquiescent and assertive, of leading and following, in peer groups, family and community.

Early Childhood Forum,
Quality in Diversity. 1998

From the perspective of the play area or classroom it has often seemed that the turmoil of innovation has inhibited rather than enhanced the maintenance of an appropriately independent environment for young learners. Practitioners are caught at the heart of this tension. On one hand they welcome the focus on education, on early learning in particular, and on providing clear guidance on common features of good practice. On the other hand they feel under enormous pressure to perform according to some national blueprint for excellence, on which they will be tested and held accountable. They feel that the demands of accountability and paperwork inevitably take them away from the core purposes of their work – observing and interacting with children. One young Reception teacher summed up anxieties felt by many: 'Yes, but suppose the children don't initiate what I need them to in order to learn what they have to?' Is it any wonder that even experienced early years practitioners are confused and lacking confidence? Practitioners who know what children need are somehow cautious and anxious about providing it. Why should it be so difficult to do what we know is right?

Problem solving involves an enquiring mind and a natural curiosity and in this respect children are natural problem solvers.

Audrey Curtis, The Curriculum for the
Pre-School Child. 1960

In 1997, the feelings of two experienced Reception teachers in a primary school involved in the EEL Project were described like this: 'Recent changes, mostly emanating from outside the school, had left them less sure about their abilities and they worried that they often were being asked to do things which they felt were not suited to the needs of their children. They were losing confidence, and their commitment to the system – although not to the children – had become increasingly doubtful ... The management of the school perceived the 'real business' of the reception class to be predominantly cognitive development, and this should be narrowed down more prescriptively to focus on National Curriculum objectives – a reality which was very different from the rhetoric of the school's public statements.'

These teachers were experiencing a feeling common to many of their colleagues at the time, a feeling that has persisted and increased in direct proportion to the pace of educational change.

Seven areas of pressure

One way of dealing with pressure is to face up to it and organise it. These are the areas of pressure currently identified by practitioners.

1. We are all so different

The range of settings within the Foundation Stage is enormous – from the childminder in a network to the Reception class in a large primary school; from the pre-school in multi-use accommodation, where every piece of equipment must be put out each session and put away again at the end, to the purpose-built nursery. The range of qualifications in these settings is also huge. For example, a growing teacher shortage is resulting in some cases in the drafting into the Foundation Stage of teachers whose entire training and careers have been with a different age group. Working towards a consistent model of good practice will take time, effort and training. Meanwhile, there is a danger that the practical nature of the curriculum will be lost and the experiences of the children impoverished.

PSHE and citizenship help to give pupils the knowledge, skills and understanding they need to lead confident, healthy, independent lives and to become informed, active, responsible citizens.

National Curriculum 2000

By the end of the Foundation Stage "you should expect to see children keen to learn, developing confidence and independence, independence in dressing and undressing, an ability to select and use activities and resources with independence."

OFSTED, Inspecting Subjects 3-11. 2001

The (EEL) project helped me to see that standing back and watching is just as important as helping and taking over.

Pascal & Bertram, Effective Early Learning. 1997

2. Children spend different lengths of time with us

The age at which children start the Foundation Stage and the length of time they spend in it depends on when they were born and where they live. There is still little recognition of the implications of this for the mental and emotional growth of children and their subsequent progress through the education system.. The balance of time spent in statutory provision (e.g. in nursery or reception classes) and in voluntary, private or independent settings (e.g. in pre-schools, playgroups, private nurseries, with childminders) also varies greatly from area to area and child to child. This makes matching opportunities to abilities even more complex, especially when national indicators are age related.

3. What is happening to the statutory school age?

The Foundation Curriculum for three to six year olds now straddles compulsory and non-compulsory phases of education. Children reach their entitlement to statutory schooling the term after their fifth birthday. 'The last year of the Foundation Stage is often described as the reception year, since most children are admitted to the reception class of an infant or primary school at some point during that year. The introduction of the Foundation Stage does not change the point at which attendance at school is compulsory.' However, there is a continuing debate about the appropriate age for children to start formal school, and a general feeling that a more appropriate age for this might be the end of the Reception year, thus bringing the UK into line with most European countries.

> The importance of appropriate communication, language and literacy learning in the early years cannot be overestimated. Early literacy impacts on the development of thought, feelings and relationships as children are helped to develop confidence, skills and independence with the written word.
>
> *QCA, Curriculum Guidance for the Foundation Stage. 2000*

Meanwhile, there are still confused and confusing messages about the nature and progression of the early years curriculum. Some of these emanate from OFSTED and LEAs, and many affect Reception or mixed-age classes in primary schools. The problems and tensions of transfer to the statutory curriculum are now being addressed by Government and Local Authorities, but teachers in Reception classes (and the practitioners in other settings with whom they work) are often still under pressure from a range of quarters to meet inappropriate targets for the National Curriculum, rather than meeting the needs of individual children by recognising their stage of development, not merely their chronological age. The emphasis when requesting pre-school information is often on literacy and numeracy, with personal and social education, play and independence given much less weight. Recent developments in identifying guidance for the Early Years Foundation Stage and the Reviews of the National Literacy and Numeracy Strategies may make a change to Statutory School Age less urgent.

> Well planned play is a key way in which children learn with enjoyment and challenge during the foundation stage
>
> *QCA, Curriculum Guidance for the Foundation Stage. 2000*

4. What about mixed-age classes?

Many classes in maintained schools contain children in the Foundation Stage alongside those in Key Stage 1. The quality of this type of provision was reviewed by OFSTED in 1993, when *First Class* raised issues about education in Reception classes in primary schools. The report found many things to praise, but also voiced concern about the way Reception was often seen merely as preparation for starting the National Curriculum. There was premature use of and over-dependence on worksheets and a lack of emphasis on speaking and listening. In one in five classes OFSTED found 'a lack of involvement in children's learning' and 'in one in four schools there was an over-emphasis on sedentary tasks.' The report remarked that unsuitable maths schemes were in use in many classes, resulting in 'little worthwhile mathematical learning.'

It also noted lacking or inappropriate resources: 'Rarely were schools able to make good provision for outdoor play ... or other valuable learning activities for example with sand and water'. The report concluded that the quality of learning through play 'presented rather a dismal picture. Fewer than half the teachers fully exploited the potential of play. In more than one third of schools, play was only recreational; it lacked educational purpose. It was largely ignored by adults, but was sometimes regarded as a useful time filler when pupils were tiring of the main work. Play was used as a reward for finishing work or as an occupational or holding device.'

In many schools these messages have still not been heard, and despite the very helpful guidance on the Foundation Stage, there is still some pressure on teachers of Reception classes to restrict play and practical activities to the afternoon 'when work is finished.'

Children became more involved in the afternoon sessions, when they were allowed more freedom and choice. Morning sessions tended to be more teacher centred and more formal.

Pascal & Bertram,
Effective Early Learning. 1997

The situation has improved recently. We now have Birth to Three Matters - a framework to support children in their earliest years (SureStart 2002) a proposal for a combined Framework for learning from birth to five in the Early Years Foundation Stage (DfES 2005) and national guidance on continuity and progression (Continuing the Learning Journey, DfES/QCA, 2005). These should all help settings and schools to ensure that the curriculum fits the child, rather than the child fitting the curriculum.

Researchers gave the highest praise to nursery schools and classes.

5. What about the effects of the Literacy and Numeracy Strategies?

The Literacy and Numeracy Strategies have been implemented in all maintained schools in England, and their effect on Reception classes has been dramatic in moving children into a formal teaching programme at a very early (and, many would say, inappropriate) age. The structure of the programmes is based on age related indicators and takes little account of children's stages of development, or the latest research on the development of the brain. The result is considerable 'top down' pressure, particularly in primary schools.

Melhuish & Sylva,
Social, Behavioural and Cognitive Development. 2001

In the reception class numeracy (and literacy) lessons will often include, or be based upon well planned opportunities for children's play.

Guidance on the Organisation of the Literacy & Numeracy Strategies, DfEE. 2000

More sensitive and helpful guidance has recently been circulated, which Foundation Stage practitioners are now advised to follow. However, at the time of writing the documents have not yet been widely available to practitioners and some settings are still getting mixed messages from their managers and advisers, and from inspectors. There is also a lack of clarity on the application of the Guidance in settings catering for younger children in the Foundation Stage. These settings are often under pressure to implement the early stages of the strategies inappropriately. One can only hope that the reviews of the NLNS (National Strategies) will help to clarify the position.

6. How do we convince parents that a change in emphasis to a more practical approach is right for their children?

Parents' expectations are not only more clear since the introduction of the National Curriculum, they are often more focused on the standards achieved by their children, rather than the quality of their experience. A recent article in *The Times Educational Supplement* reported children as young as two being sent by their parents to private tutors. Parents also feel that early years experience in a pre-school, playgroup or nursery is somehow different from the experience in a school. As children move into school, parents expect 'play' to stop and 'work' to start, and this perception has only been reinforced by what has happened to the school curriculum since the implementation of the Literacy and Numeracy Strategies and the emphasis on outcome indicators.

Most parents want their children to be happy in school, but their expectations are now often linked with an academic target reached or a National Curriculum level gained. Differing expectations of different types of setting still remain, and there is a perception that 'school is best', despite the evidence from research that children gain the greatest long term benefit from time spent in nursery settings and in designated nursery classes in infant or primary schools.

> Practitioners should "provide resources that inspire children and encourage them to initiate their own learning ... They should plan sessions to include adult and child-planned activities with uninterrupted time for children to work in depth.
>
> *QCA, Curriculum Guidance for the Foundation Stage. 2000*

7. How are we going to manage the expanding number of places, settings and qualifications for practitioners, while ensuring high standards in all?

The Government's commitment to expanding the number of places available for three and four year olds and the encouragement of diversity in provision have resulted in a wide variation in standards, approaches, methodology and staff training. Even within the same setting the quality of the provision caries from room to room and even from one part of the day to another. For example, a recent OFSTED survey has noted that in a significant number of the organisations visited the earlier and later sessions were of lower quality than the sessions offered during the core hours.

While applauding the principle of equal access to early education, we must hope that this unevenness in quality is a short-term problem. Nevertheless, it is an issue which must be faced by Early Years Partnerships and SureStarts, local authority officers, OFSTED and practitioners themselves. The provision of a common framework for the curriculum and the increase of joint training has gone only part of the way in addressing this issue.

Charles Handy, writer and thinker, said of managing change: 'If anything is to happen ... it has to start with us, individually, in our own place and time. To wait for a leader to guide us into the future is to be forever disillusioned.'

We would only add that looking at the children you work with, finding out what they already know and can do, and planning to meet their needs will help you to find that place to start.

> How are you addressing the pressures outlined in this section?
>
> Have you located and incorporated the latest guidance from the government, your local authority, your partnership?
>
> How are you managing a conversation with parents about the value of a play-based and experiential curriculum?
>
> How are you finding our about and learning from good practice elsewhere, such as Reggio Emilia, High/Scope, The Thomas Coram Centre and other Early Excellence Centres?

Summary

Brain research has shown us the importance of the early years in establishing what sort of person we grow up to be, both intellectually and emotionally.

Children learn more in the first five years of life than they will ever learn again.

Pressures of accountability have resulted in a narrowing of the curriculum for some under-fives. They have become more dependent on adults, more passive in their learning, and many are experiencing more direct teaching and less of the explorative learning necessary at this stage. The introduction of the Foundation Curriculum can and should be used to defend the rights of young children to develop all aspects of learning in a way that is appropriate to their age and stage of development.

Section 2
Developing
Independent Learning

... ride trikes with enthusiasm and growing expertise   p47

photo by Sally Featherstone

Chapter 4:

what helps a child to become an independent learner?

What are the essential skills and attributes which support independent learning?

How does independence develop? What are the key stages and what can adults do to help?

This chapter explores the nature and development of independence in young children. It includes descriptions of the aptitudes and skills associated with the child's developing independence from a range of perspectives, and the key stages in the emergence of independence from birth to five or six years old.

What is an independent learner?

A good place to start with a 'What is...?' question is a dictionary. A dictionary definition of independent is: 'autonomous; not depending on authority or control; self-governing; not depending on another person for one's opinion.' A dictionary definition of autonomous is: 'acting independently or having the freedom to do so.'

Quality in Diversity described the process of becoming independent through play like this: 'By their play, children are learning about themselves, about who they are and what they might become. They experiment with what they can do without fear of failure. They develop confidence, a sense of self worth and identity. They make and break their own rules. They try out different roles, explore and challenge stereotypes. They learn to communicate with increasing skill and confidence.'

> All the evidence that's been published is that formal instruction in language and in mathematics before about the age of seven or eight does not pay off in terms of long term benefits.
>
> *Colin Blakemore, RSA Lecture. 2001*

Identifying the key skills and attributes of independence is a useful starting point for a review of your present work. Practitioners should regularly confirm their view of independent learning and children's autonomy both as a monitoring activity and as a re-establishment of the aims for their setting in developing the whole child.

We asked a number of practitioners and others with experience of young people to list the qualities and describe the behaviours which were characteristic of children who could be termed independent learners. The selection is not an exhaustive one. Nor is it necessarily the one you might come up with – although we hope it has some elements in common with yours. It is an attempt to define some of the qualities, skills and attitudes which many parents and most practitioners seek to encourage in children, and value when they see them. The list which follows provides a framework for review and a checklist for improvement which can be used by an individual or applied across a setting. Having this or another description by us and making regular reference to it will have a direct impact on the way we work.

An independent learner –

asks questions

S/he is a child who is interested in everything and wants to know more, asking relevant questions and taking real notice of the answers.

is a problem solver

S/he is a child who shows initiative, thinks things out and tries new solutions, learning from mistakes and errors.

is a creative thinker

S/he is a child who uses equipment, resources, language and people in a creative way, combining materials and methods, constructing things and developing ideas.

is confident

S/he is a child who relates easily to adults and other children, is not afraid to try new things, speak to a group of known companions, choose a new activity.

can make choices

S/he is a child who can consider options, take time to choose, articulate needs and sustain interest in a chosen activity.

has a positive, 'can do' attitude

S/he is a child who will 'have a go', will take reasonable risks, copes well with initial failure on the way to success.

makes learning links

S/he is a child who makes connections, sees relationships and links personal experiences into real learning.

is self motivated

S/he is an intrinsically motivated 'self starter', a child who does not need encouragement to get involved in learning.

has high self esteem and a good self image

S/he is a child with a good opinion of his or her own worth, who values family, community and culture and who confidently expects to do well.

helps others

S/he is a child who readily helps others in the setting, offering assistance and support to younger or less confident children and is willing to share responsibility with them.

sets their own goals

S/he is a child with clear intentions and a good idea of how they can be achieved; s/he works hard at each stage to carry them out.

wants to understand

S/he is a child who is evidently engaging with the world, who is working hard at learning.

Chapter 4: what helps a child to become an independent learner?

wants to achieve

S/he is a child who enjoys learning and learns for its own sake, not just to please an adult, who sustains attention and concentration, who adapts and adjusts when things go wrong and who uses reference materials, books, ICT, to help in learning and to pursue interests.

uses teachers and other adults

S/he is a child who readily and easily turns to the adults in the setting and at home to help with and join in learning.

can find and select their own materials

S/he is a child who shows initiative; who does not wait to be given materials and equipment but organises space and apparatus with clear purposes in mind.

has interested parents who give encouragement at and from home

S/he is a child who receives a single message from the adults in his or her life – a message of support, encouragement and value for what they have tried to do and what they have achieved.

Most early years practitioners and many parents would probably come up with similar lists. The attributes, qualities and skills identified here are familiar to us all and are surely what we all want to see for all children. They would be as recognisable and supported by those whose work is celebrated in Chapter 2 as they are by you today. However, they do not emerge in every setting or in every child unless we first identify them and accept their value, and then put in place a framework that will help them to grow. We must then trust the children to take their own risks, manage their own activities and identify and concentrate on the things that are important to them. Doing this will affect the whole context of your work – the style of teaching and learning in your setting, the organisation of the resources, the pattern of the day, the grouping of the children, the role of the adults and your relationships with parents.

Children are individuals and need respect. A child has the right to hold their own views and should be encouraged to do so. An adult only has the right to stop a child experimenting ... if it is harmful to themselves or others.

Judy Miller,
Never Too Young. 1996

- What does this description mean for you and your setting?

- Do you encourage children to ask questions, take reasonable risks, solve problems and find things out for themselves?

- Do you make resources and equipment available so children can select and pursue their own learning?

Through acquiring these skills, children can, with our help, perceive that they are effective and competent people.

Audrey Curtis,
A Curriculum for the Pre-School Child. 1960

- Do you value the skills and attributes of independence, by noticing them, demonstrating them yourselves and talking about them with parents?

- Do you ask open questions, which allow children to pursue their own answers?

How does independence develop?

Before moving on to how we encourage and support the independent learner, we think it will be helpful to spend some time reviewing how independence develops in the early years.

Evidence from research confirms what we have all experienced and observed; children need and rely on parents, or parent substitutes, particularly when they are very young. Without them they may fail to play, to sleep well or to make good relationships with others later in life. During the first three months of life, a baby is more likely to cry if alone than when near her mother. She is least likely to cry when actually being held by her mother. Mothers have a biological need to be near their babies, and babies need to be near their mothers. Each one is anxious when the other is out of sight.

Knowing that adults, space, time and materials will be constant, the same today as yesterday, helps young children to assume more responsibility for what they do and to follow their own threads of thinking and doing without unnecessary hindrance or over-dependence on adults.

Cathy Nutbrown, Threads of Thinking. 1999

John Bowlby warned that children are in danger of failing to develop healthy relationships in later years if they lack warm and continuing attachment when they are young. More recent research indicates that in order to flourish children do not need to be with their own parent for every moment of every day, and that children can relate to several parent figures or carers equally. However, at this early stage of life the relationship with parents (or parent figures) is the single most important influence on a child, emotionally dependent on parents for at least the first year of their lives.

Jean Piaget, some of whose work we outlined in Chapter 2, used a range of questions tailored to the particular child and followed an interview model rather than a test. In contrast to what was considered normal practice in dealing with children, he interviewed many who were old enough to enter into conversation.

Mother love in infancy is as important for mental health as are vitamins and proteins for physical health.

*John Bowlby,
Childcare and The Growth of Love.
1990*

From his research, Piaget developed theories of learning and a developmental progression which had a major influence on thinking during the 20th Century. Chapter 2 introduced two major threads which are particularly relevant to the subject of this book. The first of these is the principle of schemas or mental structures, which help children to adapt to and learn from their environment. The second is that children progress through a sequence of stages of development. These stages are loosely associated with age bands, but Piaget stressed that different children may move from stage to stage at different ages.

The main developmental stages Piaget identified in children under seven are:

Stage 1 - before the age of two (the sensory motor period)

Piaget proposed that babies are born with schemas or instinctive patterns of behaviour for sucking, grasping, etc., and that these are at the centre of their development during the first two years. During this time they depend on adult carers for all their needs, and the simple schemas are triggered and reinforced through feeding, cuddling and becoming familiar with objects and events. As young babies explore, experiment, practise and begin to make sense of the detail of objects and events, they gain

> ... a schema is a pattern of repeatable behaviour into which experiences are assimilated and that are gradually co-ordinated.
>
> *Athey, in Threads of Thinking.*
> *1999*

more knowledge and understanding of the world around them. In doing so they adapt and develop their simple schemas to accommodate their new experiences.

Stage 2 — between the ages of about two and seven (the pre-operational period)

By the age of two children have a wide experience of objects and activities. However, Piaget suggested that children in the pre-operational stage have not yet established the differences between animate and inanimate objects. Animism — attributing life to inanimate objects — is a predominant feature of this stage. A young child who could not remove her shoe exclaimed in exasperation, 'Let go, shoe!'. The child who falls will blame the table for bumping his head. These behaviours are typical of the animism characteristic of this stage.

Piaget believed that pre-operational children, although more aware of themselves as individuals, are generally unable to take into account the point of view of others around them. In the early part of this stage a child will play alone or in parallel with other children, even when in a group. Later on she will join in with others as they play, but her egocentricity will encourage her to dominate the situation and this will often result in friction as individuals jockey for position in the group. Piaget always maintained that children under seven are physiologically and psychologically unable to take another's point of view into account.

> ... an infant's capacity for attachment is not like a cake that has to be shared out. Love, even in babies, has no limits.
>
> *Rudolph Schaffer, Social*
> *Development. 1996*

> The newborn acts as if the world is centred about himself.
> The young child thinks from a limited perspective ... both must de-centre.
>
> *Jean Piaget*

In Chapter 3 we noted that more recent experts in child development, for example Margaret Donaldson and Daniel Goleman, have questioned some of Piaget's conclusions about the behaviour of children at the pre-operational stage. There is now evidence that children's ability to empathise and see other people's points of view emerges much earlier than Piaget thought.

Recent research has helped us to construct a more precise sequence of development, bearing in mind that relating these to ages will always be fraught with difficulty and danger! In an attempt to head off controversy and dissent we want to establish two key points.

1. Children differ. The elements of independence appear at different ages in different children, even in the same family and even in those who have enjoyed the same stimulus and support in their early years setting. The stages we describe are broad and should be taken as applying to children in general. They are not tests for individuals, and there will be many exceptions.

2. There are several major areas of independence. For example, self esteem and relationships with others (developing as an independent person); life skills (developing the skills of independent living, such as feeding, dressing, etc.); learning how to learn (using experiences and the environment for learning, finding the things you need, asking for help, co-operating with others, etc.). A child may exhibit different stages of development in some or all of them.

Band 1: The first two years – the age of emerging independence

By about 18 months, most children have made attachments to at least one other person as well as their mother (father, brother, sister, grandparents, childminders and key workers all feature here). This stage is not a deepening dependence, but a beginning of independence, the moving on from reliance on one person to interaction with a wider group, but with no lessening of attachment to their mothers.

...babies' brains are growing fast and that the brain develops as it responds to streams of input coming from the baby's surroundings.

Goldschmeid & Jackson,
People Under Three. 1994

As well as recognising a wide range of familiar individuals, the child has learned to anticipate happenings during his day, establishing a rhythm of activities and events.

Evidence of growing independence at this stage will include attempting to drink from a bottle or cup he holds himself, or holding a spoon and bringing it to his mouth. The child will help when you dress him by holding out his arms or feet. He will reach out for objects and toys, and he can occupy himself with these for a while when he wakes after a nap. He is able to play for short periods by himself, using familiar objects which he can select, handle and explore himself. He is able to walk alone for short distances, although sometimes needing to hold on to furniture or a willing hand.

If his attention is captured (for example with a treasure basket) he can concentrate for long periods on choosing objects and investigating them. This is crucial experience in developing skills of investigation and learning how to learn.

By the time a child reaches her second birthday, she has usually mastered the fundamentals of spoken language and she is experimenting with words, phrases and sentences. She has a vocabulary of around 200 words and often learns two or three new words each day. She attaches words to objects in real life and through simple pictures in books. She is much more mobile, and may also be developing a growing independence in daytime toileting, washing and grooming and in making simple choices.

When presented with a treasure basket attention may last up to an hour or more.

Goldschmeid & Jackson,
People Under Three. 1994

Our two year old's early assertions of her independence can sometimes look like sheer wilfulness, and this often leads to altercations with other children and with adults. Not for nothing has this stage been called 'the terrible twos'! Life seems like a never-ending series of compromises, explanations and defusions of confrontation. She is old enough to have an opinion, but has not yet developed any sense of proportion. Neither is she willing to negotiate or compromise. She has not yet learnt to delay gratification. She usually has clear ideas of what she wants, and what she wants she wants now. As she becomes more verbal, parents and other carers swing between delight and despair – delight in her achievements and despair at her determination to have her own way!

The ability to choose wisely is something which children need appropriate opportunities for doing from very early days.

Goldschmeid & Jackson,
People Under Three. 1994

Sadly it is around this time that children often collect their first smack from an exasperated adult. But let us look at what is going on. It is at this stage that the child is laying down the brain pathways which will in time enable her to negotiate

Chapter 4: what helps a child to become an independent learner?

Chapter 5:

how adults can help and support children's independence

The previous chapter looked at how independence in young children manifests itself and the stages of development they go through in acquiring it. It is important to understand these. Children cannot respond to or take advantage of opportunities to develop independence unless they are offered at the appropriate stage. By planning and providing a rich array of materials and activities at suitable times, and supporting the children's thoughtful interaction with these in a variety of contexts, we can promote independence of both thought and action. This chapter looks at how we create and present the conditions in which the independent learner may grow and flourish. In other words, what we as adults need to say and do.

In *Creating Kids Who Can*, Jean Robb and Hilary Letts list the following pre-requisites for self direction, saying that 'Children will become self directed if they develop:

self reliance (relying on their own abilities)

self belief (having their own opinions)

self determination (making their own decisions)

self awareness (knowing themselves and how they feel)

self respect (having a sense of their own dignity and worth)

self control and self-restraint (ability to exercise restraint over their feelings and emotions)

self motivation (having their own incentive to do things)

self assertion (putting forward their own opinions)

self discipline (disciplining their own feelings or desires).'

> What a child can do with assistance today, she will be able to do by herself tomorrow.
>
> *Lev Vygotsky,*
> *Thought and*
> *Language. 1962*

We can recognise these as the characteristics of a well-adjusted and effective adult. So as practitioners we have many things to think about, including the steps we take to promote these dispositions in children. We will examine the implications of the Robb and Letts list under six broad headings:

self confidence and self respect (including self awareness)

self motivation

self reliance and the ability to makes one's own decisions (including self determination)

self discipline and self control

assertiveness

the ability to solve problems

What does each of these involve, and what can we do to help children develop it?

Self awareness, self confidence and self respect

Self awareness is being aware of yourself as an individual. It is knowing who you are, understanding that you have feelings and knowing what those feelings are. We have to be aware of our feelings before we can learn to control them. Ask yourself these questions about your setting:

Do we give children opportunities to learn about feelings?

Are the adults in the setting fully aware of the importance of helping children to recognise, name and acknowledge feelings?

Do the adults recognise children's feelings?

Are children given chances to think about and discuss their responses to different situations?

Do adults help children to identify and articulate their own needs?

> Children are strong, rich and capable.
>
> *Leila Gandini,*
> *Reggio Children*

If we are to fully understand ourselves we must be able to acknowledge and accept both the positive aspects of ourselves, and what may be regarded as the negative, darker sides of our personalities. Many adults find this difficult to do, and sometimes we don't make it easy for children.

> Self awareness – recognising a feeling as it happens – is the keystone of emotional intelligence.
>
> *Daniel Goleman,*
> *Emotional Intelligence. 1996*

The very youngest children find it easy to own all of their feelings. They know exactly how they feel, what they want and what will make them happy. When they feel angry they scream and stamp, when they are hurt they cry and when they are jealous they lash out. When their wishes and desires conflict with those of others they express their displeasure vociferously and naturally.

It is the way in which we deal with such conflicts that can do the most damage. Our intention is to help but the effect is often far from helpful. In our efforts to teach our children sensitivity to the feelings of others, we all too often kill their awareness and sensitivity to their own feelings. If we tell children that it's not nice to be jealous, angry or resentful, they quickly learn that we consider

> Punishment which hurts, frightens or humiliates children is unacceptable, as well as being ineffective.
>
> *Judy Miller,*
> *Never Too Young. 1996*

> ...they use praise, encouragement and comparisons to encourage children to refine their skills.
>
> *Edwards, Gandini &*
> *Forman,*
> *The 100 Languages of*
> *Children. 1996*

that part of them to be unacceptable. Consequently, the next time those feelings surface they may conceal them in order to keep our approval. Such behaviour doesn't make the jealousy go away, but it helps to convince adults that they are 'nice' children, worthy of love and respect. In short, they deny their feelings and quickly develop the ability to mask what they truly feel. Once this pattern is established it becomes habitual. For some people it is never broken. They spend an entire lifetime denying their real feelings, adopting so many masks that in the end they don't really know what they feel about anything. This makes it almost impossible for them to assert themselves and can have a devastating effect on self awareness and the facility for self direction. It is therefore of the utmost importance that practitioners:

Understand that all feelings are real for the person who is feeling them, and need to be acknowledged. Our feelings of anger and jealousy are as important as our feelings of love and compassion. Our 'negative' feelings are all part of what makes us human. What is important is that we acknowledge them, own them and deal with them constructively and appropriately. Children need to understand that it's okay to be angry, that what is important is that the anger is expressed in an appropriate way. As part of managing anger they need to be taught what the appropriate channels are.

Assess their own staff-development needs. If we are not fully confident in this area we may need further training and support.

Devise programmes of work that support children in understanding feelings, and help them to develop a 'feelings' vocabulary.

Systematically acknowledge and name children's feelings throughout the daily routine.

Understand that we can acknowledge someone's feelings without having to agree with them; acknowledgement does not equal agreement.

Make collections of stories that help children to reflect upon the feelings of others and expand their awareness of their own feelings.

By supporting the development of the children's self awareness in this way we are helping them gain the emotional literacy so necessary to independence.

> ...like any learning within their lives, children will gain in skills and satisfaction far more effectively if adults offer plenty of encouragement with constructive and accurate feedback.
>
> *Jennie Lindon,*
> *Too Safe for Their Own Good.1999*

Self confidence grows out of self respect, having a sense of personal dignity and worth. Children with self respect believe that they are equal to (but not in every way better than) other people, and this belief gives them confidence to act independently. A child who feels an all-round inferiority compared with his or her peers is much less likely to go out on a limb and exercise initiative. Believing that other children are better than they are, they will always stay in the background and wait for someone else to tell them what to do. Remember George from Chapter 1? Engaging children's co-operation without labelling them, enabling them to recognise and value themselves yet at the same time see where there are aspects of behaviour that need attention, requires good communication skills and a high degree of sensitivity. We must all the time and in every situation be aware of our own power to enhance or diminish a child's self respect.

As practitioners we are indeed powerful; the children believe us, and the labels we give them can so easily become self fulfilling. For some children, if we tell them that they are 'naughty', 'unkind', or 'argumentative' then this may well be how they come to regard themselves, even though it is untrue, even though we can all be all of these things some of the time. Equally, what a burden it must be to be labelled 'helpful', 'kind', or 'co-operative' when we might not always feel that way. If I am labelled 'kind', I might take on this label and feel that this is what I should always be. Imagine the guilt when I fail at being a constantly kind human being! If we treat children in this way we rob them of their right to fully understand what being human is all about. This will not help them to understand their own uniqueness.

Practitioners need to value all children for who they are, not what they do, and to help them to recognise their strengths and individual personal qualities. Part of this will be the strenuous avoiding of language which might label or stereotype. Children need to be supported in developing their understanding that, although we all have different strengths and weaknesses, we are all equally important.

Recognising the children's stage of development, ask yourself these questions:

What strategies do we have for enhancing children's self esteem?

In what ways do we enable the children to accept both their strengths and their weaknesses?

Do we allow children to cope with potentially challenging situations (without, of course, allowing them to become distressed)?

Do we encourage children to be adventurous, to welcome and involve themselves in new situations?

How effectively do we support children in reflecting upon and evaluating their own efforts?

If children are to have a real belief in themselves there is much to consider. This is a subtle area and it is all too easy to think we are promoting children's self esteem when what we are really doing is creating 'pseudo' self esteem – i.e. children who can only esteem themselves if they receive constant praise and approval from adults. In other words, they become reliant on our praise for their view of their own worth and are unable to esteem themselves. There are a number of things we can do to avoid this.

> The teacher is partner, nurturer and guide.
>
> *Reggio Children, Journey into the Rights of Children. 1995*

To begin with, it is important to use appropriate encouragement strategies. This requires us to refrain from empty praise like, 'I really like your picture!' 'That's brilliant!' or 'That's really lovely!' Such statements are merely personal judgements. They are evaluative rather than specific and entirely about what we think, based on our opinions and preferences. When we hold the power and we make the judgements we do little to encourage children to make up their own minds and examine their own efforts. We may even try to tell the children how they have approached their work by using statements like 'You've really worked hard!' How do we know? The child may have found the task very easy. What we have done is to make an assumption. We haven't actually asked whether they have worked hard!

> The important role of the adult is fostering progression in children's thinking: helping children to move forward ... through positive and interactive learning encounters between children and adults.
>
> *Robert Fisher, Teaching Children to Think. 1990*

Using appropriate encouragement strategies will sometimes involve us in changing the habits of a lifetime, but if we are committed to making the change we can soon adopt alternative ways of responding. For example, when children approach us with their efforts we need to make specific comments that reflect that we have looked carefully at what they have achieved and thought about it: e.g. 'Look! You've painted a big house, and I can see lots of trees by the side of it and on the door you've painted a number 1.' By describing what we see we are signalling our interest in what the child has done, but at the same time leaving the power with them. They can use our comments to help them make their own judgements, with which we can either agree or disagree.

Chapter 5: how adults can help and support children's independence

Having made specific comments and described what we see we can then move on to ask open-ended questions. We may ask, How did you paint this little bit here? What other things could you put in your picture? We return to the subject of questioning later in this chapter. All too often we tell children what we think of what they have done before finding out what they themselves think. We must encourage children to offer their own opinions about their work. If they then say they are pleased with it, we can agree and offer our praise for their efforts. When we do this we are reinforcing their own opinions, not making up their minds for them. But suppose they are satisfied with what they have done but we know they could have done even better. We can make suggestions, encouraging children to extend and build upon their efforts by focusing their attention on possibilities that may not have occurred to them. Or we can add additional materials or introduce new techniques or examples to stimulate their imagination and enable them to carry a project further.

> Observation helps educators to decide what to do next in terms of supporting, developing and extending children's development.
>
> *Cathy Nutbrown, Threads of Thinking. 1999*

> The crucial emotional competencies can indeed be learned and improved upon by children – if we bother to teach them.
>
> *Daniel Goleman, Emotional Intelligence. 1996*

Finally, we can involve ourselves practically in their task. When we do this we give value to what they are doing and show respect for their need to learn through practical experience and exploration. Later in this chapter we offer some help and advice about effective ways to become involved in children's play.

By making a conscious effort to engage with children in these ways we can support the development of intrinsic rather than extrinsic motivation and really help them to believe in their own ability to succeed.

The ability to solve problems

Problem solving has been identified as one of the six key skills required for successful learning. It is one which employers consistently put at or near the top of their lists of what they value in employees. The ability to meet the challenge of a problem, to approach it in an ordered and systematic way, to use previous experience and knowledge to develop strategies for solving it, to evaluate the success of a chosen approach, to persevere, where necessary rejecting the unsuccessful and starting again are all very sophisticated attributes. They are not, however, beyond the young child and are essential for independence of mind and thought.

> The style of interactions between the educator and the child is a critical factor in the effectiveness of the learning experience.
>
> *Pascal & Bertram, Effective Early Learning. 1997*

The DfES has suggested that these are the skills which make the most important contribution to being able to think independently and solve problems.

> Information processing skills enable children to locate and collect relevant information, to sort, classify, sequence, compare and contrast, and to analyse relationships between the things they experience.

Reasoning skills enable children to give reasons for opinions and actions, to draw inferences and make deductions, to use precise language to explain what they think, and to make judgements and decisions informed by reason and/or evidence.

Enquiry skills enable children to ask relevant questions, pose and define problems, plan what to do and ways to research, predict outcomes and anticipate consequences, test outcomes and improve ideas.

Creative thinking skills enable children to generate and extend ideas, to suggest hypotheses, to apply imagination and to look for alternative, innovative outcomes.

Evaluation skills enable children to evaluate information, to judge the worth of what they hear, read and do, to develop criteria for judging the value of their own and others' work and ideas, and to have confidence in their own judgements.

How can we create the conditions in which these skills will grow and flourish?

To begin with, we are all aware of the importance of role models for children. We know that they learn from the models we offer them of positive relationships, kind words, good manners. Models of thinking are just as important. We must practise what we preach, and demonstrate the benefits of thinking, wondering, pondering, exploring and finding out the answers to questions. We should reflect upon the degree to which we engage children in stimulating and challenging activities and conversations which promote these skills and give opportunities to demonstrate and practise them. In the setting where such skills are valued, the adult provokes, instigates, and gives status to thinking situations, observing and following children's responses and engaging in their conversations, often recording their discussions on paper or on tape.

Next, how do we create the conditions in which children will learn to approach problems with confidence and independence of mind?

Fisher (1990) suggests that there are three main factors involved in problem solving:

Attitude – interest/confidence/motivation.

Cognitive ability – application of knowledge/use of memory, thinking and reasoning skills.

Experience – familiarity with the context/materials/strategies for problem solving.

To these we would add two more:

Opportunity – the situations where skills can develop.

Example – models of others (adults and children) who have already developed such skills and demonstrate them.

We need to think carefully about whether we are creating the appropriate culture for children to feel confident about solving problems, and whether we are ensuring that the children are offered a range of support mechanisms. To begin with, do we ask relevant questions? Do we remind children of similar experiences? For example, when they are thinking about ice melting in the water tray we can remind them of how their ice lolly melted in the sun and the way the frozen puddles melted in the playground. Next, do we help them to identify existing knowledge? For example, 'Was it like the day when…?' Thirdly, do we help children to hypothesise, to plan possible solutions and try them? For example, 'Shall we try that and see what happens?' Fourthly, do we encourage children to reflect on the outcome? For example, by asking them why they think that something happened? Fifthly, do we support children in tolerating uncertainty? For example, 'I don't know either, what do you think?' Lastly, do we give encouragement when problems are not solved immediately, helping children to generate further strategies? For example, 'Can you think of another way we could try to do this?'

Self motivation

The things that motivate individuals to do things are many and varied. Consider your own reasons for reading this book. You may have picked it up in a bookshop or library and be flicking through it out of curiosity. You may be a teacher or nursery nurse in training, looking for material which will help you in your future work. You may be an experienced practitioner seeking refreshment and help in refocusing your ideas. You may be the manager or head of a setting or school in search of ways to improve the quality of your provision. If you have read this far it is presumably because you have found the earlier chapters sufficiently interesting and stimulating to make you want to go on. Or perhaps you disagree so strongly with what we are saying that you are racing through in a rage to see what outrageous statements we will make next!

> Knowing that adults, space, time and materials will be 'constant', the same today as yesterday, helps young children to assume more responsibility for what they do and to follow their own consistent threads of thinking and doing without the unnecessary hindrance of over-dependence on adults.
>
> *Cathy Nutbrown,*
> *Threads of Thinking. 1999*

The point is that all these motivations are different; there are many more which we have not listed, and they are not all mutually exclusive. Self motivation is providing oneself with a personal incentive to do things. It is not always necessary to know why we are doing something, but if we never know why much of our activity will be random and aimless. At the adult level self motivation sometimes arises from a burning interest in something, or a strong desire to carry out an action or task. Sometimes, when what must be done is less palatable, we will promise ourselves a reward for completing it. Sometimes our motivation comes from knowing that the task simply has to be done. Of course, many of these feelings and emotions we experience at a level of subtlety beyond that of young children. However, the basic motivators will be of a similar kind for them.

It is important to try to understand what is involved in promoting children's self motivation. If we are to be fully self motivated we must be able to engage in activities that excite us, capture our imagination and through which we can experience the satisfaction of achievement. This has considerable implications for the way we work with young children, and requires that we know the things that motivate and interest them. We must also be aware of the influence different learning styles and preferences have on motivation.

Practitioners need to observe children closely to find out about the choices they are making and the vehicles through which they are learning most effectively. This should help to focus involvement in children's choices and decision making, and enable us to support them in what they choose to do in ways that will help to develop their learning. Most children will usually learn much more effectively from the activities that they have chosen for themselves, so it is important to utilise the things that children most like to do as powerful vehicles for learning. Similarly, it is important to understand the ways in which we can teach children the things they need to know through the choices they make; e.g. number skills can be taught outside or in the sand just as effectively – possibly even more effectively – as at a table.

In short, we should value and respect children's choices and decisions, and support them both in reviewing what they have done and celebrating success. For children as well as adults, the motivation to try an activity again and extend it comes from the enjoyment and success experienced the last time it was tried.

Self reliance and the ability to makes one's own decisions

Making decisions that work requires practice. It also requires empowerment. In order to become self determined, young children need repeated opportunities to plan and initiate their own activities. They need to be able to set goals for themselves, and these goals need to be their own, worked out in partnership with – but not imposed by – an adult. They will also need to develop the review skills and the spontaneity to adapt what they are doing on the way to achieving their goal.

Though they do not know as much about the world as most adults, children know how they feel and what is important to them.

Judy Miller,
Never Too Young. 1996

Practitioners need to talk with children prior to periods of child-initiated learning to help them to clarify their ideas about what they wish to do. Ask the children questions about how they will achieve their goals, what materials they might need and who they might work alongside. There will, of course, be times when the intentions and goals of the child do not coincide with those of the adult. In such cases the adult will need to make judgements about whether different goals can be adapted to become compatible, whether to postpone their goals and yield to those of the child, whether to reason with the child and talk them round to doing what is wanted, or whether to insist and coerce. The latter is sometimes inevitable, but hopefully it will be rare. Children learn little from blind obedience. There is nearly always room for negotiation, and the skilful practitioner will be able to handle most children in such a way that harmony prevails.

Children are individuals and need respect. A child has the right to hold their own views and should be encouraged to do so. An adult only has the right to stop a child experimenting to progress development if it is harmful to themselves or others.

Ibid.

It is important to give support throughout the process of making and following through a decision, helping children to revise their plans where necessary and progressively enabling them to do more for themselves. Encourage children to reflect upon what they have achieved, to celebrate success while at the same time identifying opportunities for further development. The more we can do this, the more we will help children to work with purpose and intentionality, and the more we will facilitate the development of self determination.

Self discipline and self control

Disciplining our own feelings or desires involves us in doing things that we don't always want to do and is an important aspect of independence. When we support children in acquiring self discipline we help them to understand that they, and not other people, are responsible for what they do and for carrying out certain obligations. This is a subtle area and one that all too often we leave to chance. However, if children are to learn self control and self restraint then they need our thoughtful and deliberate support. They particularly need us to be consistent and explicit.

Chapter 5: how adults can help and support children's independence

Ask yourself the extent to which you help children to see the importance of self discipline to their lives. Why is it important that they should exercise their own control, rather than always being controlled? How do you support them in becoming more self disciplined?

Can you find interesting and enjoyable ways of helping children to be self disciplined and to carry out obligations? An example might be tidying up to music, or trying to do it by creeping round the room as quietly as a mouse. Children will respond well to an element of fun, and to doing routine actions in a novel and unfamiliar way. It will help if you model self discipline by becoming their partner and carry out some of the tedious tasks alongside them. However, resist the temptation to do it for them when, as you inevitably will, you feel impatient. Also beware that some children are adept at engaging adult help in an uncongenial task and then imperceptibly withdrawing, leaving you cleaning or clearing up on your own!

An important aspect of self control is the capacity to exercise restraint over feelings and emotions. Germane to this is the development of an awareness of the effects of one's actions on other people.

Ask yourself what you do in your setting to help children to understand the consequences of their own actions. In what ways do you support children in exercising control over their own actions? How effective are you in helping children to generate alternative ways of doing things? Do you systematically teach, model and reinforce conflict resolution skills? Do you support the children in understanding both their own needs and the needs of others?

You can help children take control over their own actions by having clear and consistent expectations of them and encouraging them to think about the consequences of what they do. Talk to children about appropriate individual and group behaviours and support them in learning them. For example, talk with children about the importance of listening to each other. Give positive feedback as children become increasingly able to exercise self discipline. Try to help them learn about the ways in which a good listener behaves and praise and reward good listening and good group behaviour.

In their interactions with children, Reggio Emilia teachers seek to promote children's well being and encourage learning in all domains.

Edwards, Gandini & Forman, The 100 Languages of Children. 1996

You can play games and carry out activities that enhance children's listening skills, but one of the chief ways in which you will influence children will be by the example you set through your own actions and behaviour.

Here are some practical things to do.

> talk to children about the importance of listening to each other
>
> help children learn about the ways in which a good listener behaves
>
> play games and carry out activities that enhance children's listening skills
>
> talk to the children about appropriate group behaviour
>
> support children in learning appropriate group behaviours
>
> give consistent positive feedback for good listening and good group behaviour
>
> help children to think about the consequences of their own actions
>
> support children in taking responsibility for their own actions

have clear and consistent expectations of children

teach the process of conflict resolution

It will also help children to have some strategies for dealing with the resolution of conflict. The following model, taken from High/Scope, may provide you with a useful starting point for approaching and teaching the resolution of conflict:

1. Approach calmly
2. Acknowledge feelings
3. Gather information
4. Restate the problem
5. Ask for solutions and choose one together
6. Be prepared to give follow-up support

There will, of course, be times when we need to address inappropriate behaviours and be critical of what children do. It is important at such times to focus on the deed and not on the doer. Try to acknowledge feelings by exploring with the child the situation that is causing problems. This simple formula will help.

When (describe what is happening) e.g. you shout.

I feel (name the feeling) e.g. I get annoyed.

Because (describe the consequence) e.g. other children can't hear.

So (state what you need) e.g. I need you to put your hand up if you have something to say.

And (make your expectations clear and introduce a sanction if necessary) e.g. If you continue to shout out I will have to ask you to leave the group.

Remember that survival is the most basic human drive, buried deep in the limbic brain. We are all born with a predisposition to put self first. Getting a child to become more aware of the needs and wishes of others is asking them to override this root programming. That is why it is so difficult, and why the line between independence of mind and selfishness is so delicate. Using the above prompts will help to separate the behaviour from the individual and control the former without damaging the latter.

This is a subtle area and one that all too often is left to chance. However, if children are to be helped in the difficult process of exercising self-control and self restraint then they need our thoughtful and deliberate support. Self control and self restraint don't just happen. They are disciplines that have to be learned, and in helping children to learn them we need to be consistent and explicit.

Expectations will also influence children's actual achievement: children will live up, or down, to our expectations of them.

Judy Miller,
Never Too Young. 1996

Working seriously on this requires time. We must ensure that we make time for it, and this will involve us in exploring our own beliefs and attitudes. We must ask ourselves about the extent to which we feel it to be really important, and make the same commitment to fostering in children the capability to control themselves and resolve their own conflicts as we would to the development of academic skills.

Chapter 5: how adults can help and support children's independence

Assertiveness

In many situations our ability to act independently will depend on our ability to assert ourselves. However, it is important to be clear about what is meant by assertiveness. Assertiveness is often confused with aggression, but true assertive behaviour is never aggressive. Rather, it is a direct communication designed to tell someone exactly how we are affected by a situation, at the same time as respecting the feelings of others. It relies on a sound and healthy concept of self. An assertive communication tells someone what we see (generally factual information), what we think (this may be an opinion or an assumption), what we feel and what we need.

When our communication contains all these component parts we give a 'whole' message and leave someone in no doubt about what we are saying. Failure to do this can result in a contaminated message by leaving people to make up their own minds about what we see, think, feel or need. Usually this leads to misunderstanding, and this in turn is often followed by confusion and conflict.

Ask yourself whether you are clear about what is meant by assertive communication. Do you support children in understanding how conflict arises and do you help them to sort it out so that everyone feels valued and listened to? Practitioners need to see conflict as an opportunity for learning, rather than an irritating interruption in the daily routine. Part of this will involve helping children to understand that community life is based on co-operation, compromise and consensus. It will help if you can model assertive responses to situations where conflict arises and encourage children to make direct, polite interactions with each other. Although very young children may not be able to understand this model from an intellectual point of view, they internalise it very quickly when they see it consistently applied by the adults around them.

*   *   *

We have suggested above some of the things we as adults need to address in our interactions with children in order to help them move towards independence. It is worthwhile at this point giving some attention to the nature and quality of the interactions themselves. We will need to become involved with children in their play and in their conversations with each other. The ways in which we do this will help or hinder the development of the skills and capabilities we are trying to encourage in the children in our care.

Adult involvement in what children are doing is often referred to as *intervention*, sometimes as *interaction*, which prompts the question, 'Is there a difference?' An exploration of the meanings behind these labels does expose some subtle distinctions.

Collins English Dictionary defines intervention as 'the act of intervening ... any interference in the affairs of others'. The same defines interaction as 'a mutual or reciprocal action or influence.'

It seems likely that the negotiating arrangements between adult and child are recorded in a child's brain during the second year of life. As the child grows, the pattern established will then be used whenever conflicts arise.

Sue Finch,
An Eye for an Eye. 1998

The two terms are distinct in emphasis and have a very different feel. Intervention is associated with interference and intrusion, and sometimes this is necessary. As practitioners, if we see two children attacking each other with scissors or using a hammer inappropriately we make a necessary and appropriate intervention! On the other hand, when children are engaged in meaningful play the last thing we want to do is to interfere or intrude into that process. Such an intervention could well have a negative effect, destroying the play and the potential for learning. Most of us are familiar with this scenario and struggle to avoid it happening. We are eager and enthusiastic to enter the children's play, desperately wanting to 'open doors' for them and be the facilitator of deep learning. It does little for either our self esteem or their learning when they all get up and walk away!

By paying attention to a few simple principles we can master the art of sensitive intervention, and this is very important. It is quite right that we 'interfere' in children's play to facilitate learning, but unless the initial intervention is carried out with sensitivity, meaningful interaction cannot follow. If we are truly committed to empowering children by enabling them to 'do it for themselves' we must be fully aware of the ways in which our actions might influence their play.

> *It is a way of working that is not only valid, but is also right.*
>
> *Laura Rubizzi, Diana School, Reggio*

When we understand how much young children gain from seeing themselves as problem solvers and from experiencing the satisfaction of sorting things out for themselves we realise how important it is to get this balance right. But this is only the first step. Once we have made a commitment to involving ourselves in children's play with the conscious intention of promoting independence in learning there is still a long way to go, and unless we take time to 'tune in' to what is going on things can go badly wrong. Most early years practitioners will know what it feels like to have made an enthusiastic attempt to enter children's play, only to find that the children, resenting our interference, have all got up and moved to another part of the setting! Think about these notes made during the observation of a nursery class.

> *A group of children are deeply involved in play in the home corner. Anxious to extend their play and further promote their learning the practitioner throws herself into the action.*
>
> *'Can I come in?' she asks cheerily. 'I'd love a cup of tea!'*
>
> *She sits down and begins to ask a string of questions. While not actually ignoring her, the children make polite, but lukewarm responses, and exchange glances with one another. Undeterred, the practitioner perseveres, at first unaware that some of the children have begun to remove the furniture from the home corner and set up the play some distance away. By degrees the rest of the children begin to join them. It is some time before the practitioner realises that her presence in the home corner was nothing but an intrusion. They were simply too kind to ask her to go away, preferring instead to move the location of their play.*

For children to become independent learners they need access to gifted adults who can intervene and interact appropriately and sensitively. Many of us already possess the gifts needed to do this well, and we initiate telling interactions intuitively; but by interacting more consciously and becoming more aware of what we are doing, we can become even more effective. Adopting some of the following techniques may help.

Observe before you intervene

Next time you are about to involve yourself in children's play, make a conscious effort to spend a few minutes observing the situation before you leap in.

Take time to stand back and really look at what is going on. Tune in to what the children are saying. Pay attention not only to the meaning of what they are saying but to the language they are using.

Observe how they are interacting with each other. Making a conscious effort to go through this process will enable you to really understand what is going on and make informed decisions about how to proceed. In fact, in some cases you may actually make the decision not to involve yourself, on the basis that such an involvement would have a negative effect on the play. It is a sensitive balance, but there are some occasions when the children will simply get on better without our involvement, where the play is so private and intimate and the children are concentrating so hard that any form of adult participation would be an intrusion. If we have taken the time to observe, such occasions are usually very obvious; but what if we are not sure? After all, we are there to facilitate children's learning. Doesn't this mean that we must get stuck in? In the event of such uncertainty consider trying the following approaches.

Join in sensitively in parallel

Quietly sit down near the children and begin to play with some of the materials and equipment they are using. Engage in some 'self-talk', describing what you are doing, talking to yourself rather than addressing the children. This is like a child's solitary play. It gives the children the opportunity to make clear choices. They can decide to involve you, or not. Usually within a fairly short space of time you will find the children beginning to respond to your self-talk, and starting to draw you into their play. If not, the next stage is to initiate some parallel talk. Start to comment, still to yourself, on what some of the children are doing. Copy some of their ideas and follow their lead in the play. Be careful, still, not to intrude. Watch what they are doing but avoid speaking directly to them until they speak to you.

This usually does the trick. However, any failure to respond can be taken as a clear message. If you are still talking to yourself ten minutes later you can take it as read that your involvement is not welcome! This is the cue to slip quietly away – although we have to say that in our experience this seldom happens. The point of the exercise is that it leaves the power with the children. The result is that usually they will welcome your involvement and enjoy bringing you into their world. The challenge then is about how to extend and enrich what they have started.

Extend the play

Once accepted as a partner you are in a position to move the play on in ways that may not have been possible had you not become involved. Now is the time to extend children's thinking by making suggestions, asking open-ended questions and discussing ideas as you and the children work together.

Sounds easy, doesn't it? But what will become immediately apparent as you engage in this process is that you need to give attention to the sort of questions you are asking.

Asking useful questions

Asking questions is one of the most frequent interactions between practitioners and children, and the questions usually go in one direction. A government survey noted that 75 per cent of the talk in classrooms was done by the teacher. Moreover, 75 per cent of that talk was questions. On average teachers asked one question every eight seconds! No wonder children sometimes feel bombarded by adult demands.

The first thing that this information will probably do is make you resolve to ask fewer questions. However, it is not the quantity of the questions which is significant but their quality. So many questions we ask have vague purposes and do little to extend understanding. It is often hard to monitor this yourself, so why not get some help?

Pick a colleague you know well and trust, and ask them to monitor your interaction with a group of children for 10-15 minutes. If you can manage, say, three periods of five minutes while the children are pursuing different activities the exercise will be even more helpful. Get them to write down all the questions you ask. Afterwards you will be able to undertake a simple analysis to ascertain both the frequency and the quality of your questioning. If you prefer you can carry out the same exercise by recording yourself on tape and listening to the proceedings afterwards. In either case, the aim is to collect a random sample of questions to give an insight into your questioning technique.

The teacher's role is to ask good, open ended questions that stimulate children's thinking and provoke discussion – to facilitate, orchestrate and gently guide so that the conversation does not stray too far from the subject, so that every child has a chance to participate, and so that children consider the matter at hand with all their attention and interest.

Louise Boyd Caldwell,
Bringing Reggio Emilia Home. 1997

Consider each of the questions you asked and ask yourself whether it opened up opportunities for dialogue, or restricted them. Decide whether each was:

A closed question

This is a question that can usually be answered in one word. e.g. 'What is the name of this shape?' Closed questions are often useful for a quick check on understanding. They do not generally require much thought by the answerer and do not generally provide much challenge.

A thought-provoking question

This is a question to which there is a right answer, but you have to think about it, e.g. 'When you made a cake this morning, what was the first thing that you did?'

An open-ended question

This is a question to which there is no single right answer, but a range of possibilities about which children will have to really think, e.g. 'We have got some string, sequins, paper, glue and a collection of cardboard boxes. What are some of the things we could do with these materials?'

You may well be surprised at the balance between these three types of questions when you come to analyse your own work. What proportion of your questions really make the children think? It is not unusual for most people to ask closed questions most of the time.

Here are some typical questions taken from observation of early years practitioners. What sort of questions are they? Which ones will get the child thinking?

Are you going to play with these cars or not?

We have got some wood, plastic and bubble wrap here. What are some of the things you could make?

When you made that model, what was the first thing that you did?

The glue pots keep getting knocked over. Can you think of a safer place to keep them?

Is a carrot a fruit or a vegetable?

What number comes before six and after four?

Sam is upset because his friend is not there. Can you think of something that might make him feel better?

What is your favourite story book?

How do we know if the sun will shine this afternoon?

A disgruntled four year old was once heard to enquire, 'Why do you keep asking us questions that you know the answer to?' By asking fewer questions and ensuring that the ones we do ask are quality questions we can stimulate and challenge children's thought processes and enable them to move towards greater independence in their thinking.

In the previous chapter we presented a list of the characteristics of the independent learner compiled by a group of practitioners. It is an exercise we often employ in our training, and all the lists produced are remarkably similar. Consider this one, expressed more directly in terms of behaviour and practical capabilities than the one in Chapter 4.

> The style of interactions between the educator and the child is a critical factor in the effectiveness of the learning experience.
>
> *Pascal & Bertram,*
> *Effective Early Learning. 1997*

Independent children can and should learn:

- to recognise when it is necessary for them to go to the toilet and manage the process for themselves, including washing their hands.

- to make choices about what they would like to eat at snack time, sometimes becoming involved in the preparation of food and the tidying up and washing up of utensils, etc.

- to dress themselves, do up their own buttons, put on their own socks and fasten their own shoes. It is not appropriate to always do it for them when they are perfectly able to do it for themselves. We need to manage our own impatience and realise how children will benefit from doing things for themselves.

- to access materials for themselves, selecting what they need for a particular activity.

- to help take responsibility for the care of the physical environment.

- to contribute to the welfare of those less fortunate than themselves by being involved in a variety of projects, e.g. raising money for charity.

- to undertake a range of tasks that raise their levels of co-operative consciousness and contribute to the welfare and smooth running of their community, e.g. washing paint pots, caring for living things, putting newspaper on tables for creative activities, sweeping up sand, helping to empty water trays, planting things in the outside area.

- to play co-operatively with others, taking turns and responding to conflicts constructively and with an understanding of another's point of view.

- to review and consider what they and others have done and to form judgements about its quality and value.

We all like to have in our groups children who possess these capabilities but, as we have said, they do not always come naturally. They are the right of every child but not necessarily innate in every child. Most children need to be shown how to do these things, through demonstration, example and practice. They also need the opportunity to focus on and experience key areas of development. We have tried in this chapter to isolate some of these and explore their implications, giving pointers to some of the things that adults can do to help children develop the capacity to think and behave independently.

Of course, we are not the only ones who affect children's learning. We must not forget that most children spend only a small proportion of their time in our care, and that families have a far more significant and continuing contribution to make to the development of independence in their children. Discussion with parents, carers and other significant adults will be an important part of our approach, and we offer some guidance on relationships with parents in Chapter 9. However, providing the experiences we have described will go a long way towards creating the conditions in our own settings in which the independent learner can thrive. In the next chapter we look at how the physical environment can contribute to those conditions. In Chapter 7 we look at ways of promoting independence in learning through the aspects of the curriculum.

> What can parents and practitioners do at the early stages of learning to help children to become more independent?
>
> What can you do to help parents understand and respect independence, and to distinguish emerging independence of mind from wilfulness and selfishness?
>
> How do you demonstrate to children that you value independence? How successful are you in walking the line between enabling children to act on their own initiative and adults knowing best?
>
> Before involving yourself in children's play, do you spend enough time thinking about how you can enter the play in ways that do not disrupt what is happening?
>
> Having become involved in the play, do you always think consciously about how to extend the play by stimulating and challenging children's thinking?
>
> Do you know how to ask questions that make children think?
>
> Do you have a good enough understanding of how to support children in solving problems? How could you improve these skills?

Summary

> Adult involvement is crucial to supporting emerging independence.
>
> We should identify the key skills of independent learning, particularly those associated with self awareness and self knowledge, and understand how practitioners can best support these.
>
> We should recognise that acting positively to enable independence of mind in children often requires a substantial shirt of mind-set on the part of adults.
>
> Interaction, intervention and interference are very different things, and have different effects on children's developing skills.

Chapter 6:

what the setting can do to encourage independent learning

Where does independence flourish? What is the best environment for its development?

Are there schools or school programmes where independence is encouraged and children demonstrate all the skills we value?

Consider our current obsession with house and garden 'makeovers', our continuing interest in gardening and DIY, the effort and investment that is committed to new office buildings and community spaces and the care with which we arrange our personal spaces at work and home. These all demonstrate our belief that the environment in which we work, play and take our leisure is of paramount importance to our sense of wellbeing, our work rate and even our health. In this chapter, we explore the effect of the setting, the environment and the accommodation on the development of independent learners. We have focused particularly on the environment in the pre-schools and toddler groups in Reggio Emilia in northern Italy. You can find out more about the Reggio approach in Chapter 8.

> "We want children to have the best possible start in life by giving them the best possible environment in which to learn and play."
>
> *Estelle Morris, speaking as Secretary of State for Education in 2001*

In their book *People Under Three*, Elinor Goldschmeid and Sonia Jackson write

> *The physical environment exerts a major influence on how nursery workers feel about the job and on the quality of experiences they can offer the children.*

Of course, the same must be said for children over three and the practitioners who work with them. However, many of our youngest children work and play in settings which are far from ideal. They suffer cramped conditions, low light levels, multi-purpose spaces, unsuitable equipment and furniture and little or no access to the outside. The situation is improving for some, as awareness of their needs becomes more widespread and national expectations on standards for care and education are being implemented, but the variation between the best and the worst is still unacceptably wide.

> The physical environment exerts a major influence on how nursery workers feel about the job and on the quality of experiences they can offer the children.
>
> *Goldschmeid & Jackson, People Under Three. 1994*

Some readers will be working in these less than perfect conditions, but there are solutions to most of these problems if we start from the assumption that the children in our care deserve the best we can provide. We know how important the environment is to how we feel, think and learn. In even the most modest of settings we can make our intentions clear by the way we organise and allocate space and resources.

The Reggio Emilia schools describe the environment as 'the third teacher' (the adult and the child are the other two). How can we ensure that the third teacher in our settings has the best opportunity to be successful?

We will examine the following key aspects of the learning environment:

The building

The furniture

The resources and equipment

The outside space

Movement and circulation

Let's start with a practical look at two actual settings. Here are two very different descriptions.

Room 1

The door to the room is at the end of a corridor and has a glass panel, which has been covered by notices and reminders for parents. Some of these are very out of date. They include instructions about leaving and collecting children, times for collecting part timers, addresses of suppliers of name labels, calendar dates, etc.

Inside, the room is crowded. Pictures have been displayed on the windows to prevent parents from distracting the children as they wait at the end of the day, and the lighting on this spring day is dim, despite the sun outside.

There is an abundance of furniture, which has to be negotiated by children and adults, leaving little free space for circulation. There is a very small carpet area for group times. There is no clear indication of the purposes of different

A context of overall softness means an ecosystem that is diversified, stimulating and welcoming, where each inhabitant is part of a group but also has spaces for privacy and a pause from the general rhythms. It is a serene, amiable, liveable place.

Ceppi & Zini,
Children, Spaces, Relationships. 1999

areas of the room or how resources and activities are grouped and stored. The furniture, although child sized, is old and some pieces are splintered and grubby. The low shelves for storage of materials and equipment are hidden behind curtains, which are frayed and faded, hanging unevenly from stretched wires. Where the shelves are visible, the boxes of equipment are in jumbled piles, unlabelled, often with damaged or shabby boxes.

High quality and prolonged bouts of play most frequently occurred when two or more children played together, apparently hidden from adults.

Audrey Curtis,
A Curriculum for the Pre-School Child. 1960

Display boards are placed high up on the wall, often at adult height. They hold drawings attached by pins direct to the board. There are no labels or explanations. The children's lockers have peeling labels and are leaking items of work and clothing. The adult's desk is piled high with papers, books and children's work. Sand and water trays are new but their

It might be better to create a background of unobtrusive, gentle shades on walls and ceilings, which the children then 'colour' with the work they produce. Warm whites, cream and shades of blue or green give a neutral backdrop to the setting. We can then add to the palette with experiences of light and shadow, from natural and artificial sources. Individual pieces of furniture, fabrics or an accent wall can then stand out with their own character.

How do you use colour to create a backdrop for children and their work? When you redecorate your setting, how could you use the calming colours to give a sense of unity and peace?

The way in which children's artwork is painted on transparent sheets creates interesting layering and diffused light.

Abbott & Nutbrown,
Experiencing Reggio Emilia. 2001

Floors, steps and thresholds

Floors, steps and thresholds are all important to children. Many children prefer to sit or lie on the floor to play or work. They use the spaces under tables and other furniture for hideaways and dens. They sit and stand on steps and will often pause or even set up a play situation on the threshold of a room or a space.

Flooring should, of course, always be clean but in our pursuit of hygiene we should not sacrifice comfort and texture. An ideal mixture of soft surfaces such as carpet, hard surfaces such as concrete or vinyl, and natural materials such as stone, slate, wood or cork would be wonderful! Most of us have to make do with much less, but small areas of different textures, colours and forms can make a big difference. Children can then increase their independent thinking by selecting the surface they need for the activity they are pursuing, be it building with bricks, reading, dressing up or messy work with paint or clay. The important thing is that they should have the opportunity to exercise choice.

The environment is a living, changing system ... it indicates the way time is structured and the roles we are expected to play. It conditions how we feel, think and behave; and it dramatically affects the quality of our lives.

Penny Greenland,
Hopping Home Backwards. 2000

Where possible, steps and thresholds should be wide enough for a static activity to continue without preventing passage between spaces. If you have double doors, open both; if you have steps inside or out, encourage colonisation. On a visit to an early years setting in the north of England one of the writers saw in the baby room a ramp between the indoor space and the outside. The babies used it freely to crawl between indoors and out. This allowed them to make independent choices about where they would be and what they would explore.

Do the children in your setting have a choice of floor surfaces? Is there enough space for them to work on the floor if they want to? Do you encourage them to use the floor spaces underneath furniture, on steps or on thresholds? Can they choose where they go?

Display and presentation

The display to be seen in a setting offers one of the best ways of judging its quality. The way in which the work of children, practitioners and other adults is celebrated and shown will give a clear message to any visitor by revealing the levels of respect and independence given to the children. Where children are valued their work is carefully presented and displayed work on boards, tables and centres of interest, which provide a record of past and present projects. Teachers' transcripts of children's words carefully caption the work of each child.

Adult art and artefacts are included alongside those of the children. Light flows through transparent paintings, and collage, plants and natural materials follow the passing of the seasons. Vases of flowers on shelves and in the centres of lunch tables signal a commitment to making a home-like atmosphere. Photos of children, adults and the environment are in abundance, in books and on boards.

> The environment generates a sort of psychic skin ... an energy-giving second skin made of writings, images, materials, objects and colours, which reveals the presence of the children even in their absence.
>
> *Ceppi & Zini,*
> *Children, Spaces, Relationships. 1999*

The entrance is warm and welcoming. Clear signs help new visitors, and the need for security does not get in the way of a genuine welcome. The display in this area is also carefully chosen and set up to give pleasure as well as information. The information on the parents' notice board is regularly updated and the board is decorated with children's pictures of themselves and their families.

How near is this description to what happens in your setting? Even in situations where you have to clear up every day, do you make the best use of all opportunities to display what the children do, what you intend for them and how you make your setting a real-life experience?

Texture and senses

Settings usually provide a wide range of visual stimulation in their environment, but the other senses are often neglected. Children are not solely visual learners. The environment in any setting should appeal to and stimulate all the senses. Objects to touch, smell, taste and which make sounds are just as important as display boards with colourful pictures.

We can easily add texture and form by leaving some walls natural as brick or plaster, mounting tiles and objects on surfaces or stripping furniture so the grain of the wood can be felt. Baskets and displays of natural materials such as cones, leaves, shells and flowers can be touched, handled and smelt. Displays can include three dimensional objects, textures, scents, sounds and flavours. Aromatic oils and perfumes, perfumed plants, non-caustic and non-toxic cleaning products such as 'green' polishes, the smell of lunches cooking, baking and snacks will all stimulate the sense of smell.

> In order to grow and learn, the human brain needs to be stimulated by sensory experiences which take place within a rich and varied environment. In the first months and years of life, a child needs to see, touch, hear, taste and smell.
>
> *Vea Vecchi*

Within the constant 'soundscape' of children and adults working we can offer quiet areas for rest or contemplation by using screens, partitions and curtains. Carpet or acoustic matting can help to control noise. A blanket can be pinned across a corner to deaden the sound from the rest of the room and create a quieter space. We can add wind chimes, bells and rain boards inside and out to bring the sounds of the seasons and weather indoors. We can offer tapes and headphones to ensure attention and cut out noise.

How do you offer children experiences for all their senses?

Chapter 6: what the setting can do to encourage independent learning

The outside

In the Foundation Stage the outside environment is not only important, it is a vital part of children's entitlement. Staff and children in settings where there is no safe outside place to play feel very much deprived, and rightly say they are unable to fully implement the Foundation Curriculum.

A school should be a place that 'senses' what is happening outside – from weather to seasonal changes, from time of day to the rhythms of the town.

Ceppi & Zini,
Children, Spaces, Relationships. 1999

As with other aspects dealt with in this book, we try to balance sympathy with those who have difficulties with trying to establish what is desirable. The inside of the building and the outside are inextricably linked. Even if your only outside space is a car park or a small patch of scrub, it has possibilities. The following section will, we hope, give you some way of setting priorities for improving what you have now.

Essential features described in the Italian research work *Children, Spaces, Relationships – metaproject for an environment for young children* (Ceppy and Zini, 1995) are:

The entrance This is the public area for visitors and families at the beginning and end of the day. It is the first experience given to someone entering the setting, and must give a strong message about the purposes and processes within. The path, gate, security systems, the door with its notices and views into the building – all give an initial impression which can imply an open or a closed place, transparency or opacity. The first impression for children and all visitors will be a lasting one, so make sure it is positive!

The filter places This is where the inside and the outside meet. Porches, steps, verandas, canopies and thresholds all seem important to children, and many choose to base themselves in these places which are neither inside nor outside. In these areas, children collect in ones and twos, often bringing things from inside to play on the threshold, obviously enjoying the light and air but not wishing to venture fully outside or needing to be involved in what is happening outside. It is a good idea to make as much of this sort of space available as you can. Open double doors, encourage children to colonise steps and covered ways as extensions of the inside. There is nothing you can do indoors that you cannot also do outdoors.

Outside play and the environment in general, including the large trees that overlooked the play area, were (valued) by the majority of the children.

Clark and Moss,
Listening to Young Children. 2001

The equipped and landscaped areas Grass, static equipment and hard surfaces for wheeled toys all need careful thought as you develop them. If you have a large variety of spaces and large numbers of children you will need to plan carefully if you are to avoid accidents and territorial conflict.

Because of our climate the hard area will need to be bigger than the grass. Any static apparatus should be carefully chosen and sited. It should also be as flexible as possible; an outside area should not look like a pub garden! It is a learning environment, not one created solely for recreation. Children asked about preferences for fixed or more flexible climbing apparatus gave a clear reply. They all opted for the flexibility of ropes, planks, tyres and mats, which they could manipulate themselves, using their imagination.

Areas for wheeled toys and games might be gently sloping to encourage the run off of rainwater, and can be defined by the use of permanent or temporary markings. Temporary marking using chalk will enable flexibility and encourage experiment – two keys to independent thinking.

> Well planned play, both indoors and outdoors, is a key way in which young children learn with enjoyment and challenge.
>
> *QCA, Curriculum Guidance for the Foundation Stage. 2000*

Role play settings, quiet areas for reading and thinking, natural and wild areas, trees and bushes all offer tranquility and can be provided even in relatively small spaces. The nursery garden has been a traditional element of early years education for almost two centuries. Reinstating this aspect of the outside is long overdue. Play in mud, sand and gravel and the production of plants, flowers, fruit and vegetables give children an excellent opportunity to see the cycle of life and to watch insects and other wildlife. The production of things they can eat is an added bonus. The garden also provides a tranquil place for stories, music, observing the seasons and the weather.

Installations for sound, light, weather and watching wildlife all have a place in the garden. So does the erection of sculptures, structures, mobiles, mirrors and pictures. In some settings all the available space is covered - a conservatory, a courtyard, a hall or play space. Even where access to the outside is not easy there are opportunities for the imaginative practitioner to use decoration, ventilation and light to give a feeling of outdoors.

A recommendation to all settings is to audit their own provision, listing all areas which could be used for any of the purposes above. They can then construct an action plan for fully exploiting and making the best use of the outdoor spaces available to them. The spaces, the building, the outside area, the light and the stimulation of the senses are all parts of the provided environment, controlled mostly by adults, and often affected by circumstances beyond our control. The use by children and adults of these spaces and the equipment and resources they contain are things over which we all have control.

Movement and circulation

We can't do much about the buildings in which we have to work, other than see that they are clean, safe and well decorated. But how we define the spaces inside them and encourage flow within them *is* within our control, and we have the opportunity to involve the children in this enjoyable activity.

Certain areas of both the inside and outside environment need to be allocated to particular activities. Sand, water and paint need a sweepable, waterproof floor; book and quiet areas need carpet and cushions; music, wheeled toys, woodwork, role play and gardening all have special requirements, and children need to know the boundaries and rules. However, the location of these areas does not need to be fixed for life, and those settings where packing up is a daily occurrence may have the flexibility to rearrange the location of activities more frequently than practitioners in more permanent situations. The key to this flexibility is to watch what the children do and how they use the spaces they have, and involve them in discussion of what you see.

> The school environment must lend itself to manipulation and transformation by adults and children alike.
>
> *Audrey Curtis, A Curriculum for the Pre-School Child. 1960*

Of course there is need for a balance between constant change and stagnant security. If they are to become independent, children need to know where to find things and put them away. This implies some stability, at least in some parts of the space. If the room is to meet the needs of the children, you (and they) will be making changes as a result of experiencing and observing how they use spaces and resources, and the need for development in their play. Some children are disturbed by changes in the environment, but these are few. The majority will enjoy new arrangements and ideas, particularly if they are involved in talking about them beforehand and in the move itself.

> The piazza is a place of meeting, a public place of the school, which plays the same role in the school building as the piazza does in the town.
>
> *Marianne Valentine,*
> *The Reggio Emilia Approach. 1999*

If the children are given the option of changing their own environment, they will need some help. Light, portable partitions and furniture (wheeled if possible), boxes and baskets with handles, fabric in varying sizes and colours, cones and benches all help children to be creative and make the moving more purposeful. Furniture which can serve several purposes is always useful. A screen with a window can become a castle, a shop or a puppet show; a simple piece of fabric can become a tent, a picnic rug or a partition; a portable mirror can be a shop prop, a dressing up aid or, placed on the floor, the start of a whole new way of looking at things.

How flexible are you in setting up your spaces? Do the children have any ownership of the organisation of the space they work in?

Resources and equipment

Look back at the examples on pages 68 and 69. In both settings the furniture, the resources and access to them were keys to defining the quality of the experiences available to the children.

Furniture

Furniture must be of good quality and the right size. Some settings are located in shared or borrowed spaces and have to make do with adult sized furniture. Although this is not ideal, it is not necessarily too much of a disadvantage. The way furniture is used can be more important than its size. Some children would rather stand at a table than sit on a chair, some favour cushions or bean bags, and some seem to concentrate best if they lie on the floor.

> Taking stock of everything enables staff to be conscious of and value the potential learning opportunities for the children.
>
> *Marjorie Ouvry,*
> *Exercising Muscles and Minds.*
> *2000*

Some activities may *need* full sized chairs (for example using a computer trolley or exploring the books in a library), and others may be better for them. After all, most children are used to coping with adult-sized furniture in their homes. Many practitioners find that settees, armchairs and other full sized furniture make their setting more like home and so more comfortable. Those who work in the voluntary sector, operating in church or village halls and rooms in colleges or adult centres should not get over anxious about the size of the furniture. However, furniture in this type of accommodation often gets rough use and can become splintered, broken and dangerous. The safety of the children requires that a close eye be kept on its condition, and that damaged furniture be removed from use as quickly as possible. A bonus of taking a more relaxed view is that once we accept that adult furniture has a use we are able to accept gifts of used but serviceable items from parents and friends.

When considering the furniture available to your setting, ask these questions:

Relative size
Are the tables and chairs related to each other in size and height? Can children work comfortably at the table, using the chairs we have? Can children reach the shelves and cupboard doors of the storage to which we want them to have access?

Condition and quality
Is the furniture safe and stable? Is it free from splinters on tables and chairs or chips from the paint? Does the furniture need renovating or replacing? Are catches, handles and locks safe and easy to use?

Flexibility
Is the furniture portable? Can we and the children use it flexibly to change the environment? Can we move the pieces to make screens and dividers? Is it easy and safe to move, encouraging independence and innovation?

Quantity
Is there enough furniture? Is there too much? How do you decide what is enough? What do you do with spare or unsuitable furniture?

Type
Do you use full size furniture, or would you like to? Where could you use this?

Storage

We need more storage!

How often do managers in early years settings hear this cry? But what is the storage needed for? Often many of our cupboards and shelves could be described as the 'attics' of the early years, stacked with things that 'might come in useful one day', filling space with things we can't bear to throw away, and often resulting in poor storage and access for adults and children, or shelves so full that children take their lives in their hands if they attempt to get things for themselves.

This book is about independent learning. Children cannot become independent learners if they can't see, select and access their own equipment and resources. In a setting where independence is valued the storage solutions should meet these criteria:

Access
Can children get their own things easily?

Organisation
Are things clearly grouped and labelled so children can find them and put them away?

Presentation
Are things carefully and attractively stored, preferably in transparent containers, so children can see what is on offer?

Condition
Are things checked for missing pieces, cleanliness, broken boxes, etc.?

Manageability
Are things in manageable containers which children can lift? Have they got handles? Are big sets broken into several containers for ease of carrying?

Location

Are things located near the play base where they are likely to be used (e.g. sand toy selections near the sand tray, collage materials near the sticking table)? Are the things they need spread out around the setting to avoid congestion?

Of course, furniture and storage are not the only aspects of resource management. Good management will not in itself turn poor quality, unsuitable and shabby resources into high quality learning experiences. Practitioners need to look further when checking their resources. They should check, monitor and constantly seek to improve:

Condition

Are the resources in the best possible condition? If you have to buy second hand, or cope with heavy wear and tear, do you refurbish and repair shabby furniture and resources? Do you have a policy and a budget for replacement of equipment that is worn out?

Quality

Are the resources of the highest possible quality that you can afford? Are you insistent on the best for the children? Do you discard resources and equipment which are of poor quality? Do you shop for quality as well as price? – cheap and cheerful is not always the best value for money.

Suitability

Are the resources suitable for the purpose and the children? Do they match your curriculum purposes in terms of the tool for the job? Do the scissors actually cut fabric, are plastic tools really best for digging? Do the resources match the range of needs of the children? Are the puzzles too easy? Is the construction set too small for their fingers?

Flexibility

Are the resources flexible in use, or do they only suit one purpose? Can the small world people actually fit in the doll's house? Do the cars fit the road mat as well as the garage? Can resources be mixed and matched to provide new activities and games thought up by the children?

Sufficiency

Is there enough of everything – scissors, wheels for the Lego, dressing up clothes for boys as well as girls?

Range

Do you have a good range of equipment for both boys and girls, to reflect diversity, to meet special needs? Is the range wide enough to prevent gender stereotyping? Do you provide natural and artificial surfaces and textures, to suit both the active learner and the reflective child?

Of course, practitioners need storage too. This should be acknowledged by their managers and by the children. Materials in preparation, records and planning sheets, items which need to be restricted from child access for reasons of safety, as well as personal property, all to be accommodated. A cupboard, draws or shelves which are 'off limits' to children should be a right for adults.

We have tried to present some of the questions all practitioners need to consider when thinking about the environment provided for young children. If you wish to promote independence in your setting, the questions can be used as the basis for establishing the children's right of access to materials and equipment which encourage them to manage their own learning. The systems you establish should give them choice, recognise a range of needs, enable creative thinking and support autonomy. However, being independent is not about children having access to everything and being able to do anything they like. The rules must be clear, too. If they are not, children will see choice not as something which frees and enables them but as a trap inviting them to make mistakes.

Summary

The environment is the 'third teacher' (with the child and the adult).

The outside and inside environments can and should work together.

Resources and equipment should be of the highest quality, accessible and attractively presented.

Independence and self esteem develop in a setting where building, light, colour, texture, furniture, resources, and display all celebrate and support children and their learning.

Resources should be available in a way that encourages children to make decisions and choose.

Review the way space is used and audit equipment, furniture and other resources.

Section 3
Promoting
Independent Learning

'Messy' activities are an essential part of work in all early years settings   *p123*

photo by Ros Bayley

Chapter 7:

how to improve provision to encourage independence

Authors' note.

We always intended that this chapter should be at the centre of *Foundations for Independence*. It is, after all, the part of the book which pays particular attention to advice and guidance for practitioners who want to develop and improve the opportunities for independent learning in their settings. Therefore we decided it should be a section on its own.

After the publication of the first edition we were contacted by readers who wanted more detailed help and a straightforward and simple handbook on the practicalities of promoting independent learning. We therefore reorganised and added to the material in this chapter to produce *We Can Do It!* (Featherstone Education, 2004, ISBN 190418779X), a highly illustrated, full colour collection of ideas, case studies and advice. We refer readers who are looking for more on this type of approach to *We Can Do It!.*

What can parents and practitioners do at the early stages of learning to help children to become more independent?

What are the essential skills and attributes that support independent learning?

Where does independence flourish? What is the best environment for its development?

Is independence something we can affect, something we can identify and provide for?

As we look at the setting where independence is fostered and promoted, we need to examine the different aspects of learning we offer to the children. In doing so we will see that there are plenty of opportunities to develop independence and initiative in all the aspects of learning. In this chapter, we take a range of the aspects and explore how we can use them to help children to play a greater part in decisions which affect their learning — what to do, how to do it, how to work with others to solve problems. We emphasise the importance of encouraging and allowing children to be responsible for managing themselves and their activities. We concentrate on the aspects of learning rather than the areas of learning and experience, so that our ideas and advice can be more directly related to the day-to-day life of your setting. Opportunities to develop independence and autonomy are present throughout the day and in all activities; they are part of the ethos of your setting and need your consideration as you plan how you address the Foundation Curriculum.

There are a number of factors that work against encouraging independence in children — in any setting. An organisation, even a small one, needs systems, processes and rules which make for smooth, safe and efficient operation. They are attributes of an orderly society. However, some of these will inevitably impinge on the scope of the individual to do exactly as he or she likes. It is very easy to use conditions we have had imposed on us or rules we have created for ourselves as reasons for not giving children the freedom to decide and act.

Developing independence requires time. Choosing, experimenting, exploring options, thinking and talking about possibilities all need to be allowed the space to develop. It is easy to become impatient when children take a long time to do things. How often have we all said or thought, It's quicker to do it myself than leave it to the children. Sometimes it seems as though they are being deliberately slow, and perhaps sometimes they are, although in our experience this is rare. Under pressure to get things done, to beat the clock and to meet our (sometimes self-imposed) schedules it is tempting to do things ourselves and not wait for the children. However, we should never forget that time is one of our most important resources, and we need to ensure that children are well provided with it.

The previous chapter looked at the physical setting and considered space and access. We are well aware of the variability of accommodation, of the difficult conditions some voluntary and private providers have to endure, and of the way in which Reception and Nursery classes in some schools are banished to the least attractive and convenient spaces. And of course, all settings are short of money. However, we should not use inadequacies in the environment and resources to justify not doing what we know should be done. With imagination problems can sometimes be turned into opportunities. And even when they can't, there is much that can be done within even the most basic setting to promote independence.

However, it is not always the tangibles that discourage some practitioners. There are genuine concerns about what encouraging children to be independent will mean. Will independence mean constant confrontation and conflict with children? How can I be sure children won't take inappropriate risks? Will independence be a threat to my position as an adult? What about my need to be needed? These are all natural and fair questions. We will try to answer them.

The first step is to identify the things in your own setting which prevent you from loosening the reins, surrendering some of our control, being willing to adapt or abandon careful plans and allow the children to take the lead in deciding where the curriculum should go. Sometimes it may be necessary to persuade colleagues of the value of a different approach, changing not just minds but hearts, because this is the way to change practice. It will help if you make a conscious effort to recognise the needs of young independent learners. We have already touched on many of them, but they are particularly well put by Judy Miller in her book *Never too Young*.

In order to become independent learners, Miller says, children need:

opportunity – to try things for themselves.

experience – of practising independence from an early age.

role models – of adults and other children. What we do has far more influence than what we say.

expectations – that they can and will become independent learners, given time and opportunity.

motivation – created by rewarding and praising effort and success.

information – to empower them to make choices and decisions.

Chapter 7: how to improve provision to encourage independence

With this list in mind, we shall in this chapter explore some of the key aspects of learning:

- Imaginative and role play
- Outside play
- Construction (large and small)
- Stories, puppets and plays
- Writing and reading and books
- Computers and other ICT
- Creative work (paint, modelling, collage)
- Messy activities (sand, water, dough, malleable, wood)
- Snack time and cooking
- Sound, music and dance.

In the sections which follow we discuss each aspect in turn and present some ideas and suggestions for approaches and activities that will encourage children to be independent. We show links to the Early Learning Goals, offer guidance to enable you to check on the quality in your setting, and provide for each a case study which shows children demonstrating the attitudes and qualities we are seeking. We address early years practitioners directly and include guidance on things which can be done to empower children and give them ownership. At the end of the chapter we look briefly at the ways in which planning, recording achievement, display and other fundamental aspects of organisation can support the independent learner.

In the margin beside each of the aspects we suggest resources and activities, and ideas for involving the children. We give particular attention to getting started, and because we believe that talking is one of the keys to thinking and learning, we provide pointers to stimulate the children to unlock their ideas through discussion.

Imaginative and role play

Role play is a vital part of children's education in the Foundation Stage and beyond. It forms the basis for story telling, writing and social development. It gives opportunities for children to play out the events they observe and experience. It provides experience of real-life situations in which they can practise their learning in maths, language and communication. It develops their creativity. And above all it's fun!

Links with Early Learning Goals:

<u>Language, communication and literacy</u>

> Interact with others, negotiating plans and taking turns in conversation

> Listen and respond to stories and songs

> Extend vocabulary

> Use language to imagine and recreate roles and experiences, organise, sequence and clarify thinking, ideas, feelings and events

<u>Creative development</u>

> Use their imagination in imaginative and role play and stories

Imaginative play and role play offer children endless opportunities to develop the skills of independent learning. Imaginative children will enjoy solitary role play sometimes, but **social interaction**, taking turns and sharing are vital for the success of this type of play, which makes it less easy than most to play on your own. Role play gives the chance to explore first hand the **roles of adults** in the real world (doctors, firemen, nurses, teachers, hairdressers, mums and dads). A range of **cultures and contexts** can also be offered as situations for role play, opening the door to the lives and lifestyles of the families in the local area by using implements, wearing clothes, eating food of other cultures and countries.

To experience **stories in action** (giants, bears, divers, astronauts) in imagined worlds provides a springboard to stories and poems. How can a child write an adventure story if he or she has never had an adventure? How can a child describe how a fictional feels unless he or she has practised and experimented with those feelings in role?

A four-year-old child said to her during the research: "I would love a garden and watching butterflies and digging vegetables... In the night I dream about a house for my mum and a garden with a big tree for me and my friends to climb."

Jacqui Cousins,
Listening to Four-year-olds. 1999

Children will learn to explore, express and communicate their ideas and use their imaginations when they have sufficient time to research their ideas, imitate what they see, experiment with ideas and bring their own ideas to the process.

QCA, Curriculum Guidance for the
Foundation Stage. 2000

Chapter 7: how to improve provision to encourage independence

Life skills such as using the phone, making meals, shopping and taking care of others can be practised in role without anxiety or threat. Writing in role when making lists, labels, notes, letters and appointments or taking names gives practice for emergent writing and helps to reinforce both the functions and the importance of writing. Counting, checking, selling, buying give opportunities to become aware of numbers and their uses. Negotiating and compromising give practice in social skills.

Role play allows children to shape their own learning environment by contributing to planning and providing role play situations. We should recognise this, and demonstrate our interest in their opinions by giving them real choices and handing over some of the ownership to them.

There are three major types of role play:

domestic play - where the home and family are at the centre, with jobs to do and food to prepare. These domestic situations can be familiar or new. We should aim for a variety, some rooted in the children's own experience, some encouraging flights of fancy. You could try a barbecue or a country cottage, a caravan or a lighthouse, a giant's house or a palace. Remember the opportunities outside your room as well as those within it.

transactional play - where goods, services and advice are exchanged for money. These are endlessly fascinating to children, probably because transactions are a major part of what they observe of adult behaviour. You can include shops, travel agents, vets, clinics, markets, garden centres and many others.

imagined worlds - those places where stories dwell, or places the children are unlikely to visit, such as the moon or under the sea, in a pond, a cave, the North Pole, a jungle. For city children it may be the seaside, for country children it may be a tower block. Some children may have travelled several times by air but never been on a bus. To some the dark is

Getting started

Brainstorm role play following a story or other stimulus, or at the beginning of a new topic.

Use walks and visits to discuss what people do, jobs, shops and services.

Invite visitors (the health visitor, dentist, parents, etc.) to talk about their jobs.

Collect books and leaflets about jobs.

Use items of clothing, hats, objects to start conversations about characters.

Use video clips, photos, posters, magazine articles, as starting points.

Start a collection of stories to stimulate role play. Add simple props or make prop boxes.

Use puppets to begin stories and trigger interests.

Encourage parents to get involved.

Some ideas for role play settings

a house and a food shop
a house with a baby & a baby clinic
a cave and a giant's castle
a garage and a car wash
a hairdresser's and a wedding
a garden centre and a café
an office and a train
a fish and chip shop and a house
an aeroplane and a travel agent

... and for role play outside

a sports centre
picnics
a window cleaner
painting the school (or a house)
a barbecue
a submarine
a market

familiar, to others it is the unknown. Give all children the chance to come to terms with the unfamiliar by exploring it through role play.

All three types of play can be provided in a variety of ways: through 'whole body' play with access to dressing up and life sized equipment, through small world play using Lego, Playmobil, etc. and through the use of puppets, dolls or figures. A play setting outside could link with a domestic setting inside: for instance, outside there could be a train or bus, inside there could be, for example, a clinic or shop to take the baby to.

If you can offer more than one of these types of play at the same time what results will be deeper, more complex, more intense and will offer the children richer experiences. What is the point of having a house if you can't go out anywhere? What is the point of having a shop if you can't take the food home to cook?

Ensuring quality

Role play is such a powerful learning tool, we should never neglect its impact. The domestic play area must never decline into:

a jumbled box of assorted women's cast offs as dressing up clothes

an assortment of old plastic plates and cups

some battered furniture

a couple of naked dolls in a cot with no bedclothes,

when with a little care it could have:

simple matching picnic sets

baby clothes which fit the dolls and simple baby bedding

a rack or hooks for dressing up clothes with something for the boys to wear

newly painted furniture and some new curtains.

There is so much reasonably priced children's furniture in garden centres and shops that refurbishing a play area need not be costly.

Resources to encourage independence in role play

- Lightweight furniture and screens.
- Baskets, prop boxes, access to collections.
- Well organised hanging space for clothes – hooks and loops on garments. A small bench and a mirror near a dressing up area.
- Unisex, all-purpose tabards or overalls.
- Magazines, newspapers, leaflets and forms.
- Telephones (including mobiles) – the more you have, the more they will talk.
- Light fabrics that can be tied to furniture, trees, equipment to make tents and shelters, or to tie round heads or bodies. Hats and headbands, stickers and badges.
- A tray or trolley with clipboards, notebooks and pens. White boards, blackboards, pens and chalk. Materials for making signs, notices, badges.
- Playground chalk for markings.
- Flags, streamers, shop signs and banners.
- Baskets, mats and blankets for picnics, with matching plates and cutlery.
- Plastic cones, crates and guttering for structures.
- Lightweight containers, trolleys, baskets and bags.
- Post boxes, road signs, traffic lights, steering wheels.
- A range of items from different ethnic and social backgrounds.

Look out for sales and special offers. If the children can be taken along to choose the furniture and experience the shopping it will provide another opportunity for learning.

Build up collections, boxes or baskets on different themes. These can be used in rotation to link with topics or activities, or children can decide who they want to be today. Boxes or collections for imagined places could include a story sack with a book and all the props for acting it out. Children probably need access to more (or more complicated) equipment for transactional play than for domestic or imagined play. Over time it is usually possible to make small investments in equipment, and parents or local traders can often help.

In settings where the staff and children are used to working and planning together, children are involved in decisions about the setting up, location, focus, equipment, the time for change as well as the play itself. Here is a description of a Reception class where children are accustomed to being fully involved in planning what they do.

Mrs Senga, who helps in the classroom, came to school with a new perm. The children were fascinated by her curls and followed her everywhere, intrigued by the new look. Mrs Senga and some of the children went to the school library to look for a book about hairdressing, but they couldn't find one. At group time, Mrs Senga was asked to describe what had happened at the hairdressers. The children asked some very complex questions. Mrs Brennigan, their teacher, decided that a visit was indicated and on her way home she called at a local hairdresser to ask if they would be willing to cope with a visit from the class.

A few days later the children all walked along the road for the visit. The children had already had opportunities to talk about the hairdresser, so they had some ideas of what they wanted to see and ask. The obliging hairdresser had arranged to do a free wash and set for a regular customer as a focus of interest for the visit. The children watched this process intently, taking careful note of how the rollers and drier were used.

Some children made picture lists on clipboards. Mrs Senga was in charge of the digital camera and some of the children took photos. The hairdresser gave them each a little sample of shampoo to take home. He also gave them a big bag of rollers, brushes, empty shampoo bottles, some shoulder capes and an appointment book.

Over the next few days, the children brought things from home to complete the preparations – magazines, an old hairdryer (with the flex removed), a mobile phone, empty hairspray and shampoo bottles. They also collected bowls, towels, pens and paper, purses and money. They made a price list, which included children's haircuts for the dolls. They put up posters and made a style book of pictures from magazines.

The photos from the visit were printed and mounted, including a whole series of the process of a 'wash and blow dry' from the visit. This really helped with sequencing an unfamiliar event. Chairs, tables, overalls and a booking desk complete with phone and the appointment book completed the preparations. The children decided to call their shop 'Hair Do', and with Mrs Senga's help made a big sign to go on the door.

The boys were just as keen to be involved as the girls, both as hairdressers and as clients. Visitors brought dolls from the home play area, members of staff were invited to make appointments, and parents called in to see what was going on. The children took photos of their 'salon' to send with letters of thanks for their visit.

Every child in the class became involved in this exercise, and staff observed that even the most withdrawn children took part, growing in confidence as they did so. The children often adopted their parents' names when they made appointments. Their technical language and the language of transactional situations became very sophisticated, and this affected other activities in the classroom. The concentrated play lasted for several weeks, until a spell of really fine weather stimulated interest in the school garden and the children decided to dismantle the hairdresser's and use the equipment to set up a garden centre outside.

This is an example of role play of a very high quality. These children were completely involved in setting up and organising their own learning environment. The practitioners followed the interests of the children and responded positively to the leads which they gave. They watched and listened, were sensitive to the things children were interested in, and offered resources to support them. They used these starting points to extend children's learning through first hand experiences, play and talk. This in turn stimulated the imagination and creativity of the children, and gave them wonderful opportunities to develop the skills of independent learning.

It is obvious from this description that both the children and the practitioners were used to working in that way. Those who are not often don't know how to start. Our advice is to begin with talk, and there are ideas and prompts for this in the Appendix.

If children are to be confident in leading the development of the play they must be enabled to feel ownership. Make it clear from the start that, within the parameters necessary for good manners, welfare and safety, the decisions are theirs. For example:

Storage
- wicker baskets and boxes with handles for props, picnics, role play clothes
- laundry baskets for bricks and small world play (make sure they are light enough for the children to carry)
- fit hooks and shelves in your shed, so things can be hung up and paint outlines of the objects so that the children can put them back in the right places
- small trolleys or stacking vegetable baskets keep items like balls and bean bags safe (also useful for outside collage, paint, sand toys, science, garden tools)
- child sized bags and baskets are good for clearing up; have several so that everyone can help

start the session by saying, 'Where shall we put the house today?'

set up a minimal shop, office or other setting and wait for them to ask for additional things.

put up a sign, picture or label to suggest role play ('WINDOW CLEANER', 'GARAGE', 'CAVE') then ask the children what they need to make the place work.

put a prop basket or box of items on the carpet or outside (cloths and brushes for a car wash, a doctor's kit and white coat, a trowel, fork and some seed packets).

when children lose interest in a play area, ask them what you should do. Follow their lead.

discuss purchases of new equipment, let them look at catalogues and books to choose items; when you set up a new area or topic, make a list with them and take them shopping.

Chapter 7: how to improve provision to encourage independence

after a visit, discuss how they can help to set up the new situation, where it should be, what it should contain.

observe and note the conversations going on in the role play areas. Use these as starting points for discussions, new resources and changes. See *We Can Do It!* for more examples

As part of your review of this aspect of learning we suggest you consider these questions and discuss them with colleagues:

How much independence do you allow your children in role play?

Do you encourage children to change and adapt the role play areas, furniture, equipment, etc.?

Could you involve the children more in setting up new areas?

Are the resources of the highest quality you can afford?

Do role play activities and resources reflect the groups and communities living in the area and the backgrounds of the children in your setting? Do they offer opportunities for children to broaden their experience?

Do you change the role play areas often enough?

Have you considered the benefits of having more than one role play area?

Is role play on offer outdoors as well as inside your setting?

Are there opportunities for informal and spontaneous role play as well as for play in more permanent settings?

Do you provide clothing and resources for role play which are likely to appeal to both genders? Do you encourage children away from gender stereotyping in their play? Is there equivalence between the genders in both indoor and outdoor play?

Do you encourage parents and children to contribute ideas, experiences and resources for role play?

Outside play is an entitlement for all children in the Foundation Stage. Nowadays, anxiety about children's safety and the increasingly sedentary nature of home life means that children may grow up with little opportunity to play outdoors, and many have no contact with their friends at the end of the day or at weekends. Playing in the garden or the park is unfamiliar to many, and extended periods of uninterrupted physical activity are rare, even inside our settings.

The Outdoor Environment

The QCA *Guidance for the Foundation Stage* states that

'Practitioners should:

plan activities which offer *appropriate physical challenges*

provide *sufficient space, indoors and outdoors* to set up relevant activities

give sufficient time for children to *use a range of equipment*

provide *resources that can be used in a variety of ways* or to support specific skills

introduce the *language of movement* alongside their actions

Foundations for Independence

use additional adult help to *support individuals* and to *encourage increased independence in physical activities.*' (The italics are ours.)

Links with Early Learning Goals

Early Learning Goals which are linked to outdoor play are:

Personal and social development

> continue to be interested, excited and motivated to learn
>
> respond to significant experiences, showing a range of feelings when appropriate
>
> work as part of a group or class, taking turns and sharing fairly, understanding that there need to be agreed values, and codes of behaviour for groups of people, including adults and children, to work together harmoniously
>
> select and use activities and resources independently

Language, communication and literacy

> use language to imagine and recreate roles and experiences
>
> interact with others, negotiating plans and activities and taking turns in conversations
>
> attempt writing for various purposes, using features of different forms such as lists, stories, instructions
>
> write their own names and labels and form sentences, sometimes using punctuation

Mathematical

> use everyday words to describe position

Knowledge and understanding of the world

> find out about and identify some features of living things, objects and events they observe
>
> ask questions about why things happen and how things work
>
> build and construct with a wide range of objects, selecting appropriate resources, and adapting their work where necessary
>
> observe, find out and identify features in the place they live and the natural world

Physical development

> move with confidence, imagination and in safety
>
> move with control and co-ordination
>
> show awareness of space, of themselves and others
>
> use a range of small and large equipment
>
> travel around, under, over and through balancing and climbing equipment.

In *Listening to Four-year-olds* Jacqui Cousins found that one of the things that young children place in their top three favourite activities is playing with friends and having fun (particularly outside). In some settings it is possible for children to have unrestricted access to outside play with their friends; play which gives appropriate challenges, with space and time to develop their ideas, good resources and supportive adults. However, across settings the range of outdoor play provision is wide, and some children do not have their needs met. Poor access, shared spaces, vandalism or safety issues may all limit opportunities to enjoy fresh air and space. Problems though these may be, they should not

Chapter 7: how to improve provision to encourage independence

become excuses for neglecting the contribution that the outside environment should make to growing independence. There are many things we can do, whatever the restrictions, to make the best of access to outdoor space.

Chapter 6 discussed the outside environment in some detail and suggested that there is nothing you can do indoors that you cannot also do outdoors. The opportunities to set up, share and reorganise activities are endless. If children are encouraged to get out their own apparatus and equipment from trolleys, sheds, baskets and boxes, they will always use it more imaginatively than if we decide for them. They will combine, adapt and interpret simple objects such as ropes, posts, screens and signs in many and varied ways. They will improvise from given materials to make others. They will use static equipment to support and extend temporary structures, and they will incorporate wheeled toys into their play, improving daily on what they have done before. They will bring the inside out and the outside in – if we give them ownership of their play.

Apart from the physical dimension, outdoor play gives endless opportunities for social play: learning how to negotiate, co-operate and share equipment and games, how to work in a group, to take turns, to delay their own gratification in the interests of others. The outside is often the only place where children can make noise with their bodies and voices. Large apparatus and wheeled toys encourage physical development, necessary for the co-ordination of eye, ear, hand and foot. The use of small apparatus further refines motor skills – throwing, catching, bouncing, rolling – and the chance to run, jump, hop, roll, skip, push and pull give the opportunity to revel in space and the freedom to move.

We can extend the usual features of the outside environment by bringing out activities and equipment usually reserved for indoors –

Where possible, practitioners should allow children to move spontaneously between indoor and outdoor environments. Children will improve their co-ordination, control and ability to move more effectively if they can run, climb, balance, swing, slide, tumble, throw, catch and kick when they want to and are motivated and interested in doing so.

QCA, Curriculum Guidance for the Foundation Stage. 2000

Ideas for outdoors

Screw white or blackboards to the wall or fence (make some of them big for collaborative work.

Put up a batten of wood along a wall or fence, about a metre or so from the ground; pin paper or card to the batten for painting, chalk or crayons.

offer a basket of playground chalk for games and pictures

Make or buy some clipboards and small chalk boards. Make flags, notices, signs and labels

Resources

- Barrels, tyres, boxes, planks and tubes cost little and encourage imagination.
- Lightweight fabrics and clips or clothes pegs make good shelters and screens.
- Use pop up tents and gazebos for portable shelters.
- Provide small containers with different sets (dinosaurs, people, farm/zoo animals, cars, etc.)which can be used in different places (sand, water, table top, grass).
- Small versions of metal garden tools, brushes, pans, spades, etc. are much more rewarding than plastic.

mark-making, writing, books and other table-top activities in trays, on rugs or on tables. We can provide quiet areas and wild areas. We can encourage interest in the natural environment and its care by offering weather watching, sensory gardens, flowers, bird tables and small ponds. Paint, dough, sand, woodwork and other messy materials can be available where there is space for collaborative or large-scale works. Small world, farm, jungle and zoo animals and vehicles all have a place, where chalk or paint can provide instant roads, fields and enclosures.

Providing outdoor play does not have to be expensive. Tents, gazebos and plastic furniture are all readily available, and at the end of the summer can often be picked up cheaply. As well as sales in supermarkets and garden centres look for second-hand items in newspapers and shop windows. Guttering, rope, cardboard and wooden boxes, pieces of fabric and clips for fixing them, playground chalk, clipboards and materials for signs and labels cost little and will relieve the pressure on those more expensive wheeled toys and fixed apparatus.

Ensuring quality

Consider the use of the outside environment in this account.

Storage

- boxes and baskets, light enough for the children to carry); small trolleys or vegetable baskets keep things like balls, bean bags, paints, toys, equipment for science & outdoor collage, garden tools, etc. safe
- fit hooks and shelves in your shed, so things can be hung, and paint outlines of the objects so children can put them back in the right places
- child sized bags and baskets are good for clearing up (have several so they can all help)

Have several smaller sheds, rather than one big one. Then you can store things in different ones to make access easier. You could use one for trikes, with shelves above for prop boxes. Then, when the bikes are out, the shed can become a role play area. Plan some surprises to promote language and exploration – for example a mirror, bubbles, streamers, footprints, a basket of new objects.

Brendon walks towards the outside door, which opens onto the patio area and the garden. As he passes Nazia, he says, 'Coming outside?'. Nazia looks up from the train track, nods and joins him, bringing the train with her. The two children pause on the threshold to the garden. They look around to see what is going on outside. It is autumn, and although it is sunny the gusting wind sets the wind chimes ringing and swirls leaves across the garden. It feels cold.

'I'm getting my coat,' says Brendon. 'Do you want yours?' He fetches their coats and they put them on.

The play area is busy. Bikes are popular, and a small group of children run with ribbons streaming from their hands in the wind. A basket of bean bags, small balls and quoits has been placed just outside the door. A small trolley with playground chalk, clipboards and mark makers is also at hand. A pop-up tent has been erected on the edge of the grass, with a prop basket containing lengths of fabric, assorted hats and bags and an old mobile phone. Another mobile phone is 'in use' at the top of the climbing frame.

Nazia runs back inside and soon reappears with some bubbles, which she and Brendon begin to blow. Other children come to join the game, jumping and racing to catch the bubbles. Ben (a nursery nurse) has been watching. He begins to talk about the colours in the bubbles and the way they are swept away by the wind. The children stand still and watch, commenting on what is happening.

After a while Brendon and Nazia give the bubbles to another child and go over to the edge of the hard playground, where leaves have been blown into a pile by the wind. They pick up leaves and throw them into the air, watching as they fly. Some sycamore seeds have also blown into the garden. Brendon knows about these. 'My dad calls these helicopters,' he says. 'Look how they fly.' He shows Nazia how to throw the seeds, and both children toss the seeds into the air, watching them spin and twirl. Brendon puts some seeds in his pocket to show the other children later.

Nazia says, 'I'm thirsty. I'm getting a drink. Are you coming?'

Brendon shakes his head. 'I'm going in the sand.'

Nazia fetches a drink from inside and brings it to the picnic table on the patio. She sits and watches the other children, content for a few minutes to just observe their play.

Meanwhile Brendon, Jake and Carly are building an animal park in the sand tray. They make cages for the animals with small sticks from the ground, and fetch some card from the trolley to make a notice for the park.

Sonny approaches fast on his bike. He bangs into the sand tray and dislodges the notice. He rushes off again, leaving the three park constructors standing with their mouths open. Ben has been watching. He comes over and sympathises, helping them to repair and re-erect the notice before he goes off to have a word with Sonny.

A child rings a small bell to warn that it is time to pack up the toys. Everybody helps to collect the bikes, to return balls and quoits to the basket, to clean the blackboards which are fixed to the fence, and to untie the ribbons from the tree branches. Brendon takes the 'helicopter' seeds out of his pocket and sends one flying before going inside to join the group for a story.

These children were confident. They knew what they wanted to do and had ideas about how to do it. They respected each other, listened to each other and worked together collaboratively – and when they didn't a practitioner was on hand to defuse a potentially volatile situation and talk quietly to the child who had misbehaved. There was space for children to take time out to watch what was going on. At clearing-up time they worked as a team to put things away and prepare for the end of the session.

Here are some suggestions for giving your children ownership of outdoor play.

Don't put everything out for the children before they come out. Get them involved in what goes out and where.

When you buy, involve the children. Ask them what they need, let them help with choosing new equipment and resources.

Boxes, planks, ropes, buckets and pulleys will give more scope for imagination than fixed apparatus. Watch for their ideas to emerge and, without intruding, encourage them to build on them.

Let the children choose what to grow, and don't be afraid to let them experiment. You might not be able to grow bananas in Barking but you could let children plant seeds outdoors and indoors to see what happens. If you haven't got a garden, let them plant and care for seeds or bulbs in pots, window boxes and containers.

Children love making their own dens and hidey holes. Offer cardboard boxes or fabric sheets to attach to fixed apparatus or buildings.

Encourage children to name and label their structures. Make sure there are plenty of opportunities to make their own signs, notices, flags, instructions, labels, badges, etc. to personalise their play.

Involve the children in the location and timing of snacks and drinks, stories, circle time.

Ask questions of the children to encourage them to use the resources and equipment imaginatively – for example, a small world set, some cars and some guttering have many possibilities.

Be sensitive to new ideas to support and extend their play and respond to them when they come.

And here are some questions to ask when you review the quality of outdoor play in your setting:

Is your outdoor area an exciting, flexible environment? Does it change frequently to meet the needs of the children and give them opportunities in many areas of learning?

Are the children encouraged to change and adapt the outdoor areas, furniture, equipment, etc. as they need for their play?

Could you involve the children more in selecting and buying new equipment and apparatus?

Do you consider versatility when choosing new equipment, making sure that new things have many possible uses, that they can be used by more than one child at a time, that children of different ages and stages can use them?

Is the outdoor storage accessible to the children? Can they help to get things out and put them away? Do you make full use of all the spaces available to you – e.g. sheds or other outdoor storage spaces when they are empty?

Do you put everything out for the children, or could you involve them more in deciding what goes out and where?

Do you give opportunities for children to personalise their play by, for example, offering flexible resources with many uses and providing mark-making equipment?

Do you watch children playing in this area to find out how we can enhance and extend the quality of their play?

How much independence do you allow children in this aspect of learning?

Construction

Construction using bricks, small construction sets and found materials is a feature in early years settings of all types and locations. It is one important way in which children practise and perfect fine motor control. Without good hand-eye co-ordination reading and writing become very difficult. It is sometimes an area which is neglected, considered by practitioners to be a place where 'children can get on by themselves'. Because of this it is often where most independence is given to children in deciding how and what they do, and with whom. It is also the place where real learning and language development often take place, and so should be a regular focus for observation by adults.

Recent research into brain development tells us that boys and girls develop different parts of their brains at different ages. From the beginning of nursery, boys will opt for practical activities, especially outdoors, and will choose frequent change. Girls of the same age will choose books, painting and drawing, and even at this stage they will spend twice as long on an activity as boys. This is because the left side of the brain (the side linked to analytical skills and language learning) develops earlier in girls than in boys. By providing a wide range of construction activities we help boys and girls to develop both sides of their brains. For girls, construction gives opportunities to work in three dimensions, in patterns and shapes with mathematical connections, right brain activities. It gives boys the chance to concentrate and to improve those essential skills which come from the left brain.

In some settings the construction area is dominated by boys, and in such cases it is important to consider how what it offers can be made more interesting for girls. Often it doesn't take a great deal. Simply including small world people can be enough to stimulate girls' interest.

Displaying books and pictures near construction areas helps children with ideas. They should include images of both sexes, examples of buildings and vehicles, children's plans and drawings of their own constructions, and photos of constructions, complete or unfinished, which have been made in your setting, both indoors and out.

Construction activities contribute to all areas of learning. Their relevance can be seen in the collaborative aspects of personal development, in shape and space in maths, in science, technology, physical skills and creativity.

One of the areas in which three and four year old children make the most progress concerns the development of fine motor control. This can be defined as the ability to co-ordinate the action of the eyes and hands together in performing skilful adaptive movements.

Audrey Curtis, A Curriculum for the Preschool Child. 1960

Ideas for stimulating construction

Add chalk to the basket of bricks and cars.

Put a small basket of mark makers and cards in the Lego box.

Use old, worn bricks to extend the recycled materials.

Add cars and people to brick baskets.

Try some space people figures.

Use big bricks to make houses, shops, boats for role play.

... and some ideas for locations

Take Lego outside on a concrete mixing tray.

Use a big sheet of card or wood as the base for a group construction with recycled materials.

Try a construction that is on more than one level or surface – table to floor, down a step, under a table.

Getting started

Talk about construction, encourage children to plan where they will start and what they might make.

Use pictures, stories, objects and characters as inspiration for brick play.

Links with Early Learning Goals

Early Learning Goals which are linked to construction are:

Personal, social and emotional development

maintain attention, concentration

work as part of a group or class, taking turns and sharing fairly, understanding that there need to be agreed values and codes of behaviour for groups of people, including adults and children, to work together harmoniously

Communication, language and literacy

use language to imagine and recreate roles and experiences

Mathematics

use language such as more, less, greater, smaller, heavier, lighter to compare two numbers or quantities

talk about, recognise and recreate simple patterns

use language such as circle or bigger to describe the shape and size of solids and flat shapes

use everyday words to describe position

Knowledge and understanding of the world

investigate objects and materials by using all of their senses as appropriate

build and construct with a wide range of objects, selecting appropriate resources, and adapting their work where necessary

select tools and techniques they need to shape, assemble and join the materials they are using

Physical development

move with confidence, imagination and in safety

move with control and co-ordination use a range of small and large equipment

handle tools, objects, construction and malleable materials safely and with increasing control

Creative development

express and communicate their ideas, thoughts and feelings by using a widening range of materials, suitable tools, imaginative and role play, movement, designing and making, and a variety of songs and instruments

Building with three-dimensional objects falls into three main areas:

using bricks of various sizes and in various materials.

using joining sets like Lego, Sticklebricks, Mobilo.

using recycled and found materials, such as cartons, card tubes, reels, spools, plastic containers and bottles, tops, string, wool, fabric, plastic, paper and card. These materials can be used to make temporary or permanent structures.

Chapter 7: how to improve provision to encourage independence

Many of the more permanent resources for construction need maintenance. Wooden blocks should be splinter free, stable to build with and well organised for access and storage. Regular varnishing will help to prolong their lives and protect the corners. Plastic and foam bricks should be cleaned regularly and stored in lightweight bags or crates so that children can carry them easily. Construction sets need regular washing, and should be refurbished by replacing damaged and missing parts and by adding new ones. Recycled materials must be well organised and labelled if they are not to become an uninspiring muddle, well described as 'junk'!

The ideal for avoiding frustration and conflict is to make sure that there is plenty of everything to go round. However, this is not always possible, and taking turns and waiting for a turn are important lessons for children to learn. Work with the children on devising and developing turns and routines which will give everyone a fair chance.

Each construction set needs a good mixture of standard parts and additions, such as wheels, roof tiles, arches, cogs and figures. Storing sets in several smaller containers is a way of enabling children to access them without help, and therefore enables them to be independent by working in smaller groups and different locations. Of course, children should be able to mix and combine different sets for more ambitious projects.

Construction with found materials needs thoughtful planning and organisation. It is important to make sure that glue and other joining materials, such as tape and staples, are available to children in a way that enables them to manage them independently. We need to encourage experiment without fear of failure, in an atmosphere where children go readily to each other and to adults for help, advice and guidance on the technological aspects of what they are making.

Resources

- Sometimes have a week with no glue in the construction area.
- Use found materials to make temporary arrangements of objects, collages and buildings. Draw or photograph what results.
- Offer cut card circles and split pins for wheels.
- Try to collect found materials that have their own colour.
- Boxes and containers with printed words and pictures distract children from the form of the object.
- Avoid paint unless you can be sure that it will stick to the surfaces available!
- Masking tape is easier to use than sticky tape.
- Make sure the scissors will cut the materials available.
- In the technology area, offer small scale materials to make signs and notices – cocktail sticks, plasticene, card, fine markers, photocopies of road and shop signs, pictures of people.
- Sets of people enhance play in any construction materials. Don't restrict the dolls house family to their own house!

Space is vital for constructions of all sorts, and if possible there should be a place where work in progress can be left out overnight, or put aside while glue or paint are drying. Brick play needs a flat, soft surface inside or out. A large piece of carpet is ideal. Children often prefer to work with construction and found materials on tables or benches, and these areas can include a shelf for storing models and structures.

Time is all important in planning construction activities. Children need that 'time for sustained concentration' (QCA), which gives them room to develop the play, process it in their minds and return to it later or even the next day. This is not always possible for every activity in every setting, but it is a principle that we should try to remember. Children haven't finished an activity just because we say it is time to pack away!

Ensuring quality

The following is an example of the good use of construction materials. The children have plenty of opportunities to control and shape the activities, and the result is that these lead to a range of experiences which the teacher had not planned. Note how she acts as a resource, providing just the right amount of stimulation and encouragement to keep things moving forward.

The room is set up with clearly defined areas for different activities. Four children (three boys and a girl) are playing on a carpeted area with a large set of small wooden bricks. They have made a huge layout of the bricks in a complicated design of roads, buildings, trees, parks and fields. As they work, individuals fetch additional resources – a basket of farm animals, a village set, some cars and people. Other children come to watch the construction as it grows. They contribute ideas and some get involved in the play. The teacher observes as the construction develops. She says nothing, but makes notes and takes a series of photos as the construction grows over several days with different children involved. At group times she encourages the children to talk about the construction, modelling language and vocabulary, suggesting books and stories that might be of interest.

One day she offers a set of road signs. This sparks new enthusiasm, and a flurry of writing follows. Children use materials in the technology area to make signs and notices, including one to the premises officer saying 'plese kep off'. They select small sticks, plastic bottle tops and pieces of card from the carefully organised boxes of materials, each clearly labelled with its contents, to make more signs. They give it a name: 'Brickland'.

Martha fetches a peaked cap and a shoulder bag from the prop box. She has been to a safari park and knows about tickets. She makes some from paper, cutting them out very carefully. She uses crayons to decorate each one and stands by a notice, which says 'brikland pay here'.

The teacher provides a box of money and the play develops into the next phase. Eventually the work on the village expands into all areas of the curriculum, providing opportunities in maths, language, science, technology, for visits and walks in the locality and for the development of fine motor skills. The extended building and reorganisation of the construction involves plenty of negotiation and compromise.

Here are some ideas for empowering children and giving them ownership.

Encourage children to mix and combine construction materials.

Take time and care when organising found and recycled materials for children. Transparent containers and helpful labels make access easier.

Encourage flexibility in working. Blur the edges between areas and activities, so children can move easily from construction to mark making, from inside to outside.

Help them to make links in their learning through discussion and sensitive suggestions.

Observe and document their play, and feed back what you see by sharing photos and writing down their words.

Record their constructions through photos and drawings. The records can then be displayed with books and posters and children's own words. This raises self esteem and self image, and gives the activity status with others.

Help those who are less confident to get involved by encouraging them to make labelled diagrams, signs and notices.

Use these questions to review your provision:

Do you give this area of the curriculum the status it deserves? Do you visit it, observe it and include it in your discussions?

Are the resources for construction well-organised, attractive, well maintained, high quality? Are there enough of them? Do they stimulate and sustain interest and involvement?

Are children encouraged to develop the play? Are you able to leave unfinished or ongoing constructions overnight or over longer periods? If not, what can you do about it?

Do children feel comfortable combining sets of equipment to extend their play?

Can children move from area to area, following their needs to make marks, integrate other materials, revisit activities, refer to books?

Do you consult the children when buying or collecting new items for construction?

Do children have the tools, materials and support to help them be successful when working on bigger or more permanent constructions?

Does the glue really stick? Are the scissors sharp enough? Will the paint cover the surfaces?

Stories

Stories play a crucial role in the development of young children. When they listen to a story they engage in an active process that impacts on their thinking and influences their perceptions of themselves and the world in which they live. Practitioners need to ensure that, through the stories they offer, children have the opportunity to experience a range of approaches, attitudes and responses to life. As children engage with the characters in the story they explore the experiences of others, and as part of this process relate what is happening to others to the things they have experienced in their own lives. This process will be largely unconscious, but for all that it is extremely powerful.

Practitioners should give particular attention to giving opportunities to share and enjoy a wide range of rhymes, music, songs, poetry, stories and non-fiction books.

QCA, Curriculum Guidance for the Foundation Stage. 2000

Links with Early Learning Goals

<u>Communication, language and literacy:</u>

- enjoy listening to and using spoken and written language, and readily turn to it in their play and learning

- explore and experiment with sounds, words and texts

- listen with enjoyment and respond to stories, songs and other music, rhymes and poems and make up their own stories, songs, rhymes

- use language to imagine and recreate roles and experiences

- use talk to organise, sequence and clarify thinking, ideas, feelings and events

- sustain attentive listening, responding to what they have heard by relevant comments, questions or actions

- extend their vocabulary, exploring the meanings and sounds of new words

- retell narratives in the correct sequence, drawing on the language patterns of stories

Stories have many functions and effects. They communicate messages, make statements about right and wrong, suggest ways of going about things and set up expectations. In short, stories have the potential to profoundly influence the way children behave.

When we choose stories and texts for young children we must consciously think about the messages that we are, perhaps unconsciously, transmitting. If children are exposed to a diet of stories where the heroes and heroines sit about waiting for someone else to take responsibility for sorting out their problems, then we must expect this to influence the way in which they themselves respond to problems and difficulties. If, on the other hand, the stories they hear feature strong, empowered characters ready and willing to take responsibility for the things that happen in their lives, then we are looking at probably very different outcomes.

To give an example, lets take a familiar story. Cinderella is a victim, picked on by her ugly sisters and generally exploited by her family. In fact without the support of significant others – and the fairy godmother in particular – she would probably have been condemned to a life of drudgery, doomed to live out her days in a dingy basement servicing the needs of her thoughtless and insensitive family. As she waits for her prince, passively accepting her lot, she is powerless. Her destiny is in the hands of her unscrupulous family. She does

Stories are fundamental to human experience, and stories experienced in early childhood can extend children's thinking, foster new knowledge and validate their emotions.

When children's own experiences connect in some way to those contained within a story, a match of meaning can occur. Such a match between that which children find important and the stories they read and hear makes the crucial difference between simply hearing a story and really listening with absorbed intent and making it part of their thinking.

Cathy Nutbrown,
Threads of Thinking. 1999

Chapter 7: how to improve provision to encourage independence

not even expect that life will ever be any different, and when her circumstances suddenly change no-one is more surprised than she. It is only by being whisked away by a handsome prince that she experiences a happier existence. But if we were to write the sequel to this story, what might happen to poor Cinderella, disempowered as she is? Should she in the future be faced with difficult circumstances, how would she cope? Suppose the prince fell on hard times and took up with a rich widow as a means of solving his problems; what would become of Cinderella then? It seems more than likely that she would have to return to the kitchen!

Cinderella is just one example of the sort of sub-textual message often conveyed by traditional stories. Think about some of the others – Aladdin, Jack and the Beanstalk, Sleeping Beauty – and try a similar analysis of your own. We are not condemning traditional stories or saying that they should not be used. On the contrary, they are great fun and part of children's heritage. But it is important to be aware not only of the simple narrative line but also of what the stories are saying beneath the surface, and to ensure that children are also exposed to other material which will offer alternative views.

In recent years there have been many alternative versions of traditional tales that challenge the archetypal view of the heroine as passive victim or the hero as handsome playboy. Some titles you may like to try are *Prince Cinders* or *Tarzanna* by Babette Cole and *The Paper Bag Princess* by Robert Munsch. Ask your library for more suggestions.

Some of the stories, fiction and non fiction, which mean most to us as adults are those which have some resonance with our personal experience and view of the world. Others, of course, provide escape from or a contrast with our own lives or inhabit a world of make believe and fantasy, but these are more

Getting started

Read or tell stories in which children act independently, take responsibility, show initiative and solve problems. Here are some suggestions:

Tall Inside by Jean Richardson and Alice Englander.

Pass it Polly by Sarah Garland.

Jamaica and Brianna by Juanita Havill and Anna Sibley O'Brien.

Hector's New Trousers by Amanda Vesey.

Amazing Grace by Mary Hoffman and Caroline Birch.

Alfie Gives a Hand by Shirley Hughes.

Dogger by Shirley Hughes.

The Hunter by Paul Geraghty

Make time for children to tell you their stories and be excited about what they have to say.

Share your own stories with the children. Tell them about things that have happened to you.

Record children's stories on tape, video and in writing. This gives them real value and offers lots of opportunities for talking.

Encourage children to share their own experiences and stories. Ask questions which will encourage them to talk about times when they have used their initiative to solve a problem or accomplished something through their own efforts.

Make the children's stories into books and put them in the book corner or class library.

Use puppets to model stories about characters showing independence and autonomy.

sophisticated tastes that children do not usually acquire until later. To take on board what Cathy Nutbrown says in the quotation on the right is to make a commitment to ensuring that the subject matter of the stories we tell is designed to positively engage the children. This requires us to heighten our awareness of the issues that matter to young children and to present them with flair and sensitivity. The use of soft toys and puppets can really help us to do just that. The puppet is a very potent tool. It can stimulate the imagination, extend vocabulary and help young children to move from telling stories based on their own experiences into the realm of the imagination. Puppets are tangible. Children can experience them through their senses. They can see them and touch them, identify with them, and have no difficulty suspending their disbelief.

Large humanoid puppets are now readily available in most of the catalogues of the major education suppliers, and they are not difficult to use. You do not need to be theatrical or extrovert. Simply sit the puppet on a chair and let the story making begin. The moment you introduce children to a puppet you will find that they engage with it on an emotional level, and when the emotions are engaged the learning is always deeper. Some practitioners feel embarrassed when manipulating a doll or puppet. Don't be. The children will be watching and talking to the doll, not you!

Children can be involved at all stages of the process, making decisions about what the doll or puppet should be called, where they live, who they live with and the things they like to do. In a very short space of time they will become cult figures in your setting and their personalities will continue to evolve as more and more stories develop. The events in which they figure and the things that happen to them can mirror things that are important to the children, giving them a peg on which to hang their own creative storying.

Ideas for talking

Send a letter to the children from a fictional character or a soft toy, creating a situation to which they can make a response. For example: Spot could be on his holidays and want the children to help him record his adventures upon his return; Mrs Wishy-Washy could have run out of soap; Kipper might like to have a birthday party; The Three Bears may be fed up with porridge and want advice about other things to have for breakfast.

Wrap up a parcel and have it delivered to the classroom by the site supervisor or secretary. The children can try to guess the contents and once they have opened the parcel, who it has come from and why it has come to them.

Make a collection of old photos and pictures of interesting characters. Encourage children to make up stories around them.

Invite storytellers into your setting.

Plan a storytelling event.

Start telling a story yourself and get the children to carry it on and finish it off. You could start with a story they know and move on to stories you and they make up.

Engaging in this process will in itself develop the children's cognitive skills, but if you introduce some familiar moral dilemmas you can provide even more encouragement for independence. All we need to do is to create some open-ended story starters which will form the basis for thinking and discussion. For example, disobeying the instructions of a parent or teacher (either consciously or unconsciously), going somewhere they have been told not to go, or taking something that does not belong to them.

Carrying out this sort of work is both rewarding and interesting, and an excellent way of using imaginative material to develop children's independent thinking. Open-ended stories present scenarios which have no simple right or wrong answer. They enable you to review all the possibilities and go with what your reasoning tells you is right. These are skills vital to the development of independence.

If you don't have access to large puppets, soft toys can be used effectively instead. Alternatively, you could take the bull by the horns and have a go at making your own puppets. They don't have to look particularly life-like. In fact, the more eccentric they look the more the children seem to like them!

Wherever we go we can see story telling in action: in shops, cafés, bars, on buses and on street corners people are telling their stories. Storytelling is an integral part of life and human relationships. Our stories are our identity, and as we tell them we make sense of things that have happened to us, refine our judgements, modify our point of view and reflect upon our values. In short, our stories assist us in learning more about who we are. It is through our stories that we learn about ourselves, and the world in which we live. This is just as important for children as it is for adults. Stories have great potential for enhancing children's self-knowledge and self-esteem.

Resources

- Make up story boxes containing interesting things to stimulate storytelling – dinosaurs, space, under the sea, in the jungle, at the zoo, the seaside, etc. Decorate the insides of the boxes for whatever themes or topics you have decided to cover.

- Make collections of artefacts. Try old maps, keys, binoculars, coins, etc.

- Set up a listening corner where children can select and listen to story tapes. Have a tape recorder so children can record their own stories.

- Collect a wide range of puppets which children can use for story-building. Use 'Flannelgraphs' to prompt ideas.

- Cut out some pictures from old books or magazines and mount them on card. Play a game by picking out three and making up a story around them. You'll need to do it yourself a few times to show the children how, but they'll soon pick up the idea.

- Before the children arrive for the session, put some object or artefact in the middle of the room - e.g. a very large cardboard carton, some sparkly material, a pile of conkers. Ask them who they think could have left them. Encourage them to use their imaginations and suggest unusual ideas. Or point to the box and say, 'Look! A spaceship has just landed.' Or to the material and say, 'A magician has left his cloak. Do you think it's magic? What can it do?'

This has never been more effectively realised than through the work of Vivian Gussin Paley, who uses a very simple but powerful technique in the classroom. Her exciting and innovative work goes far beyond simply developing the children's spoken language and broader literacy skills. It engages children in the storymaking process, and uses children's stories as a vehicle of instruction in special ways.

The first part of Paley's approach involves the children in dictating their story to the practitioner, who will then, if the child wishes, read the story back. Enabling the children to see their words transcribed into print places real value on what they have to say and helps them to understand the permanence of the written word. So far this is a fairly common process used by most early years practitioners, but what happens next is not. The children then dramatise their story. With the practitioner's help they count up the number of characters in the story and make important decisions about who will take what part and how the 'play' will be acted out. The story is then read by the practitioner, and the children act out the narrative as she reads. As young children's stories rarely contain dialogue this means that they have no lines to improvise or learn. If there is any dialogue the practitioner can prompt the child or say it for them.

To begin with the plays are usually quite short. In some cases they may be no more than a single line, but as the children gain in experience the stories grow in length. What is important is what is happening as the children engage in this storymaking process. Vivian Gussin Paley talks about Joseph's story of a baby who grew up and went hunting with his father. 'Having told his story and acted it out, he knows something he did not know before, and he will use the new information as the need arises'.

In Paley's classroom children were given daily opportunities for storymaking. They signed up on the story list and waited until it was their turn to have their stories written down and acted. Through this process they grew in confidence as they developed their narratives and were empowered to turn their stories into actions that supported their growing sense of self. They were also able to contribute to the development of their peers, which is in itself very empowering.

Paley's work is extensive and has a huge amount to offer children and practitioners, but the best way to find out about it is to read her many books. They are hugely interesting and give many insights into the ways in which children's own stories can be used to facilitate and enrich their development.

Ensuring quality

Consider the power of story in this account.

Lee was having a really good time in the soft play area. With a group of friends he had built an elaborate obstacle course and was enjoying himself crawling, leaping and balancing on and through a range of self-constructed challenges. The children's pleasure was obvious as they urged each other on and shrieked with the pure enjoyment of it all. Suddenly the shrieks of delight were pierced by a scream. Lee had fallen from a piece of equipment and was howling loudly as he grasped one hand in the other. As he had fallen, Lee had landed on his hand and bent his finger back. The teacher sent for the first-aider, who advised that Lee be taken to hospital to have his injured finger checked out.

All the arrangements were made. Lee was to go to the hospital accompanied by a teacher, and his mother would meet them there. Although Lee had initially been somewhat distraught he eventually calmed down and warmed to the idea of a trip out of school. Once on his way he was full of curiosity about everything around him. At the hospital he engaged first the receptionist, then the nurse and finally the doctor in a full and frank account of everything that had happened to him.

The doctor explained that Lee would have to have an X-ray to find out whether his finger was broken. Would he be able to see the pictures? Lee wanted to know. On his way to be X-rayed he showed yet more curiosity, asking questions throughout and commenting on every stage of the process.

By the time his mother arrived, looking ashen faced and worried, she must have wondered what all the fuss was about. A beaming Lee greeted her with an enthusiastic invitation to view the pictures of his finger 'to see if it was broked!'

When the X-ray was finally displayed Lee was fascinated. He could hardly believe that what he was looking at was what was 'inside his hand'. Fortunately nothing was broken, and all that was required was a sturdy bandage, which once on caused Lee to swell with pride and pleasure.

By this time, his mum was anxious to take him home but Lee was having none of it, insisting that he return to school. Once there, what ensued was to stun everyone. Lee held the attention of ten adults and 100 children as he told the story of everything that had happened from beginning to end in copious detail. As he did so he grew, visibly.

Such is the power of story! *We Can Do It!* recommends some ways of getting started on using stories to develop independence. Here are some suggestions for stimulating and empowering children through stories:

> Tell open-ended stories that pose problems and moral dilemmas. Let the children decide where the story should go and how the problems might be solved.
>
> Make books in which the children are the main characters and allow them to make decisions about content, text and format.
>
> Tell group stories, encouraging the children to contribute ideas drawn from things they have done and events they have experienced; e.g. the day our class/group went to the zoo, forest, seaside, etc.
>
> Use a small mat or rug as a magic carpet. Let one of the children sit on it and encourage the others to contribute ideas about where it is going and how it will get there, describing the journey as it progresses.
>
> Get the children to make a display of their favourite stories. Encourage them to talk about the ones they have chosen and what they particularly like about them.
>
> Set up a performance area where children can tell and act out both their own and published stories.

Use these questions to review the provision in your setting:

> Are children involved in decisions about which stories will be read and told?
>
> Do adults model the storytelling process?
>
> How often do you as practitioners 'act out' stories for the children?
>
> Do you support children in acting out their own stories?
>
> Do you talk about stories and how they are constructed?
>
> Are children encouraged to develop a critical response to the stories they hear?
>
> Do you accept children's storytelling contributions without judgement, allowing them to develop their expertise over time?
>
> Are children's stories really valued by adults? How do you show this?

Are children consulted about which new storybooks should be purchased?

Do you help parents and carers to understand the value of story to children's development?

What are you doing to improve your own storytelling skills?

How much independence do you allow children in this aspect of learning?

Writing

The QCA Guidance for the Foundation Stage suggests that we should be giving children opportunities to see adults speaking, listening, reading and writing. In an earlier chapter we emphasised the importance of example, and it is worth repeating it again here. Children pick up their attitudes to learning from what they observe of adults, so it is clear that we should be demonstrating for them in our daily behaviour the communication skills we want them to acquire. We should immerse them 'in an environment rich in print and possibilities for communication', encouraging them 'to recognise the importance of written language through signs, notices and books.' (QCA)

Authors are people who make decisions; take responsibility for the selection of what goes on paper and are sensitive to contexts and audiences.

Nigel Hall,
Writing With Reason. 1989

QCA Guidance also advises that children should have chances to share and enjoy a wide range of stories, poems, rhymes and non fiction books, to experiment with writing through mark making and to begin to understand how print works.

Links with Early Learning Goals

Goals associated with writing are found throughout the six areas as well as in Communication, Language and Literacy. Here are some of the key ones:

<u>Personal, social & emotional development</u>

continue to be interested, excited & motivated to learn

be confident to try new activities, initiate ideas

<u>Language, communication and literacy</u>

enjoy listening to and using spoken and written language, and readily turn to it in their play and learning

explore and experiment with sounds, words and texts

attempt writing for various purposes, using features of different forms such as lists, stories, instructions

write their own names and labels and form sentences, sometimes using punctuation

use their phonic knowledge to write simple regular words and make phonetically plausible attempts at more complex words

use a pencil effectively and hold it effectively to form recognisable letters, most of which are correctly formed

Chapter 7: how to improve provision to encourage independence

<u>Physical development</u>

handle tools, with increasing control

<u>Creative development</u>

express and communicate their ideas, thoughts and feelings by using a widening range of materials.

Mark-making and writing activities are some of the best ways of promoting independence and autonomy. Even in this age of ICT, writing by hand is still an important activity. Children who have good access to high quality equipment, choice, freedom, support and recognition for their efforts will become writers. Just as children need free access to play materials and the outside environment, they need access to materials and equipment for mark making, an environment rich in print, and a place where they have models of adults and other children as writers. Learning about the purposes of writing is part of the process of becoming a writer, and the best way to learn about the purposes of writing is to write, to see others writing and to practise mark-making and writing activities in real-life situations at home, within the setting, in the local community and in role play of all sorts.

Children learn by doing. They learn to talk by talking, they learn to read by reading and they learn to write by writing. Of course, they eventually need to learn the orthodox way of forming letters and they need to realise that writing has meaning which can be interpreted by the reader, but in the beginning stages of writing children need the freedom to experiment with this activity in the same way as they do with every other. They need to explore, try out, practise, adapt and expand. They need to compare the marks they make with the writing they see. As in all their learning, at first the process is much more important than the product.

If the materials, models and equipment are available, children's first experiences of writing will usually be in role play or at writing tables,

Getting started

'Plant' a letter from a story book or local character in the room for the children to find; link writing ideas with story books.

Write invitations and thank you letters to visitors; encourage everyone you know to send you and the children postcards and letters.

Scribe children's comments to put with their pictures and models; each time you put up a new caption, sign or notice, read it with the children.

Make lists of things to do, or what you need for a project or visit.

Explain the writing you do (registers, notes, messages and reminders, labels) them to the children; bring your personal writing to share - letters, cards, lists, instructions, diaries.

With the children, collect examples of different sorts of writing – lists, forms, labels, instructions as well as stories, poems, diaries, letters – so they experience a wide range of purposes for writing.

Make suggestions for writing recipes, menus, poems, recording weather, attendance, celebrating birthdays and other special events; put forms and junk mail in home corners.

Suggest that they write reminders and messages for themselves.

Ideas for writing

A café or coffee shop with bills, menus and pads for the waiters and waitresses.

writing messages, labels, lists and letters. If every role play situation, inside and outside, offers materials for writing and mark making they will be used. If every adult in the setting models writing as a useful and important activity, if they talk about what they are writing, if they read back observations, explain messages and letters, make lists with the children, write recipes, transcribe the children's thoughts and descriptions of work to use as captions and labels, children will begin to make the link between what is spoken and what is written. If every visitor and every visit involves children in writing lists, notes and letters; if children's attention is drawn to writing in offices, shops, surgeries, fire stations, garages, the school or setting; if children have the opportunity and resources to replicate the sort of writing they see being done by their parents and by practitioners (e.g. by offering forms, notebooks and diaries) they will use these experiences in their own play. The aim is for children to begin to see the relationship between their own writing and the writing they see around them.

Writing materials and equipment should echo the quality resource indicators discussed in Chapter 4. Here is a simple checklist which practitioners may find useful:

Access (Are the writing materials easy to access?)

Organisation (Are they clearly grouped and labelled so children can find them and put them away?)

Presentation (Are things carefully and attractively stored, so children can see what is on offer?)

Condition (Are things checked for missing pieces, cleanliness, broken boxes, etc.? Are they topped up so there is always plenty of choice?)

Manageability (Are writing implements appropriate to the ages and stages of development of the

Ideas for writing (continued)

A bus with home-made bus tickets.

A doctor's surgery with prescriptions.

A fire station with a message pad.

A hairdressers with appointment cards and appointment book.

An office with a computer, letters and envelopes.

A takeaway pizza place with message pads, orders and delivery notes.

Shopping lists.

Resources for writing

Try to make available -

- paper and card in a range of colours· several sizes of envelopes (recycled ones are fine)
- a range of sizes, types and colours of pens, pencils, crayons · rulers, calculators
- a letter writing table with a post box for children to send letters to each other and to the adults in the setting
- sticky labels, badges
- address books, diaries, calendars, appointment books
- ready-made books (2 or 3 sheets stapled together) for stories
- small staplers, glue sticks, sticky tape
- old keyboards, computers with word processing facilities
- stamps - you can make your own by running a sewing machine (no cotton!) across paper to make perforations – then draw the pictures
- telephones, phone books, street maps
- junk mail, forms, timetables, leaflets

children? For example, are there different sizes of pencils, crayons and scissors?)

Location (Are things located near the play base where they are likely to be used?)

Quality (Is the writing and mark-making equipment of the highest possible quality that the setting can afford? Are we insistent on the best for the children?)

Suitability (Are the resources suitable for the purpose and the children? Do the scissors actually cut, are pencils sharp?)

Sufficiency (Is there enough of everything – scissors, staplers, envelopes?)

Range (Do we have a good range of equipment for boys and girls, to reflect diversity and the local community, to meet special needs?)

... and some ideas for outside

Clip boards for scoring games.

Playground chalk for marking directions and messages.

Signs, labels, notices and instructions.

Spotter sheets for nature watching

Small chalk boards or white boards

A big blackboard screwed to the wall

Ensuring quality

This case study shows children making ready recourse to writing. David, Paddy and Shahida clearly know some of the things writing is for.

David and Shahida are in the domestic role play area. David is dressed as the mum, Shahida is dressed as a nurse. She is visiting the house to see the new baby. In her nurse's bag she has a notebook, a pen and a mobile phone.

Shahida examines the baby. She looks carefully in the baby's ears, listens to his chest and gives him an 'injection'. David asks, 'Is he OK?' 'Yes,' says Shahida. 'I'll give you a letter so you can show your husband.' She gets out her notebook and writes a note. Then she folds it up and gives it to David, who offers her a cup of tea. As he puts the note in his pocket he says, 'Your phone is ringing.'

Shahida answers the phone. 'Just a minute,' she says. 'I need to write the address down.' She writes some numbers and letters on her pad. 'I can't have a cup of tea, I've got to go to the hospital.'

Shahida leaves the house. She crosses the room and stops at the writing table, leaning over to watch her friend Paddy, who is making a card for his grandma's birthday. He has chosen a piece of orange card from the range on offer, some sequins and some feathers. He uses these to make the front of the card, saying as he works, 'This is a flower for my Nan. This is the leaves, and this is the sun – there, its finished.' He notices Shahida watching him. 'Do you wanna make one? It's for my Nan. I'm gonna write inside when its dry.' Shahida shakes her head. She continues on her way across the room, meeting one of the adults and two children in aprons as she goes. 'Do you want to come and make some biscuits with us?' they say.

Shahida joins the cooking group. She helps to read the pictorial recipe and to follow the steps it contains. When she has finished, she returns to the writing table, draws a picture of the cooking session and writes the names of the children in the group over each head, using her emerging knowledge of phonics to identify the first letter of each name. Underneath the picture she writes her own name and the word 'Bscts'. She takes her picture to one of the adults, who reads it with her and helps her to pin it on the low-level display board by the writing table.

Meanwhile, Paddy has returned to the writing corner to check on his card. It is dry, so he carefully opens it and inside he writes

'GrnHappyBrfdy
Lovefrom Paddy
XXXXXX'
He finds an envelope in the envelope drawer and writes 'Grn' on the outside. He puts the card into the envelope and takes it to his coat peg, where he balances it on top of his coat, 'So I don't forget to take it.'

We Can Do It! contains more ideas for getting started and provides a list of suggested resources. In order to give the children ownership:-

- Make the writing corner or table part of every day. Involve the children in the contents, organisation and location.
- Make sure the resources in the writing corner are interesting and easy to access. Change or add to the resources from time to time to sustain interest and give new ideas.
- When you buy new resources, get the children involved in deciding what is needed, making lists and even doing the shopping.
- Offer to act as scribe for their stories (look at the stories section in this chapter, p101), captions, thoughts and comments.
- Value their writing. Put up a pin board at child height and encourage them to pin up their own writing. Encourage them to talk about their displays.
- With the children, collect examples of different sorts of writing. Look at lists, forms, labels, instructions as well as stories, poems, diaries, letters – so they experience a wide range of purposes for writing. Help them to make their own collections.

Here are some questions you may wish to consider when reviewing your provision:

- Do you have a writing/mark-making area as a standard feature in your setting?
- Are the children encouraged to write as part of their play? Do you include writing in every role play situation?
- Do you provide models of adults as writers? What could you do to improve the models you give?
- Do you explain and share the writing you do as adults?
- Does the equipment in your writing area meet the quality criteria above? Do you offer a wide range of materials?
- Do you exploit possibilities in stories, visits, visitors and the community to explore the purposes for writing?

Are there opportunities to write outside?

Do you promote 'emergent' writing and writers? Do you value process or product in writing?

What is the balance in your setting between child initiated and adult directed writing?

Are parents involved in helping children to understand the purposes of writing?

How much independence do you allow children in this aspect of learning?

Music, movement and dance

To watch young children as they respond to and explore music, sound and movement is a magical experience. They will frequently sing and dance quite spontaneously and with few inhibitions. Running, jumping, singing, shouting, swinging and swirling come easily and naturally. The role of early years practitioners is to keep that spontaneity alive and provide experiences and materials that enable children to build on these early explorations.

Adults are often more inhibited. Perhaps for some of us, when we were young our earliest attempts to explore movement and sound were laughed at, leaving our confidence and self-esteem bruised. When this happens to children they grow up unable to sing anywhere else but the bathroom and willing to dance only in private! If we are to avoid this happening we must approach music, movement and dance with great sensitivity. Whilst only a small minority of children will go on to become professional dancers and musicians, all children can dance and make music, and the experiences they encounter in early years settings should help to ensure that they continue to do so for the rest of their lives.

> Music is a form of communication that is spiritual, emotional and intellectual. The steady pulse of the body, the rhythm of steps, the heart beat, means that the rhythm of music is natural to us.
>
> *Bernadette Duffy,*
> *Supporting Creativity and Imagination*
> *in the Early Years. 1998*

> When you ordinarily look at children playing, moving, dancing about, and doing gymnastic activities, you think of muscle development. But the major result of my research is that brain stimulation, that is, the increase of sensory activity to the brain, changes the brain cells. These changes allow for the emergence of higher levels of abilities and skills in children.
>
> *Lyelle Palmer,*
> *Kindergarten Maximum Stimulation. 2003*

Links with Early Learning Goals

The Early Learning Goals which particularly relevant to music, movement and dance are:

<u>Personal, social & emotional development</u>

continue to be interested, excited & motivated to learn

<u>Physical development</u>

move with confidence, imagination and in safety

move with control and co-ordination

show awareness of space, themselves and others

Creative development

Express and communicate their ideas, thoughts and feelings by using a widening range of materials, suitable tools, imaginative role-play, movement, designing and making, and a variety of songs and musical instruments.

Explore colour, texture, shape, form and space in two and three dimensions

Recognise and explore how sounds can be changed, sing simple songs from memory, recognise repeated sounds and sound patterns, and match movements to music

Respond in a variety of ways to what they see, hear, smell, touch, and feel

Use their imagination in art and design, music, dance, imagination and role play, and stories

Working with movement and sound enables children to develop skills, concepts and attitudes across a range of contexts. It offers opportunities to develop creativity and imagination; language, social, observation, listening, attention, memory, counting and mathematical skills; concentration ... and much, much more. These activities offer rich opportunities, and when the children are able to take on some of the responsibility for organising their own experiences then the learning is truly enhanced.

The best practice will exist within a culture of shared control and will show a sensitive balance between adult-initiated and child-initiated activities. Once we have provided the appropriate materials our role as adults is that of 'kick starting' the children by introducing them to activities that enable them to see the potential of the resources. We then need to take a back seat and allow them to explore in their own way. At this point they need our sensitive support. By observing the ways in which they work with the materials we will be able to judge what other opportunities should be made available to them, and work out strategies for moving them on with their explorations.

For young children, movement and sound are very closely linked. When they hear music they often begin, quite spontaneously, to move to

A curriculum revised to include attention to the lived body is likely to have a more profound effect because of its ability to help children discover and utilise their self-healing powers through an active and close relationship with their bodies. As the central place of the medical model within our health services becomes increasingly problematic, it is crucial to find ways of involving people in the maintenance of their own health.

Penny Greenland, Hopping Home Backwards. 2000

Getting started

Ensure that children have repeated opportunities to hear music, live and recorded.

Sing with and to the children. Dance with and for the children. Don't worry if you're not an expert – children are very forgiving and will really appreciate you joining in.

Be enthusiastic in your response to children's singing, movement and dancing.

the sound and rhythm. When they are moving and dancing they will frequently make sounds to accompany their movement.

Children in the Foundation Stage are developing their musical awareness and skills with great speed. They have increasing control over their voices, can play simple rhythm instruments and are beginning to understand concepts of tempo, beat, melody and pitch. They are also starting to enjoy making music as part of a group. If we are to keep this enthusiasm and enjoyment alive it is essential that more than anything else we make time for children to engage in musical activities initiated by themselves and their peers. It is important to furnish our settings with a rich range of resources with which the children can explore music and sound. There are some suggestions in *We Can Do It!*

Most children are fascinated by things that make a noise. Look in any shop which sells toys for the very young. Almost everything there will make a sound of some sort. Manufacturers do not do this for nothing. Watch the way young children examine and investigate new objects. As well as tasting and feeling they bang and shake to see if any sound results. And when they do find things that can produce a musical note or two, observe their delight.

Introduce the children to new instruments. You don't have to be an expert in playing them – just able to raise a sound. Try to introduce the children to musicians, both professional and amateur. Make collections of tapes and CDs so that children can listen to a wide range of music from a variety of cultures. Share control with the children, allowing them to take the lead, as and when they feel ready.

Basic timing and a mastery of steady beat appears to be necessary to any task that involves sophisticated movement, and where a person lacks beat awareness he or she usually demonstrates a motor skill deficiency. In

Getting started (continued)

Allow children time to build on what they have heard and seen modelled.

Develop children's body and spatial (kinesthetic) intelligence by helping them to become aware of all the different ways in which their bodies will move and the ways space can be used.

Ideas

Use objects, instruments, artefacts and stories as starting points for music and movement.

Play a wide variety of music and encourage children to talk about their favourites and why they like them.

Compose 'sound pictures' – let the children decide the subject, – zoo, park, seaside, forest, etc. – and encourage them to discuss various ways of making the sounds.

Let children take the lead when composing music pieces and dances.

Arrange for the children to hear adults and older children singing, playing instruments and dancing.

Resources

- Set up a 'performance area' where children can go to perform musical pieces, movement sequences and dances – it could easily be outside.
- Provide a range of objects, fabrics and artefacts to support children's movement ideas, e.g. scarves, ribbon sticks, lengths of material, hoops, beanbags, etc.

fact, recent studies show a correlation between beat competency and school achievement that exceeds two other major predictors of academic success – social class and mother's education. Practitioners have little control over these latter, but there is much we can do to support children's mastery of steady beat. By modelling and sharing action songs and rhymes and working with musical instruments we can make a real difference.

However, if we hold all the power and control then the children will be denied the opportunity to lead the group in activities. With our support, children need to be given the chance to take the lead. They need to make choices and decisions about which rhymes or songs will be sung, which instruments will be played, how loudly or softly sounds should be made or sung and the tempo at which a piece should be performed. Once they have gained experience of being in control they will gain the confidence to repeat experiences on their own.

Many researchers and early years workers are currently interested in the links between early movement experiences and future learning.

If we accept this astonishing link, that sensory stimulation of the sort provided by movement and dancing have an actual physical effect on the structure of the brain, there are important implications for our settings. We need to look at the opportunities that we provide for movement play, and at how we support children towards 'body awareness' and 'body thinking'. We need to ask ourselves whether we, as adults, have developed our own 'body thinking'. We need to look at what we are doing to help children listen to bodily-felt experience, and this is not something that is given a high priority in our culture.

Although spontaneous movement isn't currently at the heart of our culture, there are many changes taking place which suggest that physicality, and body intelligence, will become increasingly relevant; there are signs that we

Resources

- Create a music area with instruments, where children can go to compose their own musical pieces.
- Have a listening corner where children can choose music they would like to hear.
- Provide a tape recorder so that children can make recordings of their own music. They may like to take them home.

In *Hopping Home Backwards* Penny Greenland explores the concept of 'body intelligence', which she defines as the capacity we have to acquire knowledge and come to an understanding by 'direct participation with sensation, feeling and movement, and to make this knowledge and understanding useful.'

What can be done to nourish and support children's movement play?

- organise and equip your setting for movement play.
- move with children.
- notice and observe children moving.
- create situations which invite movement.
- plan activities that focus on movement, sensation and feelings.
- use the language of movement.
- support children in taking the lead in movement activities.

Chapter 7: how to improve provision to encourage independence

must balance our sophistication in intellectual and rational matters with a more developed understanding of the body. The Foundation Stage curriculum is a key place for such changes to begin.

These things take time and commitment, but in addressing them we will be helping children to take responsibility for more than just their own 'body thinking'. A well-structured, well-resourced programme which increases children's awareness of their bodies and stimulates their brains will have far-reaching consequences.

Dance depends on movement but all movement is not necessarily dance. Young children need opportunities for both. They need to see adults dancing, to dance with adults, to dance freely and expressively and to be supported in linking movement sequences together to form dances. When the time is right they need the opportunity to perform their dances to an audience of friendly and appreciative adults and peers. Settings must ensure that children can explore and practise movement for its own sake. They should be given opportunities to move in response to a wide variety of music and sounds, and learn about the ways in which movements can be combined creatively to produce a dance. Earlier we wrote about beat competence. Dance provides one of the most effective ways of feeling and expressing beat.

Look for ways of approaching other work through dance, for example by exploring the meaning of words through movement. Encourage children to use their own ideas in the composition of movement sequences and dances and to move with objects in various ways, e.g. hoops, balls, beanbags, lengths of materials and so on. When children are able to explore and experiment and are supported by adults who value their ideas and incorporate them into the dance work of the setting, children will become confident and independent in their movement and genuinely enabled to dance with joy. As Penny Greenland has written in *Hopping Home Backwards*, 'Human beings are essentially playful, physical beings who need to live in their whole bodies, not just their heads.'

Ensuring quality

Consider the power of dance and music for these children.

The children had been inspired by a dance session lead by Mrs Patel. She had demonstrated a variety of dances from her culture and then worked with the children with long lengths of beautiful fabric. This session had been met with such enthusiasm that the children's keyworker asked Mrs Patel if it would be possible to borrow the fabric so that they could use it again to build on the experience they had so much enjoyed.

As soon as it was time for child-initiated learning to begin a group of children hurried to the area, excitedly discussing their plans to 'do that dancing again!' Yasmin eagerly gave out the material while Thomas went to the CD player to start the music. Unfortunately, whilst Mrs Patel had been able to loan her fabric to the children she had needed to take the music away with her. Realising what had happened Thomas suggested that they try some other music, but after three or four alternatives the children all agreed that none of the music was suitable. 'Why don't we make up our own music?' said Omar. 'We could use the instruments!'

The music area was next to the 'performance area'. This had been a conscious decision on the part of the practitioners so that the work in both areas could overlap. Omar, Jack and Amy rushed over to the instruments and selected tambourines, a small snare drum and a 'rain stick'. After some exploration, and further negotiation about who would play what, the 'orchestra' began.

'You're playing too loud!' said Yasmin. 'We don't need it that loud!'

After several attempts and some support from their keyworker the noise level was gradually adjusted and the dancers began swaying, swirling and running with their lengths of fabric. This continued for some time until Yasmin, who was emerging as a budding choreographer, began to suggest other ways in which the fabric could be manipulated and the dance developed. All joined in except Omar, who insisted on doing his own thing.

'Look, he's spoiling it,' said Jack. 'He won't do it right.'

With a little sensitive intervention from the keyworker the problem was soon resolved and Omar's movement sequence became an extension of the dance. This resulted in other children wanting to do the same until the dance became quite long and the musicians returned to their previous volume.

'Its great,' exclaimed Yasmin. 'If we practised we could do it for everybody at circle time.' Everyone agreed that this was a good idea, and after several more rehearsals the children hurried away to the writing area to make invitations to their performance.

In this case study it is clear that the children had a great deal of control over what was going on. Here are some ways to promote decision making, independence and ownership:

- Invite children to choose which songs they would like to sing.

- When working with musical instruments, ask questions which will steer the children into offering ideas about how they could be used.

- Encourage fun with language by joining with the children to make up songs, rhymes and jingles. Set up a music area where children can use instruments and make music throughout the daily routine.

- Have a listening centre where children can listen to different kinds of music.

- Make collections of different things that children can move with, and let them decide the 'what with and how' for the movement session.

- Encourage children to compose their own pieces, movement sequences and dances. Look for something to value in every effort.

- Model possibilities and then let the children take the lead.

Use these questions to review provision in your setting.

- How much do you value music, dance and movement play? How effectively do you support the development of 'body intelligence?'

- Do you encourage the children to contribute ideas, experiences and resources for music and movement work?

- Are there enough opportunities for children to compose their own music, sound sequences and dances? Are there enough opportunities for children to perform music and dance?

- Are the children able to watch others perform? (Children learn by listening, watching and copying)

- Is there enough space for children to play instruments and move freely, without disturbing others?

- Are recycled materials available, which children can use to make musical instruments?

- Have the children been taught how to care for the resources?

- How much independence do you allow children in this area of learning?

Creativity

There is no doubt of the impact of creative development on self esteem and achievement. Both observation and research confirm this. It is essential for all of us who work with children, and especially those in early years settings, to help children realise that they are creative beings. But first we need to think about how we help children to develop their creativity. This should involve the whole team in understanding the creative process. It needs not only thought, but time for thought, and time to plan worthwhile opportunities which will stimulate the growth of children's creative capacities.

It is useful to begin by brainstorming ideas about what creativity means in your setting. We suggest you may like to compare your ideas with those of Bernadette Duffy, who has done a great deal of research into this issue. She presents her conclusions with great skill in her book 'Supporting Creativity and Imagination in the Early Years.' Creativity, she says, depends on the ability to see things in fresh ways. It involves learning from past experiences and relating this learning to new situations, as well as thinking along unorthodox lines and breaking barriers. Creative thinkers will use non-traditional approaches to solving problems, going further than the information given, and that will lead to the creation of something unique or original.

Most people find that their ideas about creativity match this definition pretty closely, but where do we go from here? We need to think about what is involved in helping children to acquire these capabilities. What opportunities and experiences should be provided? It is all very well to have creative ideas but unless we have the skills and abilities to realise them they will amount to little. We need to help children develop the attitudes and dispositions to make the most of their creative ideas and impulses, the persistence to keep going when things don't work out straight away. We also need to make allowances. Creativity can be a messy process and sometimes, as adults, our attempts to make it less messy inhibit children's independence of both thought and action.

Creativity is not simply a matter of letting go. Serious creative achievement relies on knowledge, control of materials and command of ideas. Creative education involves a balance between teaching knowledge and skills, and encouraging innovation.

DfEE, All Our Futures:
Creativity, Culture & Education. 1998

Being creative enables children to make connections between one area of learning and another, and so extend their understanding.

Children's creativity develops most productively within a rich learning environment supported by the intervention of sensitive and responsive adults.

QCA, Curriculum Guidance for the
Foundation Stage. 2000

Getting started

Share the work of famous artists with the children – you can get reproductions and posters from 'budget' bookshops. Ask the children, 'How do you think the artist did this?'

Borrow objects from your local museum and encourage the children to describe what they see, think about how it was made and talk about whether they like it and why.

Make sure that the book corner or library contains books about famous artists.

Links with Early Learning Goals

<u>Creative development</u>

Explore colour, texture, shape, form and space in two and three dimensions

Respond in a variety of ways to what they see, hear, smell, touch, feel

Express and communicate their ideas, thoughts and feelings by using a widening range of materials and suitable tools.

Getting started (continued)

Arrange for the children to visit local galleries – ask if they will consider putting on a special exhibition for young children.

Put together a display of paintings that use different media. Encourage the children to notice and talk about the different ways in which the artists have worked

Make a collection of different tools for applying paint – brushes, sticks, brooms with soft bristles, squeezy bottles. Experiment and talk about the different possibilities and effects.

Photograph children's projects at various stages of development so they can display the photographs. Help them to recall and discuss the process.

Try to get adults to dress up as various characters so that the children can observe, describe and represent what they see

Make displays of photographs and discuss the ways in which they have been taken (e.g. viewpoint, light, colours, etc.)

Creativity is fundamental to successful learning. Children need to spend time with adults who are themselves creative.

QCA, Curriculum Guidance for the Foundation Stage. 2000

A well-resourced creative area offers children a challenging and exciting context in which to develop the skills of independent learning. The creative area should be logically situated near to a water supply and there should be a suitable floor surface and space for several children to work. Where possible children should be able to choose whether to work at a table or an easel. They should also be able to work outside, for example by attaching paper to walls and fences, etc.

The children should have opportunities to investigate the properties of a wide range of materials – textiles, clay, dough, wool, printing, etc., and materials should be accessible and stored at the right height. Children should be able to call on a range of paper in various weights, colours and sizes, so that they can make decisions and choices about what they would like to use. Sometimes, if not all the time, they should be able to mix their own paint. There should be a range of brushes to enable children to select different ones for different purposes.

Adequate space is needed for work in progress, for work to dry, and for ongoing projects to be left out for completion later. There should be a range of media. Aprons, sinks and brooms should be accessible and the children should be encouraged to take responsibility for themselves and their surroundings. There should be date stamps and name stickers so children can label their own work.

As well as physical space we need to make space in the daily routine to facilitate the development of creativity. We must be flexible

Chapter 7: how to improve provision to encourage independence

enough to allow children to continue working on something in which they are deeply involved, even though we might have planned for something else. We should also try to ensure that there are opportunities for children to see other people painting, modelling and creating. This does not have to be professional artists; older children, practitioners and other adults can all provide valuable role models. We need to make time for children to be involved in the display of their own work. This often takes longer than putting it up ourselves. And we need to provide time for children to share work with others, describe what they have done and talk about the processes they went through.

Supporting the creative development of children is one of the most difficult and subtle aspects of the work of early years practitioners. Children need sensitive and focused help to develop the skills to reach their goals. The younger the children the more help will be needed. Often children know what they want to create but do not know how to achieve it. If we do not address this it will lead to frustration and stifle creative expression.

One way to help is for adults to demonstrate new materials, equipment and techniques and to draw, paint and model alongside the children. Above all, adults should openly value children's creative expressions, especially when they are being displayed. As Tina Bruce has said, how would Van Gogh have felt if his famous painting of a chair had been cut up to form part of a collage about Goldilocks and the Three Bears!? Adults can help by supporting children in taking risks and experimenting, and by making sure that there are opportunities for children to co-operate and collaborate on projects. It is also the role of adults to broaden children's minds and stimulate their imaginations by introducing them to art from cultures other than their own.

Ensuring quality

Children's work is unique and individual. Colouring a picture that someone else has drawn or creating identical cards involves little creativity or independence. It is what the individual child contributes that matters. We should always keep in mind that the process of creating has more value than the finished product. Consider what the children are experiencing in this setting.

Jessie had been fascinated when Adina, her keyworker, had taken in some of her own artwork to share with the children. Adina liked to paint with watercolours, and had shown the children how she worked. The group enjoyed looking at her paintbox and brushes, and spent a long time talking about all the different colours. They liked all the paintings, but for Jessie the picture of Adina's garden held particular significance. She asked Adina questions about what was in her garden and the way she had painted it.

The following day, as she arrived at her setting, Jessie announced her intention to make a picture of her garden, and began to talk excitedly about all the things she wanted to put in it. She was very keen to use the same sort of paint that Adina had used, so Adina found some block colours and showed Jessie how to mix water with the colour. Having selected the size of paper that she wanted, Jessie set to work, and for a period of time became so engrossed in exploring the effects of the paint that she almost forgot about her intention to paint her garden. As Adina observed she sensitively allowed Jessie to experiment with the paint, and it was not until Jessie had washed over the entire piece of paper with a mix of colours that she asked her whether she wanted to carry out her original plan. When Jessie said that she did, Adina asked her about the things that were in her garden and how she wanted to represent them.

'I want to do my swing and my slide, and the tree, and all the flowers,' said Jessie. 'We've got lots and lots of flowers.'

After thinking carefully for a moment or two, Jessie selected a medium sized brush and fetched a pot of black paint. At this point the time she had spent washing colour over the paper seemed to be of no importance at all. Jessie was now interested in the bold lines of her swing and her slide, which she painted with great deliberation. She then replaced the pot of black paint and began to look for some green. When she realised that there was none she carefully spooned some green powder paint into a pot, added water and mixed until the paint was the colour and texture she required for her tree.

Her next step was to make the flowers. At first it seemed as if she was looking for more powder paint, but instead she went to the collage table and collected some art straws and some shiny coloured paper. Laying these beside her painting she fetched some scissors to cut up the paper and art straws to make flowers. She placed the finished flowers on top of the painting, expecting them to stick to the paint. Adina watched with interest when, having written her name on a label and stuck it on her picture, Jessie began to carry her finished piece of work to the drying rack.

'Oh no!' she cried, as all her carefully cut flowers fell to the floor.

At this point Adina intervened to offer support and together they picked up the pieces.

'How do you think we could stop all your flowers falling off?' prompted Adina.

'I think I need to glue them,' said Jessie.

'You go and get the glue then,' suggested Adina, 'and I'll finish picking up your flowers.

As they worked Adina talked with Jessie about her picture. 'You've painted your slide and your swing, and your tree, and made lots and lots of flowers. Is there anything else you would like in your picture? You could paint yourself and your friends playing in the garden.

'No,' said Jessie. 'I like my picture. I like my picture!'

'So do I!' said Adina. They worked on in silence until all the flowers were stuck.

'There,' said Jessie, 'Now I can put it to dry. They are all stuck.'

With great satisfaction Jessie took her completed picture to dry.

Jessie knew what she wanted to do and was clearly in control of the creative process. She was able to call on Adina when she needed technical help. To give your children ownership:

Show them what materials will do and then stand back and allow them to use them in their own way.

Respect their ideas, even when they conflict with what you would most like; e.g. the child who paints a lovely picture and then wants to cover the whole thing with black paint. He may really need to do this!

Involve them in setting up the creative area. Start by asking questions like, 'What materials would you most like to work with today?' Let the children cover the surfaces, get the materials ready, mix the paint, make the dough, etc.

If possible, let them decide where they would like to draw, paint or model. Painting outside will provide a very different experience from painting inside and will trigger some different ideas.

Provide spaces where children can display their own two and three-dimensional representations. Ask them where and how they would most like to display their work.

Involve children in selecting and ordering resources and equipment for the creative area. They love to look through the catalogues and it helps them to understand that we cannot always have everything we would like.

Train the children to use a camera so that they can record the progress of their projects at their various stages.

Here are some questions to ask yourself about how you approach creativity in your setting:

Do you know enough about the ways in which children develop creativity? Does the staff team have the fullest possible understanding of creativity as a life-enhancing process which is crucially important to people's lives? Has the team explored the links between creativity and achievement?

How do you plan for children's creative experiences? Do your plans focus on outcomes or processes?

How sensitive are you when we interact with children in the creative area? Do you 'tune-in' to what they want to explore, listen carefully to ascertain their purpose and support them in achieving their goals (even when they are different from ours!)?

To what extent have you worked with parents and carers to help them understand the importance of process over outcome? It must be extremely distressing for a child who has worked hard on a particular representation to be greeted apathetically with, 'And what's that supposed to be?'

Could you involve the children more in decisions about which materials they would most like to work with and the ways in which they would like to use them?

Do you display children's work in ways that really respect their representations, or do you try to 'pretty' them up to make what you think would be a better display?

Do the children have access to a wide range of resources and media?

How much independence do you allow children in this area of learning?

The messy area (sand, water, malleable materials and wood)

'Messy' activities are an essential part of work in all early years settings. When children play with sand, water, malleable materials and wood, they learn skills, concepts, attitudes and approaches that are transferable to every area of learning. In a well-planned setting they do this in a way that helps the development of their independence and their initiative. But this does not simply happen; it requires that the staff team give time and energy to ensuring that such opportunities are there.

Links with Early Learning Goals

Messy activities can be used to develop every area of learning but some of the major goals are:

Personal, social & emotional development

continue to be interested, excited & motivated to learn

be confident to try new ideas and activities

work as part of a group or class, taking turns and sharing fairly

Knowledge and understanding of the world

> investigate objects and materials by using all of their senses as appropriate
>
> find out about, and identify some features of, living things, objects and events they observe
>
> look closely at similarities, differences, patterns and change
>
> ask questions about why things happen and how they work
>
> build and construct with a wide range of objects, selecting appropriate resources, and adapting their work where necessary
>
> select the tools and techniques they need to shape, assemble, and join the materials they are using

Creative development

> explore colour, shape, texture, form and space in two and three dimensions

When thinking about fostering children's independence in their approach to 'messy' and practical activities it is helpful to start by exploring how we feel about mess, and our own attitudes and anxieties; without such introspection it is easy for us to inhibit, albeit unconsciously, children's opportunities to develop individual responsibility and initiative.

This is a particular danger if we have a rigid view of what a tidy room should look like. We need to ask ourselves to what extent our own notions of 'order and tidiness' govern what happens in the messy area. Are we afraid to really share control with the children in these aspects of learning because we are concerned about the potential for chaos? Do we observe the ways children use materials so that we can fully facilitate their learning, or are we more concerned about keeping things tidy? Are we worried about how our space will appear to premises officers, cleaners, parents?

The messy area can cause a lot of anxiety because of its potential for what might seem like chaos, and on a large scale. A tight rein on the children's actions will avoid this, but it will also inhibit exploration, experimentation and learning. In such a case we will probably spend most of our time going round after the children tidying up. Staff need to agree the difference between productive and creative mess, and an untidy shambles. While the

Clay, a natural material which is used more easily outdoors, as any difficulties with mess are not as much a problem outdoors as indoors.

Helen Bilton,
Outdoor Play in the Early Years. 1998

Children need to work with a range of materials ... for example, wet and dry sand, coloured and clear liquids, compost, gravel and clay.

QCA, Curriculum Guidance for the
Foundation Stage. 2000

A lack of independence to explore can seriously affect young children's learning and their development in many ways.

Jacqui Cousins,
Listening to Four-Year-Olds. 1999

Being at the edge of what they can manage is where learning happens. It is when the environment that we set up for children enables them to be adventurous and show physical and social courage that children can begin to understand themselves and others.

Marjorie Ouvry,
Exercising Muscles and Minds. 2000

Chapter 7: how to improve provision to encourage independence

former is stimulating and exciting the latter is no use to anybody and gets in the way of learning. So they should agree the point at which materials become too untidy. The main criterion has to be the point at which the play goes off track. When this happens no-one will be able to play productively until the resources have been sorted out and a measure of order restored.

It often helps if, weather permitting, we can shunt some of the messy activities out of doors. We need to consider how effectively we make use of the outdoor area for messy play, and ensure that we make the most of the opportunities offered.

This sort of work naturally throws up issues to do with children's safety and wellbeing. We all have the safety of children foremost in our hearts, as well as having a duty of care to those in our charge. Moreover, we live in an increasingly litigious society where fears about legal action have prompted us to be cautious about children taking risks. Activities such as woodwork can cause anxieties, but many of these are lessened when the staff team agree what children may do and how they may do it. For example, certain activities require a minimum level of staffing. There will be occasions when we may not be able to guarantee that, so we need some way of making it clear to the children that these activities are off the menu. This could be as simple as covering the woodwork table with a drape, or displaying a symbol that conveys the same message. We need to strike a balance between creating conditions which protect the children and those which inhibit and restrict them. While the wellbeing of the children is paramount, we have to ask ourselves the extent to which our natural anxiety for their health and safety is impoverishing their learning.

The organisation of resources is very important. In many settings staff decide which resources will be available to the children each day. This

Getting started

Link these aspects of learning with story - e.g. *Where the Wild Things Are*; *The Rainbow Fish* and traditional tales such as The Three Little Pigs and Little Red Riding Hood. The children will extend their language imagination and creativity by using models and figures in the sand and water, and building habitats and scenes to fit the storylines.

Negotiate boundaries within which play from the different areas can overlap; e.g. constructions made in the woodwork area can be used in the sand and water, or figures made with clay or dough incorporated into other aspects of play.

Spend time observing the ways in which children are using the materials. This will enable you to 'fine-tune' the management of space, add appropriate materials and ensure that you make meaningful interactions which will facilitate purposeful play.

Ensure that children have the appropriate protective clothing for the task in hand; e.g. appropriate waterproof garments in the water area, protective goggles in the woodwork area.

Enable children to use resources from other areas with the sand, water and malleable materials – e.g. models and figures from the 'small world' area can give real life and vigour to the play in these areas.

Be clear with the children which resources may be used, which may not, and why. This will empower them to make appropriate choices.

Foundations for Independence

may mean that they have the opportunity to use a wide range of equipment and materials, but it can also lead to them being unable to think independently and use what they need at the time they most need it. If we are truly committed to the development of children's independence and initiative, then it is they who should decide what resources are to be used to facilitate their own child-initiated learning. This requires not only that we be prepared to lose some of the control, but also that we are extremely well organised.

Basic materials for sand, water, modelling and woodwork should be stored so that they are easily accessible to the children. Additional materials should be kept in labelled boxes. The labels should be appropriate for the children's stage of development. Make use of pictures and colours. But be prepared. Children will want to mix and match the resources, and this will probably drive a coach and horses through our carefully organised storage system.

Organising for quality in this area means that we need to look at the interface between adult-initiated and child-initiated learning, and explore the ways in which we are helping the children to understand the things that sand, water, malleable materials and wood will do. Children need a systematic introduction to the materials, resources and tools. They cannot make choices and decisions and exercise initiative until they are familiar with the range of possibilities available to them.

One harassed practitioner we encountered was at her wits end because day after day every single thing was taken out and put into the sand and water tray. The result was that there was so much out that no-one could play effectively with anything. The way to help her was to 'scaffold' the decision-making process. In other words, she had to get the children to understand that the decisions they made had implications for themselves and everyone else wanting to play in the messy area. It was not

Starting talking

Put up posters in the sand, water, dough and woodwork areas that promote discussion and give the children ideas for things they could try out.

Bury some 'treasure' in the sand for the children to discover – e.g. some old coins in a small treasure box, or a bundle of old keys.

Invite visitors to talk about their work – e.g. potters, carpenters, cooks, etc. – they don't have to be professionals.

Use stories, objects and characters to inspire play.

Make sure that these areas are resourced with appropriate information books.

Refer children's ideas to other children so that they can gain inspiration from each other.

Add smells, textures and sparkle to dough by using glitter, sequins, rice, colour, etc.

Add unusual things to the water tray, e.g. ice cubes with sequins or flowers frozen in them.

Use different things in the sand and water trays, e.g. noodles (cooked or uncooked), spaghetti, bark, compost, pebbles, gravel, lentils, slime, porridge, etc.

Create unusual and exciting opportunities for children to handle different materials – e.g. ice sculptures (freeze water overnight in large plastic containers, provide the children with mittens and 'safety' goggles and see what can be produced using small chisels and pounding tools).

Chapter 7: how to improve provision to encourage independence

at first easy to do this. To begin with, the children argued over the resources and tried to stake their claim on a corner of the sand tray or particular equipment. She felt intense irritation and went wading in to sort things out. In time, however, she came to see the situation as one that had the potential to facilitate deep and meaningful learning. By setting up a structure and opportunities for the children to talk through their problems and feelings, to become aware of the needs and wishes of others and to plan their use of resources, she helped them grow in confidence and independence without stifling their spontaneity or creativity. She had given the control to them.

The range of opportunities also needs our careful attention. Within these aspects of learning the possibilities that exist are in direct relation to the limits of our imaginations. Practitioners need to think laterally. Some of the most productive play with sand, water, malleable materials and wood happens when practitioners use their creative impulses and introduce unusual materials into the area. Once children have seen the new possibilities these offer, their imaginations are fired and they can go on to use these things in their own way. Try some of the ideas in *We Can Do It!*

Ensuring quality

Consider this account of some work in a setting and think about its strengths. Can you identify the particular benefits this approach brought to the children?

A group of parents had volunteered to transform an uninteresting piece of grass into a sensory garden. The project was going extremely well and some of the children were very much enjoying being involved in planning the garden and making the preparations. The final plan demanded that some areas of turf be removed and foundations laid for raised beds. As the children helped with the digging they discovered some smooth, white, round stones. The children were fascinated by these and spent a long time handling them, until one of them suggested that they might be dinosaur eggs.

Resources

- Small buckets and lengths of hosepipe so that children can fill and empty water trays for themselves
- Put a 'cooker' and a range of cooking utensils close to the modelling area, as much of the work with dough and clay involves food
- Broom handles cut down to children's size, and dustpans and brushes for sweeping up dry sand
- Well organised hanging space for aprons, wellington boots and protective clothing
- Aprons with front fastenings that children can put on and do up for themselves
- Clearly labelled baskets and boxes of additional materials for sand and water play
- A clearly labelled range of suitable tools that can be easily accessed for work with malleable materials
- A good range of safe and well organised materials for working with wood – i.e. offcuts that have been appropriately sanded to minimise the risk of splinters

Show children how to use tools and demonstrate how tools should be carried. Real tools are better and safer in the end than blunt 'pretend' versions – blunt saws can be wielded with so much force in an attempt to get a job done that children can easily lose their hold and hurt themselves. Decide if there are any tools that are just for the use of adults and if there are, give children your reasons for restricting them.

One of the diggers, Adam, said that it would be a good idea to bury the eggs in the sand so that they could hatch. He collected the stones together and made off for the sand tray. Several other children followed, and it was not long before all the stones had been buried.

'Why don't we put some dinosaurs in?' suggested Trevor. It was agreed that this would be a good idea, and Trevor headed off to the storage shelf, returning a few moments later with a box of plastic dinosaurs. For the next few minutes the small group of children became engrossed in arranging the dinosaurs in the sand tray.

Mrs Turner, who was supervising the room, had been watching carefully for some time and decided that now would be an appropriate time to initiate some discussion. Bending down beside the sand tray she began gently to question the children, to find out what they already knew about dinosaurs, where they had lived, what they ate and how they moved. As a result of this conversation the children decided that they needed some trees for the dinosaurs. They thought they would probably be able to find some in the garden, so Mrs Turner fetched the secateurs and they all headed outside. Following a discussion about what it was and was not appropriate to cut, the children selected the foliage that they needed to make trees in the sand tray and hurried back inside to put them in place. This was easier said than done as the foliage kept toppling over in the dry sand.

'We need to wet the sand to make them stand up right!' announced Sarah, whereupon she picked up a bucket and hurried over to the sink. After much wetting and patting the sand the foliage stood up and the children seemed pleased with the results.

While all this had been happening, Adam had been to the book corner to fetch a book about dinosaurs. When he returned he had the book open at the middle page where there was a stunning dinosaur picture. 'Look,' he said, 'We need some stones, there's lots of rocks in this picture!'

'We could get them from outside,' suggested Trevor, and once again everyone went back outside for a stone hunt. Large, lumpy stones were readily available but they were muddy, so the children decided to wash them in the sink. Eva filled the sink with water and the stones were soon cleaned and ready to be added to the diorama in the sand tray. As the children carried them away, Trevor remained. For him the fascination of the water on the stones surpassed the appeal of the dinosaur scene, and he continued to explore the effects for some time. Meanwhile, Adam was upset because, although they had lots of different dinosaurs, they had no pterodactyls.

'I know,' he said with determination. 'We could make some of our own.'

'How, though?' asked Sarah.

'We could do them out of clay,' said Amy.

The children searched out Mrs Turner to ask if they could have some clay, and before long were busy fashioning their own dinosaurs. As soon as these were made, they carried them to the sand tray. Some final adjustments were made, and as the warning came for tidy-up time the children seemed well pleased with their achievements.

We have emphasised the need for the adults to let go, to give children their heads – in this area perhaps more than any other. The case study above illustrates how this ownership can energise children and unlock their creative potential. Think how much more the children have learnt here, with Mrs Turner as a sensitive observer and facilitator, than if they had simply been instructed and given materials to make a dinosaur scene.

These are further ideas for stimulating creativity:

> Instead of putting out resources for the children ask, 'What do you plan to do in the sand/water/modelling area/etc. today? What things do you think you will need?'

> Tune into what children are currently interested in and reflect these interests in the resources and materials you provide and the discussions you initiate.

> Have 'themed' boxes for sand and water play. Talk with the children about what they think should go in the boxes.

> Let the children take responsibility for filling and emptying the water tray.

> Allow the children to mix their own dough and decide what colour, texture or smell they would like it to have.

> Involve the children in choosing and ordering new equipment.

> Train them to use a camera so that they can photograph projects that have gone particularly well.

> Observe and note the conversations going between children. Use these as starting points for discussions, new resources and changes.

These questions will help you review the approach taken in your setting:

> As a staff team, have you spent time looking at how you will ensure safe, enjoyable play within these aspects? (N.B. A useful publication that will help you to do this is *Too Safe for their Own Good: helping children learn about risk and life skills* by Jennie Lindon, published by the National Early Years Network.)

> Have you talked about mess v. tidiness, so that you are all more or less in agreement about what is acceptable and what is not? Can in all tell the difference between creative and uncreative mess?

> How much independence do you allow your children in these aspects of learning? Could you involve children more in the management and maintenance of these areas?

> Could you be more imaginative in the way you provide for these aspects of learning? Are there enough opportunities for children to pursue these activities outside?

> Do you give boys and girls equal stimulus and opportunity to participate in these aspects of work? Have you monitored this to find out?

> Do you encourage parents and children to contribute ideas, experiences, resources and expertise?

> Are your resources high quality and 'fit for the purpose'?

We regard the creative area as one of the most important. Creative children have the motivation, independence of mind, attitudes and skills which enable them to shape their own learning. We conclude with two short quotes from two excellent and influential pieces of government guidance.

'Creativity is possible in all areas of human activity, including the arts, sciences, at work, at play and in all other areas of daily life. All people have creative abilities and we all have them differently. When individuals find their creative strengths, it can have an enormous impact on self-esteem and on overall achievement.' *DfEE, All Our Futures: Creativity, Culture & Education. 1998*

Children need to feel safe enough to take risks, make mistakes and be adventurous. *QCA, Curriculum Guidance for the Foundation Stage. 2000*

Systems, Structures and Organisation to Promote Independence

The aspects of the curriculum discussed so far in this chapter are concerned with specific activities and resources. This section addresses some of the systems and structures within a Foundation Stage setting which will facilitate and aid the sorts of learning experiences we have discussed and described. These systems must be adapted to suit the age and stage of development of individuals and groups. How well they work will have a profound influence on children's developing independence and autonomy. Please be aware, in reading this section, of the needs of your setting and the children who attend it. We hope that some of the suggestions will be appropriate for you, while recognising that others may not.

Helping children to organise themselves and take care of their personal belongings is a constant concern for practitioners, parents and the children themselves. Parents' anxiety is shown in the way they take over from them, doing things for them that, given a little time and space, children could do perfectly well for themselves — fetching coats, organising bags, looking for lost items of clothing and so on. The anxiety of practitioners often results in banning the bringing of things from home, lining children up to check their clothing or for clean hands, restricting free access to materials or space. Children display anxiety by standing helplessly while adults organise them, or by hanging on ferociously to tokens from home so they don't get lost, or by angrily saying, 'I can do that, don't rush me!'

Here are some suggestions for helping children to organise themselves — and us:

Check the height of door handles and the ease of opening of the doors. Children must be safe, but they shouldn't feel trapped.

Make sure the pegs are at child height and far enough apart for children to manage. Space around a peg will improve access and tidiness, particularly for winter clothes. Bigger hooks make for ease of use. A shelf underneath serves as storage and a perch for changing shoes.

Have a sewing session for parents and put a tape for hanging in each child's coat. Write the child's name on it before you sew it in.

Label pegs and drawers with photos of the children. A digital or Polaroid camera makes this easier.

Write names on clothes pegs, so shoes and wellies can stay together.

A simple cloth bag hanging on each peg will accommodate small belongings such as gloves and hats. Let the children personalise them with fabric crayons.

A low shelf and some name labels will ensure safety for toys and other treasures brought from home.

A box just inside the door is useful for jumpers and other clothes removed in the garden.

Supporting children's developing sense of self image and identity is another important area of early years work. Here are some ideas:

Set up self registration with velcro cards, pockets or boxes. Have photos as well as names to convey identity. Make some for staff as well.

Photo boards and books with pictures of each child, their family and friends are sources of endless interest. Add some photos of children's homes, pets, etc.

Take the children out and let them take pictures of the community and local places of social and cultural interest.

Children love sending and receiving messages and letters. Make some message boxes from shoe boxes, and provide a message writing table.

Use names and/or photos to identify individual cups and other personal articles.

Involve the children in deciding the rules for play, what is fair and what is reasonable.

The bathrooms and toilets should be well-organised, pleasant places. Check towels, toilet paper and taps to ensure that they are easy to use and in the right place. Mirrors, flowers and plants make a lot of difference, and a chair or stool helps the place to look more homely.

Children can also be involved in planning and organising their own day and week. Of course, they need the opportunity to practise this and to realise that planning is a support, not a strait jacket. In order to do this children need:

uninterrupted time to engage in self-chosen activities.

support from adults as they plan and organise their activities.

easy access to equipment and materials.

stability in the routine of the day and the location of equipment.

easy ways of recording what they are going to do, in pictures, symbols and charts.

recognition and praise for taking responsibility for their own activities.

If they have these things they can:

decide what to do for at least part of the day.

choose when (and where) to have snacks and drinks, and contribute to their organisation and content.

think about tomorrow at the end of today.

use charts, pictures with velcro on the back, stickers or stamps to plan out their day.

decide who to play with.

make choices about joining group times.

flow freely between indoors and the outdoors.

help to plan trips, visits and outings.

comment on the organisation of the setting.

contribute to systems of rules, rewards and sanctions.

have more input into when and how adult involvement would be helpful.

Children can also be better involved in setting out and clearing up if they have more ownership of their activities. They see the importance of good organisation, they know where things are stored, they have an increased sense of responsibility for the equipment. They could:

help with the labelling and organisation of the room and the outside.

make suggestions about combinations of different sorts of materials.

contribute to choosing new equipment and resources by looking at catalogues and visiting shops.

label and caption their own models, pictures, constructions.

decide whether they want to dismantle a project or construction — whether they have 'finished with it'.

contribute to discussions about what went well and what worked.

talk about what they learned and achieved during an activity.

recognise the success of planning their own programme and the achievements of others.

make their own 'record of achievement' and collections of work.

take photos, make labels and displays, give demonstrations, invite visitors, record their own commentaries, explanations, directions either alone or with the help of other children or adults.

When examining your systems and structures it's useful to have a checklist. The one on the following page should help.

Are there:

opportunities to work inside and out?

opportunities to work alone and with others?

areas for reflection and contemplation?

places to write and read?

places to leave work that is unfinished?

tidy, well-organised spaces for storing resources?

opportunities to combine materials in new and creative ways?

opportunities to extend and complement activities outside?

places for display? Plants, pictures and artefacts to interest them, and do they reflect local cultures?

child-friendly furnishings and furniture?

Finally, are resources accessible? At the right height? Visible? Well labelled? In cupboards or drawers that are easy to reach and open? Safe for children to use?

Our original draft of this chapter offered readers an apology for its length. Now we are less inclined to make excuses! We feel that here is the kernel of what we are trying to achieve in this book. The philosophy, psychology and history of child development are very important. Case studies and accounts of practice elsewhere can provide useful ideas and pointers. But it is the actual, practical, day-to-day experiences of children in their settings which will enable and empower them as independent thinkers and set them on the way towards becoming confident, competent and successful learners. We hope you will find our advice useful, either by confirming the value of what you do already or suggesting some new ideas you could try. Or perhaps a little of both. And good luck!

Chapter 7: how to improve provision to encourage independence

Section 4
Managing the Learning

The Diana School, Reggio, Italy

photo by Sally Featherstone

Chapter 8:

identifying excellence

It is always helpful to review what other people in other places are doing. In this chapter, we describe two of the most powerful, innovative and child-centred international models of excellence in early years education. Each of them has been established for many years, and each has developed its own features which have been evolved over time. Both systems have been scrutinised, celebrated, criticised and held up as examples. Both have been proved to have a lifelong effect on children and their families. Both have been emulated elsewhere, and have influenced the practice of the many visitors, trainees and thoughtful practitioners all over the world who have encountered their work.

The two models have many similarities, and as you read about them we hope you will recognise many of the features, practices and principles which underpin this book. We, as authors, owe debts to the adults and children who have shared their practice and knowledge with us through books, training and personally in their settings. They have been our guides and inspiration as we try to identify the next steps in providing an education which truly meets the needs of our 21st century children.

Reggio Emilia, Italy. Pre-schools and infant and toddler centres

The city of Reggio is in the north of Italy, between Milan and Bologna on the plain of the river Po. It is the largest and richest region in the country. It is a region where people work hard, in the cities and on the land, and where often both the parents in a family are employed. The city is proud of the fact that the Italian flag, the tricolor, was born there in 1797. Reggio is a middle-sized city, with about 130,000 inhabitants (roughly the same size as, say, Swindon). It has a cathedral and many churches, two theatres, a bell tower, a myriad of squares, parks and fountains, museums, a fantastic market and a rather humid climate, sometimes oppressive in the heat of summer and often foggy and wet in the autumn, winter and spring. It is an agricultural region, and you can eat local Parmesan cheese and Parma Ham and drink Lambrusco or an espresso while you watch the world go by from the many local bars and restaurants.

How did it start?

The first Reggio pre-school was set up six days after the end of the Second World War, in the spring of 1945. Italy had suffered badly in the later stages of the war, and the education system was in poor shape. All the schools were provided by the church, but with hardly any money in many places there was no school available for young children. Moreover, the education available at church schools was often very traditional and academic.

Desperate about the situation in their village, a group of mothers founded and built a school to serve their small community of Via Cella, just north of the city of Reggio. They paid for the materials they needed by selling a tank, some trucks and some horses left behind by the retreating German army. Loris Malaguzzi, a young teacher, heard what they were doing and offered his services as adviser, volunteer and friend. Malaguzzi worked with the Reggio schools throughout his life, and over the next 30 years developed into a powerful and influential educational thinker.

The first school soon inspired others, not only built but organised, funded and run by parents. They had little money, so they used abandoned or donated buildings, local volunteers and home-made or improvised equipment - very much like our volunteer playgroups. Most of these schools survived and thrived until the 1960s, when the first municipal school was built. This was the first secular municipal school for young children in Italy, and broke the monopoly of the Catholic church in early education. Since the 1960s most of the original schools have been incorporated into the municipal system, which now comprises 13 Infant-toddler Centres, serving 809 children between three months and three years, and 21 Pre-schools, serving 1,437 children between the ages of three and six. Between them the municipal centres cater for about a third of the local children in each age group.

These schools grew out of their local communities, and have always worked at their heart. The children are encouraged to feel part of the community. They use the local area as a resource for learning, and make frequent visits into the city and the surrounding country. Parents are still highly involved in their children's learning. Regular meetings, briefings, written and verbal communications enrich this involvement – impressive, considering that a majority of the parents are both in employment.

What seemed a relatively simple, new way to work with young children turned out to require teachers to rethink and change their assumptions about and expectations of children, their way of organising time and their style of working, and their way of developing curriculum and planning their days and activities. It required them to develop new skills and take risks, to give extra time, to collaborate, and to critique each other. None of these changes is simple. After four years we are still struggling with some aspects of all of them.

Louise Boyd Cadwell, Bringing Reggio Emilia Home. 1997

Among the most striking things about the children in these schools are their confidence and maturity. They assume control, responsibility and planning naturally because that is what they expect. They respect and work well with each other, and draw freely on the skills of the adults around them, seeking advice or help when they feel it is needed, asking for opinions and evaluations. The schools are visited by practitioners, learning experts and government officers from all over the world. An exhibition featuring the work of some of the children, called 'The Hundred Languages of Children', has been touring the world for many years.

There some clear concepts on which the Reggio schools base their practice. They are foundation principles which have been confirmed and developed over the years. They are set out by Louise Boyd Caldwell in *Bringing Reggio Emilia Home*.

The child as protagonist, an active force in his or her own learning. Children are strong, rich and capable. They are the third protagonist, with their teachers and parents, and their rights are equal to those of the others (see Chapter 4).

The child as collaborator with others. Each child is in a collaborative relationship with other children, family, teachers and the community (see the case studies in Chapter 7).

The child as communicator. Reggio schools have a systematic focus on words, movement, drawing, painting, building, sculpture, shadow play, dramatic play, collage and music. Children have the right to use many materials in order to discover and communicate what they know, understand, wonder about, question, feel and imagine, 'making their thinking visible' (see Chapters 5, 6 and 7).

The environment as third teacher. The child's needs are central in the design and use of space (see Chapters 6 and 7).

The teacher as partner, nurturer and guide, facilitating children's exploration of themes, work on short and long projects and guiding experiences of joint, open-ended discovery and problem solving. Teachers listen to and observe children closely, asking questions, aiding discovery, feeding children's words and thoughts back to them to enable them to pursue their thinking (see Chapter 5).

The teacher as researcher. Teachers work in pairs and maintain a strong collegial relationship with all other teachers and staff, engaging in continuous discussion and interpretation of their work and the work of the children. They document their work and the work of the children, charting the progress of projects, individuals and child development in general.

Documentation as communication. Careful consideration and attention is given to the work of children and adults: commentaries, transcriptions and photographs, composed into panels, books and displays and gifts for parents are a feature of the schools. These also form an archive of the work of the school, kept centrally to act as a record of the work of the system as a whole (see Chapter 7).

The parents as partners. Parents play an essential role in the work of the schools, not as adjuncts or interferers but as full partners.

What you might see in a Reggio School

The following account is based on visits to the Diana School, and on meetings, discussions and correspondence with some of the teachers. Although every school in the Reggio group differs slightly, the environment, ethos and organisation of the Diana School are typical.

The school is in a municipal park, within easy walking distance of the city centre, the piazzas, churches and shops. It is surrounded by trees and grass, and once through the security gate the front entrance is open and welcoming. The doors and walls have glass panels and big windows, so that you can see both in and out. The foyer has welcoming notices, children's pictures and photos of children and staff.

Children arrive any time between 7:30am (for many of them have parents who must be at work by eight) and 9:00am, by which time all children are expected to be present. Parents and other carers come into the school as they bring their children, to talk with the teachers and to look at the children's work and the displays. During this first period, children are free to choose what they do, with whom and where. Small groups of friends may spend time in the piazza (a central indoor area onto which other rooms open), dressing up, reading, playing or just chatting. Others collect games and toys from shelves and cupboards. Some children talk with friends and teachers, planning what they will do during the day, sharing family news and activities.

By 9:00am all the children are present and the class groups meet in their own rooms for a sharing of news and a discussion of the day. The teachers (two in each room) introduce the planned activities, and reflect to the children on what happened the day before, reminding them of what they did, suggesting to individuals and groups how they might continue with projects or develop new aspects and ideas. Sometimes the teachers will bring in work from the previous day and talk about this, inviting comments and questions from the children; at other times they may play a recording or read from a transcript of the children's words.

Projects are undertaken by groups, or more rarely by the whole class. The membership and size of groups may change over time as the project they are working on develops. Children and teachers discuss as a whole class what each group is doing, modelling for others the development of thought and action, research, refinement and debate which attends such activities. These discussions may lead children to work in the 'atelier'. The atelier is a workshop containing equipment and materials for making things, devoted to the graphic and plastic arts. It is separate from the classrooms and contains a huge range of resources for drawing and painting, work with light, clay, found materials and natural objects. It is a specialist room with a specialist teacher, trained as an artist, available as a support to the children's work. The teacher/artist helps the children with techniques, research of forms and the production of items from their original ideas which they cannot yet, for reasons of safety or skill, undertake for themselves. In each classroom there are mini-ateliers where creative activities are planned and supported by the teachers.

At the end of the discussion session the children choose how they are going to spend the morning. Some will be invited by the teachers to join adult-initiated activities, supported and observed by a teacher. Others will decide to work on their own projects in the atelier or the mini atelier. Further groups of children go off to play in the piazza area on construction, role play, drawing or writing messages. A busy and purposeful hum of activity soon suffuses the building, rising and falling with the rhythms of the children's work and interest.

The rooms will have been carefully prepared and set out for this session before the children begin their work. Here is a typical programme.

Clay in the mini-atelier. Following observations, the teachers have noticed the children's interest in connecting diagonals, working on the flat surface of the table. The teachers want to pursue this theme, so they work with a group of children in this way, focussing on connections between diagonal lines of clay on the table.

Message table in the classroom. This table is set out with a wide range of different papers, pens, small pictures, photocopies of children's and adult's names, glue sticks, highlighters, collage bits (feathers, sequins, beads, etc.), envelopes and reduced photocopies of their own and others' pictures. In each classroom, there are individual letter boxes for each child, and many children send and receive letters every day.

Exploring joining and folding. Linking with the joining theme of the clay work, on one table there are strips of paper and staplers. The teacher has folded some pieces into zig zags. Otherwise, the children are free to explore the materials as they wish.

Exploring colour and scent. On another table is a selection of green and yellow papers, green and yellow pens and inks. A vase of scented plants and leaves has also been placed on the table. It is suggested to the children that they might 'draw the scent'.

Exploring light. In a box near the overhead projector is a collection of transparent and translucent objects, all green and yellow. Some are recycled materials, others household objects such as bowls and funnels.

In the Atelier there are natural objects, flowers, fruit, cones and pieces of wood, books, photos and pictures to delight the eye and inspire creativity. In all the rooms there are games and puzzles, construction materials and bricks, resources for domestic role play, cars and a range of other equipment on open-access shelving. The teachers in each room talk about activities offered elsewhere in the school, in the piazza and in other classrooms (music and sound, mirrors, books, etc.). There is also discussion of the current projects under way in other classes, which children may join – or simply observe – if they want to. All activities are offered to all children, although some may be specifically offered to individuals or groups the teachers wish to observe or talk with. Children are free to join and leave activities as and when they wish. They are free to visit any part of the building.

All the children leave the group session having decided what they are going to do and where they will go. They work alone or in small groups, sometimes with an adult or fetching an adult to help if they need it. During this session all the children are inside the building; the space in the building makes movement easy and no area seems overcrowded, despite the number of activities going on.

At the end of the session (around 11:00am) the children gather in a large group. On most days they spend a short recreation period in the garden before lunch at 11:30. Lunch is an important part of the day; tables are laid carefully by children, with tablecloths and flowers. Teachers join the children for a leisurely lunch, during which there is time for conversation and enough quiet for relaxation. Lunch is followed by a further free play session and a siesta. Children are collected from 4:00pm, when they are all awake and quietly playing or talking. Children can stay at school until 7:30 if a special arrangement has been agreed.

This brief account fails to do justice to the sense of purpose apparent in all the children, their drive, their enthusiasm, their ideas and creativity.

What are the special features that make the Reggio schools so successful?

The practice	How this supports independence & autonomy
The place and its people	
A factor in the success of the schools comes from the place and its people. Reggio is quite a small community, with a strong sense of identity. More important, however, is that the people of the city feel ownership of the schools – they built them (in some cases with their own hands), developed them and believe in what they stand for. There is a real commitment by families and the community, including politicians, to the schools and to children. There is community support for and pride in the achievements of the children. For example, the city tourist brochure has words and pictures by children, the theatre	Children and teachers feel confident that the people they know value them and what they do. This results in high self esteem.

Parents are true partners. |

stage curtain was designed by children. Parents and members of the community are involved in projects and visits, sharing their working expertise with the children, taking them seriously. The children 'inhabit' the city and the community, bringing it into their learning. And there is a national tradition of valuing talk, discussion, debate, and in particular the graphic and figurative arts. These are central to the work of the schools.

Learning is set in a real-life context, encouraging the development of life skills and enabling all to see the relevance of what happens within the school to the life outside it.

The schools and the system

The group of schools is a manageable size. The teachers know each other and meet regularly during the year. The schools have developed together a shared set of principles, clear values, agreed outcomes and ways of working. This means that although each school has its own 'signature' and its own identity, they are very evidently part of the same system. There is a common structure to the day for all centres and schools. The staffing and organisation is common. Features of the architecture (the central piazza, the atelier or workshop, the message boxes), the projects, the place of mealtime and naps all appear in all schools. Schools and infant–toddler centres emphasise the superiority for children of experiences over methodologies. They say it is 'invented new, not handed down.'

Teachers have confidence in the system and feel ownership of it. This encourages an outstanding commitment to their work and how they approach it.

Staff and parents work very hard. They have a commitment to 'struggle for the best' for their children. Staff stay in the schools for a long time, working with the same co-teacher for many years and developing shared expertise. There is a wholehearted commitment to the part creativity plays in learning, and an emphasis on talking, listening, play, making and thinking. There is also a commitment to process, not product, in children's learning. What is important is not the result, but how the children produced it. Staff and children are prepared to take risks in thought, discussion and in learning, because they have confidence in the support they have from other children, teachers and parents. Staff value the children's work — their words,

There is security in known systems, familiar patterns of organisation and a safe environment. This encourages both the teachers and the children to have the confidence to take risks.

thoughts, actions and artefacts. Their work is displayed with care and respect, often with transcripts of the children's words and thoughts. As a result children see their own and each other's efforts as important, and value them.

Displays reflect the respect everyone has for the words and work of the children.

The formal part of the curriculum (i.e. that which is planned and guided by the teachers), at around 2.5 hours a day, is short compared with practice in the UK.

Access to equipment and the availability of space and time all contribute to the children's involvement in their own learning.

The environment for learning

Although the schools and centres are not all in purpose-built premises, they have been skilfully and thoughtfully adapted to the children. They all have a spacious feel and plenty of light, with muted colours on walls and paintwork. Colour is provided by the children and their work. Storage is good, and areas are clearly delineated, while having an overall sense of openness. The atelier and the mini ateliers in each classroom provide access to a very wide range of accessible and well-presented resources, including recycled and found materials, tools and equipment. Message tables and message boxes for each child are a feature of all schools, and displays of natural objects (flowers, bark, shells, leaves, fruit) complement the children's work. There is plenty of room for unfinished work to be left out, and completed artefacts in all types of materials and media are displayed on the floor, on steps, shelves and tables, where they are handled and discussed. They are treated with care and respect by other children.

Resources are of the highest quality and are well displayed, so that children can get at them easily.

Writing activities are not empty exercises. They have a purpose, meaning and individuality. Every message is valued on its own merits.

There is room for role play in the central piazza and in classrooms. Construction with bricks and blocks is given substantial space. Clay and other malleable materials are offered frequently. Activities such as these are available in both child and adult-initiated contexts.

There is a good balance of child-initiated and teacher-initiated activities.

The outside spaces are gardens, with trees, flowers, fruit, grass and hard surfaces. There is provision outside for sand and water play and there are tracks for cars and wheeled toys. The outside area is mostly used for recreation.

Children have ownership of their learning.

The pace of the day and the projects

There is time during the day to talk at length, to play, to work, eat and sleep. There is enough space, so children are not overcrowded indoors or outdoors and enjoy a real sense of ownership of the environment. Mealtimes and rests have their proper place in the day. There is a clear programme and a timetable, but events flow in and out of each other without over organisation by adults or undue interruption of children's activities. When children arrive at school, there is time for free play and discussion with friends and teachers. Before they leave there is time to rest and reflect at the end of the day, and to talk about tomorrow.

There is a clear and consistent framework for the day and the use of spaces, but children own the activities which go on inside this framework. They are given time to discuss and plan what they will do.

Relationships

There is stability for staff and children. The teachers and other staff stay for long periods with one class. Children enter a class and stay with this group and their two teachers for the whole of their time in the school. When they move from room to room as they get older they stay with their group and their teachers. This means that the teachers know the children and their families extremely well, and the routines and relationships are stable. Time is not wasted getting to know each other at the beginning of each year. There is frequent contact with parents on an informal and more formal basis. There is no headteacher and there are no office staff, so there is no barrier between the children, their parents and their teachers.

Stability of staffing supports independence and confidence.

Teachers and children know each other well.

The work of the group and the individuals within it is regularly discussed at parents' meetings. On these occasions parents have the opportunity to look at, handle and discuss in detail the work of their children. Children's work is not sent home but is kept in the school, revisited and revised during projects, displayed (sometimes for quite long periods) and finally archived.

Children's work is treated as documentation of their learning. Nothing is discarded. It is kept and referred to later, becoming a celebration of achievement and a resource for future topics.

The teachers pairings last many years, so that teachers know and support each other.

The role of the teacher

There is a wholehearted commitment to co-teaching. Teachers work in pairs, both having

Observation is a vital part of the teacher's job.

equal status and equal work. They also work with a 'pedagogista' - a consultant teacher employed across several schools, who gives guidance, discusses plans, offers observations and spends time in each of the schools during the day. The teachers from different schools meet each other at regular training sessions and meetings to compare notes and discuss their work. There is a clear but flexible planning framework based on agreed guidance.

The job of a teacher is valued and given time.

Teachers spend part of every day observing, listening to children and discussing their work and ideas with them. They use these observations to plan future activities and suggestions. They also reflect children's observations and comments back to them during subsequent discussions, helping them to develop their ideas and clarify their thinking. There is an obvious respect and value for children's work, thoughts and words.

Discussion and observation are seen as an essential part of the work.

Observations are fed back to colleagues, parents and the children.

Each teacher has six hours each week of paid time to discuss their work, meet other teachers and the pedagogista, meet parents, revisit and share observations of children, and plan future activities. They also discuss common threads of child development, charting, for instance, how children's work with clay develops and how teachers can support that development. There is a strong commitment to their way of working. Teachers refer to themselves as 'researchers', working in the 'laboratory of the school', all the time discovering more about how children learn. The relatively short, formal, planned curriculum means that teachers must work with concentration during this time in order to observe and support progression in the ongoing projects.

Teachers have time to develop their knowledge of the theory and practice of education. Keeping up-to-date with recent research on learning is seen as an important part of their job.

The Reggio model has received worldwide attention and acclaim. Teachers elsewhere often envy the way things are arranged in the Reggio schools. All that space! Six hours paid time for planning and meetings! Such levels of parental commitment and involvement! Such support from politicians! However, if we want to adopt some of the Reggio methods in our own countries there are some factors which we would be wise to consider.

Firstly, the wholesale transplanting of anything carries risks. The English, the Irish, the Scottish and the Welsh are very different from the Italians. Although British and Italian parents want the same things for their children, the parents in Reggio have a different culture, different history, different values and a different view of childhood.

Secondly, the Reggio schools have invented their own system. It has taken them many years and much hard work to develop. It has been influenced by many of the methodologies and educational thinkers mentioned elsewhere in this book. If we borrow someone else's system we must take time to make it our own, to set it in our own context with our own families and children, our own political, social, economic and meteorological climate. We must be prepared to lobby our local and national politicians, we must convince the parents and others in the education system of the value of what we are doing. We must be prepared to work, to try things, to manage the failures as well as the successes, and to ensure that we are the best possible teachers. Only the best is good enough for Reggio schools – only the best should be good enough for our own children.

Above all, we must not forget the many excellent things we are already doing, and that the climate for change we are currently experiencing brings many opportunities.

> It is a mistake to take any approach and assume like a flower you can take it from one soil and put it in another one. That never works. We have to figure out what aspects are most important to us and what kind of soil we need to make those aspects grow.
>
> *Howard Gardner,*
> *The Unschooled Mind. 1982*

Having issued all these caveats, here are some things which we think can – and should – be learnt from the Reggio teachers and children. They are things which will change our settings and give our children more opportunities to become those independent, autonomous learners we all seek.

- Value the processes of play, talking, thinking. Resist the pressure to focus all the time on outcomes rather than processes.

- Value and expand creativity. Release the creative energy in the children. Build in flexibility in work and planning. Challenge children to do something large or complicated, something which will stretch them. Brainstorm with them and use what emerges to start a project.

- Provide the best resources you can afford, find, borrow. Present them with care and improve access and variety.

- Look at spaces. Bring in the light, open the doors. Remember, the environment is the third teacher.

- Give children time. Don't rush them. The Reggio day has a lot of space for thinking and reflecting. Good thinking takes time!

- Remember that observation involves listening as well as watching. So watch, listen, notice, and act on what you see and hear. Time spent in observation is never wasted. Use what you observe to make yourself think, and to affect what you offer next. Document some of what you notice, and share it with others.

- Record and display children's thoughts and words. Enhance the displays of children's work by writing down what they say and think about their learning. Deliberately and overtly show that you value their work (not the same as bland approval of everything they do!).

- Do what you know is right for you and the children. Use your professional judgement, take some risks, follow the children.

- Resist the pressures from above, and the pressure to read and write too early. Recognise drawing as communication

- Follow the Foundation guidance. It will give you the permission to do what you know is right!

- Keep children's work for longer. Refer to it as the children develop their ideas. Encourage children to return to and rework things.

- Promote parent partnership. Commit yourself to real partnership in children's learning.

- Value yourselves as practitioners.

- Identify and be proud of what you already do well.

- Hold on to the joy of working with children.

The High/Scope Approach

High/Scope features all over the world in a diverse range of settings, so that many early years practitioners are familiar with the name. Having said this, they may not necessarily know what exactly the High/Scope approach involves.

High/Scope has its roots as far back as 1962 when David P Weikart, director of special services for the schools in Ypsilanti, Michigan, initiated the Perry Preschool Project, later known as the High/Scope Perry Preschool Project. The project was designed in response to the persistent failure of high school students from Ypsilanti's poorest neighbourhoods. These were children considered to be at risk; children who, over the years, had consistently scored low marks in intelligence and academic tests. Weikart's quest, and one that has been his lifelong consuming passion, was to reverse this trend through a search for causes and cures. He was convinced that these students performed badly not because of a lack of innate intelligence, but because they had not had enough of the right sort of experiences before starting school. More recent research into the effects of early stimulation on brain development would certainly support his hypothesis.

After much consideration an ad hoc committee, comprising Weikart and three elementary school principals, was formed to explore what might be done to help these failing students. The committee held a series of discussions through which they examined such things as teaching methods, achievement and referrals to outside agencies. They explored ways in which the current patterns of failure could be counteracted. While they were engaged in this process the US Special Services Committee began to consider early intervention for

> In the High/Scope approach to early childhood education, adults and children share control. We recognise that the power to learn resides in the child, hence the focus on active learning practices. When we accept that learning comes from within, we achieve a critical balance in educating young children.
> The adult's role is to support and guide young children through their active learning adventures and experiences. I believe this is what makes our program work so well.
>
> *Schweinhart & Weikart, Significant Benefits: the High/Scope Perry Study. 1982*

three and four year olds, and Weikart was given permission to operate Michigan's first funded pre-school education programme.

Once the buildings had been found and the staff appointed, Weikart and the committee set themselves the task of designing a curriculum. They felt that if it was to support children's future academic growth and help them to break out of their cycle of underachievement, the curriculum would need to be cognitively orientated. They agreed on three basic criteria for curriculum development:

1. The curriculum should be underpinned by a coherent theory about teaching and learning.

2. Curriculum theory and practice must support each child's capacity to develop individual talents and abilities through ongoing opportunities for active learning.

3. All involved in the project should work as partners in all aspects of curriculum development to ensure that theory and practice received equal consideration.

Because there was no such approach in existence the Special Services Committee consulted a team of 'experts', who unfortunately advised against the project on the grounds that three and four year olds lacked the capacity to cope with such a curriculum! Undeterred, Weikart modified his plans and set up a carefully designed research project to compare the progress of the children in the pre-school programme with that of children without any pre-school programme experience. It was the work of Piaget that formed the basis for the first classroom programmes for three and four year olds, although over time there were disagreements about how Piaget's theories should best be interpreted in practice. This resulted in a research study of Piaget's work to see how theory and practice could be integrated in a daily classroom programme, and by a process of degrees the High/Scope Curriculum was developed, with the plan-do-review method central to the whole approach. Another key aspect of the programme was the involvement of parents and carers. Teachers worked to engage parents in thinking about the process of educating their children. A dialogue was established within which parents communicated to teachers the interests and needs of the children and their families, and teachers shared with parents information about child development and their methodology.

> Looking at High/Scope research outcomes, the best appraisal of why the igh/Scope Pre-school Curriculum works is this: The growth of children's initiative and positive social disposition in an active learning, early childhood setting can positively affect pre-schoolers' subsequent development and adult performance.
>
> *Weikart & Hohman,*
> *Educating Young Children. 1995*

In 1967 Weikart launched a further research project, The High/Scope Pre-school Curriculum Comparison Project, designed to examine the effectiveness of three diverse pre-school curriculum models. It is this study that formed the basis for the longitudinal research that has shaped so much of our thinking about the impact of early years programmes on later achievement. The study's cumulative findings and most recent conclusions are reported in *Significant Benefits: the High/Scope Perry Preschool Study Through Age 27* by Lawrence J Schweinhart and David P Weikart.

This internationally recognised research shows massively powerful results and has influenced recent developments

> ...knowledge arises neither from objects nor the child, but from interactions between the child and those objects.
>
> *Jean Piaget*

in early years education and care both here in the UK and abroad. It showed that by using the life skills and positive attitudes promoted by the High/Scope programme, these children were actually able to break out of a cycle of deprivation. Attitudes acquired during these vital early years were sustained and paid dividends in later life.

Such evidence has huge implications for what happens to people in their earliest years, and not just for children who are considered to be 'at risk'. It is true that such an approach will probably have its most dramatic effects on those suffering from social and economic deprivation, but it will benefit any child because of the way it focuses on the strengths of the individual and promotes self belief and empowerment. As children work within a High/Scope programme they learn crucial thinking skills, initiate and carry out their own learning activities and make independent decisions. The ability to do these things will benefit any child regardless of socio-economic background.

> One of the most impressive features is the children's attitude towards each other and the settling of disputes. They reason with each other and are prepared to work a solution out. They are mature, articulate and confident.
>
> *Angie Packwood, Evaluation Report, Warwick University. 1992*

The High/Scope Curriculum has been continuously evolving since 1962 but its central principles have remained constant. At the heart of any High/Scope setting you will find active learning, because the approach is founded in the strong belief that young children learn best by being doing things themselves, by being active in a stimulating environment, helped by adults who know and understand how to support and progress this way of learning. Children are not allowed to run riot; the emphasis is on *shared* control in a climate where children learn about relationships and develop their confidence and personal initiative.

The principles which guide the work of High/Scope practitioners in whatever context are:

- supporting active learning.
- observing and planning, using the High/Scope Key Experiences.
- engaging in positive adult-child interaction.
- arranging, equipping and supporting a dynamic learning environment.
- maintaining a consistent daily routine.
- observing and recording children's learning.
- involving families.
- working in teams to promote active learning.

The key elements are active learning, adult-child interaction, the learning environment, the daily routine and the plan-do-review process.

Active Learning

There are very few people working within early years who would not agree with the basic premise that young children learn best when they learn actively. This requires that they have direct and immediate experience of objects, people, ideas and events and the opportunity and support to derive meaning from these experiences through reflection.

Through the exercise of personal initiative children explore, ask questions, solve problems and search for answers. They set their own goals and learn to cope with making mistakes. En route to achieving their goals they generate and try out strategies. Active learning has its foundations in 'doing'. It involves handling, changing things, moving, making things – not just looking. Action is climbing, pretending, modelling, discovering and comparing. It is about touching, tasting, feeling and exploring. *All by yourself.*

There are four critical elements of active learning:

> direct action on objects
>
> reflection on actions
>
> intrinsic motivation, invention and generativity
>
> problem solving

Parents feel that their children operate in a mature way and that they have an understanding of, and a tolerance of those whose behaviour isn't always easy to live with.

Angie Packwood, Evaluation Report, Warwick University. 1992

An active learning environment should provide daily opportunities for children to engage in these processes.

Adult–Child Interaction

Meaningful active learning must be facilitated by high quality adult-child interaction, and practitioners in High/Scope settings spend time practising and developing positive interaction strategies. Much thought must be given to the ways in which young children think and learn, and support for active learning must be firmly embedded within the central principles of the approach. This involves adults in focusing on children's strengths, forming authentic relationships with children and adopting a problem-solving approach to social conflict. Great emphasis is also placed on the use of encouragement strategies, rather than a child management system based on praise and reward or blame and punishment.

'Oh no', she says to me, 'you don't understand. X isn't naughty, they just can't always sort themselves out.'

A parent

The quality of the personal, social and emotional education is of great importance and high priority is given to the child's emotional wellbeing.

Even at home, if his sister is playing him up, he'll sit down and sort things out with her.

A parent

Throughout the daily routine the adult is seen as the instigator of learning situations which will give children the opportunity to solve problems. The adult must constantly ask the question 'How can the teaching staff provide the key experiences most supportive of learning and development for each child while acknowledging the child's own interests?'

What makes this interaction of such high quality is that adults feel able to risk sharing control with the children. This means that for much of their time children are empowered to be in charge of their own activities. It does not mean that adults withdraw and leave the children to get on with it alone. There is real commitment to supporting children; to starting with their interests and motivations, and allowing them to explore and experiment at their own level of knowledge.

High/Scope strives for a style of interaction that enables children to express their ideas, thoughts and feelings openly and coherently. It is children who decide the direction and content of their work and conversation. Working in partnership with the adults in their setting in a climate of shared control, children gain confidence in their ability as learners. (You can read more about the quality of adult-child interaction in Chapter 5).

The Learning Environment

The environment plays a crucial part in supporting children's active learning and problem solving, and organising and managing the learning environment is a very important part of the work of a High/Scope practitioner.

The adult must provide a rich array of developmentally appropriate materials and activities from which the children are invited to select, and it is not possible for children to do this without things being well organised and accessible. Children cannot plan what they want to do unless they are aware of the possibilities, so the working areas are zoned, with each area clearly labelled. The containers for the resources and materials are also carefully organised and identified so that children can take responsibility for getting things out and putting them away again. In a good High/Scope setting there will be 'a place for everything and everything in its place'. Putting children in control demands a great deal of hard work and organisation.

> In High/Scope centres and classrooms, children are active agents who construct their own knowledge of the world as they transform their ideas and interactions into logical and intuitive sequences of thought and action, work with diverse materials to create personally meaningful experiences and outcomes, and talk about their experiences in their own words.
>
> *High/Scope Institute*

Much thought is given to the nature of the resources and materials and care is taken to include a high proportion of open-ended and 'free and found' materials, designed to promote thinking skills, problem solving and representational development. Children have free access to the materials and are supported in choosing and deciding, setting goals, making plans and following them through.

We refer you to our discussion of a high quality learning environment in Chapter 6.

The daily routine

A consistent daily routine is a key element of a High/Scope setting, where aspects of the day are arranged to best suit the needs of children, families and practitioners. This means that every day when the children arrive at the setting they know what to expect. They will also know that if there are to be any changes to the routine they will be told at the beginning of the session. This not only makes the children feel secure, vital given the emotional backgrounds and experiences of some of them, but also gives them a meaningful way of making sense of time. They can anticipate what will happen next, and this supports their active learning and gives them a high level of control over what they do during each part of the day.

Through a consistent daily routine, children have opportunities to work in a variety of groupings, through which they can engage in active learning and build a sense of community. A daily routine constructed to achieve an appropriate balance between adult initiation and child initiation will include:

Welcome Time

Small Group Time

Outside Time

Snack Time

Planning Time ⎤

Work Time   ⎥ the Plan-Do-Review Process

Review Time ⎦

Circle Time (large group time)

The parts of the day can be ordered to suit individual settings, although for obvious reasons the plan-do-review process must follow that order. This is the period of the day when children express their intentions, carry them out and reflect upon what they have done. Small Group Time is important because it allows the adults to introduce the children to new materials or reintroduce familiar ones. The things they select will be based on their observations of children's interests, key experiences and local events. Large Group Time allows for adults and children to initiate music and movement activities, re-enact stories and share play experiences and projects.

The key experiences

For three to five year olds the High/Scope curriculum identifies ten areas of learning:

- language and literacy

- initiative and social relations

- movement

- music

- classification

- seriation

- number

- space

- time

> We came away feeling quite humble, knowing that what we saw was truly education which can change children's lives.
>
> *Pascal & Bertram,*
> *Effective Early Learning. 1997*

Within these categories 66 'key learning experiences' have been identified. Working with the key experiences takes time and commitment, but it is the means by which adults discover a great deal about how three to five year old children learn and think. It is also very rewarding for the practitioners. As they make anecdotal observations of the children engaging with these experiences, the observations form the basis for planning and evaluating.

Plan-Do-Review

Plan-do-review takes place daily in High/Scope settings and is central to the whole approach. It involves the adults in asking children to plan explicitly what they are going to do. They then begin to set goals for themselves and are supported in generating and evaluating alternative solutions to problems as a means to achieve their goals.

Chapter 8: identifying excellence

As they gain expertise in managing this process, children are acquiring massively important life skills. Learning to set goals, work towards them and deal with the setbacks that occur on the way is a hugely valuable learning experience, but this does not happen without effort. Planning is a developmental process. When a three year old enters a High/Scope setting he or she probably won't have the faintest idea what a plan is. They will learn this over time as they experience the planning process embedded in the real-life, active learning provided in the setting.

All settings ... are required to plan activities and experiences that help children make progress in their development and learning.

QCA, Curriculum Guidance for the Foundation Stage. 2000

Initially a child's choices and decisions will be expressed non-verbally through pointing, and simply selecting those materials and resources that are of the greatest interest, but as time goes on they will begin to engage in the process with ever-increasing complexity. Through planning, children learn to create and express their intentions, both individually and in groups, and they experience the joys and frustrations of working towards and achieving a goal. In settings where practitioners are very experienced, children are enabled to see that there is no such thing as failure; there are only outcomes – and if we are not happy with the outcome we achieve, we change our actions to get a different outcome.

Work time involves the children in carrying out their plans. It provides adequate time for trial and error, time to generate new ideas, practise and keep going until they succeed. Throughout this time the children exercise a high degree of personal independence. Adults respect their need to explore, and understand what can be gained when self-motivated children engage in active learning.

We were taught to say that play is the work of children. But, watching and listening to t to them, I saw that play was nothing less than Truth and Life.

Vivian Gussin Paley, The Boy Who Would be a Helicopter. 1990

Review time is for children to reflect upon their experiences in a wide variety of ways. Practitioners use a range of planning and recall strategies designed to maintain children's interest and motivation, and it does not take long for the children to become adept at the process. As they gain experience they plan and review with increasing logic, verbal ability and skill. Through engaging in this process children experience both immediate and long-term benefit.

Conclusion

High/Scope is an approach to early years education that has been proved by careful studies over a long period to offer benefits to children, families, practitioners and society in general. It is only one of a number of models of early years practice, but it is a model that, well implemented, can provide excellence.

In the words of Serena Johnson, Director of High/Scope UK between 1995 and 2000:

Children, families, practitioners and society generally benefit from the approach. Families and practitioners benefit because High/Scope provides practitioners with a stimulating and rewarding method of working, encourages managers to place more value in training and encourages parents and practitioners to extend their expectations for children and themselves. Children and society benefit ... because (High/Scope) provides a learning approach which meets the developmental and cultural needs of children and also meets the demands of our fast-changing, technological society.

It provides a 'competency based' curriculum at a time when, as we know from research on the brain, children's learning potential is at its greatest. It can work in harmony with the curriculum laid down by government while recognising the needs of each child to have an 'individual learning plan' and the competencies of 'learnacy', citizenship, relating to people, managing situations and information, thus enhancing opportunities to become, in the long-term, fulfilled adults and contributors to society.

For those who want to know more about High/Scope, and particularly about how the model may be applied in a British setting, the handbook *High/Scope and the Curriculum Guidance for the Foundation Stage - Providing the Process for the Early Learning Goals* is available from The High/Scope Institute, Copperfield House, 190-192 Maple Road, Penge, London SE20 8HT.

These two case studies are not intended to provide universal solutions. We have included them because they offer clear examples of the principles we are advocating applied consistently and successfully over a long period. The sort of longitudinal studies which have been done for High/Scope do not, as far as we know, exist for the Reggio schools, but their track record is demonstrable in a different way, through the achievements of Reggio children and the culture and dynamics of the city. We hope you will gain inspiration, ideas and enthusiasm from these dedicated pioneers – as we did. However, it is important to remember that in all countries and all settings it is the impact of the adults – teachers, practitioners, carers, assistants, helpers – that will most affect the experiences of the children and the outcomes of their learning. There is no substitute for 'skilful teaching in both the nursery and reception classes, where children are constantly encouraged to feel confident about what they can achieve.' *OFSTED, Inspecting Subjects 3 –11. 2001*

Chapter 8: identifying excellence

Chapter 9:

managing change

Is the development of independence in children something we can affect, something we can plan and provide for?

If the principles of independent learning are important to you and if you want to promote them in your setting, their implementation, support and evaluation will need careful management. Everyone associated with the setting – staff, children, parents, governors and management groups, local advisers – has to be clear about what you intend, why you believe change is needed, and what their part will be in ensuring success. Judgements of quality should not be left solely to inspectors. Practitioners should know their own setting and have a good idea of the levels of quality in their provision long before an inspection team crosses the threshold.

This chapter assumes you wish to promote independence and autonomy for the children in your setting, and addresses the tasks of managing the initiatives and processes to get you there. It makes recommendations covering the way you declare your intentions, promote teamwork, manage whole setting issues, describe and promote aims and principles, train staff, change practice and involve the children and their parents. If your personal response to this book has been positive, if you feel that you want to use what you have read to identify existing good practice in your setting and to develop that quality further, this chapter will give you some starting points.

> The establishment of a foundation stage is a significant landmark in funded education in England. For the first time it gives this very important stage of education a distinct identity.
>
> *QCA, Curriculum Guidance for the Foundation Stage. 2000*

There are seven sections:

- Auditing present provision
- Coming to a shared view, and declaring intentions
- Documenting principles, procedures and practices
- Keeping everyone informed and involved
- Planning for action
- Observing and monitoring progress
- Identifying successes and areas for further improvement

The QCA Guidance for the Foundation Stage says: *These principles require practitioners to plan a learning environment, indoors and outdoors, that encourages a positive attitude to learning through rich and stimulating experiences and by ensuring that each child feels included. This is demonstrated when practitioners:*

- *encourage children to make choices and develop independence by having equipment and materials readily available and well organised.*

- *provide resources that inspire children and encourage them to initiate their own learning.*
- *give the children the space they need for their activities.*

This statement, together with others within the Foundation Stage Guidance, gives a clear lead to our practice and to the evaluation of quality in our provision. How can we know if we are achieving this high quality?

OFSTED in Inspecting Subjects 3 to 11 advises its inspectors to look for children who:

are keen to learn; developing confidence and independence

are able to show their feelings

have generally good relationships with peers and positive relationships with adults

understand basic rules for groups

are independent in dressing and undressing and taking care of their personal hygiene

are able to select and use activities and resources with independence

are able to show empathy with and understanding of others.

We will keep the QCA Guidance and the OFSTED criteria in mind as we explore what is involved in managing and guaranteeing quality provision.

Auditing present provision — why is this important?

It is easy (and dangerous) to assume that there is no existing good practice in your setting, that there are no successes, that changes and improvements start at zero. This is rarely, if ever, true. However much we want things to be better, if we look positively and realistically at present practice we can all find some foundations on which developments can be built. There is nothing more demoralising than to be told that nothing is being done, everything must change, we must start again at the beginning.

The first step is to look positively at your setting, identifying existing strengths as well as improvements for the future. By using some of the questions in this book it is possible to construct a short audit or discussion document which will help you with this evaluation.

Coming to a shared view and declaring intentions - why is this important?

If you don't come to a shared view on independence and independent learning with colleagues and parents, you will at best decrease your effectiveness, and at worst children and adults will be confused by different messages from different people.

Children who begin their education in an environment that is vibrant, purposeful, challenging and supportive stand the best chance of developing into confident, successful learners. Effective learning environments are created over time as the result of practitioners and parents working together, thinking and talking about children's learning and planning how to promote it.

QCA, Planning for Learning in the Foundation Stage

Ideally you and the parents and carers of the children will have a common view about independence, and this will have been arrived at through discussion and an honest exchange of views. These views will be clearly communicated when parents choose to send their children to your setting, and will be taken into account as you discuss their child's education and care. Remember that parents, too are early years specialists but most are not acquainted with the

Chapter 9: managing change

QCA, OFSTED, early years partnerships and so on. Therefore they do not have the professional vocabulary for articulating aims and discussing children. We recommend that in arriving at this shared view you concentrate on outcome – how you want the children to be and what you want them to be able to do. You might find it helpful to to look again at the definitions of independent learners and the descriptions of their capabilities in the middle sections of this book. They make a useful starting point for discussions. Many settings arrange for regular discussions with all parents at meetings and through questionnaires. Your brochure or prospectus will augment these by giving a clear indication of how you work and the skills and attitudes you value.

Practitioners working in settings should have regular opportunities to discuss their views on the style as well as the content of the curriculum, coming to a shared understanding of the skills children will be developing and the ways in which adults support them through sensitive observation and interaction. Sections 2 and 3 of this book (Chapters 4 - 7) will help you to consider the role of the adults, the setting and the organisation of activities to enable children to become independent learners.

It will be important to communicate the outcomes of reviews and agreements, together with any proposals for action, to management and governing committees, and subsequently to include them in prospectuses and other written statements.

A further challenge is 'the review, analysis and planning, with a group of colleagues, for further use of the information gained. This takes time, commitment and skill.'

Louise Boyd Cadwell, Bringing Reggio Emilia Home. 1997

Your documentation should make reference to the principles contained in the Foundation Guidance, but you will probably want to flavour it with the essentials of your own discussions and state in writing the commitment of your setting to independent learning. Written statements not only help you clarify your own views, they communicate to visitors such as inspectors and advisers, and provide a way into your own monitoring of your provision.

As you agree and construct statements about your curriculum, you will inevitably become aware of the links between elements of independent learning and other policy statements, particularly those dealing with equality of opportunity, special needs, cultural diversity and race relations. In school settings these statements will need to be checked to ensure that they are consistent with statements and policies in the school brochure, prospectus or handbook.

Keeping everyone informed and involved – why is this important?

The processes recommended above sometimes lead to arguments and conflicts of views, and it is as well to recognise this. There are still people around who think that young children need a formal curriculum and who see children's independence as a threat to the authority and role of the practitioners. However, if everyone is involved in discussions and decisions there is much more chance of a common intention and a common approach. Children, parents, management groups and practitioners all need to be involved at different levels and by a range of means. Meetings, discussions, questionnaires, newsletters and notices all have their place in ensuring that information is communicated and opinions are sought on current quality and future intentions.

The views of children are particularly important when developing independence. How can you develop yourself if you don't get a voice in your own learning?

Planning for action – why is this important?

One of the outcomes of your audit and reviewing processes will be suggestions and ideas of things you want to do and provide. Wish lists are by their nature long, and your list of improvements may seem very daunting – even more difficult to manage than the previous provision!

Get the list into some sort of order by constructing an action plan. This will establish priorities for action – i.e. what to do first, next and last. This will help you put the changes you want to make in a programme for development, which can be costed and incorporated in the improvement or management plan for the setting. This reduces panic by making things more manageable and showing how changes can be implemented over time and within the budget.

You might consider the following way of managing an action programme. Here are some of the areas you will probably want to address:

- Space, including improvements to the building (e.g. better access to the outside, redecoration, relocating display boards, smartening the entrance area)
- Storage (e.g. additional shelving, storage boxes and crates, replacing existing containers and boxes)
- Equipment (e.g. extending the choice of brush sizes, collage materials, outside play equipment)
- Organisation (e.g. longer access to the garden, flexible snack and drink times, circle time)
- Training and staff development (e.g. observation and intervention, understanding play, asking questions)
- Contacts with and involvement of children (e.g. discussions, observations, suggestions)
- Contacts with and involvement of parents (e.g. questionnaires, improved information, notice boards, photo books).

Your plan will need to take account of cost, urgency, importance and timescale. All these will vary.

The **cost** of implementation:

- Some suggestions will be very expensive (such as altering the building to provide access to an inaccessible play area)
- Some suggestions will be cheap (such as removing the doors from cupboards, lowering the handles on doors)
- Some suggestions can be done at no cost except for the time taken (such as rearranging the furniture to improve access to an inaccessible play area).

The **timescale** for implementation:

- Some suggestions will take a long time to implement (such as raising the money to build a safety fence, or arranging training for the staff)
- Some suggestions take little or no time to implement (such as removing or reorganising furniture or involving the children in discussions).

Chapter 9: managing change

The **urgency** of implementation:

- Some suggestions will be considered very urgent (particularly those associated with health and safety, or talking to parents about the changes you plan).

The **importance** of implementation:

- Some suggestions will be very important to you
- Some suggestions may be considered less important.

Sorting out these competing priorities can be tricky. One way to approach it is to construct a list like the one below, giving each action a priority rating from 1 (highest) to 5 under each of the above criteria. It is also helpful to associate an estimate of cost, where you can. This will enable you to separate the urgent from the important and the essential from the desirable, as well as helping you see what can be afforded.

Action	Cost	Time	Importance	Urgency
Move pinboards to child height	£15 (2)	2hrs	4	4
Remove wall between nursery & veranda	£500 (5)	3days	4	3
Replace broken stay on outside door	£5	2hrs	5	5
Introduce flexible snack time	none	1day	2	2

Observing and monitoring progress – why is this important?

We all know that it is possible to have wonderful paperwork which looks very impressive but has no relation to the reality of children's experiences. In order to make sure that what we say is what we do, we must spend time looking at the practice and the experiences of children in our settings. Direct observation is the most effective way of evaluating the quality of what we do.

Observing practice helps us at each stage of development. If we observe before embarking on change, we get a baseline for development. If we observe during times of change we get a good idea of how the changes are progressing and of any emerging problems. If we observe after the major period of change, during the consolidation stage, we have the basis for evaluating the match with our original intentions and assessing the resulting improvements in provision.

There are three different types of observation with varying degrees of formality. We will probably want to make use of them all, but to do this we need to be sure of the job of each and what it can and cannot offer.

1. We all make casual, informal observations all the time as we experience our setting. We collect first hand information by seeing, hearing, touching and even smelling the environment. We constantly make judgements as we encounter various pieces of evidence, and adjust our opinions of the quality of what we see as a result. These observations are subjective, usually without clear criteria, and are made very quickly, often while we are doing something else. They are very valuable, but they are 'scattergun' observations, often reflecting feelings rather than facts. The information we acquire in this way is usually verbal and anecdotal. We rarely write it down but nevertheless it is some of the most useful evaluation data available to us, an ongoing impression about what we have experienced.

Professionals have become much more practised at giving feedback to colleagues resulting from formal or informal observations. Parents and other visitors may well be more reserved, preferring to share judgements with others outside the setting rather than telling us. You will be familiar with the parent who talks at the gate about what she saw, sometimes in her subjectivity missing the point of what is going on and the reasons for it – 'They can have their drink any time they like, I think they should make them all sit down together like they used to do. I don't know why they have changed.' This information is important (not least in this instance by telling us that we have not communicated effectively to this parent and possibly others), but we often have to work hard to get it and sometimes only acquire it through chance or hearsay.

2. Structured observations can be undertaken by anyone who has time but are usually planned by practitioners. For a structured observation clear and agreed criteria are essential. These should be drawn from the documentation of the setting and few in number. Such observations give valuable feedback, enhanced by the practitioner's knowledge of the setting, child development and the intentions of the documentation. One member of staff may take a feature of recent development, for instance the use by children of newly organised collage materials. The practitioner will watch the children as they work in this area, making notes of exactly what happens. She may use a camera, video or tape recorder to help with the collection of evidence. This is then shared with the whole team, who are better able to judge the effectiveness of the changes they have made. Structured observations are a strong feature of all of the high quality practice we have seen.

3. Tracking individuals and groups is a method of observation which links well with your intended outcomes. If you have made a statement about the characteristics, behaviours and attitudes you hope will result from more autonomy and independence, you may want to track a child over a period of time to see whether these characteristics and attitudes are in fact resulting from the strategies you have implemented. For instance, are children making independent choices? Are they more able to resolve conflict, delay gratification, work together on projects, sustain concentration? This information is not easily acquired from a single 20 minute observation. It takes a range of perspectives from different observers (including parents and children) gathered over a period of time in different places and through a variety of activities. Such 'deep' information is rich in content, and should give you food for thought. It is the best possible way to find out whether the changes you are making are having an effect.

Where possible, observations should involve all the stakeholders in the setting, not just management and practitioners. Children, parents, members of the community, schools and other settings to which the children transfer all have a contribution to make. The important thing to remember is that these inputs won't just happen on their own; they need a structure and procedures.

Practitioners will have the best opportunity and usually the most experience of observing during sessions. However, their opinion is coloured by knowledge of the setting and their objectivity may be compromised by their closeness. Parents and other adult visitors can be involved in direct observation or through questionnaires and interviews. When you construct your questionnaire or interview questions, make sure you have included all the things you want to know and that the questions are clear, free from unnecessary jargon, and easy to understand. Children, too, should contribute their observations

Chapter 9: managing change

and feelings to the debate about quality. They may not be able to carry out systematic observations or fill in questionnaires, but if invited and encouraged they can and will give their opinions in a range of ways. Drawing, puppets, small world, role play, taking photos and playing games can expand the more usual circle time and discussion opportunities. If you encourage children to talk about how they feel as well as describing what they do, they will be able to contribute a huge amount of valuable information to add to your observations.

Children who begin their education in an environment that is vibrant, purposeful, challenging and supportive stand the best chance of developing into confident and successful learners. Effective learning environments are created over time as the result of practitioners and parents working together, thinking and talking about children's learning and how to promote it.

QCA, Planning Learning in the Foundation Stage

Identifying successes and areas for further improvement – why is this important?

We often forget to recognise and celebrate the things that are going well. We sometimes overlook the achievements and concentrate on the things that still need doing or are going less well. It gives everyone a good feeling to celebrate, and this doesn't mean forgetting the pointers to further improvement.

When you are collecting monitoring information remember to record the good things. Don't ask people to identify only the things they don't like – ask them for the things they like and feel are successful. Small children are able to draw or choose pictures of things they enjoy doing or experiencing, things that make them happy, anxious, sad or scared. Parents sometimes feel that a consultation is an invitation to complain, so give them a structure which will make sure that they also identify successful features of the setting and positive effects on their children. Make a public display of your successes. Put up a notice on the parents' board, send a letter home, give yourselves a sticker. Have a party! Giving a high priority to your successes as well as to the things you want to improve helps you to move on to the next challenges with confidence.

Finally, we can think of no better advice to a management team considering implementing a new or revised programme than that given by an early years adviser in *Effective Early Learning*, who says:

Be very clear about why you want to do it. Be convinced you are doing it for the benefit of the children first and foremost. If you are not, don't bother because you will never be focused in the way that you carry it forward because you won't know why you are doing it. And then go for it, be well organised, structure it so you can support your colleagues properly, recognise that they are going to have times of difficulty and be ready to cope with it when they need support. And manage it so that everyone feels they can play a part in shaping it.

Here are some questions that it will be helpful to consider when you review how you manage development and change in your setting.

> Do you have clear, shared, written statements setting out the way you work and the outcomes you intend? Are these tested in practice to confirm that what you say is what you do?
>
> Is observation an accepted feature of the way you work? Are practitioners in the habit of carrying out frequent, informal observations as well as contributing to the more formal structures?

Do you collect information from parents on the aspects of the setting they like, and those they feel less sure or confused about?

Do you have ways of involving children in talking about how they feel as well as what they have been doing?

Do you work in a culture where successes and achievements are recognised and celebrated?

Summary

Thoughtful and planned management is vital, especially when considering new initiatives.

You must be clear about why you want to change things, how they will be different and how you will recognise success.

Observation of the children in your setting is a vital part of evaluating quality.

Everyone should be involved (staff, children, parents and community), but there must be clear leadership or things don't actually get done.

Trust them, listen to what they have to say, and do not be afraid to let them take control   *p161*

photo by Sarah Featherstone

Chapter 9: managing change

The Last Word

We began this book with a statement about the importance of independent-minded and autonomous individuals to a free society, and by pointing out how attitudes and characteristics such as open mindedness, working with and caring for others, self control and self reliance, together with a constructive approach to problems, have their seeds in early childhood experiences.

The description of a Foundation Stage and the establishment of the goals for early learning are huge and important steps. So is the emphasis on the pre-school years and the dawning realisation that both deprivations and enrichments in early life will have a profound effect on an individual later. However, there is further to go, because it is how these new initiatives and priorities are addressed in the huge variety of early years settings which will determine whether or not they are successful.

> Low expectations, based on the stereotypical view of children as being irrational, irresponsible and selfish may affect the opportunities we offer to children. As a result, children may not have the chance to show us how capable they are, or develop their capability to make decisions, take responsibility or care for others.
>
> *Judy Miller, Never Too Young. 1996*

We have tried to give some pointers to show how this might be done, and we did this in three stages. Firstly, we traced the emergence of modern views of child development and related these to advances in brain research and child psychology. We think this is important, because while skilful practice will always be at the heart of effective early years education, it is increasingly important for us to be able to justify what we are doing and relate it to the historical views and the theory of child development. Next we offered a definition and description of the independent learner, showing how the characteristics of independence emerge in young children and exploring the influence of adults and the physical environment. In the third stage we examined two highly effective approaches to early education, in Reggio Emilia and the High/Scope Programmes, and gave some pointers to managing some of the changes you may wish to implement as a result of reading this book.

Our aim has been to produce a book that will be of practical help to everyone engaged with or in early years settings. In the hurly burly of coping with every day it is easy to lose sight of key principles. However, there is one to which practitioners should cling at all costs. It is 'trust the children'. Most children are by their nature 'programmed' to learn. They want to find out about things, to explore and to discover. Often they have ideas about how to do this. If you allow them to, you will be surprised and delighted by where they will lead you and where, with your help and support, they are able to go. Trust them, listen to what they have to say, and do not be afraid to let them take control. Give them the benefit of your mature judgement without stifling their independence and creative spirit. These things are not easy, but they are improved by sensitivity and practice. And, thankfully, they are already present in many settings. We should like to record our thanks to and our appreciation of the many excellent practitioners we have met in this country and in other places, and whose work we have been privileged to see. We could not have written this book without the benefit of their wisdom and insight. We hope we have done justice to what we have learnt from them.

The last word? No, because that, as always, belongs to the children.

Bibliography

Abbott, Lesley (Ed) & Nutbrown, Cathy. Experiencing Reggio Emilia. 2001. Open University Press

Bilton, Helen. Outdoor Play in the Early Years. 1998. David Fulton

Blakemore, Colin. RSA Lecture. 2001

Boyd Cadwell, Louise. Bringing Reggio Emilia Home. 1997. Teachers College Press

Brosterman, Norman. Inventing Kindergarten. 1997. Abrams

Brewer & Campbell. Rhythms of Learning. 1991. Zephyr Press

Ceppi & Zini. Children, Spaces, Relationships. 1999. Reggio Children

Clarke, Alison & Moss, Peter. Listening to Young Children. 2001. NCB

Cousins, Jacqui. Listening to 4 year olds. 1999. National Early Years Network

Curtis, Audrey. A Curriculum for the Pre-School Child. 1960. NFER – Nelson

DfEE. Revised National Curriculum. 2000. HMSO

DfEE/QCA. Curriculum Guidance for the Foundation Stage, 2000. QCA Publications

DfEE. All Our Futures: Creativity in Education. 1998. HMSO

DfEE. Guidance on the organisation of the National Literacy and Numeracy Strategies in Reception Classes. 2000. DfEE

Donaldson, Margaret. Children's Minds. 1978. Flamingo

Dryden and Voss. The Learning Revolution. 1994. Accelerated Learning

Duffy, Bernadette. Supporting Creativity and Imagination in the Early Years. 1998. Open University Press

Edwards, Gandini. The 100 Languages of Children. 1996. Ablex & Forman

Greenland, Penny. Hopping Home Backwards: Body Intelligence and Movement. 2000

Gussin Paley, Vivien. The Boy Who Would be a Helicopter: storytelling in the classroom

Featherstone, Sally. First Hand: making the Foundation Curriculum work. 2001. Featherstone Education

Finch, Sue. An Eye for an Eye. 1998. National Early Years Network

Fisher, Robert. Teaching Children to Think. 1990.

Early Childhood Forum. Quality in Diversity. 1998. National Children's Bureau

Gardner, Howard. Frames of Mind. 1991. Fontana

Gardner, Howard. The Unschooled Mind. 1982. Fontana

Ginsberg and Opper. Piaget's Theory of Intellectual Development. 1979. Prentice Hall

Goldschmeid, E & Jackson, S. People under Three. 1994. Routledge

Greenman, Jim. Caring Spaces, Learning Places: children's environments that work. 1988. Exchange Press

Goleman, Daniel. Emotional Intelligence. 1996. Bloomsbury

Hall, Nigel (Ed). Writing with Reason. 1989. Hodder and Stoughton

Handy, Charles. Beyond Certainty. 1995. Hutchinson

Hannaford, Carla. Smart Moves. 1995. Great Ocean

Hohman and Weikart. Educating Young Children. 1995. High/Scope Press

Holt, John. Learning All The Time. 1989. Education Now

Isaacs, Susan. The Educational Value of the Nursery School. 1954. BAECE

Johnson, Serena. Reggio Emilia. 2001. Early Years Educator

Katz (Ed). Reflections on Reggio Emilia. 1994. University of Illinois

Lindon, Jennie. Too Safe for Their Own Good? 1999. NNEN

McCarthy, Kevin. Learning by Heart. 1998. Gulbenkian Foundation

McMillan, Margaret. The Nursery School. 1919. Dent

Melhuish & Sylva. Social, Behavioural & Cognitive Development. 2001. Oxford University

Miller, Judy. Never too Young. 1996. NNEN

Neill, A S. Summerhill. 1968. Penguin

Nutbrown, Cathy. Threads of Thinking. 1999. Paul Chapman

OFSTED. First Class. 1993. HMSO

OFSTED. Handbook for Inspecting Primary and Nursery Schools. 1999. OFSTED

OFSTED. Inspecting Subjects 3 to 11. 2001. OFSTED

Ouvry, Marjorie. Exercising Muscles & Minds. 2000. NNEN

Palmer, Lyelle. Kindergarten Maximum Stimulation. 1993. Winona State University

Pascal & Bertram. Effective Early Learning. 1997. Hodder

QCA. Curriculum Guidance for the Foundation Stage. 2000. DfEE/QCA

Robb, J & Letts, H. Creating Kids Who Can. 1998

Rose and Nicholl. Accelerated Learning for 21C. 1997. Piatkus

Reggio Children. The Hundred Languages of Children (Catalogue of the Exhibition). Reggio Children

Reggio Children. A Journey into the Rights of Children. 1995. Reggio Children

Rousseau, Jean Jacques. Emile. Several editions available, inc. Everyman

Rumbold, Angela. Rumbold Report: Starting with Quality. 1990. HMSO

Schweinhart, Lawrence and Weikart, David. Significant Benefits: The High/Scope Perry Study. 1982. Blackwell

Weisman Topal, Cathy & Gandini, Lella. Beautiful Stuff. 1999. Davis

Wood D. How Children Think and Learn. 1988. Blackwell

Valentine, Marianne. The Reggio Emilia Approach. 1999. Scottish CCC1

Vygotsky, Lev. Thought and Language. 1962. Cambridge, Mass

UNITED NATIONS CONVENTION ON THE RIGHTS OF THE CHILD

Second Report by the United Kingdom

August 1999
LONDON: The Stationery Office

First published 1999

ISBN 0 11 322301 3

Printed in the United Kingdom for The Stationery Office
J89790, C20, 8/99, 5673.

TABLE OF CONTENTS

Table of Figures

Annexes

┃ INTRODUCTION

1.1.1   This report has been prepared by the United Kingdom Government building on the First Report submitted in February 1994[1], and in accordance with Article 44 of the Convention, which requires States Parties to submit reports on the measures they have adopted which give effect to the rights recognised in the Convention and on the progress made on the enjoyment of those rights. Reports are required within two years of the entry into force of the Convention for the State Party concerned and thereafter every five years.

1.2   Structure of the report

1.2.1   The report takes full account of the "general guidelines regarding the form and contents of periodic reports to be submitted by States Parties under Article 44" issued in November 1996 by the Committee on the Rights of the Child.

1.2.2   During the past five years there have been major developments in government policies in relation to children, and those changes are fully reflected in this report.

1.2.3   Those developments of law and policy affecting children have served to reinforce the United Kingdom's compliance with the Convention

---

1 ISBN 0 11 321715 3, published by HMSO.

over the past five years. But the timing and content of those developments have been dictated by the needs identified within the United Kingdom, and those needs have not necessarily arisen in a pattern which follows the structure of the Convention itself. This presents some difficulty in providing the UN Committee and other readers with a full account of relevant policy developments while following the report structure recommended by the UN Committee. Some policy developments, especially those which reflect attempts to adopt an increasingly integrated approach to provision for children, cover aspects of several different Articles of the Convention, often straddling the chapter structure which the Committee prefers to adopt. The Report sets out the relevant developments in the way most likely to give a clear account of their coverage, but to assist those working primarily by reference to the text of the Convention there are cross-references where necessary, and references in the margin to Articles which are closely connected with the policy developments which are described.

1.2.4   This Report also adopts a different approach from the First United Kingdom Report in distinguishing material related to the different parts of the United Kingdom. There are distinct cultural and traditional differences between England, Wales, Scotland and Northern Ireland, which in the case of Scotland and Northern Ireland extend to significant differences in the legal systems. This diversity of practice is underpinned and strengthened by the creation of the Scottish Parliament, the new Assembly in Northern Ireland, and the Welsh Assembly. Because this report coincides so closely with those important developments, on this occasion the Report includes chapters drawing particular attention to issues arising in Scotland, Wales and Northern Ireland. But throughout the report, frequent use of cross-references will enable the UN Committee and other readers to see how the different provisions throughout the United Kingdom add up to an increasingly coherent pattern of provision which is capable of adapting to local traditions and needs.

1.3 Main messages from 1994-95 — principal subjects of concern, and recommendations

1.3.1   The Committee on the Rights of the Child considered the initial report of the United Kingdom on 24 and 25 January 1995 and issued its concluding observations in the same month. The text of the Committee's observations is at Annex A.

1.3.2   Though they made many positive comments discussed below, the Committee was concerned about the reservations made to the Convention by the United Kingdom, discussed further at section 1.8 below, and whether sufficient consideration had been given to the establishment of an independent mechanism for the purposes of monitoring developments around the implementation of the Convention.

1.3.3   Other concerns were:

    a the adequacy of implementation of economic, social and cultural rights — a general issue dealt with throughout this Report;

    b the absence of effective safeguards to prevent the ill-treatment of children under emergency legislation in Northern Ireland;

c apparent insufficiency of measures taken to ensure the implementation of the general principles of the Convention (that is, Articles 2,3,6 and 12);

d the possible adverse effects on children of the restrictions applied to unmarried fathers in conveying citizenship to their children;

e the rights of the child to express his/or her opinion in relation to the possibility for parents in England and Wales to withdraw their children from parts of sex education programmes in schools and other decisions, including exclusion from school;

f the numbers of children living in poverty; the rate of divorce; the number of single parent families and teenage pregnancies; the adequacy of benefit allowances and the availability and effectiveness of family education;

g judicial interpretation of the present law permitting the reasonable chastisement of children within the family context;

h the administration of the juvenile justice system including the low age of criminal responsibility;

i the ethos of the guidelines for the administration and establishment of Secure Training Centres in England and Wales and the Training Schools in Northern Ireland;

j changes affecting the right to remain silent, made by the Criminal Evidence (NI) Order 1988;

k the phenomena of children begging and sleeping on the streets, and the changed regulations regarding benefit entitlement as a possible contributing factor in the increase of numbers of young homeless people;

l the situation of Gypsy and Traveller children, especially regarding their access to basic services and the provision of caravan sites.

1.3.4 Additional information and responses on those points are set out in the body of the report.

1.3.5 The Committee's Concluding Observations of 1995 on the United Kingdom's initial report included the following suggestions and recommendations:

a The United Kingdom should consider reviewing its reservations to the Convention with a view to withdrawing them;

b The United Kingdom should consider establishing a national mechanism for the purpose of co-ordinating the implementation and monitoring of the Convention;

c Ways and means should be established to facilitate regular and closer cooperation between the Government and non-government community, particularly with those non-government organisations closely involved in monitoring the respect for the rights of the child;

d The general principles of the Convention, particularly the provisions of its Article 3 relating to the best interests of the child, should guide the determination of policy making at both the central and local levels of Government;

e In line with the provisions of article 42, the United Kingdom should undertake measures to make the provisions and the principles of the Convention widely known to adults and children alike;

f Teaching about children's rights should be incorporated into the training curricula of professionals working with or for children;

g Greater priority should be given to incorporating the general principles of the Convention, especially the provisions of its Articles 3 (best interests of the child) and Article 12 (child's right to make their views known and to have these views given due weight) in the legislative and administrative measures and in policies undertaken to implement the rights of the child;

h The United Kingdom should consider the possibility of establishing further mechanisms to facilitate the participation of children in decisions affecting them, including within the family and the local community.

1.3.6   Progress on a number of these matters is set out in the report.

1.4 Main messages from 1994-95 — positive comments

1.4.1   The Committee listed as positive aspects the implementation of the Children Act in 1991 in England and Wales and the application of the Convention to many of the UK's dependent territories. There was also welcome for the initiatives to reduce the incidence of Sudden Infant Death Syndrome and to combat bullying in school.

1.4.2   The committee was also encouraged by steps taken to address the issue of sexual abuse and the advocacy and promotion of inter-disciplinary approaches in this area with the "Working Together" guidance. The Committee also welcomed the commitment of the Government to review its legislation in the area of child labour and to present new legislation in matters relating to the family, domestic violence and disability.

1.4.3   Other positive comments referred to by the Committee included:

a legislative measures planned in the area of adoption, including the intention to ratify the 1993 Hague Convention on Protection of Children and Co-operation in respect of Intercountry Adoption;

b the Code of Practice for Children with Special Educational Needs;

c the preparation by local authorities of Children's Services Plans.

1.5 NGO contributions to the preparation of the Report

1.5.1   Consistent with the spirit of partnership between government and the well developed sector of non-government organisations (NGOs) working in this field, this report has taken account of consultation with NGOs. The Department of Health, which co-ordinated preparation of the report, began this consultation at a launch conference in London in February 1998, in which a range of NGOs took part. Preparation of the report, and the procedures for involving and consulting NGOs and children, were discussed within an advisory group which included NGOs — necessarily few in number, but chosen for the breadth of their contacts with other bodies having an interest in the field of children's rights throughout the United Kingdom. The responsible departments in Scotland, Wales and Northern Ireland co-ordinated NGO participation within their countries to widen this interest. NGOs were invited to contribute points which they wanted to see reflected in the report, and many did so. NGOs also had some opportunity to comment on an early draft of the report before the Government reached final decisions on its content and coverage.

1.6 Children's participation in preparation of the report

1.6.1   The degree of participation by children in the UK's First Report was very limited. It has been possible to expand their contribution, both directly and indirectly, in preparing the present report.

1.6.2   The whole process of preparing the Second Report was launched at a conference in February 1998, opened by the responsible Minister, and including a wide range of non-government organisations (NGOs) to underline the new and more inclusive approach being adopted. This was further emphasised by the participation of a group of children, who set out their perception of children's rights in the UK.

1.6.3   Preparation of the report was significantly widened on this occasion to include consultation at local level through NGOs who were able to reflect in their replies the views of children with whom they were in touch. This consultation process was handled separately in England and Wales, Scotland and Northern Ireland, which included events aimed at drawing out the views of children.

1.6.4   In Scotland, the Government commissioned Save The Children to undertake a project, entitled "Our Lives", to seek the views of children and young people on some of the main themes of the United Nations Convention namely health, education, family life and protection from harm. The consultation took place throughout Scotland in the autumn of 1998. As part of this initiative a National Conference was held in January 1999 to consult on the findings of Save The Children Scotland's discussions with young people. Young people from across Scotland together with their teachers and youth workers attended the conference.

1.6.5   This process, and the much closer involvement of NGOs, has assisted greatly in broadening the basis of the report. There is no doubt room for further development. The degree of partnership between government, NGOs, and the voluntary sector continues to grow. It should provide the basis for closer cooperation and involvement of children by the time that the UK's next report becomes due.

1.6.6   In that connection, the United Kingdom Government noted with interest a UNICEF convened conference in December 1998. It stated that

> "the reporting process presents an important opportunity for involvement of children. Indeed, there is growing evidence that children's participation is on the increase. Yet, this evolution is

patchy at best, and reaches very few children. In most cases, they are still absent at the local, national and international levels when it comes to evaluating how their rights are promoted and protected."

1.6.7   The United Kingdom Government looks forward to examining the proposals emerging from this important initiative.

1.7   Recent developments in policies

1.7.1   Since taking office in May 1997, Government Ministers have announced a series of policy developments of relevance to the UN Convention on the Rights of the Child agenda. These are dealt with in more detail in the remainder of the report. They show how the United Kingdom Government is committed to implementing changes which will be of direct benefit to children and which fully accord with the principles of the Convention.

1.8   Reservations review

1.8.1   On ratification of the Convention, the United Kingdom entered a number of reservations. The concluding observations of the Committee on the Rights of the Child (January 1995) on the First United Kingdom Report included the following:

> " The Committee is concerned about the reservations made to the Convention by the State party. In particular, the Committee is concerned that the reservation relating to the application of the Nationality and Immigration Act does not appear to be compatible with the principles of the Convention, including those of its articles 2, 3, 9 and 10."

> and

> " The Committee wishes to encourage the State Party to consider reviewing its reservations to the Convention with a view to withdrawing them, particularly in the light of the agreement made in this regard at the World Conference on Human Rights and incorporated in its Declaration and Plan of Action."

1.8.2   The reservations have been reviewed, with the following results:-

a *Convention applicable only following a live birth*
This was an interpretative declaration, setting out the interpretation on the basis of which the Government adopted the Convention. As such it does not amount to a reservation representing less than complete compliance with the Convention, and it is likely to need to stand indefinitely.

b *Interpretation of references to "parents"*
The comment immediately above applies also in this case.

c *Immigration and Citizenship*
The position has not changed. The reasons for needing to retain the reservation, in the particular circumstances of the United Kingdom, are set out at section 7.31.

d *Employment legislation for persons under 18*
Since its first report to the UN, the United Kingdom has implemented the European Community Directive on the protection of young people at work and on the Organisation of Working Time². These Directives require EC Member States to bring their domestic law into compliance with standards in relation to the employment of young people under the age of 18. The changes to the United Kingdom law came into effect on 1 October 1980.

e *Procedures governing Children's Hearings in Scotland.*
This reservation was rendered unnecessary by the implementation of the Children (Scotland) Act 1995, and was withdrawn on 18 April 1997.

1.9 Government responsibility for the Report

1.9.1   The Government of the United Kingdom records its gratitude to the many NGOs who have contributed to the preparation of this report. They have had a considerable influence on its content, and the Government hope that many of them will see their points reflected in it. But the report as submitted to the United Nations must, under the terms of the Convention, be a report by the Government of the United Kingdom. The Government does not expect NGOs to share responsibility for the report, or to be bound by its content. Responsibility for this report rests exclusively with the Government.

---

2 Directive 94/33/EC on the protection of young people (under 18 years) at work, which came into effect on 3 March 1997; and Directive 93/104/EC concerning certain aspects of the organisation of working time, which came into effect as regards young workers on 1 October 1998. In the latter case, a young worker is defined as one who has reached the age of 15 years, is above compulsory school leaving age, and is below the age of 18.

2 SCOTLAND

Article 3, 5, 18, 19, 20, 23, 24, 25

2.1.1   Scotland has a separate legal system and in many areas has distinct legislative provisions. Relevant differences between the law of Scotland and other parts of the United Kingdom are explained elsewhere in this report, but since the United Kingdom's First Report there has been one major item of legislation which is summarised in this chapter, and which has wide effects on the treatment of children in Scotland.

2.1.2   The United Kingdom's First Report recognised the significant contribution that the Children Act 1989 made to the development of child care law in England and Wales, and noted that proposals for change in law and policy in Scotland had been published and awaited the necessary Parliamentary time. The lengthy process of both developing proposals for change and securing Parliamentary time provided a valuable opportunity to consult widely on those proposals and amend them in light of comments received from interested parties. By the time the Children (Scotland) Bill was introduced to Parliament in 1994, its underlying principles and general proposals had already been well debated by those affected by and with an interest in its provisions. The bringing together of the main private and public child care law provisions into a single piece of legislation for the first time in Scotland was, to a large extent, a recognition of the broad measure of support for a unified Act which existed in Scotland from both NGOs and statutory organisations.

2.1.3   The Bill's passage through the Parliamentary process was also significant, in that it was the first Bill to use new procedures for the taking of evidence from expert witnesses before proceeding to debate the Bill's provisions. This new procedure engendered a spirit of all-party co-operation and as a result a significant number of important amendments were made to the Bill. Among others, the definition of "child in need" was made more child-centred indicating a positive duty on local authorities to promote the welfare of children in need in their area. Also, the arrangements for the exclusion of a suspected abuser from the family home were amended to include an interim exclusion order which takes immediate effect. Equally significant, a process of dialogue with NGOs was maintained through the process which generated informed discussion on the Bill's provisions both inside and outside the debating chambers.

2.2   Principles of the Children (Scotland) Act 1995

2.2.1   The Children (Scotland) Act 1995[3] marks a significant stage in the development of legislation on the care of children in Scotland. Centred on the needs of children and their families, it defines parental responsibilities and rights in relation to children. It sets out the duties and powers available to public authorities to support children and their families and to intervene when the child's welfare requires it. For the first time in Scottish law, public and private law provisions have been brought together.

2.2.2   Prior to the 1995 Act, only parental *rights* were recognised in statute, and public child care legislation was largely focused on the service providers rather than the children using the services. The Children (Scotland) Act 1995 is clearly centred on the needs of the children themselves, with the responsibilities, rights and duties of others being focused on meeting those needs. This overarching principle, that each child has a right to be treated as an individual, is at the core of the legislative and policy developments which have taken place since the Act's implementation. This appears to be in accordance with the theme which runs throughout the Convention.

2.2.3   In addition, a number of other principles were central to the development of the new procedures

>   a   each child who can form his or her views on matters affecting him or her has the right to express those views if he or she so wishes (reflecting Articles 12 and 13 of the Convention and the Committee's suggestions made in response to the First Report);
>
>   b   parents should normally be responsible for the upbringing of their children and should share that responsibility (reflecting Article 9);
>
>   c   each child has the right to protection from all forms of abuse, neglect or exploitation (reflecting Article 19);

---

3 The Children (Scotland) Act 1995: c 36 HMSO: ISBN 0 11 805978-5

d in decisions relating to protection, the child should remain in the family home where that is in his or her best interests (Article 9); and

e any intervention by a public authority in the life of a child should be properly justified and should be supported by services from all relevant agencies working in collaboration (Article 20).

2.2.4   In recognition of these principles, three main themes run through the 1995 Act: –

a the child's views should be taken into account where major decisions are to be made about his or her future;

b no court should make an order relating to a child and no Children's Hearing should make a supervision requirement unless the court or hearing considers that to do so would be better for the child than making no order or supervision requirement at all; and

c the welfare of the child is the paramount consideration in any decision being made about the child by courts and Children's Hearings.

2.2.5   The last of the three builds on the Committee's suggestions in response to the First Report that Article 3 should be given due weight in legislation. The new provisions promote the welfare of children to a high level, equal to that required in adoption proceedings. The fact that this welfare test applies to children who have committed offences as well as those who are in need of protection is an important step in recognising that children's difficulties can be tackled by addressing their needs. In the interests of public safety, provision is made to derogate from the paramountcy principle where necessary to protect members of the public from serious harm. The Government believe this to be a necessary safeguard and consistent with its obligations to adults and other children under this and other Conventions.

2.3   Main changes

Article 5, 9, 12, 18

2.3.1   The Act introduces a number of significant new provisions designed to enhance the standing of children in Scotland. Part I of the Act deals with the private law provisions and for the first time in United Kingdom legislation sets out the responsibilities and rights of parents in relation to their children.

2.4   Parental responsibilities

2.4.1   A parent has responsibility

a to safeguard and promote the child's health, development and welfare;

b to provide direction and guidance, in a manner appropriate to the stage of development of the child;

c if the child is not living with the parent, to maintain personal relations and direct contact with the child on a regular basis; and

d to act as the child's legal representative.

2.4.2 The above responsibilities are to be fulfilled only in so far as is practicable and in the interests of the child. In addition, all except the responsibility to provide guidance exist until the child reaches the age of 16 years. The responsibility to provide guidance exists until the child is 18 years of age.

2.5 Parental rights

Article 5, 9, 12, 18

2.5.1 To enable parents to fulfil their parental responsibilities, certain rights are conferred in relation to the child, as follows: –

  a to have the child living with him or her, or otherwise to regulate the child's residence;

  b to control, direct or guide, in a manner appropriate to the stage of development of the child, the child's upbringing;

  c if the child is not living with the parent, to maintain personal relations and direct contact with the child on a regular basis; and

  d to act as the child's legal representative.

2.5.2 Those parental rights exist until the child reaches the age of 16 years.

2.5.3 Other important new provisions in family law are: –

  a a new agreement under which an unmarried father can obtain parental responsibilities and rights with the consent of the child's mother and without having to petition the Court.

  b a duty on parents and the court to seek the views of children who will be affected by major decisions;

  c an expectation that parents will take joint control in the raising of their children, even after separation or divorce;

  d replacing of the parental rights of custody and access with child centred orders of residence and contact;

  e a duty on the court not to make any order unless it considers it would be better for the child to do so than not to do so: and

  f new provisions for guardianship and the administration of children's property.

2.5.4 Section 7.25 of this report refers to developments in England and Wales related to the parental responsibilities and rights of unmarried fathers. Those developments do not apply in Scotland, but the Scottish Office is seeking views on whether similar changes should be made to the law in Scotland as part of current consultation on Scottish family law and divorce. The consultation paper *Improving Scottish Family Law* was issued in March 1999.

2.6 Child Welfare Hearing

Article 5, 18, 12

2.6.1 The aim of the child welfare hearing was to introduce an early hearing in any civil case involving an application to the court in relation to a child under section 11 of the 1995 Act. This hearing which takes place within a matter of a few weeks of the commencement of a case is designed to be held in informal conditions with the parents and, if possible, the child present. The purpose of the hearing is to enable the court to take a view firstly as to the real issues and secondly as to whether the court needs to intervene and if the latter to try to effect a settlement.

2.6.2   Supplementary to this has been the introduction of procedures refining earlier attempts to involve children in the process and to secure an indication of whether they wish to give their views. In the first place, all children above infancy are served with a specially prepared form which indicates the situation and invites them to say whether they wish to give a view. This form was prepared after very careful discussion with interested parties representing children, and had been the subject of consultation with various children and young people.

2.6.3   Children, therefore, are involved in the process and can instruct their own solicitor receiving legal aid for the purpose or can be represented by a *curator ad litem* if they are too young; or they can indicate that they wish to express a view in some other manner through a social worker or a teacher or a person whom they know and trust.

2.6.4   Once the view of the child is communicated to the court the court can consider whether or not the view remains confidential.

2.7   Mediation in Scotland

2.7.1   The courts in Scotland have a power to refer to mediation any case involving parent child relationships at any stage of the case. Thus, in the sheriff court, the child welfare hearing could be a stage at which such a referral is made.

2.7.2   Mediation services are provided by Family Mediation Scotland which has a network of local mediation services co-ordinated from Edinburgh. These services specialise in mediation in issues relating to children and have been established for several years. The techniques which they use are particularly adapted to seeking to achieve responsibility on the part of parents for the continuation of their relationships with their children and are therefore ideal for the philosophy behind Part I of the Children (Scotland) Act 1995.

2.7.3   Other mediation services are provided by solicitors under the general collective title of Comprehensive Accredited Lawyer Mediator. These mediators will deal with mediation in relation to children along with other issues notably concerning finances and property.

2.7.4   In Scotland there has been for many years a tradition of negotiation in relation to marital breakdown. This is assisted by the fact that agreements between divorcing couples can be registered for execution in the public registers and so avoid the need for court intervention. It is the general policy of those involved in family law in Scotland to seek to encourage a negotiation culture and to move away from an adversarial culture. In this, mediation has a very important role.

2.8 Public law provisions

Article 9, 19, 25, 27

2.8.1 The Children (Scotland) Act 1995 replaced most of the provisions relating to the operation of public child care law in Scotland. This section reports on some of the main changes made in support of the principles of the Convention and provides brief comments on other significant changes.

2.9 Young Offenders and the Children's Hearings System

Article 40

2.9.1 The Children (Scotland) Act 1995 carried forward the Children's Hearings System as the core of Scotland's public law provisions and strengthened its role in order to promote the interests of children referred to it. The principle underlying the system is that children, whether they have been referred for care or protection or whether they have offended, have common needs for protection, guidance, treatment or control, although the extent to which these needs are unmet will vary from child to child.

2.9.2 A Children's Hearing is not a judicial body. It comprises three volunteer members of the child's community who consider whether a child might be in need of compulsory measures of supervision, and if so, the nature of the supervision which would best meet the needs of the child. Supervision requirements last up to one year and can be extended on review if that is in the child's interests. A prime focus of the Hearing is the resolution of the child's needs in a family context. Children's Hearings are relatively informal in nature and allow all the parties – parents, children and social workers – to discuss both the reasons why problems have arisen and how they might be resolved. In order to ensure compliance with the European Convention on Human Rights, all hearings decisions can be appealed to a judicial body which may consider the matter *de novo*.

2.9.3 The Local Government (Scotland) Act 1994 established the Scottish Children's Reporter Administration (SCRA) and the office of the Principal Reporter. The SCRA formally came into operation as a national service on 1 April 1996. In practice, the SCRA brings the Children's Reporter service together under a single management structure to facilitate the coherent operation of the service and delivers consistent national practice and training.

2.9.4 Being essentially focused on resolution of difficulties within the family, certain matters falling outside this remit are dealt with by the Courts – adoption, for example. The Courts also deal with more serious offences. The document Review of Adoption Law in Scotland recognised that the same child could be subject to parallel, but distinct consideration of their welfare needs as a result of this separation and proposed a greater role for Children's Hearings in such circumstances. The Children (Scotland) Act 1995 therefore introduced provision for Children's Hearings to give advice to the Courts where such matters were being considered, ensuring that the consideration by one forum is informed by the view of the other. Early indications are that such advice is being well received and valued by the Courts.

2.9.5   Another interface which has been improved is that of long term planning for the child's future. The responsibility for such matters falls in the first instance to the responsible local authority, but this issue cannot be considered in isolation from the shorter term decisions of the Children's Hearing. New provisions now ensure that, where long term plans are being considered, the Children's Hearings are made aware of them and are in a position to give advice to the local authority. All these changes are designed to place the child at the centre of the process, and to ensure so far as is possible that all agencies and bodies involved with the child share a common understanding of the child's needs.

2.9.6   The Scottish Office continues to finance several pilot projects which aim to address and, over time, reduce juvenile offending through targeted interventions. Four projects, led by voluntary sector organisations and encompassing multi-agency working, are at different stages of development. Each project is subject to independent evaluation to assist wider discussion and debate on what measures work in addressing youth offending behaviour.

2.9.7   The Barnardos Freagarrach project is based in the Central region of Scotland; the APEX CueTen and SACRO Offenders' Mediation projects are based in the Fife region. All are well established. Through targeted and intensive programmes of intervention, the projects work with persistent young offenders from within the 10 to 16 year age group. Each aims to tackle offending behaviour and its underlying causes through individual programmes which are more intensive than currently available to the Children's Hearings system. Each project has separate but related goals for participants. Work with offenders entails addressing motivational problems, providing work experience, and developing educational and cognitive skills, social counselling and aspects of mediation and reparation involving victims.

2.9.8   A very recent and innovative project to receive Government funding targets children in the 8-14 year age group and aims to deliver packages of support measures to children identified to be at risk of potential future offending. Based in Central region and involving multi-agency working, the project is being managed by Barnardos. The project will aim to identify known risk indicators which can lead to future offending behaviour and to develop a multi-faceted approach which works with the children and their families to reduce these indicators through seeking to enhance protective factors.

2.10 Safeguarders

Article 3, 12

2.10.1   Safeguarders are independent people who can be appointed by Children's Hearings and Sheriffs to represent the child's best interests in the proceedings. Before the introduction of the 1995 Act, safeguarders were only appointed when there was a conflict of interest between the child and the parents. Now, however, the Act requires that every Children's Hearing and the Sheriff must consider in all situations whether the appointment of a safeguarder is appropriate.

2.11 Young offenders and the age of criminal responsibility

Article 40

2.12 Reservation to Article 37 and the Children's Hearings System

Article 37

2.11.1   One of the main criticisms made by the UN Committee in this area on consideration of the First United Kingdom Report was in relation to the age of criminal responsibility. Although Scotland has a low age of criminal responsibility (8 years), the vast majority of Scottish children who offend are dealt with through the Children's Hearings system. Children under 16 years are only considered for prosecution in court for serious offences such as murder and rape; and even in such instances it is not automatic that prosecution will occur. Children in these categories can be referred to the Principal Reporter who has the statutory responsibility to decide whether to refer cases to a Children's Hearing. During 1996 just over 28,000 children were referred to a Children's Hearing on offence grounds. In the same year only 47 children under 16 years were sentenced to detention by criminal courts.

2.11.2   A National Planning Group for care and education services for young people with behavioural problems, including offending, was set up in 1997. It is exploring, among other things, the means by which the admission of persons under 17 years to prison could be minimised. This forum is a good example of a partnership between Government, statutory and voluntary agencies to plan strategically for the needs of vulnerable young people. The Group published its report in May 1999, and it will be for the new Scottish Parliament to decide how these issues are to be dealt with in future.

2.11.3   The Children (Scotland) Act 1995 improved the way in which courts can deal with young offenders. Where children are prosecuted in court, the court may now refer their case to a Children's Hearing for advice on the best method of dealing with them, and the court on receipt of that advice, or in certain cases without seeking advice first, may remit the child's case for disposal by a Children's Hearing.

2.12.1   The Committee's concluding observations on the First Report welcomed the United Kingdom's intention to consider withdrawing the reservation it made to Article 37 of the Convention as it related to procedures governing the Children's Hearings in Scotland[4]. The reservation was rendered unnecessary by the Children (Scotland) Act 1995, and was withdrawn on 18 April 1997. Section 51 of the Act now provides that where a child is deprived of his or her liberty by being kept in a place of safety under a warrant by the Children's Hearing, an appeal to the Sheriff in respect of the issue of the warrant by the Children's Hearing must be disposed of within 3 days of the lodging of the appeal; and failing such disposal the warrant shall cease to have effect at the end of that period. In addition, there is an appeal from the Sheriff's decision to that of the Sheriff Principal. There is therefore prompt access to a local court and a local appellate court with access to legal representation and legal aid. These appeals may be made immediately by the children involved and/or their parents and both the Sheriff and the Sheriff Principal can overturn the lower decisions without having to refer the case back, either to the hearing or to the Sheriff.

---

4   The reservation was in respect of Article 37(d) of the UN Convention, which ensures that every child deprived of his or her liberty shall have the right to prompt access to legal and other appropriate assistance as well as the right to challenge the legality of the deprivation of liberty.

2.12.2   This more comprehensive and direct system of appeals to a Court than that which previously existed allows access to legal aid and representation. These appeal courts are also local courts which again eases the process for those involved. The maximum time a child may be kept in interim care, before an appeal to the Court must be heard, is 3 days (essentially over a weekend).

2.13 Children's Services Plans

Article 18, 20, 24, 25

2.13.1   There is now a new obligation on local authorities to produce a plan for the provision of relevant services for children. These plans are designed to ensure that the services being provided locally reflect the needs of children and young people likely to use them, and are delivered in an integrated manner. One of the main aims of children's services plans is the contribution they can make to the co-ordination of services between departments within a local authority, between different local authorities and with a wide range of other organisations and agencies involved in children's services. These include Health Boards and NHS Trusts, voluntary organisations, Reporters to the Children's Panel, children's panel representatives and housing agencies, thus ensuring that such plans are informed by the needs and views of the voluntary and statutory organisations active in the community.

2.13.2   Equally significant, local authorities are required to consult voluntary organisations which represent the interests of persons who use or are likely to use the services. This means that the views of children's representative organisations will be fully taken into account in the formulation of plans.

2.13.3   In April 1998 The Scottish Office completed a review of the first round of Children's Services Plans produced by local authorities.

2.13.4   One of the main areas of strength in the plans was that different departments and agencies collaborated in their production. Some local authorities set up strategic planning groups to take the work forward with representatives of all relevant departments and agencies. The purpose of these planning groups is seen by local authorities as promoting an integrated provision of services. Many of the plans showed extensive consultation with user and providers of services, and a number importantly underlined not only that the local authority had consulted, but had also acted upon comments received and proposed to continue to take account of views and involve users and providers in the review process.

2.13.5   The content of the plans provide a sound foundation on which further improvements in children's services can be based.

2.14 Care plans

Article 25

2.14.1   All children who are looked after by a local authority, whether they are with foster carers, in a residential establishment, or at home subject to a supervision requirement, must now have a care plan and regular reviews of their case at intervals set out in statute. Children being looked after by local authorities have experienced in the past, a lack of direction in tackling the reasons which led to them leaving their family homes in the first place. Plans are intended to provide a focus for all those involved in caring for a child, so that everyone, including the child, knows what is being worked towards and what their individual role is in day-to-day care. Children being looked after by local authorities, particularly those living away from home, are seen significantly to under-achieve educationally compared to children who do not need social work support. The Government recognises this position to be unsatisfactory and wishes to promote educational standards of such children to a level comparable with other children. This is an area which will be addressed in the forthcoming consultation exercise on the development of a Strategic Framework for Children's Services.

2.14.2 The Arrangements to Look After Children (Scotland) Regulations 1996[5] set out the processes involved in drawing up care plans. When making any care plan, wherever the child has to live, a local authority should consider a number of issues, including alternative courses of action, whether a change in the child's legal status should be sought, and arrangements which need to be made for the time when the child is no longer looked after. An additional set of considerations apply when the local authority places a child with alternative carers or in a residential home, including the issue of contact between child and parents. These plans must also identify a child's health and education needs, and must set out what is to be done to address those needs by all relevant parties, including the child, parents and local authority. The Regulations set out a clear timetable for reviewing the care plans of all children who are looked after. Where a child is looked after by a local authority and placed away from home, a first review has to take place within six weeks, a second review must happen within three months of the first and subsequent reviews are to be held at intervals of no more than six months. The review timetable for children who remain at home is a first review within three months and subsequent reviews within six months from the date of the previous review.

2.14.3 Although care plans are legally a local authority planning mechanism, parents and children are fully involved in the planning process. Local authorities are obliged to take the views of both parents and children on the proposed plan, and guidance emphasises that attendance by children and parents at reviews of the plan is to be encouraged. Although the provisions are relatively new, early indications are that a significant number of children are taking an active part in the planning for their care and education.

2.14.4 To complement these changes, a pilot system concerned to improve the planning and review process for children and young people who are looked after was launched in 1997. The Looking After Children materials, which were developed over a number of years in England and Wales, aim to improve the parenting experience of children looked after by local authorities . They set an agenda for good care by identifying the

---

5 SI 1996/3262 (S.252).

experiences, concerns and expectations of children at different ages. They also aim to further the development of outcome planning and measurement in social work practice. After positive results in the pilot, the majority of local authorities intend to start implementing the scheme proper in 1999.

2.15 Services and support for children

Article 5, 9, 12, 18, 25

2.15.1   Part II of the Children (Scotland) Act 1995 introduces duties and powers for safeguarding and promoting children's welfare. Under that Part, local authorities are required to safeguard and promote the welfare of children in need and so far as is consistent with that duty to promote their upbringing by their families by providing appropriate services. A child is considered to be in need if:

a he or she is unlikely to achieve or maintain, or to have the opportunity of maintaining, a reasonable standard of health or development unless services are provided for him or her;

b his or her health or development is likely significantly to be impaired, or further impaired unless services are provided;

c he or she is disabled; or

d he or she is affected adversely by the disability of any other person in his or her family.

2.15.2   The Government issued guidance on the range and delivery of services and support that local authorities and NGOs may provide for children in need, including disabled children, emphasising the need to involve children and families in planning and reviewing services they receive with a view to making these accessible and accountable to children and their families.

2.16 Aftercare

Article 20

2.16.1   The Government recognises that the transition to living independently can be difficult and unsettling for young people, particularly those who were previously looked after by a local authority. There is ample evidence to suggest that they are over-represented in the number of young people who are homeless. Part of the difficulty is providing a flexible level of support to meet the variety of needs of this transitional age group of 16 to 21 year olds. For some young people with a history of social work involvement there is a great temptation for them to break all ties with the statutory authorities at the earliest opportunity. Many such young people find themselves without the necessary skills or support to live independently. Planning for independence is therefore started early, and the Act imposes a new specific duty on local authorities to provide advice and assistance to prepare a child for the time when he or she ceases to be looked after by a local authority.

2.16.2   At the point where the young person leaves the local authority, the 1995 Act strengthens previous provisions by placing local authorities under a duty to advise, guide and assist any person over school age but not yet 19 years who at the time he or she ceased to be of school age was looked after by a local authority. Local authorities also have a new power to provide such assistance up to age 21, and beyond to complete a course of education. They may provide grants towards expenses of education and training and make contributions to accommodation and maintenance.

2.16.3   In recognition that not all vulnerable young people will previously have been looked after by the local authority, the Act contains a new power to allow local authorities to provide accommodation for young people aged 16 to 21 where their welfare requires it, whether or not they were previously involved with the local authority.

2.16.4   The Act now provides a sufficiently flexible legislative base to allow support to all young people in need of assistance up to the age of 21. The Government recognises that aftercare support is an area which has not been given high priority in the past, and intends promoting the innovative development of a range of support services building on the flexibility provided for in the legislation.

2.17 Children and Disability

Article 23, 24

2.17.1   The Children (Scotland) Act 1995 introduced specific provision for disabled children and those affected by disabilities. Under the Act local authority services for children "in need" must be designed to minimise the effects of their disabilities and give disabled children the chance to lead as normal a life as possible. Where a child is disabled, chronically sick or mentally ill, or where someone else in the family is disabled, the local authority must carry out this assessment of the child's and the family's needs where requested to do so by the child's parent or guardian. The 1995 Act also places a specific duty on local authorities to publish information about the services they provide for disabled children.

2.17.2   The local authority on being requested to do so must also carry out an assessment of the ability of a disabled child's carer to care for the child.

2.18 Refuges for young people

Article 19, 39

2.18.1   Before the introduction of the Children (Scotland) Act 1995 it was an offence to provide a child, who had absconded from residential care, with accommodation. The 1995 Act allows for an important exception to this. Local authorities and authorised independent persons may now provide short-term refuges, either in residential homes or in the community, for children at risk of harm who run away from home or their carers and who request refuge. These refuges will provide vulnerable young people with a safe place to stay for a short period, and information and advice to help them to decide what to do next.

2.19 Children in hospitals and nursing homes

Article 24, 12

2.19.1   The 1995 Act also introduces a new provision where a child who is accommodated in a health establishment has had, or is likely to have, no parental contact for three months or more. Those circumstances must be notified to the local authority which then has to consider whether the child's welfare needs are being adequately met.

2.20 Child protection in Scotland

Article 19, 39

2.20.1   The Children (Scotland) Act 1995 made important changes for the protection of children at risk, introducing three new court orders, which may be granted by a sheriff, designed to protect children from harm or the risk of harm: –

a   The child protection order allows anyone to apply to the Court for an order to remove the child from home. The Court may make such an order if it is satisfied that there are reasonable grounds to believe that the child is suffering significant harm because of ill-treatment or neglect or will suffer such harm if he or she is not removed to, or allowed to remain in, a place of safety. The child protection order is firmly focused on the needs of the child but contains a much higher test for removal of the child from home than its predecessor. Both the parents and the child have an early opportunity to have the order set aside or varied by the Court and such an application has to be determined within three working days.

b   The exclusion order is a new measure in the development of child protection procedures. It is designed to reduce disruption and distress to children who may have already suffered physical or mental abuse. It can be obtained from the sheriff on broadly the same criteria as a child protection order. If granted, the order requires the person to whom the harm (or potential harm) is attributed to leave the family home or not to visit it, if living elsewhere. It is therefore an alternative to removing the child from the security of his or her home under a child protection order and is a major step in reflecting the principles of Article 9. Exclusion may be authorised on an emergency basis but, as in the case of a child protection order, provision is made for early review of the order by the Court.

c   If there is good reason to suspect that a child may be suffering harm and parents refuse to allow the child to be seen in order to resolve those suspicions, a Court can make a child assessment order which gives the local authority the right to see and assess the child, or arrange for the child to be assessed by other professionals, such as a doctor or psychiatrist. The order may last for up to seven days and will not normally require the child to reside away from his or her family unless this is necessary for the purposes of the assessment.

2.20.2   Where a Sheriff is not available and there is a need to act urgently, a Justice of the Peace may authorise the removal and keeping of a child in a place of safety in certain circumstances.

2.21 Adoption

Article 21

2.21.1   The Review of Adoption Law in Scotland concluded that adoption legislation and practice in Scotland were essentially sound, but a number of significant changes were made through the Children (Scotland) Act 1995 to improve its operation. One major change was to introduce timescales within which adoption applications contested by the birth parents must be brought before the Court for resolution. Previously there was a tendency to delay such applications being made. This had the effect of creating a care planning hiatus and extending the uncertainty for the child. Such delay also acted against the interests of the birth parents, whose claim to have the child returned to them was undermined by the passage of time. The new timetabling arrangements require an application to be brought to the Court for resolution within a period of six months. The Court is now under a corresponding obligation to draw up a timetable for the resolution of the application without undue delay.

2.21.2   A further change to the legislation means that it is now possible for an adoption order to be made in relation to an 18 year old provided the application was made before the child's 18th birthday.

2.21.3   A new provision has also been introduced to ensure that a Children's Hearing involved with a child is able to give advice to a Court on an adoption application. The interface between the jurisdictions of the hearings and the Court was one which was rightly criticised in the past, with the two forums making decisions in relation to the child without having the benefit of knowing the views of the other. Early indications are that the Court is finding the views of the Children's Hearing on the needs of the child a valuable addition to its consideration of an adoption application.

2.21.4   Prior to the 1995 Act, older children for whom adoption was not a suitable form of alternative long term care would either remain in the Children's Hearings system and have their supervision extended annually, or have their parental rights assumed by the local authority. With this latter provision the parental rights and powers were vested in the local authority following an administrative resolution. This meant that parents could lose their rights without having the right to challenge that decision in court. The need for such an important step to be made within a court-based setting has been widely recognised in recent years and this particular provision has now been replaced in the Children (Scotland) Act 1995 by the parental responsibilities order — which local authorities can apply for through the Court. On the granting of the order all the parental responsibilities and rights transfer to the local authority. The grounds for granting the order are

    a that the parent is not known,

    b cannot be found,

    c is incapable of giving agreement,

    d is withholding agreement unreasonably,

    e has persistently failed, without reasonable cause, to fulfil parental responsibilities, or

    f has seriously mistreated the child.

2.21.5   These grounds are the same as those for adoption.

2.21.6   Where a child is freed for adoption and the parental responsibilities transferred to the local authority pending the making of an adoption order, the law has now been amended to ensure that parenthood remains with the birth parents until that title is removed by the subsequent adoption. These changes to the law recognise an important distinction between the child's right to have parents and the quite separate issue of the exercise of parental responsibilities.

2.22 Other relevant provisions

2.22.1   The examples above provide an overview of the main areas of change introduced by the 1995 Act since the First Report was made. Other significant changes are

a   in making a decision about a child looked after by them, the local authority must have regard to the child's religious persuasion, racial origin, and cultural and linguistic background[6];

b   clarification of the position of children who would wish to instruct their own counsel. The Age of Legal Capacity (Scotland) Act 1991[7] had left some doubt about this. Consequently, the 1991 Act was amended to make it clear that a person under the age of 16 years has legal capacity to instruct a solicitor in connection with any civil matter, if that person has a general understanding of what it means to do so. A person aged 12 years or more is presumed to have such an understanding. It is made clear that a person under the age of 16 years can apply for legal aid;

c   in making arrangements for the medical examination and treatment of children, the child's consent must be obtained where the child has "requisite capacity" in terms of section 2(4) of the Age of Legal Capacity (Scotland) Act 1991. Nothing in the 1995 Act can override that consent.

2.23 Publications

2.23.1   In order to keep local authorities and professionals working in child care informed about the implementation of the Children (Scotland) Act a free Newsletter has been issued on a regular basis. The Newsletter is a source of information on a number of aspects of implementation including training initiatives, regulations, rules and guidance, publications on the Act, legal development, local initiatives and good practice.

2.23.2   Guidance issued to local authorities and other agencies on implementation of the Act also sets out the Government's expectations about how children and young people receiving support from public agencies or looked after, will be informed, consulted and involved in decision-making generally[8].

---

6   *Valuing Diversity: Having regard to the racial, religious, cultural and linguistic needs of Scotland's Children* The Stationery Office IBSN 0 1149 5903 X.

7   c50: HMSO ISBN 0 10 545091-X

8   *Scotland's Children,* The Children (Scotland) Act 1995, Regulations and Guidance The Stationery Office ISBN 0 7480 5821 4, ISBN 0 7480 5822 2, ISBN 0 7480 5823 & ISBN 0 7480 5845.

2.23.3   A series of public information leaflets have also been produced for children and families covering various aspects of the Children (Scotland) Act 1995, including the Children's Hearings system and child protection. A children's guide has also been published on the family law provisions of the Act. Entitled You Matter[9], this booklet explains to children and young people how the changes in the law relating to parental responsibilities and rights affect them. It also explains the new court rules and procedures and shows how children and young people will be able to put forward their views to the court if they want to. Various groups of children were consulted in the preparation of these public information leaflets which are all designed in a friendly and accessible manner. A parents' booklet, entitled Your Children Matter[10], was published in October 1998. This is in line with the recommendation made by the Committee in the First Report. The booklet informs parents about their responsibilities and rights under the family law provisions of the Act.

2.23.4   Both booklets may be obtained from The Scottish Office.

2.24   Homelessness and rough sleeping in Scotland

Article 26, 27

2.24.1   Extra resources of around £300 million are being made available over the 3 years 1999-2002 for housing in Scotland, which will help to improve housing conditions for households including children among others. Homelessness continues to be a national housing priority, and homelessness among young people is being tackled by improving their rights to accommodation, and the introduction of a Rough Sleepers Initiative including projects specifically aimed at young people.

2.24.2   The Rough Sleepers Initiative was introduced in 1997 to fund action by local authorities and other statutory and voluntary bodies at local level to help rough sleepers, many of whom are young people. The initiative lays emphasis on an integrated approach by all relevant agencies, such as housing, health, social care and police. £16m has been made available over the years 1997-2000, which has been allocated to 21 local authorities. Projects assisted include some specifically targeted at young people. Examples include direct access accommodation for young men whose behaviour has meant them being refused entry by existing direct access accommodation and direct access accommodation for young women. A further £14m has been made available for 2000-01 and 20001-02. Ministers recently issued a Rough Sleepers Initiative consultation paper for comment and the future direction of the initiative will depend upon the outcome of that consultation.

2.24.3   A new Scottish Code of Guidance on Homelessness[11] came into force on 1 December 1997. By statute local authorities must have regard to the Code in exercising their functions under the homelessness legislation in

---

9   Published by the Scottish Office Home Department and Scottish Courts Administration,

10 Published by the Scottish Office Home Department, October 1998.

11 *The Code of Guidance on Homelessness* - The Scottish Office Development Department - September 1997 (updated December 1998).

Part II of the Housing (Scotland) Act 1987. The Code improves the rights of homeless children and young people by including many of them in groups who should be regarded as being in priority need under the homelessness legislation, and hence entitled to accommodation if unintentionally homeless, for example under 18s, and those at risk of sexual or financial exploitation. Young people under 21 years previously in local authority care at school leaving age or later, who are at a high risk both of becoming homeless and of being damaged by homelessness because of the problems which led to them entering care, became a statutory homelessness priority group on 1 January 1998 under the Homeless Persons (Priority Need) (Scotland) Order 1998[12]. Households containing dependent children are already a statutory homelessness priority group. More generally, the Code encourages local authorities always to seek to minimise the risk of homelessness recurring, including the provision of permanent accommodation with security of tenure, and any support services required.

2.24.4   The Code gives good practice guidance on how the Children (Scotland) Act 1995 and homelessness legislation can be used together to help homeless young people, and prevent homelessness recurring.

2.25 Subsequent developments in children's rights in Scotland

2.25.1   As a practical demonstration of the Government's commitment to young people in Scotland a Minister for Children's Issues was appointed in July 1997. In its comments on the First Report the Committee suggested that the general principles of the Convention, particularly the provisions of its Article 3 relating to the best interests of the child, should guide the determination of policy making at both central and local levels. With that in mind, the first task of the Minister is to ensure that all areas of The Scottish Office fully consider the effect that their policies will have on children.

2.25.2   A Child Strategy Statement which stresses the importance of the UN Convention has been produced which reminds all Scottish Office Departments of the need to identify and take proper account of the interests of children when developing policy. The document was the subject of consultation and it received widespread support. It was recognised that the Child Strategy Statement, whilst intended primarily for application in The Scottish Office, was equally applicable to local authorities and voluntary organisations dealing with children's issues. For that reason, the Statement was given a wide distribution throughout Scottish local authorities and NGOs.

2.26 The Children's Issues Unit of The Scottish Office

2.26.1   A Children's Issues Unit has also been set up within The Scottish Office to ensure that children's issues involving more than one policy area are properly co-ordinated. The Unit was responsible for co-ordinating The Scottish Office contribution to this Report. As well as liaison with other Scottish Office Departments, this co-ordinating role also required working

---

12 SI 1997/3049.

closely with NGOs to ensure that their views on the report were heard. To this end the Unit funded a conference, organised by the Scottish Alliance for Children's Rights (SACR), an umbrella organisation for NGOs with an interest in Children's issues in Scotland, to take their views. The Conference was well received and the comments of delegate were fed into the Scottish Office contribution to the report.

2.26.2   In recognition of the importance of taking the views of children, The Children's Issues Unit commissioned the Our Lives Project. This was a Scotland wide consultation exercise which gathered the views of young people in relation to children's rights. The project was carried out by Save the Children Scotland and was jointly funded by both parties. The Our Lives consultation process reflected the principle of Article 12 – the right of young people to be listened to in matters which affect them.

2.26.3   Over a three month period Save the Children consulted 43 groups of children and young people (326 in total), between the ages of 12 years and 18 years, from 20 local authorities, representing schools and youth groups from urban and rural Scotland and a wide spectrum of interest groups. The groups of young people were invited to discuss one of five themes: education, family life, health, protection from harm and participation; and their views were sought on how successful the implementation of the UN Convention on the Rights of the Child has been so far in Scotland. Findings were gathered from audio recordings of structured and facilitated discussions and group exercises. Further details of this consultation exercise are set out in Annex C.

2.27 Government of Scotland Act 1998

2.27.1   The Scotland Act 1998 provided for the establishment of a Scottish Parliament. The Parliament assumed its full powers on 1 July. By virtue of the Scotland Act, the Scottish Parliament has control over Scotland's domestic affairs eg: health, education, local government, law and order, etc. Westminster retains powers over matters which affect the whole of the United Kingdom e.g. UK constitution, foreign affairs, defence policy and economic and monetary policy. The Westminster Parliament remains sovereign.

2.27.2   The Scottish Executive is very much committed to young people and is keen to give them every encouragement and opportunity to make their voices heard. An inaugural meeting of the Youth Parliament took place on 30 June. The aim of the Youth Parliament is to provide a voice for young people on issues that affect them and is a channel of communication to the Scottish Parliament.

3 | NORTHERN IRELAND

3.1.1   This chapter summarises some of the most important items of legislation relevant to the Convention which have been introduced in Northern Ireland since the United Kingdom's First Report. Where necessary, the impact of these developments is explained in more detail in other chapters of this report, to illustrate relevant differences in the law and practice of Northern Ireland and other parts of the United Kingdom.

3.2   The Children (NI) Order 1995

Article 3, 5, 18, 19, 20, 23, 24, 25

3.2.1   Since the United Kingdom's First Report, the Children (NI) Order 1995[13] has been made and its main provisions have been in operation since November 1996. This Order reformed and consolidated for Northern Ireland most of the public and private law relating to children, along the lines of the Children Act 1989 in England and Wales. Many of its fundamental principles, such as the welfare principle and the non-intervention principle, serve to reinforce the application of the Convention in Northern Ireland. The Order's operation is kept under review by the Children Order Advisory Committee which was set up to monitor the workings of the court related aspects of the Order. The Committee reports to the Lord Chancellor and the Secretary of State for Northern Ireland. The Department of Health and Social Services, in consultation with the Lord Chancellor, the Department of

---

13 SI 1995/755 (NI 2) - ISBN 0-11-052707-0.

Education and the Department of Finance and Personnel, is also required to produce an annual general report on the implementation of the Children Order.

3.2.2   The Children Order, which applies to non-criminal cases, includes a wide range of measures designed to promote the welfare of children. For example, there is now a clear legal requirement for courts to make the welfare of the child the paramount consideration when making any decision concerning the upbringing of a child.

3.2.3   The Children Order contains a number of provisions designed to ensure that the wishes and feelings of the child are taken into account when decisions are being made about his or her future. In addition, there is a requirement for a *guardian ad litem*, in effect an independent social worker representing the interests of the child, to be appointed in most public law cases involving children. The Northern Ireland Guardian ad Litem Agency has been established to manage a panel of suitably qualified persons who may be appointed as guardians ad litem by the courts.

3.3   The Children's Law Centre

3.3.1   The need for the voice of the child to be heard has been further recognised by the formation of the Children's Law Centre in September 1997. This is a voluntary organisation which receives financial support from the Department of Health and Social Services to develop a range of advisory services, including a free-phone help line to children, parents and carers. It is intended that the Children's Law Centre will work in partnership with other services to offer information, advice, education, training, advocacy and commentary about the law and children's rights in Northern Ireland.

3.4   Children's Services Plans in Northern Ireland

3.4.1   The impetus for the development of Children's Services Plans stems from the commencement of the Children (NI) Order 1995. A major component of the Order is the requirement on Health and Social Services Boards to assess the extent of need for services in their areas and to provide an appropriate range and level of personal social services to meet that assessed need.

3.4.2   On 23 July 1998, the Department of Health and Social Services exercised its powers under Article 18(4) of the Children Order to place a mandatory requirement on Health and Social Services Boards to plan children's services, to consult with a wide range of statutory and voluntary agencies and to publish the resulting plans. The first Children's Services Plans have now been produced and cover the period 1999-2002. They will be reviewed and rolled forward each year, with a full review every three years.

3.4.3   Guidance on the development of Children's Services Plans was issued jointly by the Department of Health and Social Services, the Department of Education and the Northern Ireland Office in July 1998. The guidance encourages Health and Social Services Boards, who have legal responsibility for producing the plans, to reflect local circumstances and engage a wide range of organisations and individuals in the planning process.

As part of the process of consultation, each Health and Social Services Board has established an Area Children and Young People's Committee. The Committee is chaired by the Director of Social Services and membership comprises representatives from health and social services, education and library boards, the probation service, the police and the voluntary sector.

3.4.4 The development of the Children's Services Plans reflects the priority given by the three government Departments to ensuring that the provision of services to children who are assessed to be in need are fully co-ordinated at the planning and service delivery levels.

3.5 The Family Homes and Domestic Violence (NI) Order 1998

Article 19, 27, 39

3.5.1 The Family Homes and Domestic Violence (NI) Order 1998[14], which is due to come into effect in Spring 1999, is amongst the strongest pieces of legislation directed against domestic violence in Europe and the Commonwealth, it also contains a number of provisions which will significantly improve the level of protection afforded to children. In particular, two important amendments are made to the Children Order – see section 7.11 below.

3.5.2 In addition, a Family Law Systems Working Group, chaired by a senior High Court Judge and consisting of senior policy-makers and practitioners in the family law area, has been established to examine the delivery of family law in its widest context in Northern Ireland. The Group will look at the systems, structures and processes in this area, including those established by the Children (NI) Order, to ensure that they are operating as efficiently as possible.

3.6 Respect for views of children

Article 12

3.6.1 The Family Homes and Domestic Violence (NI) Order 1998 contains a provision which, when brought into operation, will allow regulations to be made specifying circumstances in which children may be separately represented under the Order. This reflects a parallel provision in the corresponding legislation for England and Wales. However, under Rule 6.6 of the Family Proceedings Rules (NI) 1996, procedures are already in place to allow for separate representation of children in any family proceedings, where it appears to the court that this ought to be the case.

3.7 Juvenile justice

Article 40

3.7.1 The Criminal Justice (NI) Order 1996[15] and the Criminal Justice (Children) (NI) Order 1998[16] introduced a number of measures which have had a significant impact on the administration of juvenile justice in Northern Ireland.

3.7.2 The Criminal Justice (NI) Order 1996 established the two key criteria that may justify a custodial sentence – "the seriousness of the offence" and the "protection of the public". The court must be satisfied that the offence, or the combination of the offence and one or more associated

---

14 SI 1998/1071 (NI 6).

15 SI 1996/3160 (NI 24)

16 SI 1998/1504 (NI 9).

offences, is so serious that a custodial sentence is justified. If the offence is of a violent or sexual nature, the court must be of the opinion that only a custodial sentence would be adequate to protect the public from serious harm from the offender. The court is obliged to state openly why it is of the opinion that the criteria apply, and to explain the reasons for the custodial sentence.

3.7.3   The Order provides for offenders, including those who are children, who are dependent on or who misuse drugs or alcohol, to be required as an additional requirement of a probation order to undergo treatment for their condition where it is associated with the offending behaviour.

3.7.4   The major changes made by the Criminal Justice (Children) (NI) Order 1998 were: –

  a to require courts, when dealing with children, to have regard to the prejudicial effect on the child's welfare of any delay;

  b to require a court to release a child on bail except where the protection of the public and the seriousness of the offence or persistency of offending mean that a remand is necessary.;

  c the introduction of the juvenile justice centre order, replacing the training school order as the main custodial sentence available to the court for those under 17 years. The order is for a determinate period of six months unless the court specifies a longer period not exceeding two years. Where a court makes a juvenile justice centre order for a period longer than six months, it is required to state its reasons in open court. The new order provides that time spent on remand in custody will count in full to reduce the custodial element of the sentence, which should further reduce the average period of detention in a juvenile justice centre;

  d it amends the Police and Criminal Evidence (NI) Order 1989[17] to allow magistrates' courts to admit children's evidence in chief by video recording.

3.7.5   These provisions are discussed in more detail in section 10.41.

3.8   The law on illegitimacy in Northern Ireland

Article 8

3.8.1   The Children (NI) Order 1995 has now reformed the law on illegitimacy in Northern Ireland to remove most of the disadvantages associated with birth outside marriage. A general principle of statutory construction, that relationships between two persons will be taken without regard to whether or not a person's parents were married to each other at a particular time, has been introduced. Any discriminations regarding succession or property rights are removed so that an illegitimate child can

---

17 SI 1989/1341 (NI12).

inherit the property of his or her more remote relations. Unmarried fathers have been given the means to obtain parental status (or parental responsibility) in respect of their children, either by court order or by agreement with the mother. The full range of financial and property orders is made available for the benefit of children of unmarried parents.

3.9 Parental responsibility in Northern Ireland

Article 9, 18

3.9.1 The Children (NI) Order 1995 amended the Guardianship of Infants Act 1886 so that in Northern Ireland married parents now have equal parental responsibility. Where parents are unmarried, the mother alone will have parental responsibility but it will be open to the father to acquire parental responsibility either by agreement with the mother or by court order. A forthcoming consultation exercise will discuss the issue of whether it should be easier for unmarried fathers to acquire parental responsibility subject to any necessary safeguards.

3.10 Fair employment in Northern Ireland

Article 2

3.10.1 At the time of the passing of the Fair Employment (Northern Ireland) Act 1989 there was an undertaking given that the effect of that Act would be reviewed after 5 years. In November 1994 the Standing Advisory Commission on Human Rights (SACHR) were asked to carry forward that review and their report *Employment Equality: Building for the Future*[18] was published on 26 June 1997. The report made a wide range of recommendations on Government policies towards fair employment and unemployment, including the persistent problem of the long-term unemployed, among whom Catholics are disproportionately represented. The report found, however, that the 1989 legislation has had a positive impact on employment equality. In terms of the potential implications for children the proposals for changes to policies and procedures in the fields of education, training and the Government initiatives on Targeting Social Need (TSN) and Policy Appraisal and Fair Treatment (PAFT) are the most relevant.

3.10.2 The Government gave the SACHR Report very thorough consideration and published its response, in the form of a White Paper, *Partnership for Equality*[19], on 11 March 1998. In regard to the PAFT initiative the White Paper put forward proposals for consultation to replace the existing PAFT guidelines, which were introduced on 1 January 1994, with a new statutory framework. The proposals would place a statutory obligation on public bodies (including District Councils and United Kingdom Departments operating in Northern Ireland) to ensure that, consistent with their other responsibilities, their functions were carried out with due regard to the need to promote equality of opportunity in those groups covered by the current PAFT guidelines. Those are:

a people of different religious beliefs or political opinions;

b people of different gender;

---

18 Cm 3684: ISBN 0 10 136842 9.
19 Cm 3890: ISBN 0 10 138902 7.

c married and unmarried people;

d people with or without dependants;

e people within different ethnic groups;

f people with or without a disability;

g people of different ages; and

h people of different sexual orientation.

3.10.3   In order to oversee the above obligations it is proposed that a new Equality Commission be established which will take over the functions now exercised by the Fair Employment Commission for Northern Ireland, the Equal Opportunity Commission for Northern Ireland, the Commission for Racial Equality for Northern Ireland and the Disability Council for Northern Ireland.

3.10.4   These proposals were subject to a consultation exercise which ended on 12 June 1998. Having taken careful account of the responses received and either made changes to meet reservations that were expressed or clarified what was intended, the Secretary of State announced in Parliament on 10 July 1998 her intention to create a unified Equality Commission and to impose a statutory requirement on the public sector to promote equality of opportunity. This was included in the Northern Ireland Act 1998 which received Royal Assent in November 1998.

3.10.5   The White Paper set out plans for a new, more effective Targeting Social Need (TSN) initiative, combined with measures to promote social inclusion. New TSN will continue to be based on objective need, but with a particular focus on measures to combat unemployment and enhance employability. Other departmental programmes will target people and areas in need and key inequalities such as health, housing and education, all of which have implications for children. Under New TSN Northern Ireland will establish a Promoting Social Inclusion (PSI) initiative which will seek to tackle the long term causes of exclusion and will emphasise prevention.

3.11 Housing matters in Northern Ireland

Article 26, 27

3.11.1   The Housing (NI) Order 1988 sets out the duties of the Northern Ireland Housing Executive. Where necessary, the NI Housing Executive secures immediate temporary accommodation for applicants who are homeless, in priority need and not intentionally homeless. This includes people with families, young persons at risk of sexual or financial exploitation, single parents and other vulnerable members of society. Such accommodation is provided either in one of the Housing Executive's own hostels or in a private sector "bed and breakfast" establishment. Applicants are usually allocated a secure tenancy within two months, depending on their area of choice.

3.11.2   The NI Housing Executive provides advice and assistance to other homeless people in their attempts to find accommodation and helps to fund a number of voluntary bodies which operate hostels for young people. The NI Housing Executive, in partnership with the voluntary sector, has an effective strategy for dealing with homelessness, which is less of a problem in Northern Ireland than in some parts of the United Kingdom. The most common reason for homelessness given by applicants has been a breakdown in sharing arrangements with family, friends or partners (some 30% of cases). There is also evidence that around 40% of hostel residents in Belfast have some form of mental health problem.

3.11.3   In taking measures to tackle violence against women, the Department of the Environment also funds housing for women with special needs, including women with children. Five years ago the Department, in consultation with the Women's Aid Federation, undertook to make additional resources available to increase provision for vulnerable women and children. Over the five year period housing association provision for this group has more than trebled from just over 100 places to 367, with a further 80 places under construction. Plans are in hand for further provision of almost 150 new places by March 2002.

3.12 Children's involvement in human rights issues in Northern Ireland

Article 12, 42

3.12.1   The School of Education at the University of Ulster completed a study of young peoples' understanding of Human Rights in Northern Ireland. The results of this study were published[20]. The research formed part of a wider Commonwealth study involving 915 pupils from 23 schools in Botswana, India, Northern Ireland and Zimbabwe. The results from the international study were published by the United Kingdom Department for International Development[21].

3.12.2   The Northern Ireland report indicated that whereas pupils at ages 14 and 16 had some understanding of human rights principles in relation to specific issues, they had no coherent, integrated understanding of human rights concepts and the majority (93.5%) were not aware of the UN Convention on the Rights of the Child.

3.12.3   The Northern Ireland report also contained a human rights audit of the NI curriculum and interviews with pupils, teachers and education advisers. These sections suggest that human rights education is not well integrated into the Northern Ireland curriculum and that pupils and teachers alike would welcome a more explicit focus for such work within the curriculum. In this respect, as part of an overall review of the statutory curriculum, the Northern Ireland Council for Curriculum, Examinations and Assessment is examining how the broad concept of citizenship and education for democracy can be addressed within the curriculum. Approval has been given for the introduction of a pilot programme in schools from September 1999 and CCEA will evaluate this programme before making any proposals for change.

---

20 Smith, A. and Birthistle, U. (1977) *Human Rights Education: A Study of Young People's Understanding of Human Rights in Northern Ireland*, School of Education, University of Ulster, Coleraine.

21 Bourne, R. et al (1977) *School-based Understanding of Human Rights in Four Countries: A Commonwealth Study*, Department for International Development, Serial No. 22, ISBN 1 86192 095 4.

4 WALES

4.1.1   This chapter summarises recent legislative and administrative changes specific to Wales and relevant to children's services. It refers to action being taken to further strengthen the safeguards for children in public care, and to protect children at risk of harm or neglect. It also illustrates the practical steps that have been taken in Wales to make sure that children and young people have been able to express their views on a range of issues that concern them.

4.1.2   For the most part, the position on particular services for children and young people is broadly the same as in England. Distinctive arrangements in Wales are highlighted in the appropriate chapters of this report.

4.2 Welsh Language Act 1993

Article 2

4.2.1   This Act established the principle that, in the conduct of public business and the administration of justice in Wales, the English and Welsh languages should be treated on the basis of equality.

4.2.2   The Act promotes the development and use of the Welsh language. It established the Welsh Language Board, one of whose activities is to grant aid organisations concerned with the promotion of the language. The Board has invested about £550,000 annually in the Welsh nursery school organisation, Mudiad Ysgolion Meithrin, and about £250,000 in the Welsh youth organisation Urdd Gobaith Cymru. (See also paragraph 9.36.)

4.3 Local Government (Wales) Act 1994

4.3.1 This Act established 22 unitary local authorities which from April 1996 replaced the 8 County Councils and 37 District Councils in Wales. These new unitary authorities are responsible for delivering all local government services, including education, leisure and social services, to the people in their areas, including children and young people.

4.4 Government of Wales Act 1998

4.4.1 The Government of Wales Act established a National Assembly for Wales, elected for the first time in May 1999. From July 1999, the Assembly took over most of the responsibilities and functions of the Secretary of State for Wales and the financing of most public services in Wales. The Assembly will operate within the framework of primary legislation enacted by the United Kingdom Parliament and has substantial scope for the enactment of secondary legislation distinctive to Wales.

4.5 Minister for Children in Wales

4.5.1 In 1997, the Government designated one of the Ministers at the Welsh Office as Minister for Children in Wales. The Welsh Office subsequently adopted an objective for children of promoting their social development and protecting them from abuse or neglect; improving their health and well-being; and raising their standards of educational achievement. In support of this objective, a Departmental Committee on Children's Issues was established in 1997 with the job of improving effectiveness of policy co-ordination on children's issues and promoting a coherent structure of children's services across Wales. Following the election of the Assembly, an Assembly Cabinet post has been designated with special responsibility for children's issues.

4.6 Strategic approach to children's services

4.6.1 The Government is committed to the development of a strategic approach to children's services in Wales, as set out in the Social Services White Paper for Wales 'Building for the Future'[22], published in March 1999. The strategy will aim to set out clear objectives and principles for the development and delivery of all services for children in Wales. It will take note of the United Nations Convention on the Rights of the Child, and related European Union commitments to child welfare and will provide context for the development of all services for children. In advance of the strategy a number of initiatives are being taken forward in health, social services and education.

4.6.2 The *Children First*[23] programme in Wales was announced in April 1999, broadly along the lines of the *Quality Protects* initiative announced by the Department of Health. The *Children First* programme aims to modernise public services for children in need, particularly for children looked after. It will focus on outcomes for children, taking account of the views of children

---

22 Building for the Future Cm 4051 published by The Stationery Office: March 1999 ISBN 0-10-140512-X

23 Welsh Office Circular 20/99: *The Children First Programme in Wales: Transforming Children's Services* published by Welsh Office, Children and Families Division, Cathays Park, Cardiff CF10 3NQ

themselves and their parents. As part of the programme, local authority elected members have been reminded of their corporate parental responsibilities for children in the care of their authorities. £5 million has been made available to begin implementation of the programme in 1999-2000.

4.6.3 Also in April 1999, the Welsh Office announced details of the Sure Start programme in Wales, designed to increase opportunities for very young children and their families, especially in more deprived areas and to help give those children the best possible start in life. £25 million has been allocated to this programme over the next three years. A further £25 million over the same period is being used to establish a Children and Youth Partnership Fund. This will promote local initiatives which will lift youngsters' educational achievement, engage them in creative activities in their communities and encourage them away from crime, drugs, vandalism and truancy.

4.7 Children's Services Planning in Wales

Article 4, 5, 9, 16, 19, 20, 39

4.7.1 The Welsh Office issued guidance to local authorities in Wales in 1993 on *Accommodating Children – A Review of Children's Homes in Wales*[24]. This advised authorities that their plans for residential child care facilities should form part of an integrated strategy for children within each authority.

4.7.2 In 1994, local authorities in Wales were advised[25] that they should prepare comprehensive plans for children's services. In April 1996, that guidance was strengthened and made mandatory.

4.7.3 The introduction and development of Children's Services Plans in Wales has been widely welcomed and accepted. This is the key mechanism for ensuring that all agencies work together in planning for and providing support for children in need. The effectiveness of the arrangements is monitored by the Social Services Inspectorate, Wales.

4.7.4 The plans produced by local authorities for 1996-97 were analysed by consultants on behalf of the Welsh Office. A report of this work was published in 1997[26]. The analysis has helped inform the preparation of revised plans and has provided a baseline from which to monitor progress in planning for children's services.

4.7.5 In September 1998, the Welsh Local Government Association (WLGA) launched its report *Developing a Strategy for Children in Need in*

---

24 Welsh Office Circular 34/93: published by Welsh Office, Children and Families Division, Cathays Park, Cardiff CF10 3NQ in 1993 and 1994.

25 Welsh Office Circular 11/94: published by Welsh Office, Children and Families Unit, Social Services Policy Division, Cathays Park, Cardiff CF1 3NQ in 1993 and 1994.

26 *Analysis of Children's Services Plans of Welsh Local Authorities 1997*. Published by Welsh Office Social Services Inspectorate, Cathays Park, Cardiff CF1 3NQ. November 1997.

Wales – The Local Government Role[27]. The document, which takes account of the views of many organisations in Wales representing the interests of children, brings together the key local authority responses to children in need. It identifies the main issues for the future from the local government perspective, taking as its principal standpoint the requirements of the Children Act 1989 and the UN Convention on the Rights of the Child.

4.7.6 Proposals for consultation on ways to bring together the various separate requirements for children's services planning were made in the Social Services White Paper for Wales. The aim is to establish ground rules for unified children's services plans, with a view to introducing integrated planning from April 2001.

4.8 Children in public care in Wales

Article 20

4.8.1 Following the convictions for child abuse of some former members of staff at children's homes in the North Wales area, the Secretary of State for Wales decided in April 1995 to appoint a barrister to review the papers held by the North Wales Police and what were then the County Councils of Clwyd and Gwynedd. Her conclusion and recommendation was that no public inquiry was necessary, but that there were concerns about the adequacy of the local authorities' procedures in certain respects.

4.8.2 Subsequently a team of experts, the North Wales Child Care Examination Team, was appointed in January 1996 to examine the child care procedures in the two North Wales counties and the arrangements planned by their successor authorities (from April 1996). The Team reported in June 1996[28]. Their recommendations embraced many aspects of the work involved in ensuring effective delivery of services for children. These covered strategic planning, child protection, child care planning, residential care, foster care, management, inspection and children's rights. Local authorities throughout Wales were asked to implement those recommendations applicable to them and a Development Fund of £500,000 was allocated by the Welsh Office to support authorities in doing this.

4.8.3 In response to continuing public concern, the Secretary of State for Wales decided in June 1996 that a full inquiry should be held into widespread allegations of abuse in the child care system in North Wales. Under the Tribunals (Evidence) Act 1921, Sir Ronald Waterhouse (a retired High Court Judge) was appointed, together with two assessors, to conduct a full judicial inquiry into allegations of abuse at children's homes in North Wales since the mid 1970's. The North Wales Child Abuse Tribunal (NWCAT) heard evidence between January 1997 and March 1998. The Tribunal's report to the Government is awaited and the Government will respond as soon as practicable to the Tribunal's findings.

---

27 *Developing a Strategy for Children in Need in Wales - The Local Government Role* : Report of the Advisory Group on Children's Services, September 1998. Welsh Local Government Association, 10/11 Raleigh Walk, Atlantic Wharf, Cardiff CF1 5LN ISBN 1 901719 10 3.

28 *Report of the Examination Team on Child Care Procedures and practice in North Wales* - Return to an Address of the Honourable the House of Commons dated 17 June 1996. Published by HMSO ISBN 0 10 277896 5.

4.8.4   By the time that the NWCAT was substantively engaged in taking evidence, good progress had been made by local authorities in implementing the recommendations of the North Wales Child Care Examination Team. However, in the light of the evidence submitted to the NWCAT and the recommendations made in Sir William Utting's report *People Like Us*[29], it was evident that more remained to be done. The Welsh Office therefore established a 'Looked-after Children Development Fund' and made available £880,000 to support local authorities in Wales in 1998-99. This was aimed at further improving local procedures and good practice in providing services for children in public care in Wales.

4.8.5   The report of the North Wales Child Care Examination Team on child care procedures in North Wales recommended an increase in the staff of Social Services Inspectorate, Wales (SSIW) to provide more effective advice to Ministers and local authorities on children's services in Wales. The Children's Development Unit within SSIW has since been strengthened to help support a programme of work for the development of children's services by new unitary local authorities in Wales. In addition, the Inspectorate's capacity for inspection and advisory services has been strengthened by the appointment of four officers.

4.8.6   The Welsh Office has established an inter-disciplinary group including social services, health and education interests to spearhead work to improve the quality of life and outcomes for children in public care in Wales.

4.9   Child protection in Wales

Article 9, 18, 19, 39

4.9.1   Social Services Departments across Wales have been striving to address wider child protection issues and ensure that front line social services recognise the signs of abuse or neglect and act upon them without delay. Collaborative working between all the agencies involved is crucial to the success of child protection policies and local authorities, health authorities, schools, the police and the voluntary sector continue to work actively together to secure the safety of all children. The guidance on Area Child Protection Committees (ACPCs), *Working Together*, has been extensively reviewed over the last year. Revised guidance is expected to be issued later in 1999. The Assembly will continue to work with ACPCs, and all the agencies involved in them, to ensure that child protection procedures are kept under continual review and that they remain robust, appropriate and effective.

4.9.2   The Assembly has retained the standing Child Protection Committee established within the Department by the Welsh Office. The key function of the Committee is to analyse the reports of local inter-agency reviews of child protection cases causing concern and to identify and disseminate best practice issues to all the agencies concerned in child

29 *People like us:* The Report of the review of the safeguards for children living away from home, by Sir William Utting. Published by the Stationery Office on behalf of the Department of Health and the Welsh Office. ISBN 0-11-322101-0.

protection. A specific grant has been made available annually to local authorities to assist the development of inter agency working in child protection.

4.10 Childcare Strategy for Wales

Article 28

4.10.1 The Out of School Childcare Initiative which started in Wales in 1993 saw about 4,200 new out of school childcare places created in three years. Since 1995, the Welsh Office has also funded the development of a childcare initiative to improve facilities for children under five. The initiative sought to involve employers in provision of childcare for their employees' children in an attempt to retain and recruit parents, particularly women.

4.10.2 Welsh Office funding for Chwarae Teg (Fair Play – an equal opportunities organisation) has assisted them to conduct two audits of childcare provision in Wales: one in 1992 and one in 1996. Chwarae Teg has also helped to set up a Wales Childcare Database, which parents can use at Libraries and Job Centres to find out about the childcare services available locally.

4.10.3 In June 1998 the Minister for Children in Wales launched a Green Paper *A Childcare Strategy for Wales*[30]. The Strategy is part of a United Kingdom-wide framework of Government initiatives, including family-friendly employment, welfare reform and help with the costs of childcare for working families. In addition to existing and enhanced Welsh Office programmes, an additional £1.51 million was made available in 1998-99 together with a similar level of funding in 1999-200, to support infrastructure developments to pave the way for implementing the Strategy in Wales.

4.10.4 The Strategy is being taken forward at local level by local childcare partnerships co-ordinated by local authorities. Starting in 1999 for a period of three years, substantial resources will be available from the National Lottery New Opportunities Fund to set up new out of school childcare places in Wales.

4.10.5 The emerging strategic approach to children's services will encourage childcare and early years developments to be linked effectively with other relevant programmes operating in Wales including the Strategic Development Scheme and Welsh Capital Challenge; and the People in Communities, Sure Start and other programmes designed to improve the quality of life for children and their families by promoting social inclusion.

4.11 Support for Child and Family Services Grant Scheme

Article 24, 26, 27

4.11.1 Since 1991 this scheme has helped to cover the core costs of a number of children's voluntary bodies in Wales and thereby enabled those organisations to promote the interests of children more generally. For example, at present, it helps to fund Children in Wales, the national umbrella body promoting children's interests in Wales; Childline (Wales), which runs a

---

30 *The National Childcare Strategy in Wales - A Consultation Document* Cm 3974 published by The Stationery Office: June 1998 ISBN 0 10 139742 9.

helpline for children; Voices from Care, representing the interests of children in the public care system; and the Wales Pre-School Playgroups Association, whose members provide pre-school education and care for children under 5.

4.11.2   The scheme also assists projects that deliver services to children in need. Examples include

a   the Access for Black Children with Disabilities (ABCD) project in Cardiff to help children have access to appropriate health services;

b   the Children's Society's Advocacy Unit which operates in South Wales and provides independent representation and advocacy services for children looked after by local authorities;

c   young carers projects in Carmarthenshire, Merthyr Tydfil and Flintshire;

d   a project in Wrexham to provide therapeutic treatment for children who have suffered sexual abuse; and

e   a community childminding scheme in Powys.

f   The grant scheme has responded to emerging priorities. In 1999-2000, these were identified as promoting services for children with disabilities and Advocacy services for children looked after by local authorities. In line with these priorities, £108,000 was made available for six new projects to provide services for disabled children and £120,000 for four Advocacy projects (including the National Youth Advocacy Service independent advice service for children looked after in North Wales, and Childline's Children in Care helpline).

4.12 Publicity and research about the rights of the child

Article 42

4.12.1   In July 1994, the Welsh Office published a leaflet in Welsh about the UN Convention on the Rights of the Child.

4.12.2   The Welsh Office commissioned a research study, undertaken over six months in the later part of 1998, on the extent and efficacy of existing advocacy services for looked-after children in Wales.

4.12.3   The International Centre for Childhood Studies at the University of Wales (Swansea), recently published *Children and Decision Making*[31]. This is a summary of the Centre's research study of children's participation in decisions about their care during the time when they are looked after by local authorities. Copies of the report have been made available by the Social Services Inspectorate, Wales, as part of their development programme to help those working with looked-after children. The Assembly is funding the development of a training pack for use of these materials to promote active participation of children in making decisions on their care.

31 *Children and Decision Making: a study of children's participation in decisions about their care.* International Centre for Childhood Studies, University of Wales Swansea, Singleton Park, Swansea SA2 8PP. February 1998.

4.13 Opportunities for Children and Young People to express their views in Wales

4.13.1 Development funding made available by the Welsh Office in recent years has stimulated a wide range of initiatives across Wales to enable children and young people to express their views about policies which affect them. These initiatives have involved both local authorities working in partnership with voluntary sector organisations and work instigated by the voluntary sector itself.

4.13.2 Children and young people have primarily been able to express their views through consultation processes or through participatory conferences at both national and local level. Examples include :-

4.13.3 ALL-WALES

a Children in Wales: conference in May 1998 about the 50th Anniversary of the Children Act 1948. Participants included 30 children and young people aged 8-17, representing groups from across Wales.

b Contribution to the Utting Safeguards Review: representatives of children "looked after" expressed their views directly to Sir William Utting and his team as a contribution to the Safeguards Review.

c Children and Young People and the National Assembly: 50 children and young people from across Wales attended each of two events in September 1997 and September 1998 at which they were able to discuss their views with policy makers.

d Voices From Care: as a self help organisation for children "looked after", Voices From Care regularly consults its membership and feeds back the results of those consultations to policy makers in central and local government.

4.13.4 LOCAL/REGIONAL GENERAL CONSULTATIONS

a Anglesey Youth Forum Consultation: a one day consultation was held in March 1998 on issues facing children and young people in Ynys Mon (Isle of Anglesey) and the potential development of a forum of young people. 30 young people aged between 13 and 18 took part from across Ynys Mon.

b National Society for the Prevention of Cruelty to Children (NPSCC): consultations with 7 groups of children and young people connected to NSPCC projects around Wales were held between April and June 1998. The purpose of the consultation was to look at how the voice of young people could be influential in the work of NSPCC Wales. 35 children and young people aged between 12 and 18 took part.

c Right On - Cardiff Youth Network: consultation took place between September and December 1998 with young people aged between 13 and 18 on a Cardiff housing estate looking at issues affecting social exclusion as part of an initiative with Save

The Children Fund, Centrepoint, Pilotlight and Demos. 10 young people took part.

d Aberaeron Young People's Association: a large consultation was undertaken in November 1997 with children and young people living in Aberaeron and the surrounding area in Ceredigion looking at issues broadly affecting young people. The consultation was completed via questionnaires with children and young people aged 11-17.

e Dynamix: approximately 60 children and young people aged 6 to 18 took part in an outreach consultation with children and young people on a large housing estate in Swansea. The consultation focused on the needs of young people in the local community and was mainly conducted through interviews on the street.

f Consulting children and young people in Merthyr Tydfil: group consultations and a one day conference looking at health service, social services, play and leisure, education and housing were organised as part of the process of developing the Children's Services Plan for Merthyr Tydfil and this was facilitated by the Children's Society. The activities were held over 1997-1998 and 75 children and young people took part in the conference.

g Ynys Mon (Isle of Anglesey) Children's Services Plan: views of children and young people were sought by the local authority in developing the Children's Service Plan for Ynys Mon. It involved a focus group of children and young people from across the island and a forum for other young people from each school.

h Denbighshire Youth Strategy: a consultation was undertaken with young people in Denbighshire to identify their needs as part of the development of a youth strategy for the county.

4.14 Rough sleeping in Wales

Article 24, 26, 27

4.14.1 The Assembly will be reviewing advice given to local authorities to make clear that young people who have been in the care of a local authority are deemed to be vulnerable and thus classified as in priority need under section 19 of the Housing Act 1996. It will also be considering whether further action is needed to ensure these young people receive the services and support that they need.

4.14.2 The Assembly will also be devising a strategic programme to address the problems of rough sleepers. The project will include a review of the relationship between local authorities' housing and social services departments and the guidance and support on housing given to young people leaving care.

5 GENERAL PRINCIPLES AND GENERAL MEASURES OF IMPLEMENTATION

This chapter covers articles: –

2 *Discrimination*

3 *Action and decisions affecting children to be undertaken in the best interests of the child*

4 *Commitment to implement*

6 *Right to life*

12 *Right to express a view and to be heard*

42 *obligation to promulgate provisions of Convention*

44 *Reporting obligations*

5.1 Harmonising national law and policy with the provisions of the Convention

Article 4

5.1.1 The Human Rights Act received Royal Assent on 9 November 1998. It will give further effect in United Kingdom law to the rights and freedoms contained in the European Convention on Human Rights (the European Convention). Many of the Articles in the European Convention are similar to those in the UN Convention on the Rights of the Child, for example those relating to the prohibition of torture, the right to respect for private and family life, freedom of thought, conscience and religion, freedom of expression, and freedom of assembly and association. These provisions are not, of course, directed exclusively at the rights of children. They will be of general application, but will be of benefit to children too.

5.1.2 The Act operates through two main provisions. First, all legislation, both past and future, will have to be interpreted, so far as possible, in a way which is compatible with the European Convention rights. The Government expects that it will be very rare for a court to be unable to construe primary legislation consistently with the European Convention. Where a court cannot do so, it will be required to give effect to that legislation, but the higher courts will be able to make a declaration of incompatibility in respect of it. It will then be for the Government and Parliament to decide how to respond. Where there are compelling reasons for doing so, it will be possible for the incompatible legislation to be amended quickly by a Ministerial order (subject to the approval of Parliament). Where a court cannot interpret subordinate legislation compatibly with the European Convention rights, it will (subject to limited exceptions) be able to set that legislation aside to the extent necessary to give effect to those rights. Courts will also have to develop the common law consistently with the rights under the European Convention.

5.1.3   Second, the Act will (with limited exceptions) make it unlawful for a public authority to act in a way which is incompatible with a European Convention right. The term "public authority" is widely drawn so as to provide a correspondingly wide protection of human rights.

5.1.4   The Act will also place a requirement on Government Ministers to publish a statement on the compatibility with the European Convention of Bills they have introduced into Parliament. This will ensure that full consideration is given to the human rights implications of new measures both during the policy development stage and during debates on the Bill in Parliament.

5.1.5   The Government believes that the Act will assist the United Kingdom in complying with the European Convention on Human Rights, and in so doing will directly support compliance with related Articles in the UN Convention on the Rights of the Child. The Act will also have a more general benefit by promoting a culture of human rights within the judicial system, within government, and within society as a whole.

5.1.6   Ministers have decided that the main provisions of the Act will be brought into force on 2 October 2000 to take into account the arrangements necessary for implementation. Time is needed to complete a comprehensive programme of judicial training, to make whatever court rules are necessary before implementation, and to allow government departments to prepare for implementation.

5.1.7   The European Convention on Human Rights also has a direct effect in relation to the position of children in Scotland and Wales. It applies to the Scottish Parliament and the Scottish Administration broadly as it will apply in England and Wales, as described at paragraph 5.1.2.

5.2   Children's Services Planning in England and Wales

Article 4, 5, 9, 16, 19, 20, 39

5.2.1   Children's Services Planning is a critically important mechanism for improving the broad range of services for children in need and their families. Planning was made mandatory in April 1996: local authorities must now assess the need for children's services in their area, consult various bodies in planning how that need will be met, and publish the resulting plans.

5.2.2   In 1992 local authorities were advised that they should produce plans for children's services. The results were studied by the Social Services Inspectorate (SSI) and reports were published in July 1994 and November 1995[32]. These reports showed that, although most local authorities had

---

32 *Children's Services Plans: an analysis of Children's Services Plans 1993/94,* by the Social Services Inspectorate of the Department of Health, Published by the Department of Health 1995.

produced plans, they varied in content and effectiveness. Planning presented local authorities with significant technical challenges in mapping needs and the supply of services and in bringing parties from several agencies relevant to children's welfare together to plan coherent services.

5.2.3   These problems of achieving coherent services across several agencies were discussed in the report of a study by the Audit Commission into community child health and social services for children in need[33]. A key recommendation of this report, which was published under the title *Seen but not heard* in 1994, was that children's services planning should be mandatory, jointly prepared by relevant agencies and published. A study commissioned from the National Children's Bureau (NCB) by the Department of Health, and published as *Crossing the Boundaries* in 1995[34], explored ways of encouraging better co-ordination of services across departmental boundaries.

5.2.4   The Government responded to the Audit Commission recommendation by amending the Children Act 1989 so as to require local authorities to plan children's services, to consult specified agencies, to publish the plans and to review those plans from time to time. This was implemented in April 1996 by the Children Act 1989 (Amendment) (Children's Service Planning) Order 1996[35]. The plans prepared under that Order were required by 31 March 1997. The guidance accompanying the Order superseded the earlier circular and although the mandate for planning related only to services for children in need, it encouraged joint planning for the welfare of children generally.

5.2.5   A report of a third SSI study, entitled *Partners in Planning*[36], was published in 1998. This showed considerable energy going into joint working at local level and a gaining of experience of working across traditional barriers. Success depended upon the drive of key individuals, the extent to which participants could identify coinciding interests and their influence over resources.

5.2.6   There are indications that real change is occurring slowly. This is borne out by a further report from the NCB[37] of a small study which looked at the extent to which the shape of services has changed in response to planning. There is real enthusiasm to plan better services for children jointly, but this is in the context of a struggle to take on board the technical aspects of measuring and analysing needs and reshaping services.

---

33 *Seen but not heard:* by the Audit Commission, published by HMSO 1994.

34 *Crossing the boundaries: a discussion of children's services plans* by Paul Sutton, published by the National Children's Bureau 1995.

35 SI 1996/785

36 *Partners in planning: Approaches to planning services for children and their families,* by the Social Services Inspectorate of the Department of Health. Published by the Department of Health, 1998.

37 *Children's Services Plans: Analysing need, reallocating resources.* Barbara Hearn & Ruth Sinclair. Published by the National Children's Bureau, 1998.

5.2.7   In recent years other Government Departments have proposed or introduced planning requirements which affect children. Some of these new requirements require plans to set out objectives and targets. It will be necessary, in the medium term, to revise the current framework for planning children's services to take account of these developments.

5.3   Monitoring Children's Services Plans

5.3.1   The Department of Health will continue to monitor Children's Services Plans. As part of the Department's work programme for 1997-98, a study has been commissioned from the National Children's Bureau to look at how planning has led to adjustments to the shape of service delivery in a selection of local authorities children's services plans.

5.3.2   This year the SSI will be conducting an inspection of children's services planning activity in eight authorities. SSI regional offices expect to receive copies of plans as part of their monitoring function. And the Department can, if necessary, call for copies of all the plans. Planning activity for children's services is in its early days and there is much work to be done, but there are some encouraging initial signs that agencies are finding ways of planning services together.

5.4   Policy and practice of youth work in Northern Ireland

Article 28, 29, 12

5.4.1   In October 1997 the Department of Education for Northern Ireland published a curriculum document for the youth service, *Youth work: A Model for Effective Practice*. One of the key points in this guidance document was the stress placed on participation as one of the underlying principles of youth work. The document advises youth groups and organisations to involve young people fully in the making of decisions on matters which affect them. Such matters might include policy-making, the planning and implementation of programmes, and management and organisation of facilities.

5.4.2   All members, irrespective of ethnic origin, sex or disability should be encouraged to assume relevant responsibilities, commensurate with their age and experience. This, it is hoped, will help young people to shape and develop their own experiences.

5.5   The promotion of children's rights and United Kingdom aid policy

Article 4

5.5.1   The Government's objective is 'the achievement of human rights for all people – and that includes every woman and child'[38]. The Department for International Development (DFID) is committed to a rights based approach to development in poorer countries[39]. This means putting people first, giving particular attention to the needs and the voices of the poor and disadvantaged among whom children are a special priority, focusing on those rights essential for eliminating poverty, and achieving sustainable livelihoods and dignity for all.

38 Speech by Clare Short, Secretary of State for International Development, 30 June 1997.

39 *Eliminating World Poverty: A Challenge for the 21st Century*, White Paper on International Development. Cm 3789 published by The Stationery Office, November 1997.

5.5.2   The objective of DFID in promoting children's rights is to support international efforts to enhance children's well-being through implementation of the Convention on the Rights of the Child, promoting children's protection and participation, alongside the provision of effective and sustainable services for children's survival and development. In partnership with governments and civil society organisations, DFID supports, and if necessary assists in meeting the rights set out in the Convention on the Rights of the Child. Provision of services such as health care, education, and welfare is an essential part of the United Kingdom's contribution to promoting children's rights in the countries where DFID works. At the same time, the United Kingdom is placing a stronger emphasis on combining provision for children with children's protection and participation in the development process.

5.5.3   All projects sponsored by the Department for International Development (DFID) have policy information markers which provide a measure of the extent to which projects[40] are pursuing key policy areas. DFID has introduced such a marker for 'Promotion of the Rights of the Child'. This will provide information on numbers of projects and associated expenditure on promotion of the rights of the child and hence will assist the Government to fulfil its reporting obligations to the Committee on the Rights of the Child. For a project to score against this marker, the approach and components of the activity must be informed by an analysis of the situation of children, including children's own perceptions, and children should also have contributed to the design of the activity as their evolving capacities allow (Article 12 of the Convention).

5.5.4   **DFID activities** that support or demonstrate a contribution towards the rights of the child[41] include:

a **Services responding to children's survival and development needs in education, health, water and sanitation, shelter etc. and which are especially relevant to the needs of excluded and disadvantaged children**. For example, a key focus of the DFID assisted District Primary Education Projects in Andhra Pradesh and West Bengal in India is improving access to education for vulnerable groups, including child labourers. DFID in India is also preparing plans for projects to reach children and adolescents, and to support the National Literacy Mission. In Bangladesh, DFID is providing support to child workers through the UNICEF Basic Education Programme for Urban Hard to Reach Children, and UCEP which provides opportunities through education and training for poor urban working children and promotes children's rights. Some of the

---

40 Markers apply to projects and programmes with a commitment value of £100,000 or more and do not therefore capture smaller projects.

41 These examples are drawn mainly from the *Annual Report on Human Rights*, Foreign and Commonwealth Office and Department for International Development, April 1998.

education programmes of the larger NGOs that are supported by DFID, are involved in an ILO project for former child garment workers. In Malawi, the Primary Community Schools Programme is involving remote rural villages in the building of up to 100 schools. Community participation is central to ensuring enrolment and continued attendance of children from disadvantaged rural backgrounds in these schools.

b **Programmes which assist Governments and civil society organisations to support families in bringing up their children, to re-unite children separated from their families and to support children without families in ways which avoid institutionalisation**. For example, in those parts of Africa with a high prevalence of HIV/AIDS, such as Zambia, many children are orphans; these children are more likely to have their rights denied or violated and their property taken away from them. DFID works with governments and civil society to protect such children. DFID has supported family tracing and reunification programmes with the International Committee of the Red Cross and Save the Children in the Great Lakes and Angola. In Eastern Europe the key issue in a number of country programmes is the de-institutionalisation of childcare with a view to both reducing the numbers in institutional care and improving standards in the institutional network. The other side to this reform is the introduction of a system of fostering and adoption. DFID, through the Know How Fund, is supporting projects along these lines in Romania and Bulgaria and a small pilot project in Estonia.

c **Programmes which have concentrated on a child rights approach**. For example, DFID will promote programmes which integrate training in the Convention on the Rights of the Child such as natural resources extension programmes. In Malawi, DFID funded an Estate Land Utilisation study which produced data on child labour. DFID already supports a number of NGOs which have mainstreamed a child rights approach and is drawing on their experience to mainstream a child rights approach in its own work. In Bangladesh, DFID is commissioning a scoping study on children's work as part of a broader child rights agenda, to enhance DFID's knowledge about the complex issue of children's work, and identify potential initiatives. This will ensure a more informed response to child rights issues through sectoral project work; and may identify strategic support to child-centred initiatives in the field of children's work.

d **Advocacy programmes which seek to influence societal attitudes towards children**. In Uganda, DFID supports the Uganda Society for Disabled Children which helps children with disabilities to live independent and productive lives by promoting self-help and community support. Local people have said this community based programme has resulted in increased awareness and confidence, changed attitudes, and better livelihoods.

e **Programmes which encourage the participation of children and young people in decisions which affect them, for example in planning, needs assessment, drafting legislation and research**. For example, DFID part funded an ACTIONAID research project in which children were central and active participants. The research has led to a better understanding of children's work in the household, and the factors which affect the roles of girls and boys. This informed design of practical projects which were implemented following the research. In Egypt, DFID supported a Participatory Poverty Assessment which is highlighting children's perspectives on poverty to be fed into the formulation of the Egyptian Government's National Strategy on Social Development. In Guyana, DFID is funding participatory research, involving children, on constraints on regular attendance at school.

f **Activities which increase the awareness of children and adults of children's rights and human rights broadly**. In Bangladesh, DFID supports Shoishab which raises awareness of children's rights for community members who keep children in their households as domestic helpers. On a regional level, the DFID funded Pacific Regional Human Rights Resources Team (a winner of the UNICEF Maurice Pate Award) has focused on children's rights through family law issues such as violence against women, divorce, maintenance and adoption. On an international level, DFID has provided support to the UN Special Representative on Children and Armed Conflict whose mandate is to raise awareness of the plight of children in armed conflict and to stimulate international action. In June 1998, DFID hosted an international conference in London which was successful in highlighting the work of the Special Representative and raising awareness of rights, protection and welfare issues related to children affected by armed conflict. The United Kingdom was also active in securing the inclusion of use of child soldiers under fifteen in the definition of war crimes in the statute of the newly established International Criminal Court.

g **Programmes which protect children from exposure to violence, danger, exploitation and abuse at home and in the wider community, or which help and support children who have suffered from such exposure**. For example DFID is funding a number of NGO projects which address the needs of street children in Central and South America and helping to address the problem of violence against street children through the provision of safe havens. In Central and Eastern Europe DFID is supporting the transition of state police forces to community police services by improving skills and changing police behaviour and attitudes, emphasising the involvement of local communities and improving the treatment of victims of crime, especially women and children. In Pakistan DFID supports a project implemented by Save the Children which provides social support for children leaving the football stitching industry. DFID supports the International Labour Organisation's International Programme for the Elimination of Child Labour and has funded action oriented research in South Asia and South East Asia on trafficking of children and their exploitation in prostitution and other intolerable forms of child labour. DFID supports projects which protect the rights of children affected by conflict and supports rehabilitation of children affected by conflict including child soldiers. DFID are working in this field in partnership with the Office of the UN High Commissioner for Human Rights (OHCHR), the International Committee of the Red Cross (ICRC), the United Nations High Commission for Refugees (UNHCR) and the UN Special Representative on Children and Armed Conflict. DFID also funds projects with NGOs, for example, rehabilitation projects with child soldiers in Liberia and Angola through Handicap International and UNICEF. In Jordan, DFID supports a pilot Family Protection Unit for abused women and children and is currently developing this into a larger programme with the Jordanian police service.

h **In Bangladesh**, DFID is exploring support to a street children's programme called Chinnamul Shishu Kishore Sangstha (CSKS) which, in addition to learning opportunities and a safe haven, provides access to legal aid for children held without trial in jails and vagrancy centres. DFID will be addressing juvenile justice issues as part of a broader accessible justice strategy under development.

i **Reviews of national legislation** to ensure compatibility with the Convention on the Rights of the Child and creation of mechanisms in central and local government to ensure effective co-ordination of policy towards children. For example, DFID has begun discussions with the government of Zambia on reform of the law on children. In Uganda, DFID, with Save the Children, is in discussions with the Government concerning support to piloting the implementation of the 1996 Children's Statute.

j **Establishment and strengthening of effective and appropriate national organisations, within government and civil society** who are concerned with promoting and co-ordinating implementation of the Convention on the Rights of the Child and with monitoring progress. DFID is currently exploring how best it can support activities in this important area of work.

k **Knowledge generation and dissemination concerning the rights and needs of children.** Because the specific needs of children within households and communities are often not understood or explicitly acknowledged, their needs and interests are often overlooked and subsumed by the needs of other household members, who have more power to express themselves. In many societies girl children tend to do the hardest work, have less to eat and are denied the opportunity of an education. In DFID's support to the education sector in Tanzania and Kenya, DFID is helping its partners find out more about the social and economic processes affecting who goes to school and who stays there, and who is excluded and for what reasons. In Pakistan, DFID is providing a Junior Professional Officer on Child Rights to the UNICEF office.

l **Family tracing in relation to the Kosovo crisis.** DFID is supporting the International Committee of the Red Cross for family tracing and re-unification of refugees fleeing Kosovo.

6 CIVIL RIGHTS AND FREEDOMS

This chapter covers articles: –

7 *Registration and nationality*

8 *Identity*

13 *Freedom of expression*

14 *Respect for freedom of thought*

15 *Respect for freedom of association*

16 *Protection of privacy, family, home, correspondence*

17 *Freedom of the press, and the child's access to it*

37 *Protection against torture*

6.1 Freedom of thought, conscience and religion

Article 14

6.1.1   Where a child is being looked after by a local authority the authority is required to have regard to the child's religious persuasion, racial origin and cultural and linguistic background when making decisions about him. The authority has also to take into account the child's wishes and feelings. Children accommodated in children's homes are required by regulation to be given the opportunity to practise their religion. Positive steps are taken to facilitate their doing so.

6.2 Religious Teaching

6.2.1   The statutory requirements for the provision of RE and daily collective worship remain broadly unchanged under the School Standards and Framework Act 1998. The Act applies the current arrangements, with minimal changes, to the new school framework which comes into effect on 1 September 1999. Under the Act:

a   RE provision in community schools, and foundation and voluntary schools without a religious character will essentially be the same as is currently in county schools;

b   collective worship provision in community and foundation schools without a religious character will essentially be the same as is currently in county schools;

c   collective worship provision in voluntary schools without a religious character will essentially be the same as is currently in voluntary schools;

 d RE and collective worship provision in foundation schools and voluntary controlled schools with a religious character will essentially be the same as is currently in voluntary controlled schools; and

 e RE and collective worship provision in voluntary aided schools with a religious character will essentially be the same as is currently in voluntary aided schools.

6.2.2 There is a number of existing important provisions that will remain:

 a in certain circumstances, parents can make arrangements with a school for a child to be taught alternative RE. For example, arrangements can be made for a child attending a community school or a foundation or voluntary school without a religious character to receive denominational RE; and

 b community schools and foundation schools without a religious character are able to apply for a 'determination' which lifts the 'wholly or mainly of a broadly Christian character' requirement from their daily collective worship. Such schools may then choose to provide alternative worship which is distinctive of a particular faith.

6.2.3 Parents of children attending any maintained school retain the right to withdraw their children from RE and daily collective worship either in whole or in part. It is open to parents to take account of their children's views in exercising their right of withdrawal from RE and collective worship. This is presently a matter for parents and the Government has not issued any advice to that effect.

6.2.4 There is a large number of voluntary schools maintained from public funds representing particular faiths or denominations. It remains open to independent promoters to propose further new schools to be maintained from public funds. All such proposals are considered on their merits.

6.3 Privacy and data protection

Article 16

6.3.1 Paragraph 4.26 of the United Kingdom's First Report referred to data protection legislation. Further changes have been made since that report.

6.3.2 United Kingdom law does not provide for a statutory right of privacy (but see section 5.1 above which deals with the incorporation of the European Convention on Human Rights into United Kingdom law). Children are afforded the same protection as adults under the general law (for example the law on defamation and on interference with correspondence). The Data Protection Act 1984 which provides for safeguards against the misuse of computerised personal information also applies to the personal data of children. The Data Protection Act 1998, which gives effect to the 1995 EC Data Protection Directive, is due shortly to replace the 1984 Act. The new Act applies to certain manual records as well as to computerised information and strengthens individuals' rights.

6.4 Privacy in Children's Homes in England and Wales

Article 16

6.4.1   Children's homes in England and Wales are required under the Children's Homes Regulations to provide suitable facilities to allow children to meet privately with their family and a range of other people.

6.4.2   Children's homes are required by Regulations to have a telephone where children can make and receive telephone calls in private.

6.4.3   Homes are also required to consider how to provide special privacy in which to allow a child to pursue his religion.

6.5 The future of emergency legislation in the United Kingdom

Article 13

6.5.1   Specific counter-terrorist powers are available to the police throughout the United Kingdom, and a number of further powers are available in Northern Ireland alone, to enable the security forces and the criminal justice system to deal effectively with the particular terrorist threat which has existed there. The Government seeks to retain the balance between providing the security forces with powers which are appropriate and proportionate to the threat of terrorism and protecting the rights of individuals.

6.5.2   Both in Northern Ireland and in the rest of the United Kingdom, these special counter-terrorist powers are independently reviewed annually, and their renewal is subject to debates in Parliament. The Government has now undertaken a major review of counter-terrorism legislation, its use and effectiveness. A consultation paper was issued in December 1998, which considers all aspects of current counter-terrorist legislation, including the Northern Ireland (Emergency Provisions) Act 1996 and the Prevention of Terrorism (Temporary Provisions) Act 1989, and sets out proposals for new, permanent legislation which is intended to be available throughout the UK to deal with all types of terrorism. The proposals were made available for consultation until 16 March 1999 and responses are now being analysed with a view to drawing up firm proposals for legislation. As part of the review, the Government will ensure that the proposals put forward for new legislation are compatible with the European Convention on Human Rights and other relevant human rights commitments, including the Convention on the Rights of the Child.

6.5.3   The Committee was particularly concerned about the emergency provisions in Northern Ireland in the context of the Convention. There has been no official assessment of the particular impact upon children of the emergency legislation in Northern Ireland, but allegations of harassment of children are very rare. Any such allegations would be treated extremely seriously, and the procedures for dealing with them are widely publicised.

6.5.4   The detention, treatment and questioning of persons arrested under the terrorism provisions in Northern Ireland are carried out according to statutory codes of practice, which include special safeguards for the rights of detainees. These ensure that in the rare event of the police having to interview anyone who appears to be under the age of 17, the well-being and rights of the interviewee are given the highest priority, and the interviewee must be accompanied by an appropriate adult. The Northern Ireland emergency legislation permits a constable or a member of the security forces to stop and search any person in specific circumstances laid down in legislation. If it is necessary to search a child under 14, this is normally done by a female police officer or a female soldier. For a juvenile older than this, the search is carried out by a police officer or soldier of the same sex as the child.

6.5.5   Similarly, the PACE codes of practice, under which the police operate in England and Wales, contain specific guidance for the police when dealing with cases involving juveniles. In Scotland, when a child under sixteen has been either detained or arrested, the police are under a statutory obligation without delay to tell the child's parent or guardian that the child is in custody at a specified place. The parent or guardian has a statutory right, unless there is reasonable cause to suspect that he himself has been involved in the alleged offence, to be permitted access to the child.

6.6   Children of unmarried fathers: acquisition of citizenship

Article 7

6.6.1   The Committee commented on "restrictions applied to unmarried fathers in transmitting citizenship to their children". The Convention provides that a child shall have the right to acquire nationality; it does not require that there shall be a right to transmit nationality from father to child. The law of the United Kingdom makes comprehensive provision for children to acquire British nationality as required by the Convention, including provision for according that status where the child would otherwise be stateless. Further, although there are practical difficulties about automatic provision for transmission of nationality in the male line regardless of legitimacy, provision exists, where an unmarried father with British nationality is prepared to take responsibility for his minor child resident in the United Kingdom, for the grant of British nationality to that child if he does not already enjoy that status. That may be done by means of an application for a certificate of registration made to the Nationality Directorate of the Home Office.

7 FAMILY ENVIRONMENT AND ALTERNATIVE CARE

This chapter covers articles: –

5 Respect for responsibilities of parents to provide direction and guidance to child in child's exercise of convention rights

9 Right to live with parents

10 Freedom to enter or leave country for family reunion

11 Measures against abduction and non-return from abroad

18 Responsibilities of parents and guardians

19 Protection from violence and abuse, neglect and exploitation

20 Obligations to children without parents

21 Adoption: authorisation procedures, inter-country arrangements

25 Right to review of those in care

27 *Right to standard of living and parental responsibility for maintenance*

39 *Protection of child victims of neglect and abuse*

7.1 Supporting families

Articles 5, 9, 18

7.1.1   On 4 November 1998, the Government published a programme of measures to strengthen family life by supporting families with children. The consultative document *Supporting Families*42 focuses on the Government's responsibility to support families though its policies and to help parents to meet their children's needs.

7.1.2   The consultation paper concentrates on five areas where Government can make a difference. The Government intends to:

a Provide better support to parents to ensure that every parent has access to the advice and support they need.

b Give better financial support to families to improve family prosperity and reduce child poverty.

c Help families balance work and home so that it is easier for parents to spend time with their children.

d Strengthen marriage to help protect the interests of children and reduce family breakdown

e Tackle the more serious problems of family life, including domestic violence and school age pregnancy.

---

42 Published by the Stationery Office, November 1998 ISBN 0-11-341225-8.

7.1.3   This is the first consultation paper on the family, fulfilling the Government's manifesto commitment to strengthen family life. Although the consultation did not cover Scotland many of the measures referred to in the consultation document extend to Scotland. Over the past year, the Government has developed a range of new measures which will give practical support to families. These include new financial support, such as the increase in Child Benefit and the introduction of the Working Families Tax Credit; £540 million for the new Sure Start Programme to help families ensure that their children are ready to learn when they start school; and the measures announced in the White Paper *Fairness at Work* to help families balance work and home. Some £42 million was made available for the corresponding programme in Scotland.

7.1.4   The consultation paper sets out a major programme of action to support families. The consultation period ended on 15 March 1999. The Ministerial Group on the Family published a summary of the responses to the consultation document on 8 June 1999. The responses to *Supporting Families* will be used in the ongoing development of family policy across Government.

7.2   Education for parenthood in England and Wales

Article 18, 28

7.2.1   The Government wishes to strengthen parenting education in schools. It has set up a National Advisory Group to advise on a framework for personal, social and health education. As part of its work, the Group will develop proposals to help all secondary schools teach their pupils about the responsibilities of parenthood.

7.3   Education for parenthood in Scotland

Article 18, 2828

7.3.1   In Scotland the curriculum is not prescribed by statute and the responsibility for the delivery and management of the curriculum rests with education authorities and head teachers. Guidance is, however, provided by the Scottish Office Education and Industry Department. The National Guidelines in Environmental Studies include a section on relationships in which education for parenthood could be introduced.[43]

7.3.2   In addition the materials *Personal Relationships and Developing Sexuality* provide teachers with a curriculum framework covering pupils between the ages of 5-18. These materials offer advice on what issues should be covered at different stages in Scottish schools. The Scottish Qualification Authority also offer a Standard Grade examination in Social and Vocational Skills in which the three themes covered are home, work and community.

7.4   Family Learning in England and Wales

Article 18, 28

7.4.1   The Government has recognised that more needs to be done to improve support for parents. In its consultation paper *Supporting Families*[44] it sets out proposals for providing such practical support. The consultation

---

43 Curriculum and Assessment in Scotland National Guidelines - Environmental Studies 5-14, SOED, March 1993.

44 Published by the Stationery Office, November 1998 ISBN 0-11-341225-8.

document invites views on many issues covering families, including ways of improving parental involvement in children's education, parental support for schools and schools' support for parents, and the best ways to develop education on parental responsibility in schools. The National Family and Parenting Institute will have as part of its remit, the development of parenting support programmes and activities, including those which help parents to help their children learn.

7.4.2   Family Learning can involve: families learning together; parents, grandparents, and other carers helping children; and children helping their parents. Family learning can be an effective approach for families of all sorts, and it can and should be fun.

7.4.3   The Government sees the value of effective family learning both in promoting lifelong learning for adults and raising the attainment of children, both key objectives for Ministers.

7.4.4   The Government is particularly aware that family learning can reach some of the most disadvantaged in society at risk of exclusion, and it can help ensure disadvantaged children get the help they need to lay the foundations for effective learning.

7.4.5   The Government supported Family Literacy Initiative illustrates this point. It reaches parents with poor basic skills and their children particularly in areas of social disadvantage. Independent evaluation has shown it to be effective in assisting both children and parents to improve their literacy skills.

7.4.6   Family Literacy is doubling in size in 1998-99 and will continue to grow so that all LEAs will have access to provision from 1999-2000. Around 120 LEAs have been offered £4m funding for 1998-99 to reach around 6000 parents and their children, an average of 4 courses per LEA. From 1999-2000 Family Literacy will be available nationally.

7.4.7   From next year the Government will be supporting Family Numeracy projects with a grant totalling £1 million. The aims are to: provide greater support in the home for numeracy; offer a quick start into numeracy for pre-school and reception children at risk of under attainment; and offer a re-start for their parents' numeracy. Successful pilots have been run, meeting all these aims.

7.4.8   In Wales, the Basic Skills Agency, with funding of £923,000 since 1996 from the Welsh Office, has developed and implemented a successful series of family literacy projects in partnership with primary schools, parents and all 22 local authorities in Wales. The Agency is working up family numeracy projects based on the Family Literacy model.

7.4.9   The Government believes that it is important to embed family learning in mainstream education. That is the way to secure the wider value of family learning for both adults and children. That is the message that the

Government is giving to all those involved in providing education, as teachers, managers, or funders. It is also important to promote the potential value of family learning more widely, and that is why the Government supports a range of educational organisations who do so.

7.5 Family education – Scotland

Article 28, 18

7.5.1   In Scotland, the Government has committed £15 million to supporting the role of parents in their children's education. The funds will be made available to education authorities over three years, to expand provision of family literacy schemes and home-link teachers, and to develop parent support groups.

7.6 Looked after children

Articles 18, 20, 25

7.6.1   In 1995, the Department of Health launched the *Looking After Children: Good Parenting, Good Outcomes*[45] (LAC) materials. They provide the opportunity to engage children, wherever they are placed, in their own care plans and encourage communications between all those involved in the care of the child.

7.6.2   The materials have been designed to improve the parenting experience of children looked after by local authorities and other agencies. They set an agenda for good parental care by identifying the experiences, concerns and expectations of children of different ages and stages by bringing to the attention of those responsible for their upbringing the probable consequences of different actions. One of the broad aims of the materials is to introduce ideas about outcomes into social work practice.

7.6.3   Since May 1995, most local authorities in England have committed themselves to implementing LAC with the aid of a support programme offered by the Department of Health. The LAC materials are also being used internationally, including Hungary, Canada (6 Provinces), Australia (2 States), Norway, Sweden, Belgium and Russia.

7.6.4   In Wales, use of the LAC materials was the subject of guidance[46] issued in the context of implementation of the recommendations of the North Wales Child Care Examination Team. The LAC forms were produced in Welsh. The Department has undertaken a two year programme of work to assist local authorities in Wales to implement the LAC system, which involves a systematic approach to multi-agency assessment planning and review for looked-after children.

7.6.5   Developments in Scotland in arrangements for looking after children are reported above in Chapter 2.

---

45 Published by the Department of Health 1995.

46 Welsh Office Circular 35/96 *Child Care Procedures and Practice in North Wales –* Implementation of the Report of Ms Adrianne Jones (NWCCET). Children and Families Unit, Welsh Office, Cathays Park, Cardiff CF1 3NQ. July 1996.

7.7 Child Protection in England and Wales

Articles 19, 30, 39

7.7.1   The Government is firmly committed to ensuring that all children within the community are safeguarded and protected from abuse. The Children Act 1989 was designed to promote appropriate and decisive action to protect children from abuse and neglect.

7.7.2   Good co-operation and joint working by all agencies – social services, health, education, the police, probation and the voluntary sector – is an essential prerequisite for safeguarding the welfare of children. *Working Together Under The Children Act 1989,* the key Government guidance issued in 1991, provides a solid foundation for inter-agency co-operation in child protection work and real improvements have been made in tackling serious cases of abuse.

7.7.3   In 1995, the Government published a report *Child Protection: Messages from Research.* This gave details of the key messages arising from a major programme of research into child protection, which included 20 individual studies. One of the conclusions reached from the research was that real benefits could arise if there was a focus on the wider needs of children and families rather than a narrow concentration on the alleged incident of abuse.

7.7.4   It is for this reason that the Government began in February 1998 a process of consultation and debate in order to inform the development of new guidance on joint co-operation and working. A consultation paper has been issued which examines the general issues and principles which need to be considered. The key message which the Government wishes to promote is a new emphasis on looking more widely at the needs of the most vulnerable children and families in the community. Families need help at an earlier stage to tackle their problems before parenting difficulties escalate into abuse. However, the Government recognises that an effective child protection system will continue to be needed to deal with cases of abuse. Work on the new guidance will also be informed by the improvements in understanding and knowledge in many areas of child abuse which have occurred over the past decade.

7.7.5   Public consultation on the revision of the *Working Together* guidance on child protection procedures was undertaken in Wales in parallel with consultation in England.

7.7.6   The Government is also developing a framework for a needs-led assessment of children and their families. The framework will focus on assessing the needs of children and the capacity of parents or family members to meet those needs in both the short and long term. It will be underpinned by the latest knowledge of the impact that domestic violence, alcohol and drug misuse, mental health and sex offending can have on child development.

7.7.7   Following a consultation period with all organisations and individuals with an interest in services for children as well as from those who can speak for children themselves, the Government's intention is to issue new guidance.

7.8 The Review of Safeguards for Children Living Away from Home

Articles 19,20,39

7.8.1   In November 1997 the Secretary of State for Health published the report of the *Review of Safeguards for Children Living Away from Home* conducted by Sir William Utting and others. This report, which related to England and Wales, followed a series of convictions of people in North Wales for multiple abuse of children in their care[47]. The Secretary of State also announced that he would chair a Task Force "to help the Government prepare costed responses to the principal recommendations of the report and then monitor progress with their implementation". It includes 10 Ministers from across Government, and advisers from both inside and outside Government. Its terms of reference are

> "To help the Government prepare costed responses to the principal recommendations of the report *People Like Us* and then to monitor progress with their implementation."

7.8.2   The Review made a number of principal recommendations, and over 150 other recommendations and suggestions for detailed change. These affect a wide range of issues including:

a the quality of local authority care for children they look after, and the support of those children and young people after they leave care

b education and health care for looked-after children

c the regulation of foster care and children's homes, and boarding schools not already regulated

d checks on the suitability of people recruited to work with children

e the criminal justice system, including the prosecution of alleged child abusers, child prostitution and child pornography

f the youth justice system and the protection of children in custody.

7.8.3   The Government accepted the general principles of the Review report and a large majority of its detailed recommendations. The report made 20 principal recommendations and over 130 other recommendations with the aims of: improving protection for children in foster and residential care, in schools and the penal system; to provide more effective safeguards and checks to prevent abusers from working with children; provide more effective avenues of complaint and increase access to independent advocates; provide more vigilant management; provide more effective disciplinary and criminal measures; provide effective systems of communication between agencies about known abusers.[48]

---

47 *People like us:* The Report of the review of the safeguards for children living away from home, by Sir William Utting. Published by the Stationery Office on behalf of the Department of Health and the Welsh Office. ISBN 0-11-322101-0.

48 *The Government's Response to the Children's Safeguards Review:* Cm 4105, published by the Stationery Office November 1998. ISBN 0-010-141052-2..

7.8.4   The Government's response covers a number of discrete areas namely: public care; care leavers; regulation; education; health; inter agency working; stopping dangerous people from working with children; juveniles in the penal system; criminal justice. Individual Government Departments will be monitoring implementation of action within their areas of responsibility. In addition, the Ministerial Task Force on Children's Safeguards will monitor the overall programme of action. Some of the proposals cannot be taken forward until there is time in the legislative programme.

7.8.5   The Government has taken into account the costs of the changes in setting the increased level of funding available for individual Departments under the Comprehensive Spending Review. To help finance the improvement in services, the Government has introduced a Children's Special Services Grant totalling £375 million over three years.

7.8.6   In Scotland Roger Kent, a former Director of Social Work, was commissioned in 1996 to carry out a wide ranging review of the arrangements for looked after children living away from home, to make recommendations about improved safeguards for such children and to report. The Kent report, which was entitled the Children's Safeguards Review, was published in November 1997 and it identified a number of areas as key issues in ensuring the safety of children in such circumstances. These included better recruitment arrangements for those working in residential child care, raising the status and professionalism of the care task, better communication between families and organisations caring for children, greater rigour and independence in the inspection of children's homes and the development of a culture that does not tolerate abusive behaviour.

7.8.7   The Kent report was the subject of a consultation exercise which concluded in March 1998. Over 80 responses were received, commenting on the 61 recommendations in the report. There was widespread support for the vast majority of the recommendations.

7.8.8   The Government decided to implement a significant package of measures designed to take forward the key recommendations in the Kent report. A Government response to the report was published in November 1998. The Minister has committed himself to a national strategic framework for children's services and the development of national standards. An essential part of this will be the first round of local authority children's services plans which have provided an opportunity to set and review progress towards strategic outcomes for children's services. Individual care plans already require the inclusion of plans for the child's health and education.

7.8.9   The Government has piloted a more rigorous means of selection for people who work with children in residential settings. As part of the process social work, education and health authorities can check if an applicant for a position which gives substantial access to children has criminal convictions. The Government intend to add to this by establishing a statutory consultancy index which will allow authorities to access non-conviction information.

7.8.10 It is the Government aim to reduce the number of children looked after by local authorities living in a residential setting and to expand the availability of foster carers. Children in foster care should have the same level of protection as children living in residential settings and so the Government has proposed the inspection of foster care services.

7.8.11 Extra resources totalling £36.7m over the three year period commencing 1999/2000 have been available to improve children's services. This included £15 million specifically for the implementation of the key proposals in the Children's Safeguards Review.

7.8.12 At the heart of these proposals for reform are the children themselves. The Government has recommended to local authorities the increased use of Children's Rights workers and *Who Cares? Scotland* workers. The Government has provided additional funding to *Who Cares? Scotland* in order that they can meet these additional demands.

7.9 Role of the education service in England and Wales in protecting children from abuse

Article 19

7.9.1 The Department for Education and Employment issued in October 1995 Circular 10/95 *Protecting Children from Abuse: The Role of the Education Service* which went to schools, including for information to independent schools. This replaced previous advice on child protection. The Circular makes it clear that children have a fundamental right to be protected from harm. The primary responsibility for child protection rests with social services departments (SSDs). The police and the NSPCC also have responsibilities for investigating allegations of abuse. The Circular makes it clear that education staff should not investigate allegations or suspicions of abuse, but should refer cases to the local SSD. However, the guidance recognises that teachers are in a good position to identify signs, or hear allegations, of abuse.

7.9.2 The main recommendations of Circular 10/95 are that —

a all staff should be alert to signs of abuse and know to whom they should report their concerns or suspicions;

b all schools and colleges should have child protection policies, which should include procedures to be followed if a member of staff is accused of abuse;

c all schools and colleges should have a senior member of staff with designated responsibility for child protection, who should receive appropriate training.

7.9.3 Similar guidance was issued in Wales.[49]

---

49 Welsh Office Circular 52/95 Published by Welsh Office Education Department, Cathays Park, Cardiff CF1 3NQ 1995.

7.9.4 In 1995-96 and 1997-98 the DfEE helped to fund the training of teachers with designated responsibility for child protection through the Grants for Education Support and Training (GEST) programme of grants.

7.10 Role of the education service in Scotland in protecting children from abuse

Article 39

7.10.1 The Scottish Office has published inter-agency guidance on child protection, *Protecting Scotland's Children – A Shared Responsibility*. On the basis of the new guidance, it is intended that an update to circular 10/90 on education services' responsibilities for child protection will be prepared and distributed to education authorities.

7.10.2 National guidance was published in November 1998 for all agencies, including social work, health, police and NGOs on how they should work together to tackle child abuse and neglect. This guidance, entitled *Protecting Children – A Shared Responsibility*[50] was consulted on in 1997 and amended in the light of comments and views from a wide range of interests. Related guidance on child protection for health professionals has been prepared by a working group and will be issued later in 1999. SOEID intends to review guidance for education professionals in the light of the new inter-agency guidance.

7.11 Protection of children from violence in the home – Northern Ireland

Article 39

7.11.1 The Family Homes and Domestic Violence (NI) Order 1998 increases the protection available to children under the existing law, in a number of ways.

7.11.2 First, it amends the Children (NI) Order 1995 to enable the court, when making an emergency protection order or an interim care order, to include the requirement that the suspected abuser be excluded from the home, rather than the child having to be removed, as is the case at present.

7.11.3 In addition, when considering making an occupation order or a non-molestation order, the court must take into account as a factor the health, safety and well-being of any child involved.

7.11.4 In common with the Children (NI) Order, the Family Homes and Domestic Violence (NI) Order also allows children (under 16) themselves to apply for remedies with the leave of the court, provided the court is satisfied that they have sufficient understanding to do so.

7.11.5 Further, a new provision has been inserted into the Children Order so that when a court is considering whether or not to make a contact or residence order in favour of someone who has a non-molestation order made against them, it will consider any harm which the child has suffered or is at risk of suffering through seeing or hearing the ill-treatment of another person by the person who has the non-molestation order made against them. This provision therefore recognises an increased understanding of the

---

50 Published by The Stationery Office on behalf of The Scottish Office November 1998

harm that can come to children through witnessing the abuse of another person; and also that if a parent has suffered violence from their partner, there is a high risk that the children are also vulnerable to abuse.

7.12 Physical punishment of children in the home

7.12.1   An application was made by a child to the European Commission on Human Rights on the basis that the injuries sustained by the child were in breach of Article 3 of the European Convention on Human Rights, which provides that "no-one shall be subjected to torture or to inhuman or degrading treatment". The Court concluded that there had been a breach of Article 3 in this particular case and that domestic law in the United Kingdom did not give adequate protection to the child. However the Commission made clear that its finding "does not mean that Article 3 is to be interpreted as imposing an obligation on States to protect, through their criminal law, against any form of physical rebuke, however mild, by a parent of a child."

7.12.2   Before the hearing, the Government had already announced its intention to issue a consultation paper with the aim of seeking the widest possible consensus on how any necessary and appropriate changes to the law relating to physical punishment of children in the home might be made.

7.13 Corporal punishment within child care

Article 19

7.13.1   In England, Wales and Scotland, Regulations made under the relevant legislation and accompanying guidance have given effect to the Government's policy that corporal punishment has no place in the public child care setting. In addition, because of the special vulnerability of children in children's homes, Regulations also prohibit a range of other punishments in homes.

7.13.2   Several NGOs, including Barnardos and the National Children's Bureau, made clear their opposition to any form of physical punishment of children when commenting on the existing law in relation to corporal punishment in private schools and the defence of 'reasonable chastisement' in relation to the use of corporal punishment in the home.

7.13.3   Section 131 of the School Standards and Framework Act 1998 now outlaws corporal punishment for all pupils in maintained and non-maintained schools, and for children receiving nursery education in England and Wales. These provisions are expected to come into force on 1 September 1999. Similar legislation in Scotland will be a matter for the Scottish Parliament.

7.14 Corporal punishment in Northern Ireland

Article 19

7.14.1   Corporal punishment in grant-aided schools in Northern Ireland has been unlawful since 1987. The relevant provisions do not at present extend to independent schools, but it is intended to extend the existing provisions to such schools as soon as a suitable legislative opportunity occurs.

7.14.2   Corporal punishment has not been used in any of the training schools in Northern Ireland since the 1950s. Early in 1999 new statutory rules under Article 52 of the Criminal Justice (Children) (NI) Order 1998[51]

---

51 SI 1998/1504 (NI 9).

will remove the statutory right of training school managers to inflict corporal punishment upon those children ordered to be detained in training schools.

7.15 Safety Review by the Chief Inspector of Social Services

Articles 19, 39

7.15.1   To support the work of the Children's Safeguards review, and against the background of concerns raised by the child abuse cases, the Chief Inspector of Social Services wrote to all local authorities in England in May 1997 asking them to review the ways in which they had implemented the provisions of the Children Act and subsequent guidance and to provide a report to local authority Committees and the Social Services Inspectorate of the Department of Health (SSI) by 31 July 1997. Those reports provided the basis for a major inspection of management and practice in a number of local authorities. The Chief Inspector will be reporting to Ministers his assessment of the current procedures for ensuring the safety of children and young people in public care.

7.16 Children in public care

Article 20

7.16.1   A local authority has a duty to look after a child when that appears to be the best way of safeguarding and promoting the welfare of the child. A local authority will seek a suitable placement for the child. This may be through a relative looking after the child, or if no one is suitable then an attempt will be made to place the child in the community. Siblings looked after by local authorities should generally be placed together. In all cases, the guiding principle is that decisions should be made in the best interests of the child.

7.16.2   The placement is always intended to promote the best interests of the child. The views of the child and the child's parents are considered before the placement. The child's religion, racial origin, cultural and linguistic background are also taken into account. The placement might be with foster carers, or a children's home or a residential school. Some two thirds of looked-after children live with foster carers.

7.16.3   Children may only be placed with approved foster carers. Placements are subject to continuing supervision by the local authority to ensure that the welfare of the child is being furthered. Foster carers are expected where it is appropriate to maintain links between the child and the child's natural family.

7.16.4   Anyone proposing to foster a child privately has to notify the local authority and to notify when the arrangement ceases. The local authority has a duty to visit the child to promote and safeguard the welfare of the child.

7.16.5   In England and Wales, all children's homes, except small private children's homes (accommodating three or fewer children) and 'exempt' homes, such as holiday homes, are subject to the provisions of the Children Act 1989 and Regulations. The Government intends to introduce legislation so that small private children's homes in England and Wales are also subject to provisions of the Children's Homes Regulations. In Scotland, homes where a substantial part of the function is to provide services for the purposes of the Children (Scotland) Act 1995 are similarly required to be registered. The relevant Regulations set out the need for responsible authorities to ensure that the number of staff of each home and their experience and qualifications are adequate to ensure that the welfare of the children accommodated there is safeguarded and promoted at all times.

7.16.6   All homes covered by Children's Homes Regulations are required to be inspected at least twice yearly by the regulating or local authority (one visit unannounced) to ensure that the homes are complying with the standards set. The relevant legislation in both England and Wales and Scotland also allows for the inspection of any children's homes by the appropriate Social Services Inspectorate if necessary.

7.16.7   The position in Northern Ireland is broadly similar to that described above.

7.17 Incidence of care among children of ethnic minority parents in England and Wales

7.17.1   There is some evidence that children of certain ethnic groups appear to be over-represented in the total of looked-after children. However, there is no centrally collected information on the numbers of ethnic minority children entering and leaving care. The Department of Health is undertaking a programme of work, in consultation with the Welsh Office, to develop national statistics on the ethnic origin of social services staff and service users, including children.

7.18 Co-ordination between government departments over children in care – views of NGOs

7.18.1   The Government have noted the comments of the Who Cares? Trust during the preparation of this report. While by no means uncritical of some areas, the Trust noted several developments since 1994 which they welcomed. These included, at the level of government co-ordination, the following: –

a   The introduction of mandatory Children's Services Plans – although with concerns whether children at local level are involved in the planning process, and about how effective the plans are in practice.

b   Department of Health *Looking After Children* materials (see section 7.6) which measure the progress of children across seven dimensions and attempt to assess the outcomes of care. The Trust would like there to be more training on the purpose of the materials for them to be used more effectively to benefit children.

c   Audit Commission/SSI Joint Reviews which measure how well local authorities deliver social services, a key principle being the views of service users, including looked-after children.

d   the establishment of a General Social Care Council.

e   The Health Select Committee Inquiry into Looked-after Children.

f   The creation of the Children's Services Strategy Group in the Department of Health.

g   The creation of the Social Exclusion Unit with its focus on the most marginalised groups, such as the homeless and those excluded from school, amongst whom are to be found disproportionate numbers of young people from care.

h   The review of social work training.

7.18.2   The Trust see a need, however, for

   a   arrangements to require local authorities to monitor, at the
       point young people leave care and prior to their 21st birthday,
       where they are accommodated, their educational attainment
       and employment status.

   b   An amendment to the Code of Guidance under the Housing Act
       1996 to require local authorities to develop strategies for youth
       homelessness which should make specific reference to meeting
       the housing needs of care leavers.

7.19 Divorce and separation in England and Wales: The Family Law Act 1996

Articles 9, 18

7.19.1   The Family Law Act 1996[52] was passed on 4 July 1996. **Part I** sets
out four general principles for the court to consider in exercising functions
relating to Parts II and III:

   a   that the institution of marriage is to be supported;

   b   that the parties to a marriage which may have broken down are
       to be encouraged to take all practicable steps, whether by
       marriage counselling or otherwise, to save the marriage;

   c   that a marriage which has irretrievably broken down and is being
       brought to an end should be brought to an end –

       ·   with minimum distress to the parties and to the children
           affected;

       ·   with questions dealt with in a manner designed to promote
           as good a continuing relationship between the parties and
           any children affected as is possible in the circumstances;

       ·   without costs being unreasonably incurred in connection
           with the procedures to be followed in bringing the marriage
           to an end;

   d   that any risk to one of the parties to a marriage, and to any
       children, of violence from the other party should, so far as
       reasonably practicable, be removed or diminished.

7.19.2   **Part II** deals with divorce and separation; it provides for
compulsory attendance at an information meeting before a statement of
marital breakdown is filed, and a period for reflection and consideration.
Section 22 of the Act has been implemented. The Government announced in
June 1999 that it did not intend to implement the remainder of Part II in 2000
as previously planned. Before implementation, the Government must be
satisfied that the new divorce procedures will work. The preliminary
research results from the information meetings have been disappointing.
The full research results from the pilots, will be available in early 2000, when
the Government will consider whether further research is necessary.

52 c 27 Stationery Office ISBN 0-10-542796-9.

7.19.3 Under section 11 of the Act, in any proceedings for a divorce or separation order the court must consider whether the circumstances of the case require it to use its powers under the Children Act 1989 in respect of the welfare and upbringing of the child and, if it so decides, it may delay granting the divorce or separation order. The child's welfare is paramount in deciding this issue. The court will also have particular regard to:

a the wishes and feelings of the child in the light of his age and understanding and the circumstances in which those wishes were expressed;

b the conduct of the parties towards the child;

c the principle that in the absence of evidence to the contrary the child's welfare is best served by regular contact with those who have parental responsibility for him and with other members of his family;

d the aim that the child should have as good a continuing relationship with his parents as possible; and

e any risk arising from arrangements for his care and upbringing.

7.19.4 The provision of legal aid funding for mediation in family disputes under **Part III** of the Act is already available in many areas and will be made available throughout England and Wales. Currently the Legal Aid Board is granting contracts to suppliers of mediation services to permit phased implementation, so as to ensure that sufficient quality-assured services are available to meet the demand for mediation services. A total of 140 mediation services in all areas of England and Wales have already been awarded contracts and a further 110 contracts will be awarded by the end of July 1999. Under the terms of the legal aid franchises, suppliers are required to meet the following standards:

a Suppliers must have documented child protection procedures and must be able to demonstrate how child protection cases are identified and referred to the appropriate bodies.

b Suppliers must have documented procedures to show that, where children are consulted directly as part of the mediation, they have addressed the issues of :

- parental consent;

- the purpose of the consultation;

- preservation of absolute child confidentiality except where child protection issues arise.

c Suppliers must have documented procedures designed to ensure that clients are encouraged to consider:

- the welfare, wishes and feelings of the child;

- whether and to what extent each child should be given the opportunity to express his or her wishes and feelings in the mediation.

7.19.5 In addition section 29, requiring those seeking legal aid in family proceedings first to attend a meeting to consider whether mediation might be suitable for their case, is being introduced on an area by area basis as adequate provision becomes available. The provisions of this section will also be implemented throughout England and Wales.

7.19.6 **Part IV**, providing a single set of civil remedies to deal with domestic violence and to regulate occupation of the family home, was implemented on 1 October 1997. With the leave of the court, and provided the court is satisfied that the child has sufficient understanding, a child under sixteen may apply for an occupation order or a non-molestation order. Non-molestation orders prohibit a person from molesting another adult or child associated with them. Occupation orders deal with the regulation of the occupation of dwelling houses, and would be available only to a child with existing rights in the property.

7.20 Adoption, fostering and family proceedings – views of NGOs

Article 21

7.20.1 The British Agencies for Adoption and Fostering (BAAF) have welcomed the steps being taken by the Government to conclude bilateral agreements with other countries on inter-country adoption. They have however expressed a desire to see stronger measures for ensuring the child's right to be heard in judicial and administrative procedures affecting the child, and for the child's rights to have his or her views given due weight need to be strengthened. In particular:

a the child is not normally entitled to party status in adoption proceedings

b in England and Wales, the child may have no representation or other voice in proceedings between parents concerning residence and contact, or in applications by fathers for parental responsibility.

7.20.2 The BAAF have made clear their strong support for the Utting and Kent reports, and in particular the recommendation for the registration of private foster carers.

7.21 Recent legislative measures: regulations to prohibit the placement of children with persons who might put them at risk

Articles 19,39

7.21.1 In October 1997 an important measure for the further protection of children was effected by the introduction of the Children (Protection from Offenders) (Miscellaneous Amendments) Regulations[53.] The purpose of the 1997 Regulations, which came into effect on 17 October 1997, is to prohibit the approval by adoption agencies, local authorities or voluntary organisations acting as responsible authorities of any person as a foster carer or adoptive parents where either that person or any adult member of that person's household over the age of 18 years is known to have been convicted of, or cautioned for, a specified offence. To this end, the 1997 Regulations amend the Adoption Agencies Regulations 1983, the Foster Placement (Children) Regulations 1991, the Children's Homes Regulations 1991 and the Disqualification for Caring for Children Regulations 1991.

---

53 SI 1997/2308.

7.21.2 Specified offences include those offences, other than the offence of common assault and battery, specified in Schedule 1 to the Children and Young Persons Act 1933, offences in Schedule 1 of the Sexual Offences Act 1956 (rape), section 1 of the Protection of Children Act 1978 and section 160 of the Criminal Justice Act 1988 (offences relating to indecent photographs of children). These offences are now included in the Schedule to the Disqualification for Caring for Children Regulations 1991[54].

7.22 Recent legislative measures in England and Wales: making information available to adopted children

Article 21

7.22.1 New regulations were introduced in July 1997 which require the adoption agency to make available to the adoptive parents information about the child and his or her background, at the latest when the adoption order is made. The purpose of the information is to assist the adoptive parents to tell the child something of his background. The Adoption Agencies and Children (Arrangements for Placement and Review) (Miscellaneous Amendments) Regulations 1997[55] provide that such information as was made available by the adoption agency should be made available to the child before he reaches his eighteenth birthday. Ideally, the information should be given to the child gradually as he grows up so that he will be aware of the fact of his background and adoption and be comfortable with that knowledge.

7.23 Intercountry adoption

Article 21

7.23.1 Where a State of origin is prepared to allow some of its children who have no family to be adopted by families living overseas, the United Kingdom, as a receiving State, is in consequence obliged in practice to accept that the State of origin cannot provide alternative families for these children. Conditions in these States of origin are well documented and the extent of availability of child welfare services is well known. However, the United Kingdom takes appropriate measures to satisfy itself about conditions which exist in some countries including making fact-finding visits.

7.23.2 Adoption legislation in the United Kingdom provides for a child who is adopted overseas to be provided with safeguards and standards of care equivalent to those enjoyed by children born and adopted within the United Kingdom. Also, one of the effects of the making of an adoption order in a United Kingdom court, or recognising the effects of an adoption order made in certain specified ('designated') countries, is that the adopted child is to be regarded in law as if he or she was a child of the adopters' marriage. The same legislation makes it an offence for an authorised person or body to obtain improper financial gain from making arrangements for adoption.

7.23.3 The local authority or approved adoption agency who arranged the adoption will be required to monitor the progress of the child until an adoption order is made – at least one year from the time the child entered the United Kingdom. Where a child has been adopted in a country whose adoption is recognised by the United Kingdom, that child is automatically regarded as a child of the marriage of the adoptive parents and therefore the

---

54 SI 1991/2094.

55 In Wales this guidance was issued as Welsh Office Circular 30/98, published by the Children and Families Unit, Social Services Policy Division, Welsh Office, Cathays Park, Cardiff CF1 3NQ. 2 September 1998.

adoption agency has no further involvement in the process once the child enters the United Kingdom.

7.23.4 The United Kingdom played a full part in the 1993 Hague Conference on Protection of Children and Co-operation in Respect of Intercountry Adoption and formally signed the Convention on 12 January 1994. The United Kingdom is working with several countries with the aim of entering into formal intercountry adoption agreements; these agreements are firmly based on the principles of the 1993 Convention and set out the process and procedures which will permit United Kingdom citizens to adopt children in the respective country.

7.23.5 The Government passed the Adoption (Intercountry Aspects) Act 1999 which enables the United Kingdom to give effect to the 1993 Hague Convention on Protection of Children and Co-operation in Respect on Intercountry Adoption. The Act also places a responsibility on the public bodies to undertake intercountry adoption work and makes it an offence for a person to bring a child to the UK without approval. Its provisions will enable a more efficient process to be introduced for improving intercountry adoption.

7.23.6 The legislation will allow the UK to join 34 other countries which to date have ratified or acceeded to the Convention. Ratification is expected to take place before the end of the year 2000. The Act provides effective measures to protect children living overseas and also places intercountry adoption on a firm legislative footing along with domestic adoption.

7.23.7 Article 21 embodies the sound legislative provisions and principles of good social work practice which the United Kingdom recognises, most of which is already contained in existing adoption law and practice.

7.23.8 Statistics on intercountry adoption in the United Kingdom are below: -

Number of Overseas adoption applications

Country	1993	1994	1995	1996	1997	1998	1999 Jan-Apr	Total 1993-1999
Albania	1	1	1	1	0	0	0	4
Algeria	0	0	0	0	0	0	1	1
Argentina	0	0	0	0	0	0	0	0
Amenia	0	0	1	0	0	0	0	1
Bahrain	0	0	0	0	0	0	1	1
Beluras	0	0	0	0	1	1	1	3
Bolivia	1	0	1	0	0	0	1	3
Brazil	3	3	7	4	4	3	0	24
Bulgaria	2	3	0	2	0	4	1	12
Burundi	0	0	0	0	1	0	0	1
Canada	0	0	0	0	0	0	0	0
Cambodia	0	0	0	0	0	2	0	2
Chile	1	1	1	0	4	4	0	11
China	3	1	1	4	4	7	0	20
Colombia	0	0	0	0	1	0	0	1
Czech Republic	0	0	0	0	1	0	0	1

FIGURE 1: OVERSEAS ADOPTION 1993-1997 (Part 1)

Country	1993	1994	1995	1996	1997	1998	1999 Jan-Apr	Total 1993-1999
Egypt	0	0	0	1	0	0	0	1
Eire	0	0	0	0	0	1	0	1
El Salvador	1	3	1	0	0	0	0	5
Estonia	0	0	0	0	3	0	0	3
Ethiopia	1	0	0	0	0	0	0	1
Greece	0	0	0	0	1	0	0	1
Guatemala	2	3	12	16	26	20	2	81
Honduras	0	1	0	0	0	0	0	1
Hong Kong	1	0	0	1	0	0	0	2
Hungary	1	1	1	0	1	0	0	4
India	16	20	22	29	21	22	8	138
Indonesia	1	0	0	0	0	0	0	1
Iran	0	0	0	1	0	0	0	1
Israel	1	0	0	0	0	0	0	1
Jamaica	2	0	0	0	1	0	0	3
Japan	0	0	0	0	0	1	0	1
Jordon	0	0	0	0	1	0	0	1
Latvia	1	0	0	0	0	0	0	1
Lebanon	0	2	0	0	1	0	0	3
Lithuania	0	0	0	0	0	1	0	1
Madeira	0	0	0	0	1	0	0	1
Mauritius	0	0	0	0	1	0	0	1
Mexico	0	0	1	0	0	2	0	3
Nepal	1	1	1	1	1	2	0	7
Nicaragua	0	0	0	1	0	0	0	1
Nigeria	0	0	0	0	0	0	0	0
Pakistan	1	2	3	1	3	2	4	16
Panama	1	0	0	0	0	0	0	1
Paraguay	8	16	6	1	1	0	0	32
Peru	1	0	0	0	1	1	0	3
Phillippines	7	2	1	5	4	4	0	23
Poland	2	1	2	1	1	2	0	9
Romania	22	14	9	10	5	17	4	81
Russia	1	4	4	3	3	13	5	33
Serbia, Republic of	0	1	0	0	0	0	0	1
Sierra Leonne	0	0	1	0	0	0	0	1
Singapore	0	0	0	1	1	0	0	2
Sri Lanka	4	6	3	2	3	0	1	19
Taiwan	0	0	0	0	0	1	0	1
Tanzania	1	0	0	0	0	0	0	1
Thailand	4	10	5	10	10	13	8	60
Trinidad	0	0	0	0	0	0	0	0
Turkey	1	1	1	0	0	0	0	3
Ukraine	2	0	1	0	0	2	0	5
USA	4	0	8	4	5	8	2	31
Vietnam	0	1	1	1	3	2	0	8
Venuzuela	0	0	0	0	0	0	0	0
Yugoslavia	0	0	0	0	0	0	0	2
Total	101	115	154	308	223	258	86	1245

FIGURE 2: OVERSEAS ADOPTION 1993-1997 (Part 2)

7.24 Nationality consequences of adoption

Articles 7, 21

7.24.1   The present law on acquisition of British citizenship through adoption is contained in the British Nationality Act 1981. Under this Act, a child adopted in the United Kingdom by a British Citizen becomes such a citizen automatically from the date of the adoption provided at least one of the adopters is a British citizen at the time the adoption order is made. There is at present no similar provision for children adopted by British citizens outside the United Kingdom. Instead, the Home Secretary is normally prepared to use his discretionary power to register any minor as a British citizen where at least one of the adoptive parents is a British citizen otherwise than by descent and he is satisfied that the adoption was not arranged merely to facilitate the child's admission to this country. In the Government's view this practice enables the United Kingdom to meet its obligations under the 1967 European Convention on the Adoption of Children.

7.24.2   The possibility of providing for the automatic acquisition of citizenship by children adopted overseas was considered prior to the introduction of the 1981 Act. A number of potential problems were identified. Such acquisition might have caused some children to lose their original citizenship, either at once or on reaching adulthood. The arrangement might also have resulted in the widespread acquisition of British citizenship by people having no connection with the country beyond the adoptive parent-child relationship. The stated purpose of the 1981 Act, on the other hand, was to limit the acquisition of British citizenship to those with rather more substantial United Kingdom connections. Finally, it was feared that in some cases, inter-country adoptions might have been arranged with the sole aim of circumventing British immigration controls, perhaps by unscrupulous third parties for financial gain.

7.24.3   The advantage of the registration procedure is that the adoptive parents (and, where appropriate, the child) can be made aware of the possible consequences of acquiring British citizenship and so make an informed decision on whether or not to proceed. It also enables the Home Secretary to refuse citizenship where there are concerns about irregularities in the adoption process.

7.24.4   It is hoped that the 1993 Hague Convention on Inter-country Adoption, when fully implemented, will serve to eliminate some of the worst abuses of the inter-country adoption process. The United Kingdom intends to ratify the Convention in due course but, like other signatories, will first need to make some changes to its domestic law on adoption. An individual Member of Parliament has recently introduced a Bill on intercountry adoption which seeks to amend the British Nationality Act 1981 so that once the United Kingdom has ratified the Convention, children resident outside the United Kingdom who are the subject of 1993 Convention adoptions by British citizen parents who are resident in the United Kingdom would acquire British citizenship automatically. If the Bill is successful the United Kingdom will be able to ratify the Convention in the year 2000.

7.25 Consultation on possible changes in the determination of paternity and the parental responsibilities of unmarried fathers

Articles 9, 20, 27

7.25.1   The Government carried out a public consultation in the spring of 1998[56] to seek views on possible changes to the law on the determination of paternity through the courts and on the acquisition of parental responsibility by unmarried fathers.

7.25.2   **Paternity:** At present there are two separate procedures in England & Wales for obtaining a determination of paternity through the courts. The consultation addressed the feasibility of establishing a single procedure.

7.25.3   **Parental responsibility:** The Children Act 1989 introduced a new concept of "parental responsibility", defined as "all the rights, duties, powers, responsibilities and authority which by law a parent of a child has in relation to the child and his property". The Act confers parental responsibility automatically on all mothers, married or unmarried, and on married fathers. It also introduced a new procedure for an unmarried father to acquire parental responsibility by making an agreement with the mother, which must be properly witnessed and registered with the court. In cases where the parents are unable to reach agreement the father may apply to the court for a parental responsibility order.

7.25.4   The consultation discussed two main questions – whether it was right in principle to make it easier for unmarried fathers to acquire parental responsibility for their children, subject to any necessary safeguards, and whether automatic parental responsibility should be limited to certain categories of unmarried fathers, such as a father who registers the child's birth jointly with the mother.

7.25.5   Following consideration of the results of the consultation, the Government announced on 28 June 1998 that it had concluded that parental responsibility should be conferred on unmarried fathers who sign the birth register jointly with the mother. More than 70% of unmarried fathers already do that.

7.25.6   A separate consultation has been carried out in Scotland (see section 2.5.4 of this report). Any legislation there, will be a matter for the Scottish Parliament.

7.26 Recovery of maintenance for the child

Article 27

7.26.1   The Government believes that all children are entitled to the financial and emotional support of both their parents, wherever they live. The child support scheme, which applies in England, Wales and Scotland, aims to ensure that non-resident parents fulfil their financial responsibilities towards their children. Regular payments of child maintenance can transform the lives of lone mothers and their children, providing a stable income that

---

56 *Review of Procedures for the Determination of Paternity and of the Law on Parental Responsibility for Unmarried Fathers*; Consultation Paper issued by the Lord Chancellor's Department: March 1998.

can help lone mothers off Income Support and into work. An equivalent scheme operates in Northern Ireland.

7.26.2   The Child Support Agency assesses maintenance and either collects it or arranges for it to be paid direct from the non-resident parent to the parent with care. At May 1998, the Agency had a caseload of 786,000 and in 1997-98 it collected and arranged almost £550 million in maintenance.

7.26.3   The child support scheme has not yet gained the co-operation of all non-resident parents. In the quarter up to May 1998, only 35% of non-resident parents paid all their regular maintenance due. Support among parents with care has also declined recently: as many as 7 in every 10 who have made a claim for Income Support tried to avoid applying for child support. Steps are being taken to improve the compliance of parents, including using the telephone more actively and interviewing parents with care about child support when they claim benefit. In addition, an extra £15 million is being invested in the Child Support Agency this year and next, specifically aimed at increasing the amounts of maintenance which are paid.

7.26.4   Where a non-resident parent refuses to pay, the Child Support Agency may secure regular payments by serving a deduction from earnings order on his employer. If the non-resident parent is not working for an employer, or a deductions from earnings order is ineffective, an application can be made to the magistrates' court for a liability order. Such an order authorises the use of enforcement action to recover the debt (entering the liability order on the Register of County Court judgements which may affect the parent's credit rating, or sending bailiffs to seize goods to the value of the maintenance due).

7.26.5   A fundamental problem with the current scheme is the complex formula used to calculate maintenance liability. Up to 100 pieces of information may be required, leading to lengthy processing times, high error rates and providing every opportunity for the potentially unco-operative parent to frustrate the process. The Agency spends 90 per cent of its time assessing cases and keeping assessments up to date and only 10 per cent of its time enforcing payment.

7.26.6   In July 1998, the Government published a Green Paper *Children First: a new approach to child support*[57] setting out proposals for a new, local, customer-focused child support scheme based on a radically simpler method of assessment.

7.26.7   To ensure that women and their children on the lowest incomes see financial benefit from co-operating with the Child Support Agency a Child Maintenance Premium is proposed. Parents with care on Income

---

57 Cm 3992, 6 July 1998, published by the Stationery Office.

Support would be allowed to keep up to £10 per week of the maintenance paid for their children.

7.26.8 The proposed child maintenance service will have a simple transparent formula, enabling parents to know before they apply for an assessment roughly how much child maintenance to expect. For those fathers who earn £200 a week or more, liability will be based on a simple percentage of net income: 15 per cent for one child; 20 per cent for two children; and 25 per cent for three or more children. There will be a flat rate of £5 for those fathers with incomes of less than £100 a week and a sliding scale for those with incomes between £100 and £200. There will also be an allowance for any children in the non-resident parent's new family.

7.26.9 The new scheme will improve the situation for lone mothers – maintenance should be assessed quickly and accurately, providing a vital bridge from dependency on benefit to the world of work. The scheme will also work better with other support for families such as mediation. It will support continuing contact for non-resident parents and make improved provision for parents who have shared care of their children.

7.26.10 The consultation period on the Green Paper ended on 30 November 1998. Extensive consultation has been undertaken, and over 1500 responses to the Green Paper received. MPs, academics and NGOs have been invited to meet the Minister and officials. The results of this exercise have not yet been fully analysed, but will be published in due course. Legislative and operational constraints mean that the new scheme cannot be introduced immediately. However, a number of improvements are already under way or planned within the Child Support Agency to pave the way for radical reform, including:

    a extended working hours;

    b a simpler and more efficient process for making and appealing decisions;

    c reorganisation to centralise processing work and free local staff to concentrate on providing advice face to face for those clients who require this service.

7.26.11 An extra £12 million has been allocated to the Child Support Agency in 1998-99 for a number of customer-focused initiatives including improvements to the telephone service and more user-friendly forms and letters.

7.27 Hague Convention on the Civil Aspects of International Child Abduction

Article 11

7.27.1 The 1980 Hague Child Abduction Convention provides procedures for the return of wrongfully removed or wrongfully retained children to their country of habitual residence.

7.27.2 The Hague Conference organises a rolling programme of reviews of the various Hague Conventions in which all contracting states participate. The most recent Special Commission to review the 1980 Convention took place in March 1997. The United Kingdom proposed, and the review meeting accepted, that contracting states had a responsibility to ensure the safety of children returned to their country of habitual residence. The Hague Conference is considering how to take this forward.

7.28 European Convention on Family Matters (Brussels II)

Article 11

7.28.1   A Convention on Jurisdiction and Recognition and Enforcement in certain Family Matters[58] was signed by Ministers of the European Union in May 1998. The Convention will ensure that orders in Member States in divorce and similar cases, including orders affecting children made at the time of the divorce, will generally be recognised throughout the European Union with the minimum of procedural requirements.

7.28.2   The Convention has three main elements:

a It lays down the circumstances in which courts in Member States are to have competence to hear proceedings for divorce, nullity and judicial separation, and proceedings for parental responsibility orders made in the context of matrimonial proceedings.

b It lays down rules to regulate the situation where there are concurrent matrimonial proceedings in courts of different Member States involving the same parties, but not necessarily the same type of case, for example where there are divorce proceedings in one country and, at the same time, nullity proceedings in another.

c There is provision for the recognition and enforcement throughout the European Union of matrimonial decrees and orders made under the Convention. This includes limited grounds for refusal of recognition and enforcement in appropriate cases.

7.28.3   This Convention has been drafted with the intention that its provisions should not interfere with the operation of the 1980 Hague Convention on International Child Abduction.

7.29 The 1996 Hague Convention

Article 3, 5, 11, 18, 20

7.29.1   The United Kingdom participated in the negotiations leading up to the 1996 Hague Convention on the Protection of Children[59]. The Government expects to consult on whether to ratify the Convention. Issues to be addressed include the grounds of jurisdiction applicable to orders relating to children, provision for the transfer abroad of such jurisdiction and grounds of recognition and enforcement of such orders. This Convention has been drafted with the intention that its provisions should not interfere with the operation of the 1980 Hague Convention on International Child Abduction.

---

58 Official Journal C221, 16 July 1998.

59 The Hague Convention of 19 October 1996 on Jurisdiction, Applicable Law, Recognition and Enforcement and Co-operation in Respect of Parental Responsibility and Measures for the Protection of Children.

7.30 International enforcement of maintenance orders

Article 27

7.30.1   The United Kingdom has agreements with a number of countries for the reciprocal enforcement of maintenance orders. Some of these agreements have been negotiated with individual countries and others arise from international conventions on maintenance which the United Kingdom has signed and ratified. These arrangements are designed to assist a parent in one country to recover maintenance, on behalf of themselves or a child, from the absent parent residing in the other.

7.30.2   The Hague Conference on private international law arranged a Special Commission to consider the conventions on Maintenance Obligations, which met in April 1999. The meeting examined problems and decided to seek solutions in this area. The United Kingdom will participate fully in this work.

7.31 Reservation relating to immigration and nationality

7.31.1   The Committee raised the concern that the reservation relating to the application of the Immigration and Nationality Act might not be compatible with the principles and provisions of the Convention, including those of its articles 2, 3, 9 and 10. The Committee asked the United Kingdom to review the reservation with a view to withdrawing it and has suggested that a review be undertaken of nationality and immigration laws and procedures to ensure their conformity with the principles and provisions of the Convention.

7.31.2   The Government believes that the United Kingdom's immigration and nationality law is entirely consistent with the Convention. In fact the United Kingdom makes generous provision both for the admission of foreign children to join parents settled here, and for the acquisition of citizenship. In the years 1986-1996, 98,000 children were granted settlement and 103,587 were registered as British Citizens.

7.31.3   It should be borne in mind that the chairman of the working group which drafted the Convention explicitly stated that Article 9 on the separation of children from their parents was intended to apply to domestic law, and not to international situations; and that Article 10's family reunion provisions were not intended to affect the general right of states to establish and regulate their immigration laws in accordance with their international, obligations. In other words, the Convention is not intended to establish any new rights in relation to immigration.

7.31.4   Notwithstanding this, to avoid argument about the extent to which the fine detail of immigration and nationality law is or is not in keeping with the letter or spirit of the statements, necessarily generalised, about children's rights contained in the Convention, the United Kingdom entered a reservation which made it clear, for the avoidance of doubt, that nothing in the Convention was to be interpreted as affecting the operation of United Kingdom immigration and nationality legislation.

7.31.5   The United Kingdom has made similar reservations, for the same reason, to several other human rights conventions, including the International Covenant on Civil and Political Rights.

8 | BASIC HEALTH AND WELFARE

This chapter covers articles: –

6 *Right to life*

18 *Responsibilities of parents and guardians*

23 *Rights of disabled children*

24 *Right to health care*

26 *Right to social security and insurance*

27 *Right to standard of living and parental responsibility for maintenance*

8.1 General policy on child health

Article 24

8.1.1   Health is a constant theme of Government policy, which is concerned with taking determined action to deal with the social and economic influences which undermine health: —

- The Welfare to Work budget has set in hand a New Deal to fight joblessness;
- The worst excesses of low pay will be tackled through a national minimum wage;
- Social exclusion will be the subject of a long-term, determined and co-ordinated Government effort;
- Repairs and new building will provide decent housing, paid for by the phased release of councils' accumulated proceeds from the sale of council houses;
- An integrated transport and environment policy will ensure better public transport and a healthier environment for all;
- Tough measures on crime will help ensure that families and communities have the chance of healthier lives; and
- Education reforms, such as nursery education, smaller classes and higher standards, will give families the means to better themselves and so improve their health.

8.1.2   The Government intends to take action to ensure that all those responsible for the provision of health and social services pay particular attention to those at greatest risk and those who have the most difficulty in having access to health and social care. There are three levels for action to deliver the agenda for better health: central Government; regions and communities; and individuals. Central Government cannot do everything, but it can set the agenda and priorities for local and community action.

8.2 The Parliamentary Select Committee on Health: Reports on Health Services for Children and Young People

Article 23, 24

8.2.1   Since the United Kingdom's First Report the all-party Parliamentary Health Select Committee has conducted a wide ranging inquiry into all aspects of children's health service provision. The Committee published its terms of reference and an appeal for evidence in summer 1995 — in order to give all those organisations working in the field of child health ample opportunity to prepare and submit evidence. The Committee received over 500 submissions from some 400 organisations and individuals. There followed a series of oral hearings, starting in February 1996 and continuing into January 1997 at which the views of professional and voluntary organisations with an interest in child health issues were fully represented. Government Ministers were interviewed, as were the Chief Medical Officer, Chief Nursing Officer and a number of health officials, all working in the administration of health services for children. The Committee appointed a team of specialist advisers in paediatric nursing, paediatric medicine and child mental health to supply information otherwise not readily available, and to elucidate matters of complexity. The Committee also made a series of visits to a number of centres of child health service provision.

8.2.2   The Committee published its findings in four reports[60], from February 1997 to March 1997, just prior to the Dissolution of Parliament, election and appointment of a new Government. The Committee decided to express its views by highlighting such concerns as it felt necessary and making appropriate recommendations to the incoming Government. A Command Paper setting out the new Government's response to the Health Committee's inquiry into health services for children and young people was published in November 1997[61]. The Government chose to make a single response because of the common themes running through the Committee's four reports.

8.2.3   In their reports, the Committee looked at the health needs of children and adolescents and the extent to which those needs are met by the National Health Service and other agencies. Their reports considered the health needs of healthy children as well as those of acutely ill children,

---

60 *"The Specific Health Needs of Children and Young People"; "Health Services for Children and Young People in the Community, Home and School"; "Hospital Services for Children and Young People" and "Child and Adolescent Mental Health Services".*

61 *Government Response to the Reports of the Health Committee on Health Services for Children and Young People, Session 1996-97: "The Specific Health Needs of Children and Young People" (307-1); "Health Services for Children and Young People in the Community, Home and School" (314-1); "Hospital Services for Children and Young People" (128-1); "Child and Adolescent Mental Health Services" (26-1). Cm 3793, Dd 5067751. Published November 1997 by The Stationery Office.*

children with chronic illnesses or disability, children with a life threatening or terminal condition and child and adolescent mental health services. The Government welcomed the reports, as they make a substantial contribution to the debate about children's health. The Government appreciated the Committee's view that, while the overall state of children's health is encouraging with a steady fall in childhood mortality rates and significant improvements in both incidence and severity of childhood diseases, there is scope for further progress.

8.2.4   The Government particularly welcomed the Committee's endorsement of the principles set out in the existing guidance documents on children's health services – *The Welfare of Children and Young People in Hospital*[62], *Child Health in the Community – A Guide to Good Practice*[63] and *A Handbook on Child and Adolescent Mental Health*[64]. These will continue to be important guidelines for the service. In Scotland *At Home in Hospital – A Guide to Care of Children and Young People* and *Caring for Sick Children* provide similar guidance on the provision of care and treatment of children in hospital[65].

8.2.5   The Government agreed with the Committee that the health needs of children are significantly different from those of adults, that some children may be vulnerable, and that the provision of effective health services for children depends upon a thorough understanding of their special needs. The future strategy for children's services in the National Health Service will be founded on this important understanding and based on the following basic principles which lie at the heart of the Government's health policy: –

promoting fairness
- with a public health policy which will reduce the inequalities in health status of the population by tackling the fundamental causes of ill health;
- by reducing variations in access to and use of services;
- by working together across government, in the public and private sectors, to ensure the importance of children's needs is recognised.

---

62 *Welfare of Children and Young People in Hospital*, Department of Health, ISBN 0 11 321358 1, 1991, HMSO.

63 *Child Health in the Community*: A Guide to Good Practice, NHS Executive, H86/009 0703, 1996, Department of Health.

64 *A handbook on Child and Adolescent Mental Health Services*, Department of Health Social Services Inspectorate, Department for Education, G61/008 2942, 1995, published by the Department of Health.

65 *At Home in Hospital - A Guide to Care of Children and Young People*, The Scottish Office Home and Health Department, 1993 Published by The Stationery Office; and *Caring for Sick Children: A Study of Hospital Services in Scotland*, Scottish Office Audit Unit 1994.

improving the quality of services, especially
- the effectiveness of treatment, in terms of outcome for the patient;
- the skill, care and continuity with which the service is delivered;
- the accessibility of the service in terms of distance, time, physical access, language and understanding
- the delivery of the service, covering the physical environment of care, and ensuring the service is managed and delivered in an efficient and courteous manner.

promoting partnership and co-operation, between all agencies within health, social services and education to deliver a seamless service.

8.3 Child health – views of NGOs

8.3.1   NGOs commented on the existence of evidence for improvements in the status of children's health, as reflected in the independent Health Select Committee's investigation and subsequent series of reports.

8.3.2   The evidence base for the Health Select Committee's view of improvement is significant and covers a range of morbidity. Cystic fibrosis and cancer treatments offer examples of this, with a substantial improvement in life expectancy over the last 30 years following the introduction of new intensive treatments for cystic fibrosis. Mortality rates for childhood cancer halved between 1970 and 1985. However the Government recognises a number of areas for development, modernisation and improvement. As an example, although rates of infant mortality have fallen significantly, as indicated in the table below, it is recognised that further work needs to be done to reduce rates further.

8.3.3   Infant mortality (death under 1 year) rates have continued to fall since the UK's First report to the UN, the lowest rate ever recorded for England and Wales is now (1998) at 5.7 deaths per 1,000 live births. One contributory aspect to infant mortality is the incidence of Sudden Infant Death – a condition where babies predominantly under the age of one year die without there being apparent cause. The incidence of such deaths has decreased by 60% since 1991, when the Chief Medical Officer's expert advisory group produced guidance on avoiding risk factors associated with the occurrence of cot death. This work and the publicity campaign *"Back to Sleep"* and *"Reduce the Risk of Cot Death"* to advise new parents on the avoidance of cot death continues in liaison with the voluntary sector, and in particular with the organisation the Foundation for the Study of Infant Deaths. The Government also continues to fund the work of the Confidential Enquiry into Stillbirths and Deaths in Infancy (CESDI) which produces an annual report on matters of significance to the health care of children under one year of age.

Infant Mortality Rates, All deaths at ages under one year England and Wales (rates per 1,000 live births)	
Year	Rate
1946	42.9
1951	29.7
1956	23.7
1961	21.4
1966	19.0
1971	17.5
1976	14.3
1981	11.1
1986	9.6
1991	7.4
1996	6.1
1997	6.0

FIGURE 3: INFANT MORTALITY

8.4 'Our Healthier Nation'

8.4.1   The Government published a consultation document, *Our Healthier Nation*[66], in February 1998, with a general consultation period which ran to 30 April 1998. The Green Paper discharges commitments to tackle the root causes of ill health – poverty, unemployment, poor housing and polluted environment. There are two key aims:

a to improve the health of the population as a whole and

b to improve the health of the worst off.

8.4.2   The strategy covers the entire population including the health of children, and includes three key settings: schools, workplaces and neighbourhoods, with a focus on joint working at and across all levels. The Paper covers the contribution of a decent education to the capacity to make healthier choices and the link between poor educational achievement and unwanted pregnancy in the early teenage years. It goes on to identify healthy schools as one of three settings offering the opportunity to focus the drive against health inequalities and improve health overall.

8.4.3   The Green Paper consultation process drew over 5,500 responses, of which more than 90% were supportive of the Green Paper proposals. Analysis of the responses will be a key strand in the development of a definitive White Paper, to be published shortly – which will also include the findings of Sir Donald Acheson's Independent Inquiry into Inequalities in Health, the Chief Medical Officer's Project to review the public health function, and an interim review of the Health of the Nation initiative.

66 *Our Healthier Nation*: A Contract for Health, Cm 3852, Dd 5067877 2/98, 1998, The Stationery Office.

8.4.4   One of the Government's 18 interdepartmental neighbourhood renewal Policy Action Teams, set up from September 1998, has highlighted the contribution participation in arts and sport can make to improving physical and mental health. The Government has welcomed the report and intends to implement many of its recommendations.

8.5   Health care in Scotland

Article 24

8.5.1   Similarly, in Scotland the Government's policy is to ensure that all children and their families have equality and ease of access to an appropriate, seamless, comprehensive and co-ordinated service, which is integrated with services provided by the local authority, such as education, social work services, housing and the environment.

8.5.2   The Chief Medical Officer in Scotland undertook a comprehensive review of the role of acute hospital services in the network of clinical services in Scotland in 1997-98. The review paid particular attention to the needs of children, according special recognition to the services for them in the NHS in Scotland. A sub-group of the review considered the treatment services for children, assessing future needs for paediatric nursing, paramedical staff, paediatric surgery, neonatal care, networking, community child health and general paediatrics.

8.5.3   The review recognised the need to deliver a combined service of care separate from adults across a continuum of primary, secondary and tertiary care with appropriate links to maternity and adolescent-adult services. Services should be "child-centred" with provision of in-patient facilities that are separate from those of adults, adolescents having the freedom to choose between child and adult in-patient facilities should special provision for them not be available.

8.5.4   The review endorsed the importance of the continuing development of a integrated service for children in which the work of the NHS in Scotland is integrated with that of Local Authorities, Education and Social Work Services and in the case of non-accidental injury and child abuse, with police forces.

8.5.5   The review suggested retaining local access to services but recognised that certain high technology services will have to be concentrated in order to be sustainable and of high quality. The review also endorsed the recommendation that Health Boards should have a designated commissioner of services for children.

8.5.6   The Department of Health will be taking forward the work of the review.

8.6 Towards a Healthier Scotland

Article 24

8.6.1 A White Paper *Towards a Healthier Scotland*[67] was published in February 1999. It sets out a new strategy for improving public health through a 3 level approach based on tackling life circumstances, lifestyles and priority health topics. The Paper has the overarching aim of reducing health inequalities. Partnership working between agencies – including the NHS, local authorities, private and voluntary organisations and local communities – is central to the strategy.

8.6.2 Ministers are still considering the White Paper but they have accepted the key principles of the strategy.

8.6.3 The White Paper is concerned with the health of the population as a whole but places particular emphasis on the health of children and young people. Child health is included in the list of priority health topics. A child health resource pack will be produced to assist agencies to plan and implement co-ordinated programmes to support children and their families in fulfilling their potential.

8.6.4 One of the key initiatives in the White Paper is the establishment of 4 demonstration projects which will point the way towards integrated working between agencies and encourage the dissemination of best practice. Two of the demonstration projects will concentrate on children. "Starting Well" will focus on the promotion of health and protection from harm in the period leading up to birth and throughout the first 5 years of life. "Healthy Respect" will foster responsible sexual behaviour on the part of Scotland's young people with emphasis on the avoidance of unwanted teenage pregnancies and sexually transmitted disease.

8.6.5 In addition to the "Healthy Respect" project, funding will be provided for expertise to be made available to many more schools in Scotland in order to promote a more informed and responsible approach to sexual matters on the part of young people.

8.6.6 On diet, the framework of *Eating for Health: A Diet Action Plan for Scotland*[68] is endorsed. The Plan recognises the need to influence diet from a very young age. The White Paper also announces that a national dietary co-ordinator will be appointed to give impetus to implementation of the Plan; breastfeeding will be one of the areas on which the co-ordinator will focus.

8.6.7 Headline targets included in the Paper, as a focus for action, cover a range of topics. Those targets relating to children and young people include smoking, teenage pregnancy and dental health. Relevant second rank targets relate to diet, alcohol misuse and physical activity.

---

67 Cm 4269, The Stationery Office, Edinburgh, ISBN 0-10-142692-5.

68 Published by Her Majesty's Stationery Office, 1996, ISBN 0-7480-3138-3

8.6.8   The Oral Health Strategy for Scotland was published in December 1995. This strategy identified that everyone should have the opportunity of a healthy functional mouth throughout life; by adoption of a healthy diet, by sensible use of preventative measures and by access to dental treatment for oral healthcare when required. It added a new target for children that by the year 2005 children aged 12 are to have an average of no more than 1.5 permanent teeth decayed, missing or filled. The strategy emphasised the need for a multi-disciplinary collaboration at national and local level with Health Boards, the dental profession, the medical and allied professions, local authorities, schools, nursery schools, playgroups, the media, employers, manufacturers and retailers, all being identified as having an important contribution to make to the improvement of oral health. It identified areas of action to achieve national targets – diet, health promotion, fluoridation, the role of the individual and clinical prevention of dental decay. This supports other strategies identified in Scotland including *The Scottish Diet*[69].

8.7 Northern Ireland's agenda for health and wellbeing

8.7.1   Northern Ireland's regional strategy for health and social wellbeing 1997 - 2002 *Health and Wellbeing into the Next Millennium*[70] identifies family and child health and welfare as a key area for action, and sets the following targets:-

a by 2002 there should be a 10% reduction in stillbirths and deaths in children under one year old;

b by 2002, of the children assessed by Health and Social Services Boards as being in need, those below compulsory school age should receive good quality early years services within their homes or elsewhere, or a combination of both; and those of school age should receive family support services operating out of school hours;

c by 2002 there should be a reduction of at least 25% in the total number of acute hospital bed days occupied per annum by children aged 0-15 years;

d by 2002 there should be a 50% reduction in the number of children abused or re-abused who are on child protection registers.

8.7.2   In December 1997 the Department of Health and Social Services for Northern Ireland launched *Well Into 2000: a positive Agenda for Health and Wellbeing*[71] which sets out the Government's approach to tackling health and social problems in Northern Ireland.

---

69 *The Scottish Diet*, HMSO, 1993, ISBN 0 7480 0797 0.

70 *Health and Wellbeing: Into the Next Millennium*; Regional Strategy for Health and Social Wellbeing 1997-2002, published in 1996 by the Department of Health and Social Services for Northern Ireland.

71 *Well into 2000; a Positive Agenda for Health and Wellbeing*, published in 1997 by the Department of Health and Social Services for Northern Ireland.

8.7.3   *Well Into 2000* recognises the Government's commitment to economic, health and social policies which promote good health and wellbeing for all on an equitable basis. Its vision is the development of high quality cost-effective care with respect for the rights of the individual, and with strong local communities participating in decisions about needs and services.

8.8   'Better Health; Better Wales'

Article 24

8.8.1   In May 1998, the Welsh Office launched the Public Health Green Paper *Better Health; Better Wales*[72], which advocates a new approach to improving the health and well-being of the people in Wales by addressing a wide range of social, economic and environmental factors which impact on health.

8.8.2   *Better Health; Better Wales* proposed a new approach to tackling the underlying causes of ill-health which focuses on the concept of sustainable health and well-being – through the encouragement of sustainable communities, a healthy lifestyle and better environment. The aim of the new strategy is to prevent disease and improve the health and well-being of the people in Wales and bring the level of those with the poorest health up to the level of those with the best health.

8.8.3   The Green Paper sought views on a wide range of issues including those relating to lifestyle, schools, housing, environment, transport and organisational structures. It sought to identify how public policy should be developed to protect children and families and how all sectors of the community could develop caring roles. It also raised questions of how education and training can best be used to inform people about health and how a new partnership approach can benefit the health of children in schools.

8.8.4   The consultation exercise is now complete and the responses will provide the basis for an Action Plan . The ensuing strategy is intended to be taken forward by the National Assembly for Wales in 1999.

8.9   Health of Children in Wales

Article 24

8.9.1   The Welsh Office *Report on The Health of Children in Wales*[73] was commended to health and local authorities in Wales in January 1997. It provides a clear policy statement for children's health services, identifying the statutory and policy requirements, and includes good practice guidance for Health Authorities, Local Education Authorities, Social Services Departments and the Voluntary Sector. Implementation of the report's recommendations is being taken forward by these organisations at the local level in the context of local need.

---

72 *Better Health; Better Wales* : A Consultation Paper. Cm3922. Published by The Stationery Office: ISBN 0 10 139222 2.

73 DGM(97)06 sent to Chief Executives of: Health Authorities; NHS Trusts; and Local Authorities in Wales, January 1997. Published by Welsh Office Health Department, Cathays Park, Cardiff CF1 3NQ.

8.10 Health in Schools in Wales

Article 24

8.10.1   Health in Schools in Wales will be a key component of the strategic framework taking forward the *Better Health; Better Wales* Green Paper proposals. This includes the concept of the 'health promoting school', in which the whole life of the school has a role to play in promoting the health of young people. In Wales this is taken forward by Health Promotion Wales (HPW). Six primary schools and six secondary schools in Wales took part in the European Network of Health Promoting Schools (ENHPS) project, which is managed by HPW. A major aim of the ENHPS project is to ensure that good classroom teaching is matched by efforts to improve the school environment. Among the initiatives undertaken are health promoting playgrounds, links with local sports centres, healthy tuckshops, drugs education, safety initiatives and No Smoking Day activities.

8.11 The National Healthy Schools Award – 'Investors in Health'

Articles 18, 23, 24

8.11.1   Health in schools will be a key component of the strategy of *Our Healthier Nation*. The strategy will aim to build on the concept of the healthy school to promote not just excellence in educational achievement, but to foster emotional wellbeing and enable young people to improve their quality of life and that of the wider community. This does not just mean young people spending more curriculum time on personal, social and health education as a formal subject. The ethos of all school activities should encourage awareness of relationships, responsibility for self and leading on from that responsibility to others.

8.11.2   The first step in development of a National Healthy Schools Award was an expert consultative seminar in February 1998. A key element of the Healthy Schools Award is joint working between Health Authorities and Local Education Authorities. In phase one of the Award, schemes were piloted in each of the eight NHS regions in England. One LEA in each region worked in partnership with its corresponding Health Authority to set up a pilot project which developed models and criteria which can be used by new Health and education partnerships and pump priming support of £150,000 for each project was made available jointly by the Department for Education and Employment and the Department of Health in 1998-99. Each of the pilot partnerships was independently evaluated by the Thomas Coram Research Unit at the Institute of Education. Government will look to expand involvement in the future so that, ultimately, all schools will have the chance to participate. The National Healthy Schools Scheme will provide an opportunity and support to all schools to encourage them to work towards becoming healthy schools through the criteria and standards emerging from the pilot projects.

8.11.3   The elements of the Healthy Schools initiative are:

 a a National Healthy Schools Award and Associated Fund;

 b a Healthy Teacher Focus;

 c a National Healthy Schools Network within the National Young People's Network;

d the Wired for Health Website to be accessed through the National Grid for Learning ;

e the development of Strategies for Safe Travel to School;

f the development of a "cooks academy" in schools during school holiday periods.

8.11.4   The "healthy school" or "health promoting school" concept has already been adopted by many schools nationwide, often backed by local initiatives set up between health promotion departments and local education authorities and/or schools. Such schools recognise their role in shaping positive attitudes to health amongst staff, pupils and parents, for example through attention to the effects of environment on mental and physical wellbeing and the benefits of positive role models from staff. Schools undertake formal personal, social and health education but development of positive health and welfare goes much deeper than that in the "healthy school".

8.11.5   Healthy Schools will not be the only focus of Government strategy. There are many young people beyond school age or who are not currently within the school system who need help and support. Government funding of the Young People's Health Network has helped to encourage co-operation and the sharing of experience between those agencies who deal with the various problems young people face and encourage the involvement of the young people themselves. The Government will work with young people to promote the understanding that good health, including mental health is central to the enjoyment of life. The aim is to provide practical support to enable them to adopt healthy behaviours that will benefit them through their life and be passed on to their children.

8.12 Child nutrition

Article 24

8.12.1   The Government commissioned a National Diet and Nutrition Survey (NDNS) covering children between the ages of 4 -18. The report of the survey will be published during 1999. It will provide information on the diets of approximately 2000 young people between the ages of 4 to 18 years. Findings of other recent surveys and studies, although not as comprehensive in coverage as the NDNS, give an indication of the trends in the nutritional status of children aged between 4 and 18 years. These generally indicate that although children are growing taller on average than ever before, they are also getting fatter.

8.12.2   The Government's new public health strategy *Our Healthier Nation* has identified schools as a setting to focus attention on improving the health of children. The Healthy Schools Initiative aims to improve the health and well-being of children and as part of this it will encourage healthy eating through a whole school approach to food. Also, the Government intend to produce Regulations on compulsory national nutritional standards to school lunches and a consultation paper setting out proposals was published at the end of 1998.

8.13 Infant feeding – England and Wales

8.13.1   The Government has mounted a continuing publicity campaign to increase awareness of the importance of taking folic acid before and during the first twelve weeks of pregnancy to prevent neural tube defects in babies. The latest results show that spontaneous awareness amongst women has risen from 9% in 1995 to 49% in 1998 and prompted awareness from 51% to 89% over the same period.

8.13.2   The Government promotes breastfeeding in the following ways. The National Network of Breastfeeding Co-ordinators (NNBC) has been established to promote breastfeeding at a local level and to share ideas nationally with a view to increasing both the number of mothers breastfeeding and the length of time they continue to breastfeed. Each year the four United Kingdom Health Departments support National Breastfeeding Awareness Week to increase public awareness of the benefits of breastfeeding. The Government has also appointed two part-time Infant Feeding Advisers to act as a focus for developing and implementing strategies for promoting breastfeeding. In particular, to increase the incidence of breastfeeding amongst groups where breastfeeding rates are lowest. This is where their expertise lies.

8.13.3   The Department provides financial support to the four main voluntary organisations in this area, the National Childbirth Trust, La Leche League, the Breastfeeding Network, and the Association of Breastfeeding Mothers. Close links are also kept with UNICEF's Baby Friendly Initiative which includes a Departmental observer sitting on the Steering Committee of the UK BFI. The Department offers support for research into breastfeeding through the Quinquennial Surveys of Infant Feeding Practice – the report of the 1995 survey was published in 1997. This showed that the incidence of breastfeeding had increased significantly between 1990 and 1995 in all countries in the United Kingdom. The Department also receives and publishes expert advice on breastfeeding through its advisory committees, such as COMA's[74] Panel on Child and Maternal Nutrition.

8.13.4   The Government is committed to the promotion and protection of breastfeeding which is universally accepted as the best form of nutrition for infants. The Infant Formula and Follow-on Formula Regulations came into force in March 1995. These regulations implement EC Directive 91/321/EEC, which embraces the principles of the WHO Code of Marketing of Breast-milk Substitutes 1981. The regulations place statutory restrictions on the composition, labelling, advertising and export of infant formulae.

8.13.5   School lunches and, in some areas, drinking milk are provided free to children from families in receipt of income support or an income based jobseeker's allowance. The Welfare Foods Scheme also provides free milk

---

74 COMA: the Committee on Medical Aspects of Food and Nutrition Policy.

and vitamins to pregnant and breastfeeding mothers and their children up until the age of five who are from families in receipt of income support or an income based jobseekers allowance. The Government provides these benefits as a nutritional safety net for children in low income families.

8.14 Breastfeeding – Scotland

8.14.1 In 1994, a national target was set for breastfeeding in Scotland (50% of mothers still breastfeeding at 6 weeks by 2005). Health Boards were invited to set local targets and to put in place arrangements to monitor these. Most Boards have now set targets and Scotland's Chief Medical and Chief Nursing Officers have taken steps to encourage professional support for breastfeeding and to improve professional practice. The recent Priorities and Planning Guidance for the NHS in Scotland 1999-2002 reiterated the importance of continuing work towards the national target.

8.14.2 In order to advise on and monitor work in this area, the Scottish Office Department of Health set up, in 1995, the Scottish Breastfeeding Group and appointed a National Breastfeeding Adviser. The Group, which is chaired by the Department's Chief Nursing Officer, is a multi-disciplinary body representing a range of professional and lay organisations with an interest in breastfeeding issues. The National Breastfeeding Adviser's remit is to provide training, advice and support to NHS personnel and lay workers, to act as a facilitator to local breastfeeding initiatives, and to report progress to the Scottish Breastfeeding Group. A dedicated website "Breastfeeding in Scotland", which includes information on research, statistics, good practice, and other resources, has recently been set up[75].

8.14.3 The recent White Paper *Towards a Healthier Scotland*[76] identified the health of children as a key area for action. It recognised that breastfeeding and good care in early life can significantly improve a child's chances in life; and it set out proposals for a health demonstration project to focus on the promotion of health from birth and throughout the first 5 years of childhood. One of the potential aims of this project will be to encourage good nutrition through breastfeeding.

8.14.4 In recent years, breastfeeding has been more closely integrated with mainstream health education campaigns. Integrating breastfeeding in this way helps to establish it as a normal, everyday occurrence and works to encourage a positive shift in attitudes and behaviour towards it.

8.15 Health inequalities – England and Wales

Article 23, 27

8.15.1 *Our Healthier Nation* emphasises that the Government's priority is to do more to prevent people falling ill in the first place and to ensure early intervention as required. This means tackling the root causes of the avoidable illnesses. In recent times the emphasis has been on trying to get people to live healthy lives, where necessary by changing their lifestyles. The emphasis now

---

75 This site is at www.show.scot.nhs.uk/bf/
76 Cm 4269, The Stationery Office, Edinburgh, ISBN 0-10-142692-5.

is to look for more attention and action concentrated on the things which damage people's health which are beyond the control of the individual.

8.15.2 Ill health is both a cause and effect of social exclusion: the very worst off in society, facing unemployment, lack of training opportunities and poor housing are much more likely to fall ill, and in turn illness reduces the chances of being able to get a job or go back to college. This circle of deprivation can create serious difficulties for children's health and development. Government policy will therefore be directed to tackling the root causes. As a first and important step the main causes of inequalities in health were addressed by an Independent Inquiry into Inequalities in Health, set up under Sir Donald Acheson (former Chief Medical Officer), which considered issues of social and economic deprivation and social exclusion. The Government asked Sir Donald to report on the main trends in health inequalities and to identify the areas of policy which evidence suggests are most likely to make a difference. Sir Donald's report was published on 26 November 1998 and its findings are being fed into work on the *Our Healthier Nation* White Paper which is due to be published shortly.

8.15.3 In Scotland, health inequalities are being tackled through the White Paper *Towards a Healthier Scotland*, which is described in more detail in section 8.6.

8.16 Young People's Health Network (YPHN)

Article 24, 27

8.16.1 The Network is being co-ordinated by the Health Education Authority (HEA) and funded by the Department of Health. The HEA won the contract to run the Network after an open tender exercise. The initial contract is for three years (1996-97, 1997-98 and 1998-99) and funding of up to £200,000 per year is available. It is planned that the YPHN will incorporate a schools network as part of the Healthy Schools initiative. Details of this will be settled in the future.

8.16.2 The Network was launched in June 1996. Its aim is to keep those interested in young people's health issues in touch with one another and, through facilitating the exchange of experience and ideas, promote the health of young people. The network project is overseen by a steering group comprising officials from the Department of Health and the Department for Education and Employment. There is also an advisory group whose membership will include some of the main voluntary organisations active in the youth field such as the British Youth Council and Youth Clubs United Kingdom. Also included on the advisory group are Young Minds. Feedback is positive and the HEA have sent out over 19,000 communiques.

8.17 The Patient's Charter – Health Services for Children and Young People

Article 24

8.17.1 To emphasise the importance which the United Kingdom Government gives to the child's right to health, a booklet was issued in March 1996 supported by implementation guidance to the NHS which amplified and strengthened the rights and standards set out in the Patient's Charter so far as they apply to children and young people. In particular the booklet offers:

In the community

- a child's right to be registered with a doctor;
- a programme of health checks to ensure healthy development;
- provision to care for a sick child at home wherever possible, and support for doing so;

In hospital

- the choice for adolescents of being admitted to a children's ward or an adult ward.;
- the aim that each child should have a named paediatric nurse to be responsible for the child's nursing care;
- the aim that each child should be under the care of a consultant paediatrician or paediatric specialist;
- opportunities for children to see the ward before admission;
- provision of play and educational facilities.

8.17.2   In accordance with the Government's commitment to "a new Patient's Charter concentrating on the quality and success of treatment", a group of advisers will make recommendations to Ministers about the content and format of a new NHS Charter.

8.17.3   The implementation of the Patient's Charter in Scotland was reviewed in 1997. Consultation on a revised Charter for Scotland will be similar to the action being taken in England.

8.17.4   In Scotland the Priorities and Planning Guidance published on 25 September 1998 will require Health Boards and NHS Trusts to give special attention to children's needs and to plan services for children in the context of the five strategic aims – improving health, reducing inequalities, promoting primary care, promoting community care and reshaping hospital services.

8.18 Measures to prevent HIV/AIDS and other sexually transmitted infections (STIs)

Article 24

8.18.1   The UK is a relatively low prevalence country for HIV and other STIs. By the end of March 1999, 37,875 HIV diagnoses and 16,201 AIDS cases had been reported but most were acquired through sex between men. Mother to child transmission is the major infection route for children and accounts for about 85% of paediatric AIDS cases. A total of 232 children aged under 16 years were treated for HIV infection in 1997, 43% were less than 5 years and 46% were between 6 and 8 years. Reported STIs are increasing and data for England and Wales show that the biggest increases have been amongst teenagers and young people. Amongst 16-19 year olds, cases of chlamydia rose by 53% between 1995 and 1997, cases of gonorrhoea by 45% and cases of genital warts by 24%. The reasons for this increase are not clear but the sexual health strategy will consider how to reverse this trend.

8.18.2   New diagnoses of selected conditions by sex, and number of teenage infections for England in 1997 are shown below.

	Infectious syphilis	Uncomplicated gonorrhoea	Uncomplicated chlamydia	Herpes simple first attack	Genital warts first attack
Males	97	8358	16093	5565	30041
Females	49	3945	22528	9444	28342
Total	146	12303	38621	15009	58383
Males <16	2	47	49	10	96
Female <16	-	140	501	104	438
Male 16-19	1	1024	1772	252	2356
Female 16-19	3	1411	7221	1729	7825

Figure 4 Teenage Infections for England 1997

8.18.3 Nationally funded HIV/AIDS health promotion for the general population in the UK is focussed mainly on 16-24 year olds and includes information on prevention of other STIs. Work undertaken by the Health Education Authority included the launch in 1999 of a safer sex Website, work with the National Union of Students and with young people's magazines and national and local radio. Messages have included the role of condoms in preventing HIV and STIs, where to go for advice and overcoming peer pressure to have sex. In addition, the Government has recently set up two pilot opportunistic screening programmes on Chlamydia to assess the efficacy of this approach and its likely impact on prevalence and long term sequelae.

8.18.4 The Department of Health is taking forward a number of initiatives aimed at increasing ante-natal HIV testing. A leaflet for pregnant women, *Better for your baby*, was launched on World AIDS Day 1998 together with a leaflet for midwives *HIV testing in pregnancy – helping women choose*. This was produced jointly with the Royal College of Midwives and recommends that all women should be given information about HIV testing and offered a test as part of their antenatal care. Other initiatives include developing targets aimed at reducing mother to child transmission.

8.18.5 Over the coming year, the Department of Health will develop a new national HIV/AIDS Strategy which will cover aspects of treatment and care and prevention. The Department will consult on the Strategy before publication.

8.19 Child and Adolescent Mental Health Services (CAMHS)

Article 23, 24

8.19.1 An increase in problems causally related to psychosocial adversity has been reported throughout the Western World. Conduct disorder and depression in young people are two examples. The Parliamentary Select Committee on Health, when inquiring into the state of children and young people's mental health, commended the Government for taking steps to improve co-ordination between agencies and for making it mandatory that Children's Service Plans be drawn up. The "four tier" approach to service provision was equally commended, as was the importance given to CAMHS and initiatives to raise the profile of this important area of health services. Guidance was issued to health and local authorities in 1995.[77].

8.19.2   All information requirements are kept under regular and rigorous review and there have been a number of improvements in the Central collection of statistics over the last few years. For child and adolescent mental health services this is a complex task and the need for accurate and useful information has to be balanced against the potential bureaucratic burden that may be created. However a number of NHS Regional Offices have undertaken reviews of CAMHS in collaboration with Social Care regional groups and these have provided up-to-date information of services in their region. A number of national projects will also contribute significantly to the information base:

> a The Audit Commission is due to report shortly following a detailed review of child and adolescent mental health services in order to assess progress in policy implementation.
>
> b A voluntary organisation, the Mental Health Foundation, has undertaken a wide-ranging inquiry into the factors affecting the mental health and emotional development of children and young people in the UK and its report is also expected shortly.
>
> c A national survey of child mental health morbidity has been commissioned from the Office for National Statistics to provide up-to-date information on the prevalence of mental health disorders in children, the level of impairment and the usage of services (report expected late 1999).
>
> d In Wales, the Welsh Office has commissioned consultants to map services and thus identify deficiencies and other problems.
>
> e In Wales, the Welsh Office is working with consultants and the voluntary sector to provide guidance for primary school teachers on the signs of emotional and mental health problems in children.

8.19.3   There are differing systems for categorising children's problems and these differences often reflect the legitimate and specific priorities of the relevant agencies of intervention as well as the range of perspectives that exist amongst the professionals concerned and within society at large. The Government's Public Health strategy as outlined in Our Healthier Nation aims to establish broader ownership of children's problems across Government Departments and across the agencies at local level. A 'common language' will take time to develop but the increased cross-Departmental activity to explore these issues will help break down the false barriers created by the different categorisation systems.

77A handbook on Child and Adolescent Mental Health Services, Department of Health Social Services Inspectorate, Department for Education, G61/008 2942, 1995, published by the Department of Health.

8.19.4 *The Framework for Mental Health Services in Scotland* was published by the Scottish Office in September 1997[78]. It requires every Health Board to lead the development of a joint, comprehensive mental health strategy focusing on the needs of people with a severe and/or enduring mental health problem, ensuring that inadequate services for particular groups including children and adolescents are made good.

8.19.5 The Government supports voluntary sector projects through direct grant aid. These projects are awarded for up to three years and organisations are able to apply for new grants on expiry of the current awards. In addition the Government announced in May 1998 the award of £1 million to Home-Start, one of the organisations recognised by the Health Select Committee as valuable in the area of CAMHS.

8.19.6 The mechanisms for funding and commissioning all specialist services are being considered within the context of the implementation of the proposals outlined in the Government's White Paper, *The New NHS*[79].

8.19.7 The Department of Health is aware of a number of local initiatives to develop child mental health services within primary care. Research has recently been commissioned to provide a comprehensive national picture of the nature, organisation and cost-effectiveness of CAMHS within primary care. In addition, a study to explore the role and distribution of in-patient psychiatric care has been commissioned. The information that emerges will assist in the planning of such provision on a more rational and equitable basis. The mechanisms for commissioning specialist services are also being addressed in the context of the implementation of the proposals in the two recent White Papers; *The New NHS* relating to England and Wales, and *Designed to care-Renewing the National Health Service* in Scotland[80].

8.19.8 Improving the mental and emotional health of children and young people is vital to reducing social exclusion and increasing life opportunities. Improved CAMH services, provided by the NHS or social services departments, will contribute to wider government programmes including Sure Start, Quality Protects, family policy initiatives, the crime reduction strategy and interventions to assist children with special educational needs.

8.19.9 A new national target on CAMHS for health and social care is being introduced for the first time this year under the National Priorities Guidance, 1999/2002. This will be backed by an additional investment of some £84 million over three years and aims to:

---

78 *The Framework for Mental Health Services*, The Scottish Office, September 1997, Published by The Stationery Office, J13702 9/97.

79 *The New NHS*, Cm 3807, Dd 5067946 2/98, 1998, The Stationery Office.

80 *Designed to Care – Renewing the National Health Service in Scotland*, Cm 3811, Edinburgh: The Stationery Office ISBN 0 101381123.

"Improve provision of appropriate, high quality care and treatment for children and young people by building up locally-based Child and Adolescent Mental Health Service (CAMHS). This should be achieved through improved staffing levels and training provision at all tiers; improved liaison between primary care, specialist CAMHS, social services and other agencies; and should lead to users of the service being able to expect:

- a comprehensive assessment and, where indicated, a plan for treatment without a prolonged wait;

- a range of advice, consultation and care within primary care and Local Authority settings;

- a range of treatments within specialist settings based on the best evidence of effectiveness; and

- in-patient care in a specialist setting, appropriate to their age and clinical need."

8.19.10 The development money for CAMHS will be made available via the Modernisation Fund (£60m over three years) and the Mental Health Grant to local authorities (£24m over three years) with effect from April 1999. The NHS Executive and Social Care Regions are working together to identify priority areas for joint investment. The focus is on building up core services – and reducing inequalities – and promoting innovative practice.

8.20 Child mental health – views of NGOs

8.20.1 Several non-government organisations which contributed to preliminary discussion of this report mentioned their concern about the incidence of mental health problems among children and adolescents - they included Young Minds, the Mental Health Foundation, the Faculty of Child and Adolescent Psychiatry, the National Children's Bureau (NCB), the Who Cares? Trust (WCT) and the Trust for the Study of Adolescence (TSA). They pointed out that evidence given to the Health Committee by the National Health Advisory Service claimed that 20% of children and young people suffered from a diagnosable disorder with 40% having mental health problems of some sort.[81]

8.20.2 The Mental Health Training Initiative funded by the Department of Health for three years has recognised the need for raising awareness of the mental health issues of young people, particularly with regard to the high rates of suicide among young men and Asian young women.

8.20.3 The TSA, with the support of the Home Office, has devised and delivered training for prison officers in Male and Female Young Offenders Institutions improving the understanding of the age range and providing opportunities for prison staff to consider their roles and implement

---

81 Para. 187-190, Health Committee 4th report on *Child and adolescent mental health services, vol II: minutes of evidence and appendices*, 1997

'child-oriented' policies within the youth justice system. This work is continuing.

8.20.4   Major funding from the National Lottery has been granted to the TSA with Youth Access to provide accredited training for counsellors of young people and for those who use counselling skills in their work. Within the next three years a range of counselling and counselling skills training will be available for the voluntary and statutory sectors at a nationally accredited standard for those who work with young people in a wide range of services.

8.20.5   The Economic and Social Research Council's Programme of Research on Youth Citizenship and Social Change represents a major, publicly-funded contribution to knowledge about young people in the United Kingdom and Europe. It also aims to address issues concerning young people's empowerment and the right to have their views heard and respected. The research will examine their views on schemes designed to help young people channel their views to local policy-makers and service-providers, and will explore and evaluate ways of involving young people in all stages of the research process, from design through to dissemination.

8.20.6   In the last two years the Trust for the Study of Adolescence has been running a Youth Empowerment Project, funded by the National Lottery, which aims to help young people get their views about mental health across to adults in training. Young people have been actively involved in training adults at events in several places in the United Kingdom and their views have been disseminated by newsletter to many more.

8.20.7   NGOs have also drawn attention to the Health Select Committee's reservations over levels of CAMHS provision across the country. The Government acknowledged that there were considerable variations in CAMHS services due to a significant extent to historical factors. This is being addressed in the National Priorities Guidance objectives for CAMHS described above.

8.20.8   Twenty-four innovative CAMHS projects were established in 1998, financed initially from the Mental Illness Specific Grant to Local Authorities. Each three year project will be evaluated within the terms of the grant and the voluntary organisation "Young Minds" has been commissioned to draw together the lessons to be learned from these projects with a view to publishing the results as a stimulus to good practice. Future funding for these projects will be provided under the new Mental Health Grant.

8.21 Reducing the rate of teenage conceptions – England and Wales

Article 24, 27

8.21.1   The Government recognises and is concerned by the high rate of teenage conceptions in the United Kingdom – one of the highest in the developed world.

8.21.2   Under 16 conception rates rose throughout the 1980s reaching a peak in 1990 of 10.1 per thousand girls aged 13-15 in England and Wales.

Although a slight improvement is apparent from 1996 to 1997, they remain a cause for concern with a rate of 8.9 in 1997. Teenage conception rates (aged 13-19) are similarly worrying. The 1997 rate is 62.3 per thousand, although there was a slight drop in the mid-1990s. The rates of under 16 and teenage conceptions in England over the last 17 years is shown in the table below: –

Teenage conception rates per thousand teenage girls (England)

	Under 16s	Under 20s
1980	7.2	58.6
1981	7.3	56.9
1982	7.8	56.1
1983	8.3	55.6
1984	8.7	59.5
1985	8.6	61.3
1986	8.8	61.9
1987	9.3	65.8
1988	9.4	66.5
1989	9.4	67.5
1980	10.0	68.8
1981	9.3	64.8
1982	8.4	61.4
1983	8.0	59.3
1984	8.3	58.3
1985	8.5	58.7
1986	9.3	62.5
1987	8.8	61.9

FIGURE 5: TEENAGE CONCEPTION RATES IN ENGLAND

8.21.3 There is a wide regional variation in under 16 conception rates (see Annex D). Areas of higher teenage conception tend to be areas of higher social exclusion. The Government believes that teenage pregnancy is all too likely to be a cause as well as a symptom of social deprivation.

8.21.4 The rate of teenage conceptions in Scotland is also at a comparatively high level. Teenage pregnancies rose between 1986 and 1991 from 44.4 to 50.5 per 1000 women in the 13-19 years age group. Although the rate fell to 43.1 in 1996, it remains a cause for concern. Among 16-19 year olds, the rate peaked in 1991 at 77.8 per 1,000 females in this age group and declined to 69.6 by 1996. Among 13-15 year olds, the rate increased from 7.5 per 1,000 females in 1986 to 9.6 in 1996.

8.21.5 As in other parts of the country, teenage pregnancy in Scotland is more likely among the less well off. Incomplete education, limited educational attainment, poor employment prospects, low income and poor social and environmental circumstances can all contribute to situations where conception is more likely. Teenage pregnancy is clearly related to social deprivation categories. In 1996, the pregnancy rate for 13-19 year olds ranged from 17.2 per 1,000 in the least deprived areas to 68.6 in the most deprived.

Article 24, 27

8.21.6   Under the umbrella of the public health strategy, the Minister for Public Health nominated in November 1997 four people to work in their respective subject areas towards establishing national priorities as part of a programme aimed at reducing the rate of teenage conceptions. The Social Exclusion Unit published its report on 14 June 1999. The four task areas are:

a   sex and relationships education (where a great deal of "prevention" work can be carried out),

b   vulnerable and hard to reach groups (with the socially excluded – for example children who are or have been in care),

c   contraceptive and sexual health services and

d   research.

8.21.7   The report sets out a national programme with two specific goals: to halve the rates of conceptions among under 18 year olds in England by 2010 and to lessen the risks of young parents suffering the consequences of social exclusion by getting more teenage parents back into education, training and employment. The programme will include:

a   a new task force of Ministers, led by the Minister for Public Health, to co-ordinate the policy across Government supported by an implementation unit in the Department of Health;

b   a national publicity campaign to reinforce the report's key messages – targeting young people and parents with the facts about teenage pregnancy and parenthood, with advice on how to deal with pressures to have sex and with messages that underline the importance of using contraception if they do have sex;

c   improved access to NHS contraception and sexual health services for teenagers, including young men;

d   a new national helpline to give advice to teenagers on sex and relationships;

e   new guidance to be issued on sex and relationships education in school;

f   better support for teenage parents and their children, providing supervised, semi-independent housing with support for 16 and 17 year olds who do not live with their parents, and support to ensure that under 16s who have children will finish their education (in addition to pilots to encourage 16 and 17 year olds to stay in education); and

g   special action targeted on prevention for the most vulnerable groups including children looked after by a local authority, those excluded from school and young offenders.

8.21.8   In addition, the Department of Health with the help of an external reference group will be developing, over the next twelve months, a Strategy on Sexual Health. The Government will work in partnership with health services, voluntary and community groups, professionals and others to develop this overarching framework for sexual health. Although the strategy will cover all the groups at high risk, of all ages, it will have a critical role to play in contributing to a national strategy to reduce teenage pregnancy. It will join up current initiatives in sexual health including HIV/AIDS strategy, work on Chlamydia, the Social Exclusion report and the report of the Personal and Social Health Education Advisory Group.

8.22 Teenage conception rates – Scotland

8.22.1   The rate of teenage conceptions in Scotland is also at a comparatively high level. Teenage pregnancies rose between 1986 and 1991 – from 44.4 to 50.5 per 1,000 women in the 13-19 years age group. Although the rate fell to 43.1 in 1996, it remains a cause for concern. Among 16-19 year olds, the rate peaked in 1991 at 77.8 per 1,000 females in this age group and declined to 69.6 by 1996. Among 13-15 year olds, the rate increased from 7.5 per 1,000 females in 1986 to 9.4 in 1996.

8.22.2   As in other parts of the country, teenage pregnancy in Scotland is more likely among the less well off. Incomplete education, limited educational attainment, poor employment prospects, low income and poor social and environmental circumstances can all contribute to situations where conception is more likely. Teenage pregnancy is clearly related to social deprivation categories. In 1996, the pregnancy rate for 13-19 year olds ranged from 17.2 per thousand in the least deprived categories to 68.6 per thousand in the most deprived.

8.22.3   The Government addressed the issue of sexual health and young people in its recently published White Paper, *Towards a Healthier Scotland*[82]. Among other things, this sets a national target of a 20% reduction in the rate of pregnancy among 13-15 year olds for the period 1995 to 2010, and also announces funding for a demonstration project to be called "Healthy Respect". The focus of this project will be to promote sexual health and prevent sexually transmitted diseases as well as reducing unwanted pregnancies. Bids are currently being sought from bodies interested in running the project. We will be looking for bids which can develop measures to nurture self-respect in young people and discourage coercive or manipulative sexual behaviour as well as addressing improved methods of sex education and advice for young people about sexual health and contraception.

82 Cm 4269, The Stationery Office, Edinburgh, ISBN 0-10-142692-5.

8.23 Programme to reduce the rate of teenage conceptions – Scotland

Article 24, 27

8.23.1   Scotland does not have a specific current national target for reducing teenage pregnancies – the general policy has been that targets are best set locally in the light of local circumstances. Local targets have, therefore, been set at Health Board level. Twelve of the 15 Scottish Health Boards have set local targets to reduce the number of pregnancies amongst teenagers. Typically they are expressed in terms of a percentage reduction in conception rates for teenagers or a reduction in the number of teenage abortions.

8.24 Programme to reduce the rate of teenage conceptions – Northern Ireland

8.24.1   In Northern Ireland the Regional Strategy for Health and Personal Social Well-being has set a target to reduce the overall number of births to teenage mothers by 10% by 2002. Northern Ireland is also participating in the national programme to reduce the rate of teenage conceptions.

8.25 Measures to reduce accidental death or injury in childhood

Article 18, 24

8.25.1   The number of children dying or seriously injured each year as a result of accidents has declined steadily since the previous report. The Department of Health mounts or supports financially a number of initiatives to ensure that the downward trend is maintained.

8.25.2   Financial grants are provided by the Department to support the work of specialist organisations such as the Child Accident Prevention Trust and the Royal Society for the Prevention of Accidents. In conjunction with the Department, these organisations have been, or are, involved in the development of standards to improve the safety of children's environment and products, accident prevention programmes to assist health and safety practitioners at regional and local level, and public awareness campaigns to inform parents, teachers and children about effective accident prevention.

8.25.3   The Departments of Health, Education and Employment, Trade and Industry and Environment, Transport and the Regions support "Child Safety Week", an annual awareness raising campaign in the summer, which is designed to inform parents, carers and children on how to prevent accidents and injuries. This high profile campaign uses national, regional and local press to maximise the impact of the campaign. The Department has evaluated the success of the campaign over the past three years. Since 1997, the Department has also funded an extension of the campaign so that activities can take place in the winter and the spring.

8.25.4   The Department funds the Child Accident Prevention Trust to develop and conduct trials of a publicly accessible information service on accident prevention. It is expected that this service will enable parents with literacy difficulties to have access to individual advice.

8.25.5   The Department caters for the needs of minority ethnic groups by funding, via the Child Accident Prevention Trust, the translation of safety leaflets into four Asian languages. These leaflets are produced in consultation with the relevant communities.

8.25.6   The Department, working with colleagues in other government departments and the Royal Society for the Prevention of Accidents, has developed a training resource called *Together Safely* which aims to teach children, parents and carers the principles of general risk assessment, including road safety.

8.25.7   The Department has helped to fund a specialist training programme in child pedestrian safety. The package, which includes video training, uses four schools which have adopted the recommended methods. The strength of this approach is the active participation of the children themselves in contributing to their own safety as pedestrians.

8.25.8   In the wider context, the Department is working closely with colleagues in the Department of the Environment, Transport and the Regions to ensure that accidents, including child accident prevention measures, are effectively highlighted in the Government's new integrated transport policy. A range of proposals are under consideration. These include measures to promote traffic calming, safer cycling, safety training in schools and communities, and greater emphasis on pedestrian safety.

8.26 Child road safety – progress since the First United Kingdom Report

Article 18, 24

8.26.1   The Government's White Paper on the future of transport *A New Deal for Transport: Better for Everyone*[83] makes clear that improving road safety, especially of children, will continue to be an important objective for the Government. The principal way in which these commitments will be taken forward is a new road safety strategy and target for Great Britain. The main objectives of the new strategy will be the effective enforcement of legislation; publicising the risks and educating road users (particularly children and young people) about the need to use the roads with thought and care; and promoting better engineering standards for roads and for vehicles. The Government's new public health strategy[84] announced its intention not only to reduce the number of accidents by a fifth, and to reduce the rate of serious injury from accidents by at least one tenth, by 2010, but also to tackle the pronounced bias towards childhood accidents in the lower socio-economic groups. Accordingly, the Department of Health has commissioned the Child Accident Prevention Trust to set in motion a series of discussions with children and community development agencies to discuss how these inequalities in the incidence of child accidents could be targeted effectively.

---

83 Cm 3950: ISBN 0-10 139502-7, published by the Stationery Office.

84 *Our Healthier Nation: A Contract for Health*, Cm 3852, Dd 5067877 2/98, 1998, The Stationery Office.

8.27 Child road safety – progress on existing target

8.27.1   The current road safety target is to reduce casualties by a third by the year 2000 (based on the 1981-85 annual average). Progress in achieving the target for reducing the number of children killed or seriously injured has been encouraging.

Age	0 to 4	5 to 7	8 to 11	12 to 15	Total
Pedestrians	535	734	1322	1363	3954
Cyclists	15	136	354	511	1016
Car Passengers	262	206	283	520	1271
other categories	14	9	44	144	211
Total	826	1085	2003	2538	6452
1981-85 baseline	1380	2027	3501	4773	11681
reduction	40%	46%	43%	46%	45%

FIGURE 6: ROAD ACCIDENTS – CHILD CASUALTIES IN GREAT BRITAIN, 1997

8.27.2   The 255 children (aged 0-15) killed in road traffic accidents in 1997 was 55% lower than the 1981-85 annual average of 563. The 44,289 children injured on the roads in 1997 was 11% less than the 1981-85 average of 49,770.

8.28 Child safety in the Government's new transport policy

Article 18, 24

8.28.1   The Government shares the concern of many that pedestrians and communities should be given full consideration in the development of transport policy, so that traffic needs do not necessarily take precedence.

8.28.2   This point has been addressed by the Government. The objective of the policies set out in the White Paper is to improve the safety of more vulnerable road users, including pedestrians (particularly children) and cyclists in a way that is consistent with encouraging more walking and cycling. Children should be able to walk to school in safety and initiatives to provide safer routes to school will support both safety and environmental aims.

8.28.3   The aim is, in particular, to improve road safety education in schools and by parents, by assessing the effectiveness of existing training aids and developing new ones; and to assess local measures to achieve safer routes to school, and in producing a best practice guide. The transition from primary to secondary school marks an important milestone in the development of children. It coincides with increasing responsibility and independent travel. But it also coincides with the peak in pedestrian and cycling accidents among children, so work is focusing in particular, on preparing children for the transition from primary to secondary school.

8.28.4   Children are more likely to become road traffic casualties when they first get behind the wheel of a car. Drivers aged 17-20 comprise under 5% of licence holders, but 15% of drivers involved in road traffic accidents. When account is taken of their mileage, the risk is even higher. That is probably because of their immaturity and their lack of experience. Young drivers tend to be relatively competent at handling their vehicle but not at anticipating the actions of other road users.

8.28.5   Following a consultation exercise in 1993, various measures have been taken to improve the knowledge, behaviour and perception of risks by new drivers including a separate theory paper in the driving test and a requirement that drivers who commit certain offences within two years of qualifying must re-take the driving test. The content and structure of the practical driving test is currently under review.

8.28.6   Traffic calming is one of the most effective ways to reduce the number and severity of accidents involving children. Research has shown that 20 mph zones supported by physical measures such as road humps, pinch points and rumble devices reduce the number of child pedestrian and cyclist casualties by 67%. The Government made £50 million available to local authorities in 1998-99 for this sort of local road safety scheme. There is now a separate budget for small schemes on trunk roads to deal with specific safety problems and the majority of schemes in the Government's programme of major improvements have safety as a major objective.

8.29 Cleaner air

Article 24, 27

8.29.1   The Government is committed to delivering cleaner air for everyone. The National Air Quality Strategy 1997 set standards and objectives for the main air pollutants to be achieved in the United Kingdom by 2005. These standards are set at levels which represent no or minimal risk to people's health. Action is under way at local, national, and international levels to ensure that those standards and objectives are met. The strategy is being reviewed to see what further measures might be introduced.

8.29.2   Transport is now the main source of urban air pollution. Vehicle emissions and fuel have been subject to increasingly tight controls over the last few years, for example by the introduction of lead-free petrol and compulsory catalytic converters for cars. The Government's taxation policies are designed to promote the use of cleaner fuels and low emission vehicles. Regulations enable local authorities to enforce vehicle emission standards at the roadside. The United Kingdom and its EU partners have recently agreed even tighter fuel and emission standards under the auto oil programme.

8.29.3   The White Paper *A New Deal For Transport: Better For Everyone*[85] published in July 1998 looks at ways of reducing the impact of transport on air pollution. It sets out a package of measures to provide a real choice of transport which is environmentally sustainable and not health-threatening. It aims to reduce traffic congestion and cut pollution by improved management of roads, and by promoting the use of less polluting forms of travel such as cycling and walking.

8.29.4   The United Kingdom contributes to the reduction of trans-boundary air pollution through EU membership and under UNECE protocols for sulphur, persistent organic compounds, and heavy metals. In June 1998, under the EU air quality framework directive, the United Kingdom secured agreement to the first set of "daughter directives" which set new air quality limits for nitrogen dioxide, sulphur dioxide, lead, and small particulates.

8.30 Planning – transport and noise

Article 24, 27

8.30.1   Planning Policy Guidance Note (PPG) 13 on Transport was issued in March 1994. This encourages policies designed to reduce reliance on the private car while maintaining and improving choice for people to walk, cycle or use public transport rather than drive between homes and facilities which they need to visit regularly.

8.30.2   The White Paper *A New Deal For Transport: Better For Everyone* further strengthens this shift in emphasis, and will lead to updated planning guidance on locations for major growth and travel generating uses with the emphasis on accessibility to trip destinations by foot, bicycle and public transport, taking into account the needs of all in society. This emphasis on accessibility will improve the quality of life for children.

8.30.3   This New Deal for Transport will improve the environment in towns and cities and create conditions for people to move around more easily. More road space and priority will be given to pedestrians, cyclists and public transport, through a different approach to traffic management. This should also increase safety and help cut air pollution. Local authorities will be expected to take a strategic view of traffic management when preparing Regional Planning Guidance and development plans. Local transport plans will set out how these measures will be delivered at a local level.

8.30.4   PPG 24 on Planning & Noise, issued in September 1994, provides guidance to local planning authorities to minimise the adverse impact of noise. It outlines the considerations to be taken into account in preparing development plan policies and in determining planning applications both for noise-sensitive developments and for those activities which generate noise. It introduces the concept of noise exposure categories for residential

---

85 Cm 3950: ISBN 0-10 139502-7, published by the Stationery Office.

development, encourages their use and recommends appropriate levels for exposure to different sources of noise. It also advises on the use of conditions to minimise the impact of noise.

8.30.5   The Government is working with local authorities to set up a number of pilot schemes to assess the viability of Home Zones. These initiatives, adapted from European measures, are aimed at reducing the impact of road traffic in residential areas so that they are better living places for residents, particularly children.

8.31   Disabled children – effectiveness of benefits

Article 23

8.31.1   Since the United Kingdom's First Report, there has been research by the University of York on the needs and circumstances of families caring for disabled children. *Expert opinions: a national survey of parents caring for a severely disabled child* was published in 1995[86].

8.31.2   There has also been more recent research, funded and published by the Joseph Rowntree Foundation based in York (JRF), on the needs and circumstances of families caring for disabled children[87]. The report examines the benefits system which recognises that both disabled adults and children incur extra costs because of their disability. The study says that little is known about the nature and extent of these costs, particularly for children. The report describes minimum essential budget standards for children of differing ages and with a range of disabilities. The researchers have documented the experiences of some 300 parents of severely disabled children and drawn up a list of the agreed minimum necessary to enable disabled children to develop to their full potential.

8.31.3   The report details the priorities and experiences that influenced the parents' decisions. It examines the implications of the findings for benefit provision and service delivery. The study concludes that parents of disabled children are still "paying to care" and that the minimum essential cost of raising a severely disabled child is, on average, three times more than for a child without a disability.

8.32   Report on the rights of disabled children – independent research by an NGO

Article 23

8.32.1   The children's charity Barnardo's recently commissioned and published a research report *Accessing Human Rights: disabled children and the Children Act*[88]. The report acknowledges that a lot of effort, time and resources go into providing social services for disabled children and asks whether disabled children are getting what they really need.

8.32.2   The report details what disabled children need, and what they have a right to, as defined by the UN Convention on the Rights of the Child.

---

86 Beresford, B. (1995). *Expert Opinions: A National Survey of Parents Caring for a Severely Disabled Child*, published by the Joseph Rowntree Foundation.

87 *Paying to Care - the cost of childhood disability* by Barbara Dobson and Sue Middleton, published by JRF, July 1998, ISBN no 18999 87754.

88 By Dr Jenny Morris, published by Barnardos September 1998.

Against this measure the author points to shortfalls in the Children Act and its implementation with regard to disabled children and shows how they stem from an underdeveloped understanding of inclusion. Dr Jenny Morris goes on to look at where direct services for disabled children are failing, and offers examples of various approaches developed by individual projects. The report ends with a detailed illustration of delivering a fully inclusive service, demonstrating ways within existing resources to meet previously unsatisfied need.

8.32.3   The Government has confirmed that it is committed to providing special allowances to help with the extra costs which disabled people may incur, and that it intends to maintain Disability Living Allowance as a universal, national benefit for those who meet the conditions of entitlement. Under these arrangements

a Disability Living Allowance is payable for some 196,000 children aged under 16, at the same rates as for adults.

b Of these children some 72,500 receive the highest rate care component and some 45,500 receive the higher rate mobility component.

c Increases in the child's disability premium, introduced in April 1990, is now helping 61,000 children.

d The carer premium, introduced in April 1990, to help those caring for disabled children is now being received by 183,000 carers.

8.33 Children with mobility problems

Article 23

8.33.1   The Department of the Environment, Transport and the Regions is implementing the transport provisions of the Disability Discrimination Act which will require all new public transport (buses, coaches, trains, trams and licensed taxis) to be fully accessible. The requirements for access to trains and trams came into effect from 31 December 1998. Requirements for new single deck buses are expected to take effect from 1 January 2000; new double deck buses from 1 January 2001; and new taxis from 1 January 2002.

8.33.2   On the specific issue of children with mobility problems, the Department of the Environment, Transport and the Regions has produced a video and supporting literature entitled *It's not my problem*. This is designed to promote better quality special needs transport services for children and young people who need specialised provision to get to school, attend a youth club, or go on holiday, for example.

8.33.3   The Government proposes to extend the mobility component of Disability Living Allowance to 3 and 4 year olds.

8.33.4   The Government proposes to introduce a new Disability Income Guarantee for severely disabled people. The guarantee will take the form of a new higher rate of disability premium and a new higher rate of disabled child premium, paid as part of Income Support (IS), income-based Jobseeker's Allowance (JSA), Housing Benefit and Council Tax Benefit, for those who receive the highest rate care component of Disability Living

Allowance. The help will benefit over a third of families on IS and JSA(IB) in 2001 with disabled child premium. Approximately two thirds of those helped will be lone parent families.

8.34 Social Security and childcare services and facilities

Article 26, 27

8.34.1   The Government, through the Social Security system, aims to:

- support all families with children, especially poorer families;
- help workless parents into the labour market by lowering the barriers to work, especially the lack of affordable childcare;
- support working parents; and
- ensure that financial and emotional support from parents continues even after separation.

8.34.2   The Government believes that the best support for children is that provided by parents, ensuring they grow up with as high a standard of living and as high hopes for the future as possible, in a household where work, not benefit dependency, is the norm. Parents will be helped into the labour market through the Working Families Tax Credit (WFTC), by better childcare provision and by the extension of family-friendly working practices. One million children and their parents will be helped over the next five years by the Government's national childcare network.

8.34.3   Child Benefit remains the primary benefit for families, providing a contribution to the cost of bringing up children. It is a universal, non-means tested benefit payable at a flat rate in respect of each child, with a higher rate for the first child. This benefit is normally paid to the mother as the primary carer for the child.

8.34.4   A similar benefit is paid in Northern Ireland as well as England and Wales and Scotland.

8.34.5   Those families who assume the responsibility of caring for an orphan can receive Guardian's Allowance in addition. Recipients of contributory Social Security benefits who have dependent children normally qualify for a child dependency increase, which is paid on top of Child Benefit.

8.34.6   However, for low income families with children, the main source of help is Income Support, an income related benefit payable to people who work less than 16 hours a week. An allowance is paid according to age in respect of each child and a flat rate additional premium is paid for each family. In addition, families receive help with housing and local taxation costs which is also linked to family size and the age of the children.

8.34.7   For low income families working 16 hours or more a week help is provided through Family Credit. This benefit, available to both employed and self-employed, gives extra income to families so that they can move into or remain in work. A means tested benefit, it also takes account of family size and the age of the children. Again, a similar benefit is paid in Northern Ireland.

8.34.8 In October 1994 additional help with childcare costs was introduced into Family Credit improving the level of help available for those families previously prevented from taking up work. The amount of help with childcare costs available in Family Credit was increased from June 1998.

8.34.9 Although the family remains a fundamental building block of society, it is often children and families who bear the brunt of economic change. There is no agreed definition of poverty in the UK, but:–

a In 1996/7, almost three in ten children were in families in the bottom fifth of the overall income distribution. Around four in ten children were in families in the top half of the income distribution.

b Between 1979 and 1995/96 (where this represents the combined financial years 1995/6 and 1996/7) and including the self-employed, the proportion of children living in families without a full-time worker rose from 18 per cent to 32 per cent.

c Between 1979 and 1995/96 the proportion of children below fractions of contemporary average income increased substantially. Excluding the self-employed, in 1979 8 per cent (on the Before Housing Costs (BHC) measure of income) and 9 per cent (on the After Housing Costs (AHC) measure) of children lived in households with less than half 1979 average income; by 1995/96 24 per cent BHC and 34 per cent AHC were in households with less than half 1995/96 average income.

8.34.10 The Government announced in the Budget in 1998 their intention to increase support for all families by:

a increasing the Child Personal Allowances for children under 11 years by £2.50 in the income related benefits from November 1998; and

b increasing the standard rate of Child Benefit for the eldest child from April 1999 by £2.60. The same amount will be added to the family premium in Income Support, Jobseeker's Allowance, Housing Benefit and Council Tax Benefit to ensure that the poorest families benefit from the change.

8.34.11 From October 1999 the Working Families Tax Credit will replace Family Credit providing a more generous level of help to those families on the lowest incomes and extending help further up the income scale. There will also be improved help with childcare costs allowing families to receive 70% of their childcare costs, which will be subject to an overall ceiling. Families on lower incomes will be able to receive up to 95% of their child care costs through the combined effect of the WFTC, Housing Benefit and Council Tax Benefit. The qualifying age for children is currently the September following their 12th birthday. Under Childcare Tax Credit (CTC) the qualifying age will be increased to cover all children up to age 14 – and in the case of children who are disabled, and who have greater needs, until the school leaving age of 16.

8.35 The Sure Start programme for children aged 0 to 3

Article 6, 18, 24

8.35.1   During 1997-98 the Government conducted a comprehensive review of the expenditure programmes of all government departments, and this review included a cross-departmental review of services for children aged 0 to 8. The review looked at the multiple causes of social exclusion affecting young children, and considered whether they could be more effectively tackled at the family and community level using a more integrated approach to service provision.

8.35.2   As a result of this review a new programme – Sure Start – was announced in July 1998 which will provide support for 0-3 year olds and their families in deprived areas. This new support will be specifically targeted at tackling the early causes of social exclusion. The new programme will be based on evidence of what works best in preventing social exclusion, building on existing services, and will involve consultation with local parents.

8.35.3   The Government will put in place arrangements to ensure that this new investment is well spent, and will consider ways of improving the co-ordination and effectiveness of existing services for young children.

8.36 The National Childcare Strategy

Article 26, 27

8.36.1   The United Kingdom Government is committed to supporting families and children. A vital component of this support is the development of a National Childcare Strategy to ensure good quality, affordable childcare for children aged 0-14 in every neighbourhood, including both formal childcare and support for informal arrangements. The Strategy is founded on a commitment to promoting the well being of children, offering equal opportunities for parents, especially women, and to supporting parents in balancing work and family life.

8.36.2   The framework and consultation Green Paper *Meeting the Childcare Challenge*[89] (May 1998) set out proposals to raise quality, make childcare more affordable and make childcare more accessible. This is to be achieved by working in partnership at a local level with local authorities, private and voluntary childcare providers, parents, Training and Education Councils (TECs), and employers. Some 600 responses to the Green Paper were received and the Government is considering how to take the Strategy forward. *Guidance to Early Years Development and Childcare Partnerships* was published in October 1998[90].

8.36.3   Further action is in hand to raise the quality of care – plans include the better integration of early education and childcare and at least 25 new Early Excellence Centres which will provide models of good quality integrated education and childcare; better support for parents and informal carers; a more consistent regulatory regime covering education and

---

89 *Meeting the Childcare Challenge. A framework and consultation document*, May 1998. Cm 3959. Published by The Stationery Office. ISBN 0-10-139592-2

90 *Early Years Development and Childcare Partnership:* Planning Guidance 1999-2000. Ref: EYDCPG Produced by the Department for Education and Employment. ISBN 0 85522 880 6.

childcare; establishing high quality programmes of regular out of school learning activities; new standards for early education and childcare; a new training and qualifications framework for childcare workers; and more opportunities to train as childcare workers.

8.36.4   The Government also aims to make childcare more affordable, as explained at paragraph 8.34.11.

8.36.5   Childcare will be made more accessible by increasing places and improving information – the United Kingdom Government is encouraging a diversity of childcare provision to meet parents' preferences. Funding of £300 million in England will be used to set up new out of school childcare places over the next five years. Plans also include a new national information line which will link parents with local childcare information services which meet national standards.

8.36.6   In Scotland similar structures have been put in place and £91 million is being made available from the Comprehensive Spending Review: £49 million to support the childcare strategy in general and £42 million for support for families with very young children. The New Opportunities Fund will also provide £25 million specifically for out of school care.

8.37 Out of school childcare

Article 27

8.37.1   Since 1993 the United Kingdom Government's Out of School Childcare Initiative (OSCI) has created 122,745 good quality, affordable out of school childcare places in England. The Initiative offers parents, especially women, the opportunity to participate more fully in the labour market. Before the Initiative there were only 500 after school childcare schemes. Now there are over 4,000 schemes most of which would not have opened without Government support. The Initiative was delivered locally by Training and Enterprise Councils (TECs) in England in partnership with local authorities, school, voluntary organisations and employers. (Similar but separate arrangements exist in Wales, Scotland and Northern Ireland).

8.37.2   As part of the National Childcare Strategy, there will be a massive expansion in out of school childcare places. In its last year of funding places, 1998-99, increased funding of £22.1 million led to 41,376 extra childcare places in England. From 1999 the Lottery New Opportunities Fund will invest £220 million in supporting the setting up of new out of school childcare provision in the United Kingdom, of which £20 million is for integrated childcare and education projects. The intention is that out of school childcare will become available for every community which needs it, helping up to 1 million children.

8.38 Health and housing for Travelling people in England and Wales

Article 2, 24, 27,

8.38.1 With regard to health services, regional health authorities in England are required to take account of Travellers' needs in drawing up their plans. The Department of Health funds a number of special schemes aimed at improving access to primary health care for people without permanent accommodation.

8.38.2 There have been changes since the United Kingdom's First Report in relation to accommodation for Gypsy and Traveller families. Under Part II of the Caravan Sites Act 1968, local authorities had a duty to provide caravan sites for Gypsies resorting to or residing in their area. From 1978 to 1994, under the Department of Environment Gypsy sites grant programme, over £128 million was expended on grant-aiding site provision. Permanent sites usually have internal roads, hardstandings, amenity buildings containing bath or shower, toilet, basin, sink, working areas, electricity to each pitch, and street lighting. The sites should be in areas frequented by Gypsies and have reasonable access to shops, schools and essential services. Under the grant programme the number of caravans on local authority sites increased from just under 3,000 to nearly 6,000. Part II of the Act was repealed in November 1994 with 330 sites in existence. The emphasis is now on encouraging Gypsies to provide sites for themselves through the planning process. The Department for the Environment issued advice to local authorities in January 1994 that, when drawing up their development plans, they should address the accommodation needs of Gypsies. There are now some 4,000 Gypsy caravans on private sites compared to just under 3,300 in January 1994. Altogether, in January 1998, 80% of Gypsy caravans were on authorised sites, the highest proportion ever.

8.39 Housing for Travelling people – Northern Ireland

Article 2, 26, 27

8.39.1 The Department of the Environment for Northern Ireland is involved in the provision of accommodation for the travelling community in the form of serviced sites for Travellers. It offers 100% grant-aid to District Councils who provide the sites. On 5 August 1998 the Department of the Environment published as a consultation paper the *Report of the Working Party on Accommodation*[91] *for Travellers*. This proposed a number of options for Traveller accommodation. The consultation period finished on 31 October 1998 and over 40 responses were received. While they were being considered the Minister for the Environment in the Northern Ireland Office asked the Northern Ireland Housing Executive to carry out pilot exercises on 4 sites throughout Northern Ireland. The revised policy should issue shortly.

---

91 Report of the Working Party on Accommodation for Travellers, issued by the Department of the Environment for Northern Ireland.

9   Education, Leisure, Cultural Activity

This chapter covers articles: –

28 *Right to education*

29 *Education to be directed towards development of talents*

31 *Right to rest and play, and participate in culture*

9.1   Raising standards in schools

Article 28

9.1.1   The Government's aim is to ensure the best possible quality of teaching and learning in every school and to enhance excellence in education. Through its White Paper *Excellence in Schools*[92], the School Standards and Framework Act and the Teaching and Higher Education Act, the Government has developed a programme of action in England and Wales designed to raise standards in schools and increase the morale and professionalism of teaching and reducing exclusion from school. The measures planned or under way include those set out in sections 9.2 to 9.8 below.

9.1.2   During 1997-98 the Government conducted a comprehensive spending review of the expenditure programmes of all government departments. Under this review the proportion of UK GDP devoted to education will rise from 4.6% in 1998-99 to 5.0% in 2001-02. The cash sums for education will rise from £38.2bn in 1998-99 to £47.8bn in 2001-02.

9.2   Local authority education development plans in England

Article 28, 29

9.2.1   Local Authorities were required to draw up Development Plans (EDPs) by 1 April 1999. Local Education Authorities will work with schools and, in particular, support them in meeting their performance targets on

92 Cm 3681: ISBN 0-10-136812-7.

literacy and numeracy and on reducing school exclusions. The Secretary of State for Education and Employment approved all EDPs on 26 March 1999 - 144 for all the full three years, and 6 with the requirement to re-submit their EDPs within one year.

9.3 Class sizes in England, Wales and Scotland

Article 28

9.3.1   Research has shown that by allowing teachers to spend more time with individual children, smaller classes benefit pupils in those vital early years when they need to acquire the basic skills of literacy and numeracy. For that reason, the Government has passed legislation to reduce infant class sizes for 5, 6 and 7 year olds to 30 or below by September 2001 at the latest, using money from the Assisted Places Scheme. In 1998 the percentage of pupils leaving primary school with the level expected for their age in English was 65%. For mathematics it was 59%.

9.3.2   The Government wants this target to be achieved early — by September 2000 wherever possible – and has made available £620 million to put this into effect. £217 million has already been invested in additional teachers and new classrooms. The remaining £403 million will be made available over the next two years to provide some 2,400 new classrooms and around 6,000 more teachers.

9.4 The National Literacy and Numeracy Strategies in England and Wales

Article 28

9.4.1   The Government is committed to raising standards of literacy and numeracy. These skills are the foundation for future learning, and the key to developing a child's full potential. The Government has set ambitious national targets for 2002 when it is expected that 80% of all 11 year olds will achieve the standards expected for their age in English and 75% will achieve the standards expected in mathematics.

9.4.2   The National Literacy and National Numeracy Strategies are the top priority for primary schools over the next few years and the Government will provide teachers with practical support to raise standards. Both strategies are supported by substantial resources and an entitlement to a programme of professional development for all primary teachers. The strategies will guarantee training for all primary teachers in the best methods of teaching literacy and numeracy, translating into action the Government's pledge to help teachers do their job well and acquire practical skills for the classroom. The new national curriculum for initial teacher training will help to ensure that new teachers entering the profession are also equipped to teach literacy and numeracy to a high standard.

9.5 National Literacy and Numeracy Strategy in Scotland

Article 28

9.5.1   The Scottish Office Education and Industry Department has embarked on a national strategy for improving their level of achievement in literacy and numeracy, by:

    a Expanding the Early Intervention Programme aimed at raising standards of literacy and numeracy in the early years to £60 million over 5 years;

    b Developing a framework for setting targets to raise levels of literacy and numeracy in line with national benchmarks of 80% pupils achieving relevant stages in primary and 75% in S2;

c New guidelines for initial teacher training to emphasise literacy and numeracy;

d £30 million over 3 years to support in-service training of teachers in literacy and numeracy;

e £15 million over 3 years to support family literacy schemes;

f Support for the National Year of Reading including £7.8 million to allow every school in Scotland to buy books for their libraries.

9.6 New professional requirements for headteachers and teachers in England and Wales

Article 28,29

9.6.1 In order to help raise teaching standards, under the Teaching and Higher Education Act newly appointed head teachers will be required to hold a professional headship qualification, and people employed as teachers will be required to complete an induction period satisfactorily.

9.7 Specialist Schools in England and Wales

Article 29

9.7.1 The Specialist Schools programme was established in England in 1993. Specialist schools are maintained secondary schools which, in addition to providing the full National Curriculum, specialise in technology, languages, sport or the arts. A specialist school seeks to bring about school improvement through teaching and learning in its chosen specialism. All such schools must have drawn up a three year development plan setting out how this will be achieved. Specialist schools are also responsible for raising private sector sponsorship and building on-going links with sponsors. Capital and annual grants are available from the public sector to complement business sponsorship in order to help specialist schools implement their development plan.

9.7.2 The White Paper Excellence in Schools included an announcement on the relaunch of the Specialist Schools programme. In order to spread the benefits of the programme, specialist schools are required to set objectives and related targets for sharing good practice and their facilities with other schools and the wider community. Specialist schools can also be a focal point for revitalising education in Education Action Zones, working with other partners to help bring about school improvement. The Government has stated its commitment to extending the programme, which it believes will promote diversity and excellence in secondary education. In September 1998 there were 300 designated specialist schools in England.

9.8 Education Action Zones in England and Wales

Article 28,29

9.8.1 The Government is determined to ensure that all pupils have the opportunity to gain the qualifications and skills they will need to participate in society and work, and will have the confidence to continue learning throughout life. To achieve this aim in areas facing particular challenges requires a partnership approach and a willingness to innovate.

9.8.2   For this reason, the Government launched the Education Action Zones programme in the White Paper *Excellence in Schools* in summer 1997. Since then, 25 zones have been established and are in operation. Another 47 zones have been shortlisted in the first stage of the second round process and are awaiting final approval.

9.8.3   Education Action Zones are groups of schools working in partnership with local and national partners typically including the local education authority, parents, businesses, community organisations and other statutory agencies to drive up standards of education in areas of social challenge. They are testbeds for innovative ideas. For example, some zones are using cutting edge IT programmes for accelerated learning, tackling disaffection, and improving links between home and classrooms and between primary and secondary schools. Another zone, through a one-stop shop bringing together education and social services, is providing a complete family support service within the schools.

9.8.4   Funding for zones in the first round comprises £250,000 per zone per year from businesses and up to £750,000 from Government per zone each year. 12 zones started in September 1998; a further 13 will start in January 1999. However, funding for zones in the second round comprises up to £750,000 a year. £500,000 will be guaranteed; and up to £250,000 more will be available to match pound per pound funds the zone can raise from its business and other partners. Each zone can therefore receive up to £1 million per year.

9.9   Raising standards in Scottish schools

Article 28, 29

9.9.1   In Scotland, all the Government's initiatives in school education are part of a major agenda to improve standards and achievement. In particular, starting from the 1998/99 school year, the Government have developed with schools and education authorities a framework for setting targets and measuring achievement in relation to those targets. This enables schools to focus on improving standards. It will also provide a much more meaningful measure of school achievement than examination results alone and allow more, better and clearer information to be provided for parents – enabling them to participate as active partners in the drive for improvement.

9.9.2   The targets are set by schools themselves in agreement with their education authority, taking into account the individual starting point of each school and the particular local circumstances which they face. The targets set are stretching but realistic.

9.9.3   Targets are being introduced and set, initially, in the four key areas of literacy, numeracy, examination attainment and attendance. It is open to schools to set targets in other areas such as ethos, learning and teaching and other subject areas. The approach is to challenge schools to do as well as better performing schools with similar characteristics – and to challenge the top performing schools to continue to improve.

9.10 New Community Schools in Scotland

Article 28

9.10.1 New Community Schools are central to the Government's strategy to modernise schools, to raise attainment and to promote social inclusion.

9.10.2 New Community Schools bring together in a single team professionals from a range of services. This will enable action to be taken early to address the needs of vulnerable children and to meet those needs in the round. The focus is firmly on the pupil and his or her family. New Community Schools will ensure integrated provision of school education, social work and health education and promotion services. These are the core services but authorities are encouraged to consider other services and be innovative and flexible in their approach. Services in New Community Schools will be integrated and management structures will include a single reporting and accountability framework.

9.10.3 New Community Schools will set targets for raised attainment, raised attendance and reduced inclusion; improved service integration; improved social welfare; and improved health.

9.10.4 At present the Government is funding five development projects which build on previously existing activity in relation to integrated approaches and illustrate some of the practical aspects of the New Community Schools model. The New Community Schools Prospectus, which gives authorities details of how to apply for funding for pilot projects, was published in November 1998. Pilot projects will begin from 1 April 1999. Over the three years from April 1999, the Government will invest £26 million from The Scottish Office Excellence Fund to support at least two projects in the area of each local authority.

9.10.5 Over the three years from April 1999, the Government will invest £26 million from The Scottish Office Excellence Fund to support at least two pilot projects in the area of each local authority. In the first phase, from April 1999, there are 37 pilots, involving single schools or clusters of schools arranged in a number of ways (e.g. groups of primary schools or a secondary school with the primary schools associated with it).

9.11 Education, leisure and cultural activities in Scotland

Article 28, 29, 31

9.11.1 The Scottish Office Education and Industry Department administers a grant scheme – the Further Education (Approved Associations) (Scotland) Grant Regulations 1989 – which supports national community education voluntary organisations.

9.11.2 The grant scheme assists national voluntary organisations working in the field of youth work, adult basic education and community development with the cost of maintaining a headquarters presence in Scotland (in 1998-99, grants totalling over £1.5 million). This helps organisations to co-ordinate and develop their contribution to informal education. There is a diverse range of voluntary activity in the informal education sector and voluntary organisations make a significant contribution to the economic, social and environmental life of Scotland. Included in the scheme's aims are: to complement and influence statutory educational provision and to encourage participation by all members of the community including children and young people in the processes of personal and social development and education, both individually and collectively.

9.11.3 At present, local authorities provide community education as part of their duty, under section 1 of the Education (Scotland) Act 1980, to secure the adequate and efficient provision of further education (allocation in 1998-99 £101.5m). That includes social, cultural and recreational activities and physical education and training either as voluntary organised activities designed to promote the educational development of persons taking part or as part of a course of instruction. The functions of community education provided by authorities are adult education, educational support for community development and work with children and young people. In all these fields, authorities are able to make provision themselves or through or in partnership with other organisations, particularly voluntary bodies.

9.11.4 In particular youth work is concerned with the personal and social development of young people, who through their participation in youth work programmes will grow and develop as individuals having particular knowledge, skills and the confidence to participate fully in their organisations, projects, communities and society in general. Statutory and voluntary community education organisations offer a wide range of leisure and recreational activities and initiatives for young people which stimulate personal and social development and decision making and independent living skills. Peer education is particularly successful with young people, for example in health education programmes. These skills not only assist young people in their personal development and growth to maturity but encourage the development of self-esteem giving them the confidence to participate in formal education and training programmes.

9.11.5 Community Learning Scotland (CLS), the Government's advisory body on community learning (building community capacity, investing in community learning and promoting personal development) has a Youth Work Forum which brings together a cross-section of organisations associated with youth work to provide information and advice to local authorities and facilitate collaborative youth work developments. The "Connect Youth" network aims to involve young people between the ages of 13 and 19, particularly those with little or no previous experience of formal youth activities. A number of councils have established forums and encouraged representatives of a wide range of service departments to attend meetings. CLS is involved in the design and delivery of the training provision and in networking between the various groups. There is widespread interest in the establishment of a national forum which would facilitate collaborative approaches, provide a national resources unit as well as a platform for debating and taking forward issues of national importance to young people. A National Voice for Youth – a Youth Parliament – is receiving support to establish links with the Scottish Parliament. Such a Youth Parliament will help young people gain experience of politics, establish partnerships and make links with young people across Europe.

Empowerment of young people to have an informed and active role in determining the decision and conditions that affect their lives does much to promote active citizenship in individuals and communities.

9.11.6   Community education is also involved with the pre-school sector in stimulating adult learning to help parents understand child development and improve parent's self esteem to the benefit of the child. This provision is part of the wide ranging adult education programmes available throughout Scotland and will be integral in the development of adult basic education policy. Increasingly other agencies such as further education colleges and training providers are developing literacy and numeracy support programmes.

9.12 Spiritual, moral, social and cultural development and citizenship in England and Wales

Article 28, 29, 31

9.12.1   Many schools offer education for citizenship as part of their provision for preparing pupils for responsible life in a free society. The Government recognises that whilst there is good practice in some schools it is by no means universal. It established a National Advisory Group on Education for Citizenship and the Teaching of Democracy in Schools to build on and extend current good practice and to giver greater coherence to this work in all schools in England and Wales.

9.12.2   The final report of the Advisory Group on Education for Citizenship Education and the Teaching of Democracy in Schools was published in September 1998. It recommended ways in which schools can develop in young people the knowledge, skills and aptitudes to make their voices heard and play a positive role in their communities.

9.12.3   The Secretary of State for Education and Employment has accepted the recommendations of the Citizenship Advisory Group that, while there is much good practice in schools, citizenship education needs to have greater coherence. He has also accepted the recommendation of an inter-departmental neighbourhood renewal team, Policy Action Team 10, that the Government should "encourage schools, through the use of creative and sporting activity as part of Personal and Social and Health Education to build pupils' confidence and self-esteem".

9.12.4   The Secretary of State for Education and Employment announced his proposals[93] for the review of the National Curriculum on 13 May 1999. The Government asked the Qualifications and Curriculum Authority to consult on the proposals to enhance the teaching of citizenship and democracy in schools - at Key Stages 1 and 2 as part of a non-statutory framework including personal, social and health matters, and at Key Stage 3 and 4 as a distinct statutory entitlement. The Government intends that this

93 The review of the national curriculum in England The Secretary of State's proposals. Ref:QCA/99/405.

will be a light touch approach, with a programme of study based on learning outcomes to allow scope for schools to develop their own approaches for delivering teaching in citizenship, and to be innovative, for example by drawing on knowledge and understanding gained across other subjects in the curriculum, and encouraging political activities in the community. In order to allow schools time to build good practice in this area, we propose to implement the statutory order in September 2002. The Government will also develop proposals for supporting the training of teachers, and provision of guidance and resource materials.

9.12.5   The proposals for PSHE and citizenship are designed to build on and extend current good practice, establish coherence and secure consistency and continuity and progression of learning. They set out a learning framework across the key stages to enable schools to:

a   promote their pupils' personal and social development, including their health and well-being effectively;

b   develop pupils' knowledge and understanding of their role and responsibilities as active citizens in a modern democracy; and

c   equip them with the values, skills and knowledge to deal with the difficult moral and social questions they face.

9.12.6   The framework consists of:

a   joint non-statutory framework for personal, social and health education and citizenship at key stages 1 and 2; and personal, social and health education at key stages 3 and 4; plus

b   a statutory Order for a foundation subject in the national curriculum for citizenship at key stages 3 and 4.

9.12.7   The Government believes that for citizenship at key stages 3 and 4, where provision is not so well established, it is important for young people to have a clear statutory entitlement to learning about their duties, responsibilities and rights as citizens, the nature of democratic government and the skills needed to play an active part in their school, neighbourhood, communities and society.

9.12.8   The proposals for PSHE and citizenship are designed to be a basic framework within which schools can develop their own approaches. They include opportunities for active learning through community involvement and the practical development of the key skills of communication, working with others, the application of number, information technology, improving own learning and performance, and problem solving. They recognise the contribution which personal, social and health education and citizenship can make to combating racism and promoting equal opportunities through teaching about fairness, justice, rights and responsibilities and through developing an understanding and appreciation of diversity.

9.12.9   Citizenship is complementary to and not a substitute for history, spiritual and personal social and health education. Together with these subjects it will help develop the citizens of the future. For example, the framework proposes that by the end of Key Stage 4, to develop knowledge and understanding, pupils should understand the legal and human rights and responsibilities underpinning society, and how they relate to citizens, including the role and operation of the criminal and civil justice system. There will, therefore, be opportunities for schools to teach about the main human rights charters and conventions, including the UN Convention on the Rights of the Child.

9.12.10 NGOs have expressed concerns that the Citizenship Education Advisory Group's report argues against any statutory requirement to introduce mechanisms directed to ensuring that children are provided with opportunities to express their views on the running of schools and their education.

9.12.11 In a survey for the Institute of Citizenship Studies - *Citizenship Education in Primary Schools* (Kerr 1996), 14 per cent of the 144 schools responding said they had a school council; some 75 per cent said they involved pupils in negotiating rules on behaviour. In a similar survey of secondary schools – *Citizenship Education in Secondary Schools – a national survey* (Fogelman 1991) – around 60 per cent of the 455 schools surveyed said they had school councils.

9.12.12 Many schools, therefore, already have school councils or involve their pupils in decision making in other ways. We expect this will spread when citizenship has a higher profile in schools. The Government will encourage schools to involve their pupils in these ways but does not wish to overburden them at this time of change in the education sector by introducing statutory requirements.

9.12.13 The Government recognises the importance of continuing citizenship education after the end of compulsory schooling, including in FE colleges. Many colleges and schools already offer a wide range of opportunities, both formal and informal, for 16-19 year old students to enhance their knowledge and understanding of their rights and responsibilities as citizens. Ministers will be considering how best to encourage institutions to develop those opportunities further as part of their consideration of the Government's overall strategy for citizenship education.

9.12.14 The Deputy Prime Minister and the Secretary of State for Education and Employment announced a national Children's Parliament on the Environment, to build on the interest that young people have in this area and to stimulate them to think about what can be done – in particular what they can do themselves – to secure a healthy future for everyone. The initiative provided children with the opportunity to develop an understanding of, and take an active role in, the democratic process and help them to understand their duties, responsibilities and rights as citizens. The competition had two strands: a debating competition and an essay competition. It culminated with the winners presenting an action plan to the Prime Minister. The Government will now respond to the issues raised by the children during the Parliament.

9.13 Spiritual, moral, social and cultural development and citizenship in Scotland

9.13.1 In Scotland, the 5-14 Curriculum Programme for pupils between those ages offers a number of opportunities for pupils to learn about spiritual, moral, social and cultural development and citizenship under the national guidelines on Personal and Social Development, Religious and Moral Education and Environmental Studies.

Article 28, 29, 31

9.14 Citizenship education, and other developments in the National Curriculum - views of NGOs

9.14.1 The National Children's Bureau (NCB) believe that dissemination of the Convention remains piecemeal. They would like to see copies of it more widely available in schools, more reference to it in teacher training, and that of others who work with children, and a wider range of material including internet sites, age-appropriate printed material, and library resources related to the Convention

9.14.2 The Government supports the widest dissemination of the principles of the Convention, although for many children that can more appropriately be achieved by referring to the Convention in the course of other work, and in language more suited to children than the inevitably legalistic tone of the Convention itself. These views of NGOs on dissemination of the Convention therefore link closely with the issues related to citizenship education described above.

9.14.3 There have been other suggestions from NGOs for widening of the National Curriculum, for example to include sex and relationship education. They noted with approval that the QCA consultation report on citizenship education[94] specifically asks about its relationship with personal and social education: and that the DfEE has appointed a national advisory group on personal and social education.

9.14.4 The Social Exclusion Unit published its report on teenage pregnancy on 14 June 1999. Following the report the DfEE will issue new draft guidance on sex and relationships education by the end of the year which will underline how vital it is that pupils are taught sex education which is appropriate for their age. The Government wants teachers to be better trained to teach children about sex and relationships. The Teacher Training Agency will shortly produce proposals for the accreditation of specialist sex and relationships education teachers. In addition, the Government wants all Ofsted inspections to cover sex and relationships education and to make sure their inspectors are properly trained to do so. Parents will continue to have a major say in the sex and relationships education offered at schools and will work in partnership with staff and governors on the development of school sex education policies. They will also retain their right to withdraw

---

94 *Education for citizenship and the teaching of democracy in schools.* Final report of the Advisory Group on Citizenship 22 September 1998. Ref: QCA/98/245.

their children from all or part of sex education, but as now the Government expects that very few will choose to do so.

9.14.5   The Personal, Social and Health Education Advisory Group's report was also published on 14 June 1999. It makes a strong educational case for PSHE and suggests how the best practice in our most successful schools can be built on to develop a coherent approach within and beyond the curriculum. Good Personal, Social and Health Education is a major means by which schools promote their pupils' personal and social development, health and well being.

9.15 Personal Learning Plans – Scotland

Article 29

9.15.1   The Government believes that children need to be recognised as individuals and given the personal support and encouragement they require. They are therefore introducing personal learning plans, to be piloted in new Community Schools. The plans will set out a programme of learning for each child, taking into account their individual needs, experience and progress. Key features will include an assessment of children soon after entry into education, forming the starting point of the plan; an agreed programme, including targets for achievement which will be regularly reviewed and updated to ensure that it remains relevant to the pupil's needs throughout his or her time at school; and an outline of the main responsibilities of the school, parent and pupil in relation to the learning plan. The plan will initially be agreed with parents, with the pupil taking increasing responsibility for the plan as they move through school.

9.16 Peer Education and Peer Counselling

9.16.1   Through the National Mentoring Network (NMN), the Department promotes mentoring, including peer tutoring opportunities for pupils in schools, to help motivate, inspire and raise aspirations and achievement. DfEE is currently funding a cross-age tutoring project in Birmingham (Secondary School pupils acting as tutors in local primary schools), and another in Bedfordshire, in which post-16 students act as "buddies" to incoming Middle school pupils.

9.16.2   The DfEE has recently undertaken a survey of Secondary Schools to establish the extent of different types of mentoring being used, including peer tutoring.

9.17 Improving attendance at school in England

Article 28

9.17.1   Improving school attendance of registered pupils of compulsory school age (5-16) is a key element in the Government's drive to raise educational standards. The price young people pay for irregular attendance is all too apparent: only 8% of persistent truants obtain five or more GCSEs at grades A-C, compared with 54% of those who have never truanted in year 11. In addition the Youth Cohort Study shows that young people who truant are less likely to have a good job offering training and more likely to be unemployed or inactive than those who attend regularly. There are also wide social consequences. The 1996 Audit Commission report "Misspent Youth" indicated that 65% of school-age offenders sentenced in court were persistent truants or had been excluded from school.

9.17.2   Each year in England almost a million registered pupils miss at least one half day without the school's authority. About 50,000 are so absent on any one day. The 1998 National Pupil Absence Tables published by the DfEE on 1 December 1998 indicate a slight increase in the time lost to unauthorised absence in maintained schools - 1.1% compared to 1.0% in 1997. In primary schools, levels of unauthorised absence have remained at 0.5% of scheduled schooling missed.

9.17.3   The Government has therefore set an ambitious goal of reducing the learning time lost due to unauthorised absence by one third by year 2002. To assist schools and local education authorities meet this target, a new major grant programme has been introduced. £500 million over three years is being made available to cut truancy, unruly classroom behaviour and unnecessary exclusions. The programme will involve co-operation between schools, local councils and police in a package of measures including computerised registration facilities to monitor attendance, additional staff to follow up unexplained absences and support for initiatives such as truancy watch schemes.

9.18 Improving attendance at school in Scotland

Article 28

9.18.1   In 1995 the Scottish Initiative on Attendance, Absence and Attainment (SIAAA) was set up jointly between HM Inspectorate of Schools and the University of Strathclyde. Its aims were:-

a to raise awareness of the importance of attendance and attainment,

b to highlight and disseminate examples of good practice;

c to encourage schools, School Boards and parents to improve their skills and knowledge on attendance matters; and

d to highlight disruption caused to a pupil's learning by high levels of authorised and unauthorised absence.

9.18.2   It offered a national programme of staff development courses on attendance policy, monitoring and evaluating attendance, working with parents and School Boards and raising pupil and teacher expectations. A regular newsletter *The School Supporter* was issued to all schools.

9.18.3   Many innovative approaches to combat truancy have been developed and publicised by individual schools. These include the preparation of absence and lateness notification slips to overcome the reluctance of parents to provide notes to explain absence smart card systems for senior pupils, mailshots to all parents including a newsletter and an attendance print-out for all pupils, positive letters home for good attendance and incentive schemes based on attendance. The work of schools has been brought together in *Close to the Mark*[95], a publication of good practice launched in December 1997. It has been produced by the

---

95 *Close to the Mark*, ISBN 1 85098 56 7, published July 1997, Scottish Initiative on Attendance, Absence and Attainment, University of Strathclyde.

SIAAA and presents a wide range of examples on good practice, as well as examples to help a school evaluate and develop its own practice.

9.18.4   As part of the Government's initiative to raise standards in schools, a national objective to minimise levels of levels of absence in Scotland has been announced. Within that it will be for schools and education authorities to set detailed targets and develop strategies for improving performance on attendance.

9.19 Improving attendance at school in Wales

Article 28

9.19.1   The Welsh Office has accepted targets recommended by the Social Exclusion Unit, in its report on school exclusion and truancy, for a reduction in the level of exclusions and truancy by one third by the year 2001. The Department will issue guidance on school attendance and related matters *later in 1998.*

9.20 Nursery education in England and Wales

Article 28, 29

9.20.1   The Government is committed to high quality early education integrated with childcare and family support where needed ; and to co-operation and partnership between the state, private and voluntary sectors in the planning and provision of services.

9.20.2   The nursery voucher scheme established by the previous Government was discontinued at the end of the summer term 1997. This was replaced by a new planning approach in which representative partnerships work with local education authorities to produce Early Years Development Plans (EYDPs) for their areas.

9.20.3   The first EYDPs were approved in March 1998. These guarantee nursery education places from September 1998 for all 4 year olds whose parents want such facilities for their child. This means free places for up to 650,000 four year olds in England, and requires LEAs to work closely with approximately 16,000 voluntary groups and private nurseries. For the longer term, EYDPs will show how childcare and education will be integrated, and how provision will be extended to include three year olds.

9.20.4   In July 1998, the Government announced:

a the launch of the Sure Start programme, an inter-departmental approach to integrated service provision for vulnerable children aged 0-3 (see section 8.35); and

b a doubling of nursery education places for three year olds by 2002, entailing 190,000 extra free places.

9.20.5   Early Years Development Plans have also been prepared for 22 Welsh local authority areas. From 1 September 1998 all 4 year olds are entitled to at least a part-time early years education place. Welsh plans also take account of the need to plan for the provision of early years education through the medium of the Welsh language.

9.20.6 The Government has also introduced a pilot programme of Early Excellence Centres (EECs) to help develop and test high quality, integrated, family-oriented early years services. The immediate target is to establish 25 over three years and, at the time of writing, 11 had been approved. As "beacons of excellence", EECs will work with other agencies and providers to develop integrated services and raise standards.

9.21 Pre-school education in Scotland

Article 28, 29

9.21.1 The Government are committed to an ambitious programme of expansion. By the winter of 1998, all parents in Scotland with children in the pre-school year had access to a high quality, part-time pre-school education place for their child. At present over 90% of eligible children undertake pre-school education. Local authorities have responsibility for planning, co-ordinating and delivering places in their area. They may do so through their own managed centres, or by commissioning places in the private and voluntary sectors. Local authorities are funded by direct grant.

9.21.2 The Government are also committed to extending universal provision to all 3 year olds, from the term after their third birthday, by 2002. With their partners local authorities expect to educate around 60% of three year olds in school year 1999-2000, which represents good progress towards the target. An additional £138 million has been allocated to early education over the period 1999 to 2002 to fund this expansion. This brings the total budget for pre-school provision for this period to £384 million.

9.21.3 At present, pre-school education and day-care of children are regulated under differing streams of regulation. Local Authority nursery schools and classes are regulated under Education legislation, whereas pre-school outside school sites and day care for children 0-8 is regulated under 'Children's' legislation. This has resulted in differing staffing and other standards being applicable in different settings, where the same type of activity is being conducted. The Scottish Office has recently issued a consultation paper on this issue, *Regulation of Early Education and Childcare*[96], which discusses the possibilities of harmonising the regulatory standards which apply in pre-school education and childcare settings. Responses to this consultation paper are due by June 30, 1999 and Scottish Ministers will then consider appropriate methods of progress.

9.22 Access to pre-school education in Northern Ireland

Article 28, 29

9.22.1 In Northern Ireland the Government has established a Pre-school Education Advisory Group (PEAG) in each Education and Library Board area to prepare and assist with the delivery of a pre-school education expansion programme beginning in September 1998. The expansion programme is designed to provide a full year of pre-school education to all children in the

96 Published by the Scottish Office Education and Industry Department, March 1999.

year before they enter compulsory education, and will be delivered through partnership between the statutory, voluntary and private sectors. The phasing of the programme will be dependent on the available resources. The PEAGs will work closely with existing Area Early Years Committees in co-ordinating the planning of pre-school education with other early years services.

9.23 Education and academic attainment of boys

Article 28

9.23.1   The Government is concerned at the gap in some areas of the curriculum between the performance of boys and girls at school. A report by the Government Office for Standards in Education ("Recent Research on Gender and Educational Performance", Ofsted (1998)) has analysed recent research on the causes of this gap. It shows there are many complex reasons and that there is no simple, single solution.

9.23.2   The Government has taken action in a number of areas to address this issue. Local Education Authorities are now required to demonstrate in their Education Development Plans what action they will take, where relevant. Trainee teachers are being made aware of the need to set high standards, regardless of gender. The Government is encouraging and enabling schools to analyse the performance of groups of pupils by gender. The Government is also funding projects which address boys' underachievement, particularly in literacy.

9.24 Discrimination in school exclusions – views of NGOs and the Government's response

Article 28, 2

9.24.1   Some NGOs commented that there was evidence that children of ethnic minorities were disproportionately represented among those excluded from school. The Churches' Commission for Racial Justice pointed out, for example, that a report of September 1996 by the Office for Standards in Education found that African/Caribbean pupils were up to six times more likely to be excluded than white children. Some 150 African/Caribbean children in every thousand were excluded (1993-94 figures). The Children's Society argued for ethnic monitoring to inform policy in this area, and to enable the possibility of discrimination to be systematically guarded against.

9.24.2   The Government has taken action on these points. The Government's White Paper on Education *Excellence in Schools*[97] made clear the Government's commitment to raising educational standards and to equality of opportunity for all pupils. It recognised that children from ethnic minority backgrounds now form a tenth of the pupil population in British schools. These children bring with them cultural richness and diversity, but some are particularly at risk of under-achieving. The Government is determined that all must have a full opportunity to succeed and has introduced many policies which will benefit ethnic minority pupils alongside other children, for example a new focus on literacy and numeracy, and other measures to raise standards and effectiveness, such as smaller class sizes,

97 Cm 3681: ISBN 0-10-136812-7.

especially at the infant stage, enabling more attention to be given to children needing particular support.

9.24.3   The Department for Education and Employment has set up an advisory group on raising ethnic minority achievement to help forge a new partnership at national and local level, and to take action to:

a   spread the successful methods of schools that have been most effective in raising ethnic minority pupils' achievement;

b   consult on how best to monitor ethnic minority pupils' performance at national, local and school level, and how to create and implement effective plans of action where monitoring reveals under-performance;

c   provide guidance on best practice in raising awareness of important ethnic considerations, in tackling racial harassment and stereotyping, in promoting attendance and reducing exclusion of ethnic minority pupils, and in creating a harmonious environment in which learning can flourish; and

d   review the level and delivery of specialist support in schools for raising the participation and achievements of ethnic minority pupils to ensure that the support meets continuing needs.

9.24.4   In the light of the Social Exclusion Unit report on Truancy and School Exclusion (published in May 1998), the Government will be pursuing the following initiatives aimed specifically at reducing ethnic minority exclusion in England and Wales:

a   publishing full data on exclusions including a breakdown by ethnic minority group;

b   requiring OFSTED to conduct special inspections of high-excluding schools, including those disproportionately excluding ethnic minority pupils;

c   promoting community mentoring in ethnic minority communities;

9.24.5   In Scotland forms for recording exclusions from schools have recently been changed to include details of ethnicity in order that this can be monitored.

9.25 Children's right to be heard with respect to their exclusion from school – England and Wales

Article 12, 28

9.25.1   The Government accepts that it will often be appropriate for the child to address the governors' discipline committee or the appeal panel about his or her exclusion from school. The Government's statutory guidance, "Social Inclusion: Pupil Support" (Circular 10/99 issued by the Department for Education and Employment in July 1999), states that exclusion panels should allow the pupil to attend the hearing and speak on his or her behalf, if he/she and his/her parents so request, unless there is good reason to refuse.

9.26 Children's right to appeal against school exclusion – Northern Ireland

Article 12, 28

9.26.1   Under Article 124 of the Education Reform (Northern Ireland) Order 1989, a principal must determine measures for promoting self-discipline and good behaviour on the part of pupils and for their enforcement. In determining these measures a principal must have regard to any guidance provided by the Board of Governors: in a number of secondary schools mechanisms are in place to allow the views of pupils to be expressed.

9.26.2   Article 39 of the Education and Libraries (Northern Ireland) Order 1993 requires school authorities to prepare schemes specifying the procedures relating to the suspension and expulsion of pupils from school. The Regulations made by the Department of Education for Northern Ireland to specify the matters to be included in the schemes require the schemes to provide for the parent or the pupil himself where he has attained the age of eighteen to be advised of his right of appeal against a decision to expel the pupil from school.

9.27 Exclusions from school in Scotland

Article 12, 28

9.27.1   The Scottish Office commissioned a major research project into exclusions from school from Moray House Institute of Education in 1994, which was completed in 1997[98]. The study found that while there was a general agreement that exclusion from school was a severe sanction which should be used as a last resort in reaction to serious or criminal misbehaviour, there were differences in practice across the country and within authorities. The Government therefore issued draft national guidance on exclusions for consultation and issued a final version in April 1998. In encouraging consistency in handling exclusions from school, the guidelines emphasise a multi-agency, inclusive approach and highlight good practice.

9.27.2   The Committee criticised the fact that children do not have the right to express their opinion when decisions are made to exclude them from school. As in England, for the same reasons, the legal right to appeal rests with the parent, or with the pupil if he is over school leaving age. However, the national guidance launched by the Government in Scotland in April 1998 highlights the need to take account of the provisions of the United Nations Convention on the Rights of the Child, stressing in particular articles 3.1 and 12.

9.27.3   Schools and authorities are setting targets to reduce exclusions in order to achieve the Government's target of a reduction of a third by 2002. The Government recognises that additional resources will be necessary and has therefore committed £23 million in additional funds to support children at risk of exclusion or who have been excluded. The funds will also be used

---

98 Exclusions from School and Alternatives Series, all published by Moray House Institute of Education.
Education Authority Policy and Procedures: ISBN 189979509X, 1997.
Alternative Education Provision for Excluded Pupils - A Literature Review: ISBN 1899795103, 1997.
The Headteachers' Perspective: ISBN 1899795111, 1997.
Case Studies of School Practice: ISBN 189979512X, 1997.

to provide, by 2002, a full timetable for every pupil excluded for over three weeks. The Government has stressed in providing these funds that reducing the need for and incidence of exclusion should be addressed in an inclusive manner; treating all pupils equally and offering them all an educational experience of value.

9.27.4   The funds are in addition to those provided from 1997-2000 to pilot projects offering alternatives to exclusion. The projects being supported under this programme include those which offer personal learning or behaviour plans to pupils; work placements which meet the needs of individual children better than the standard curriculum; and multi-disciplinary teams focusing on the whole needs of the child. They are being evaluated by HM Inspectors of Schools.

9.28 Training for work: The New Deal for Young People – views of NGOs and the Government's position

Article 26, 29

9.28.1   Non-government organisations support the New Deal, the government's programme to tackle youth unemployment. This is a major programme based on novel methods of long-term funding for the life of the present Parliament, and involving new partnerships with employers in the private and public sector, and with the voluntary sector.

9.28.2   Some NGOs have expressed concern at the lower age limit of the scheme, which is available to 18-24 year olds. They fear that 16 and 17-year-olds who are neither in education, training nor employment – and ineligible for social security benefits – might suffer by their exclusion. They also raise concerns about the level of benefit and whether the amount payable is adequate.

9.28.3   The Government believe that this point raised by NGOs is not well-founded. Although 16 and 17 year olds are not eligible for the New Deal, they already have access to education and training programmes which will help them achieve recognised qualifications and also help them to achieve work skills. The Government believe that 16 and 17 year olds should be in education, training or work involving some kind of learning, rather than dependent on the benefits system. That is why young people who leave full-time education are guaranteed the offer of a work-based training place with an allowance – though in some cases the training will give those concerned employed status with a wage. The Government's aim is that every young person should be on the road to achieving a proper qualification.

9.28.4   The Government is firmly committed to tackling poverty and improving the living standards of the poorest households. But the Government believes that the best way out of poverty is by helping people into work and giving them the opportunity to improve their lifestyle for themselves, where they are able, and by providing extra help where they are not. There is no objective way of deciding what are adequate benefit rates. Levels of benefit need to take account of the competing demands on public expenditure and work incentives.

9.28.5   For those who cannot work the Government have devoted an extra £1.2bn a year to supporting children and tackling child poverty. The Government have also increased the child personal allowance for children under 11 in Income Support, Income-based Jobseeker's Allowance, Family Credit, Disability Working Allowance, Housing Benefit and Council Tax Benefit by £2.50 per week, per child from 9 November. And, from April 1999, child benefit will be increased by £2.95 for the eldest child for this group. The Government have also announced a disability income guarantee for the most severely disabled people.

9.28.6   The Secretary of State for Education and Employment launched the Investing in Young People Strategy in December, 1997. In July 1999 he announced an enhanced strategy – called *Connexions* – for making sure that far more young people continue in education and training until at least 19. This will build on current initiatives including:

a   ensuring young people have the help, support and guidance that will raise their aspirations and tackle any personal and family problems standing in the way.

b   encouraging employees aged 16-17, who did not receive good qualifications at school, to take advantage of the new right to study or train for approved qualifications with the support of their employer.

c   ensuring that the range of qualifications and courses is attractive and motivating, both to individuals and to employers.

d   building on the best work being done in schools, in colleges and in work based training to drive up quality and standards of delivery across all models of learning; and

e   tackling barriers to learning; including financial barriers.

9.28.7   Increasing the number of young people who want to learn – and improving their success in getting the skills and qualifications – will make the difference for individuals between a lifetime of low skills and low wages, and making a real contribution to society and gaining proper reward for it. All young people need to access to high quality, comprehensive and impartial careers information, advice and guidance.

9.28.8   New Start is a key strand of *Connexions*. This initiative, announced on 24 November 1997, aims to motivate and re-engage 14-17 year olds who have dropped out of learning or are at risk of doing so. It is not a new programme replacing existing provision but a strategy to tackle disaffection amongst this age group.

9.28.9   An important part of New Start is the development of multi-agency partnerships working at local level building on and drawing together existing initiatives. DfEE is currently funding 17 projects. All projects were asked to identify the scale and nature of disaffection in their area; the effectiveness of local learning provision; the scope to strengthen existing or introduce new provision and to develop a strategy and an action plan based on this research.

9.29 A new Learning Gateway For 16 and 17 Year Olds

Article 26, 29

9.29.1   As part of *Connexions* the Government is committed to providing better opportunities for all young people to participate in learning and achieve to the highest level possible. It is particularly concerned to engage in learning those 16 and 17 years olds who lack the basic skills, qualifications and attitudes to enter education and training opportunities at NVQ level 2 or who have become detached from learning altogether.

9.29.2   A Learning Gateway for this group of 16 and 17 years old will be introduced from this September 1999. Building on the lessons learned from New Start partnerships projects and other similar initiatives the Learning Gateway will provide a client centred approach to support young people who have drifted away from learning and need additional help to enter mainstream learning opportunities.

9.30 Modern Apprenticeships and National Traineeships:

9.30.1   Modern Apprenticeships were introduced in 1995 as a challenge from Government to industry to increase radically the supply of skills of young entrants to the workforce at craft and technician level, NVQ3. National Traineeships were introduced in 1997 engaging young people in training to NVQ2 level.

9.30.2   MAs and NTrs are available throughout the UK, albeit in slightly different form in Scotland and Northern Ireland to reflect the particular features of their education and training systems. In England and Wales training frameworks are available in 82 sectors, with another 15 under development, extending industry approved Apprenticeship training to new sectors vital for competitiveness including IT and Telecommunications. There are 47 frameworks for National Traineeships. The top 5 sectors in terms of starts are business administration, engineering, manufacturing, retailing, motor industry and hotel and catering. Training frameworks must include an NVQ level 2 or 3, Key Skills, and the underpinning knowledge and skills required by employers.

9.30.3   MA is open to young people aged 16 to 24 and is the main work based training option for those aged 19 plus. NTr is open to young people aged 16-24, but for the priority group aged 16 to 18 mainly. Over 250,000 young people have embarked on MA since its national introduction, with substantial year on year increases for young people in training, now 133,000, which represents 45% of all workbased training for young people. There have been 30,000 starts on National Traineeships since its introduction.

9.31 Time for Study or Training Legislation

9.31.1   From 1 September 1999, young employees aged 16 or 17 who have not attained a certain "standard of achievement" in their previous education or training will have the right to reasonable paid time off to study or train. The "standard of achievement" is in essence level 2, ie: 5 GCSEs grades A*-C, and NVQ level 2, Intermediate GNVQ, or certain other qualifications set out in regulations. Study or training can be undertaken in the workplace, in college, through open or distance learning or elsewhere. Employees who are aged 18 will have the right to time off to complete the study or training they have already begun. There is no exemption for small firms and no qualifying period of employment for the young employee.

9.31.2 There will be new arrangements for support for FE students and pupils in school posts –16 from September 1999. These arrangements, which include a means-tested Education Maintenance Allowance (EMA) for young people who stay on in learning, will be reviewed by DfEE after about three years of operation, and the Government will then decide the shape of longer term provision. The EMA pilots will operate in selected areas to July 2002.

9.31.3 The Government does recognise that certain groups of vulnerable young people should be eligible for benefits. Those in certain vulnerable groups (for example those leaving local authority care) or those at risk of severe hardship are able to claim Jobseeker's Allowance (JSA). The vast majority of 16 and 17 year olds applying for assistance under the JSA severe hardship provisions are successful. There is no evidence to suggest that young people in need are being wrongly denied benefit. Young people who are not available for work, for example those with disabilities or certain lone parents, are entitled to Income Support.

9.31.4 DfEE is closely monitoring the impact of the New Deal on the availability of work based training opportunities for young people. Initial evidence in Pathfinder areas suggests that opportunities for 16-17 year olds have not been significantly affected.

9.31.5 In Northern Ireland the Employment Rights (Time Off for Study or Training) (NI) Order 1998 replicates those sections of the Teaching and Higher Education Act 1998 (ss 32 and 33) which give young persons the right to paid time off work for study or training, by amending the Employment Rights (NI) Order 1996.

9.31.6 In addition to right to time off, the Order enables an employee to seek a remedy by taking a complaint to an industrial tribunal if he or she claims to have been unreasonably refused permission to take time off work or to have been denied payment for time taken off to study. By doing so it keeps Northern Ireland employment rights legislation in line with Great Britain

9.32 New Deal for Lone Parents

Article 26, 29

9.32.1 The Government is concerned that the children of lone parents should not live a life of poverty and social exclusion. The key to this is to ensure that lone parents enjoy the same choice as parents in couples to avoid that social exclusion by obtaining work. The New Deal for Lone Parents has been introduced to provide tailored advice and assistance to individual lone parents to help them overcome the barriers they face as they seek to improve the lives of their families through obtaining paid employment. It is a voluntary programme targeted principally at lone parents on Income Support whose youngest child is of school age, but those with younger children are welcome to take advantage of the service.

9.32.2   The New Deal for Lone Parents was introduced in eight prototype areas in July 1997. The programme was extended nationally to lone parents making a new Income Support claim from April 1998 and was extended further to all lone parents already on Income Support from October 1998.

9.33 Bullying in school – England and Wales

Article 28, 19

9.33.1   Research undertaken for the former Department for Education by Sheffield University between 1991 and 1993 showed that 10% of primary and 4% of secondary pupils were bullied at least once a week; and 27% and 10% of primary and secondary pupils respectively were bullied at least sometimes. Subsequent surveys have broadly confirmed these findings. It is clear that bullying is widespread and no school is immune from it.

9.33.2   The Government attaches a high priority to helping schools prevent and combat bullying. Since 1994, the Department for Education and Employment has taken a number of measures to provide schools with guidance so that they can tackle the problem of bullying themselves. These have included :

    a   releasing two short public information films on the theme *Don't Suffer in Silence* which were shown widely on television;

    b   publishing leaflets giving practical advice to parents and children;

    c   publishing an anti-bullying pack, made available free on request to all maintained schools in England; and

    d   publishing research on the pack which showed that schools just starting out on their anti-bullying work found the pack invaluable; although most schools had a policy on bullying, either separately or as part of a wider behaviour and discipline policy, some still did not and most schools thought there had been a reduction in the number of bullying incidents since using the pack.

9.33.3   In July 1997 the White Paper in England *Excellence in Schools*[99], and in Wales the White Paper *Building Excellent Schools Together*[100], reminded schools that effective strategies to deal with bullying should form a central part of their behaviour policies. Section 61 (4)(b) of the School Standards and Framework Act 1998 now requires the head teacher to determine measures to prevent all forms of bullying among pupils. This will come into force on 1 September 1999. The Government will also be taking more active steps to spread information on good practice in combating the problem.

9.33.4   The Government recognises that it is important to involve pupils when drawing up a school's discipline policy. It is good practice which is already recommended in the DfEE's guidance on pupil behaviour and discipline. And the Government is reinforcing the point in new integrated guidance on 'Social

---

99   Cm3681: ISBN 0-10-136812-7, published by the Stationery Office.

100 *Building Excellent Schools Together* Cm 3701. Published by The Stationery Office for the Welsh Office. ISBN 0 10 137012 1.

Inclusion: Pupil Support' which is to be issued for consultation shortly. However, Ministers rejected amendments to the School Standards and Framework Bill to require the governing body and the headteacher to consult pupils in the development of the school's discipline policy.

9.33.5   The Government believes it is important to determine when pupils could best make a contribution to drawing up the school's discipline policy. But that should be for individual schools to decide in the light of their particular circumstances. In some cases that may be before the governing body makes its statement of general principles; in others, headteachers may decide that it is best to consult pupils when determining the school's rules and codes of conduct. Schools need flexibility over who and when to consult; that is best left to be covered in guidance.

9.34 Bullying – Scotland

Article 28, 19

9.34.1   In 1994 The Scottish Office issued to all schools a leaflet aimed directly at children entitled *Let's Stop Bullying: Advice for Young People*[101]. In August 1995, the Department issued a further leaflet providing advice for parents and families entitled *Let's Stop Bullying: Advice for Parents and Families*[102]. In autumn 1995, the Scottish Schools Ethos Network was set up in response to the demand from schools to share information, ideas and ways of improving school ethos. The Network is sponsored jointly by Moray House Institute of Education and The Scottish Office and now has over 750 members. Last year, the Government asked local authorities for information on progress in implementing their anti-bullying policies. The review revealed that while there were a number of examples of good practice in tackling bullying, overall awareness of the problem and effective strategies to tackle it were variable.

9.34.2   In October 1998 the Government announced its intention to set up a network to disseminate good practice in tackling bullying and to make advice and support available to schools across Scotland. Expressions of interest in running the network have been invited; the network should be up and running in early 1999.

9.34.3   Information on good practice in anti-bullying polices was also included in *Close to the Mark*[103] published in 1997. In February 1998 the Government pledged £34,000 in financial assistance to ensure that the ChildLine Scotland dedicated Bullying Helpline continues.

9.35 Teacher training

Article 29

9.35.1   The United Kingdom Government has introduced new standards for the award of qualified teacher status and a national curriculum for initial teacher training covering the core subjects of English, mathematics, science and information and communications technology.

101 *Let's Stop Bullying: Advice for Young People*, Dd 8403820 10/97, 1994, The Stationery Office.

102 *Let's Stop Bullying: Advice for Parents and Families*, Dd 8433579 8/95, 1995, The Stationery Office.

103 *Close to the Mark*, ISBN 1 85098 56 7 7, 1997, Scottish Initiative on Attendance, Absence and Attainment, University of Strathclyde.

9.35.2 Whilst the new standards do not explicitly mention the UN Convention on the Rights of the Child they fall within the spirit and philosophy of the recommendation in article 29. They do this by expecting all trainee teachers to meet all the standards including:

a establishing and maintaining a purposeful working atmosphere;

b setting high expectations for pupils' behaviour, establishing and maintaining a good standard of discipline through well focused teaching and through positive and productive relationships;

c establishing a safe environment which supports learning and in which pupils feel secure and confident;

d using teaching methods which sustain the momentum of pupils' work and keep all pupils engaged;

e exploiting opportunities to improve pupils' basic skills in literacy, numeracy and IT, and the individual and collaborative study skills needed for effective learning, including information retrieval from libraries, texts and other sources;

f exploiting opportunities to contribute to the quality of pupils' wider educational development, including their personal, spiritual, moral, social and cultural development;

g setting high expectations for all pupils notwithstanding individual differences, including gender, and cultural and linguistic backgrounds;

h providing opportunities to develop pupils' wider understanding by relating their learning to real and work-related examples;

9.35.3 Additional elements in the training of teachers of pupils aged 3-11 are: –

a providing structured learning opportunities which advance pupils' personal and social development, communication skills, knowledge and understanding of the world physical development and creative development;

b understanding their responsibilities in relation to school policies and practices, including those concerned with pastoral and personal safety matters, including bullying;

c recognising that learning takes place inside and outside the school context;

d understanding the need to liaise effectively with parents and carers; and

e having a working knowledge and understanding of teachers' legal liabilities relating to the Race Relations Act 1976, the Sex Discrimination Act and section 3(5) of the Children Act 1989.

9.35.4   The Government will consider including explicit mention of the UN Convention on the Rights of the Child in the standards for Qualified Teacher Status when the Teacher Training Agency reports and advises Ministers on the standards. The TTA is due to report by December 2000 taking account of OFSTED evidence and the review of the pupils' National Curriculum. The Government does not propose to revise the standards, which took effect in May 1998, at the present time.

9.35.5   The standards for the award of Qualified Teacher Status set out above only took effect in May 1998. Therefore, we do not propose to revise them at this time. The Teacher Training Agency is due to report and advise Ministers on the standards for QTS by December 2000, taking account of OFSTED evidence and the review of the pupils' National Curriculum.

9.36 Teacher training in Wales

Article 28

9.36.1   The Welsh Office has introduced new criteria which all courses of initial teacher training must meet, and has specified the English, Mathematics and Welsh curricula which must be taught to all trainees on all courses of primary initial teacher training. The criteria set out the standard of knowledge, understanding and skills all trainees must demonstrate in order successfully to complete a course of initial teacher training and be eligible for Qualified Teacher Status.

9.36.2   In addition, the Welsh Office is consulting on the content of the national curriculum for initial teacher training for Primary Science, Secondary Science, Secondary English, Secondary Welsh, Secondary Mathematics and the use of information and communications technology in subject teaching.

9.37 Teacher training in Scotland

Article 28

9.37.1   There are separate arrangements in Scotland for teacher training. All courses of initial teacher education must comply with guidelines issued by the Scottish Office Education and Industry Department. These guidelines have recently been reviewed and revised guidelines, which come into operation from academic session 1999-2000 were issued on 5 November 1998.

9.37.2   The guidelines make clear that new teachers must be committed to promoting pupil achievement and raising pupils' expectations of themselves and others, in collaboration with colleagues, parents and other members of the community. They must value and promote equality of opportunity and fairness, and adopt non-discriminatory practices, in respect of age, disability, gender, race or religion. The guidelines set out the skills to be attained by beginner teachers. These include : –

    a being able, whether at pre-school, primary or secondary level, to play a full part in developing pupils' skills in literacy and numeracy;

    b demonstrating a knowledge of, and ability to play a part in, personal and social education, health education, enterprise and, when appropriate, vocational education;

    c motivating and sustaining the interest of all pupils in a class;

d   setting expectations and a pace of work which make appropriate demands on all pupils and ensure that more able pupils are effectively challenged;

e   identifying and responding appropriately to pupils with difficulties in, or barriers to, learning and recognising when to seek further advice in relation to their special educational needs;

f   responding appropriately to gender, social, cultural, linguistic and religious differences among pupils;

g   encouraging pupils to take initiatives in, and become responsible for, their own learning;

h   demonstrating that he or she knows about and is able to apply the principles and practices which promote positive behaviour and underlie good discipline;

i   being able to create and maintain a stimulating, purposeful, orderly and safe learning environment for all pupils, including those with special educational and health needs;

j   demonstrating a knowledge of, and being able to contribute to, strategies to prevent bullying;

k   demonstrating a working knowledge of his or her contractual, pastoral and legal responsibilities;

l   demonstrating an understanding of the roles of, and how to communicate and co-operate with teachers in other schools; members of other professions and agencies concerned with pupils' learning, welfare and career development; and members of the community served by the school;

m being able to report to parents about their children's progress and discuss with them in a sensitive and productive way matters related to their children's personal, social and emotional development; and

n   demonstrating an understanding of international, national and local guidelines on child protection and teachers' roles and responsibilities in this area.

9.38 The needs of disabled children – views of NGOs

Article 28, 29, 23

9.38.1   Mencap commented, during the preparation of this report, on the increasing recognition among professionals of the rights of disabled children to express their views in respect of Care Plans made within the provisions of the Children Act. But they were worried that there might be a need for new ways of translating this awareness into everyday practice. Research by Minkes et al 1994 and Morris 1997 detail the rarity of consultation with disabled young people about plans to accommodate them away from their family.

9.39.2   This links with the need, in Mencap's view, to equip field and residential social workers with the necessary skills in attending to the messages given by disabled children. There is an urgent need to develop both guidance and a range of multi-media materials to assist staff in consulting disabled young people about their wishes and feelings. There is also a need to develop the parental awareness of children's rights and the value of involving disabled children in plans and especially in their own Transition Plans. The Department of Health have recognised these risks, and commissioned independent research, recently published, as a contribution to improving the abilities of professionals in ascertaining the wishes and feelings of disabled children.[104]

9.38.3 Mencap and other organisations have noted the efforts in the United Kingdom to re-focus Social Services from protection towards prevention. In the case of disabled children, they are concerned to ensure that this does not harm the progress being made in protecting disabled children from abuse. The emphasis on neglect and emotional abuse contained in the recent Consultation Paper Working Together[105] is very much welcomed as these forms of abuse are particularly prevalent among children with learning disabilities.

9.38.4 The United Kingdom Government maintains its efforts to ensure that disabled children have access to education tailored to their needs. Mencap have warned that the emphasis on the National Curriculum and on league tables must not be allowed to have a negative impact on the educational opportunities available to disabled children. They are concerned about the need to provide adequate training for Learning Support Assistants, and that so far as possible disabled children and their parents should have the same degree of choice of school as other children. A particular concern, which the Government recognises, is the risk that disabled young people, and particularly those with challenging behaviour, are vulnerable to exclusion. Mencap feel that there is a small and largely hidden group of children with complex health needs who are excluded from school by a failure at national and local levels to develop inter-agency protocols to meet health needs in educational settings.

9.38.5 These comments were echoed by the Children's Society, who noted with approval the establishment of the Disability Commission, but pressed for continued progress on including disabled children and children with special needs in mainstream education.

9.39 Government action on the education of disabled children

Article 28, 29, 23

9.39.1 The Government has taken action which already addresses these points. From September 1998, all schools are required to set annual targets for school improvement. In addition, to the statutory core of performance targets, schools will be encouraged to set additional targets that reflect their needs and local priorities. This will take account of children with special education needs including children with disability. The Government has funded research into target setting within special schools and guidance was

---

104 Russell P. (1998). *Having a Say! - Disabled Children and Effective Partnerships in Decision-Making,* published by the Council for Disabled Children.

105 *Working Together to Safeguard Children: New Proposals for Inter-Agency Cooperation* published by the Children's Services Branch of the Department of Health, February 1998.

published in November 1998. This guidance included assessment criteria designed to help with whole-school target setting.

9.39.2 The Government, in its November 1998 document *Meeting Special Educational Needs: A programme for action*[106], addressed the issue raised by Mencap of the need to provide adequate training for Learning Support Assistants (LSAs). DfEE has commissioned research to look at both existing training available and good practice in the deployment and training of LSAs.

9.39.3 The Government recognises the importance of inclusion and choice and asked in the Green Paper "What priority measures should we take to include more pupils with special educational needs in mainstream schools?". In response the SEN Action Programme announced the intention to review the statutory framework for inclusion. In addition, the Disability Rights Task Force (DRTF) has been reviewing the present exclusion of education from provisions of the Disability Discrimination Act. If the Government's review or that of the DRTF confirm a need for changes, the Government will make them.

9.40 Special Educational Needs

Article 28, 29, 23

9.40.1 The *Code of Practice on the Identification and Assessment of Special Educational Needs (SEN)*[107] was published in 1994 to provide guidance for schools and Local Education Authorities (LEA) on their responsibilities towards all children with special educational needs. Local Education Authorities and schools have now accepted the Code as the principal guide for improving the quality of education for pupils with SEN. The Code continues to have a positive impact on schools, it has led to an improvement in provision for pupils with SEN, and the procedures recommended in the Code are becoming increasingly embedded in schools' policies and practice.

9.40.2 The Green Paper, *Excellence for All Children: Meeting Special Educational Needs*, published in October 1997 set out proposals for raising the standards of provision with SEN. Practical steps for implementing this vision were set out in *Meeting Special Educational Needs: A Programme of Action*[108], published on 5 November 1998. Key aspects of the three year programme include:

a developing a more inclusive system, e.g. by requiring LEAs to publish their policies on inclusion of children with SEN in their Education Development Plans, providing support through the Standards Fund for promoting inclusion and developing links between mainstream and special schools, increasing the Schools Access Initiative and reviewing the statutory framework for inclusion;

---

106 *Meeting Special Educational Needs: A programme for action*, ISBN 0 85522 906 ; published 1997 by DfEE.

107 *The Code of Practice on the Identification and Assessment of Special Educational Needs (SEN)*, ISBN 0 85522 444 4; published 1994 by HMSO for the Department for Education.

108 *Meeting Special Educational Needs: A programme for action*, ISBN 0 85522 906 ; published by DfEE.

b providing financial support for projects to improve provision and raise achievements of children with emotional and behavioural difficulties;

c a clear expectation that all LEAs should provide access for all parents and carers of children with SEN to parent partnership and mediation services, with a commitment to legislate if necessary;

d greater emphasis on listening to and taking account of the views of the child;

e developing the role of special schools in an increasingly inclusive education system;

f developing the knowledge and skills of all staff working with children with SEN; and

g promoting partnership between LEAs and with other local agencies to support children with SEN.

9.40.3 The Welsh Office issued a separate Green Paper in Wales *The BEST for Special Education*[109]. The Welsh Advisory Group on Special Education has been set up with a similar remit to that of the National Advisory Group. It will work to the same timetable.

9.40.4 There is a number of collaborative initiatives being undertaken by the Department for Education and Employment and the Department of Health. These include the development of Behaviour Support Plans and proposals for addressing the needs of children who have Special Educational needs as a result of emotional and behavioural difficulties. Children's rights organisations, including the NCB, were involved in preparing guidance for LEAs on Behavioural Support Plans. These initiatives have been considered by the National Advisory Group for Special Educational Needs. The Government's Social Exclusion Unit is also specifically focusing on truancy and exclusion from school.

9.40.5 Welsh local education authorities have to prepare Behaviour Support Plans in line with guidance issued by the Welsh Office in June 1998[110].

9.41 Special Educational Needs (Scotland): update

Article 28, 29, 23

9.41.1 In March 1996 The Scottish Office published a circular *Children and Young Persons with Special Educational Needs: Assessment and Recording*[111]. The main purpose of this circular is to advise education authorities, and to inform others, about the statutory arrangements in Scotland for providing for children and young persons with special educational needs and, particularly, for the undertaking of assessments and the opening of Records

---

109 Cm 3792. Published by The Stationery Office. ISBN 0 10 137922 6.

110 Welsh Office Circular 19/98 LEA *Behaviour Support Plans*. Published by the Welsh Office Education Department, Cathays Park, Cardiff CF1 3NQ. June 1998.

111 Circular 4/96, *Children and Young Persons with Special Educational Needs [Assessment and Recording]*, Edinburgh, The Scottish Office, 1996

of Needs. Education authorities throughout Scotland adhere to the principles and practices contained in it.

9.41.2   In May 1998 The Scottish Office issued A Discussion Paper *Special Educational Needs in Scotland*[114] which invited views on how existing educational arrangements may be improved and made even more responsive to the needs of children and young people with special educational needs and their families. In November 1998 the Government announced a number of measures, worth £8 million per year, including the establishment of a national SEN information and advice service for children and families, additional resources for staff development and training, and increased support for organisations working in the area of special educational needs.

9.41.3   The Discussion Paper also announced the formation of an Advisory Committee to undertake a strategic review and make recommendations on the co-ordination and provision of education for severe low incidence disabilities. This committee will submit recommendations to Ministers in early 1999.

9.41.4   The Scottish Social Inclusion Network has been established to assist the Government develop a social inclusion strategy for Scotland, a key element of which will be to focus on promoting inclusion among children and young people.

9.42 Children belonging to a minority or indigenous group

Article 28, 29, 31, 2

9.42.1   It is a fundamental objective of the United Kingdom Government to enable members of ethnic minorities to participate freely in the economic, social and public life of the nation, with all the benefits and responsibilities which that entails, while still being able to maintain their own culture, traditions, language and values. Government action is directed towards addressing problems of discrimination and disadvantage which prevent members of ethnic minorities from fulfilling their potential with the same opportunities as other members of the community.

9.42.2   The Race Relations Act 1976, which applies to the whole of Great Britain but not to Northern Ireland, makes racial discrimination unlawful in employment, training and related matters, in education, in the provision of goods, facilities and services, and in the disposal and management of premises. The Act gives individuals a right of direct access to the civil courts and industrial tribunals for legal remedies for unlawful discrimination.

9.42.3   The Race Relations (Northern Ireland) Order 1997 came into operation on 4 August 1997. The legislation follows the general lines of the

---

114 *Special Educational Needs in Scotland: A Discussion Paper*, Edinburgh, The Scottish Office, 1998.

Race Relations Act 1976. It gives individuals a right of access to the courts and industrial tribunals for legal redress. The Order also established the Commission for Racial Equality for Northern Ireland to help enforce the legislation and promote equality of opportunity between people of different racial groups. The traditional Irish Traveller community is defined as a racial group for the purposes of the legislation.

9.43 Development of respect for the natural environment

9.43.1 Environmental education provides opportunities for pupils to develop respect for the natural environment. The National Curriculum provides a range of opportunities and requirements for children aged 5 to 16 to study environmental matters. In particular, secondary school pupils must be taught about living things in their environment, ecosystems, population and resources, settlements and their effect on land use, economic development, and the managing and sustaining of environments. The current review of the National Curriculum will be informed by, amongst other things, the recommendations of the Sustainable Development Education Panel, an external panel of education, business and environmental experts. The Panel is considering developing a variety of initiatives to reach all sectors of the population, including the young, with appropriate messages about sustainable development.

9.44 Welsh language education in Wales

Article 28, 29, 31

9.44.1 The Government is committed to a strong system of Welsh medium education: the 1997 Education White Paper *Building Excellent Schools Together*[113] gave a clear undertaking that parents who want their children to be educated in Welsh should have every opportunity to exercise that choice; and that all pupils in Wales should be given the opportunity to learn Welsh at whatever school they attend.

9.44.2 In Wales, Welsh is taught to all pupils between the ages of 5-14 either as a first or second language. Schools also use Welsh as the medium of teaching. Some 27% of primary schools use Welsh as the sole or main medium of instruction and a further 6% use it for part of the curriculum. Nearly 21% of secondary schools use Welsh as the medium of instruction for at least half their foundation subjects (such as history, geography, design & technology and music).

9.45 Wales Youth Agency

Article 28, 31

9.45.1 The Wales Youth Agency was established in 1992 to assist the development of provision of informal education for young people aged 11 to 25 in Wales, across all sectors. It distributes grant to national voluntary youth organisations operating in Wales to support the local services which they provide.

9.45.2 The Agency, in association with the Wales Youth Forum, has worked with a range of young people across Wales and from different organisations to create a voluntary Charter of Entitlement for Young People.

---

113 *Building Excellent Schools Together:* Cm 3701. Published by The Stationery Office for the Welsh Office. ISBN 0 10 137012 1.

The Charter is based on young people's views of services they consider should be available to them.

9.45.3   At a meeting on 14 July 1998, the elected member working group on Youth Issues at the City and County of Swansea formally adopted the Charter as a Pledge for Young People. This pledge will form the basis of a corporate approach to developing services for young people.

9.45.4   The Agency is currently working with the Welsh Office, local authorities and voluntary groups to develop new collaborative programmes to tackle exclusion from secondary school, and to promote greater co-ordination of services for young people in line with the Government's agenda for lifelong learning.

9.46 Gaelic education in Scotland

Article 28, 31

9.46.1   The Government in Scotland makes available specific funding for Gaelic-medium education where there are sufficient numbers of children whose parents request it. In 1997-98 1736 children attended Gaelic-medium units in 55 primary schools. Cultural activities related to the Gaelic language are organised by a number of organisations some of which receive Government funding, for instance An Comunn Gaidhealach organise the annual Royal National Mod.

9.47 Irish medium education in Northern Ireland

Article 28, 31

9.47.1   There have been a number of significant developments since 1994 in the arrangements for funding and supporting the development of Irish medium education in Northern Ireland. In the past 3 years a total of 5 schools providing teaching in the Irish language – 4 primary and 1 secondary – have been given grant-aided status. This means that of the overall enrolment of 1,375 pupils in Irish-medium schools over 90% are in schools which receive 100% grant-aid.

9.47.2   Provision is now available for GCSE examinations in the medium of Irish, and a unit has been established recently to provide curriculum materials for use in Irish medium schools.

9.47.3   Under the Education (NI) Order 1998 the Department of Education will have a duty to encourage and facilitate the development of Irish medium education. This will place the sector on a footing similar to the integrated education sector.

9.48 Integrated education in Northern Ireland

Article 28, 31

9.48.1   There has been significant expansion of, and investment in, the integrated schools sector since 1994: total enrolments have increased from just under 4,000 to over 11,000 at October 1998.

9.48.2   In addition, following the issue in 1997 of policy guidelines to all schools in Northern Ireland about the procedures for transforming to integrated status, 12 existing schools have been given approval to become integrated. As a result the integrated pupil population has increased by over 25% since the introduction of the guidelines, from 8,100 to over 11,000.

9.48.3 Between 1994-95 and 1998-99 capital investment in new integrated schools has totalled £30m and a further £16m is already planned over the next two years.

9.48.4 The Government has established a Working Group initially chaired by the Minister of Education in the Northern Ireland Office, to examine ways of enhancing the contribution of all schools to the promotion of a Culture of Tolerance, as outlined in the Belfast Agreement. The Group issued to all interested parties a progress report in December 1998 –*Towards a Culture of Tolerance – Integrating Education*. The consultation period closed on 26 February 1999 and the responses are being considered in determining how best to implement some of the recommendations of the working party.

9.48.5 The Education (NI) Order 1998 provides for the recognition and grant-aid of integrated nursery provision for the first time.

9.49 Education for Gypsy and Traveller children in England and Wales

Article 28, 29, 31, 2

9.49.1 Gypsy and Traveller children are entitled to have access to schools in the same way as all other children. The Government provides funding under Section 488 of the Education Act 1996 to meet the additional educational needs of Gypsy and Traveller children in England. This specific grant programme is supporting Traveller Education Services in some 120 Local Education Authorities in England improving access, attendance and achievement for these children. There is a separate programme in Wales.

9.49.2 The Department for Education and Employment has recently produced a video for Gypsy and Traveller parents aimed to improve attendance and achievement at secondary school level.

9.50 Education of Travelling people – Scotland

Article 28, 29, 31, 2

9.50.1 The Secretary of State's Advisory Committee on Scotland's Travelling People placed considerable emphasis on the consideration of the education of Traveller Children during its 1995-97 term of office. The Committee recognised that Traveller Children suffer from problems of interrupted learning. It has recommended that local authorities should support the regular attendance of Traveller Children at school and should monitor this. They also recommended that local authorities should seek to educate the settled community in the way of life and culture of Travelling People and promote mutual understanding.

9.50.2 The Scottish Office Education and Industry Department regard the question of the access of Traveller children to education as an equal opportunities issue. The issuing of detailed guidance on the promotion of equal opportunities in education is, however, a matter for education authorities and similarly the responsibility for providing an education for Traveller children falls to schools and education authorities.

9.50.3 In order to assist in this the Scottish Office support with funding the work of the Scottish Traveller Education Programme (STEP). The remit of STEP includes advising schools and education authorities on the needs of

Traveller communities and how to improve educational provision for these groups.

9.51 Traveller education in Northern Ireland

Article 28, 29, 31, 2

9.51.1   The Education Reform (Northern Ireland) Order 1989 requires that all pupils of compulsory school age in grant-aided schools should have access to a balanced and broadly based curriculum, with their progress regularly assessed and reported to their parents. These provisions apply to all children including Traveller children. The legislation provides parents with the statutory right to express a preference about the school they wish their children to attend.

9.51.2   The policy of the Department of Education for Northern Ireland is that Traveller children can only be effectively provided for in schools which provide a non-discriminatory environment which is understanding of, and sympathetic to, the way of life of Traveller families, which respects and values the uniqueness of Traveller culture and which positively welcomes Traveller children.

9.52 The National Lottery

Article 31

9.52.1   The United Kingdom's National Lottery was established in 1993 by Parliament to raise money for worthwhile causes. It was launched in November 1994 and by 31 December 1998 had raised over £6.3 billion for the six good causes, and supported over 34,000 projects nationwide.

9.52.2   The distributors of lottery funds in the United Kingdom (the four national Arts Councils, the four national Sports Councils, the Heritage Lottery Fund, the National Lottery Charities Board (NLCB), the New Opportunities Fund and the Millennium Commission) are already funding many thousands of projects which, either directly or indirectly, benefit children. The Arts Councils aim to help people across the United Kingdom enjoy, and take part in, the broadest possible range of arts activities. Their *Arts 4 Everyone* scheme has placed a particular emphasis on young people and projects which support and develop their talents. The National Lottery Charities Board gives grants to help those at greatest disadvantage and to improve the quality of life in the community. The first three grant programmes included "youth issues and low income". The Heritage Lottery Fund preserves, restores or acquires the nation's most treasured heritage, which makes up the fabric of the nation's history and culture. The Millennium Commission aims to fund projects which will make a substantial contribution to the community, and will be seen by future generations as marking a significant moment in their history. The Sports Councils distribute lottery funds to encourage and enhance sport for all.

9.52.3   Schools have received 1,769 awards worth £123.9 million, playgroups have received 255 awards worth £2.9 million, and youth organisations have received 271 awards worth £8.4 million. In total the youth sector has received 1,328 awards worth £174.1 million.

9.52.4   Specific examples include:

a a grant of £80,000 by the Arts Council of England to Bingham Infants Self-Help Group in Nottinghamshire towards development of a multi-purpose hall for arts usage. The hall will benefit both school pupils and the wider community in an area which has suffered from recent pit closures;

b a grant of £48,986 by the Sports Council for Wales to Vale of Glamorgan County Borough Council for the provision of skate-boarding facilities in a safe environment for a large number of youngsters in the Vale of Glamorgan;

c a grant of £7,000 by the Heritage Lottery Fund towards the development of a play centre in Battersea Park, London under its Urban Parks Programme.

d a grant of £382,375 by the Scottish Arts Council to the Scottish Library Association to donate specially selected sets of thirty six Scottish books to every one of Scotland's 400 secondary schools.

9.52.5 Information from the National Lottery Charities Board (Wales) shows that pre-school education in Wales received 218 grants, totalling £1,394,908; whilst play projects received 228 grants, totalling some £1.75 million. 294 grants totalling £1,768,572 have been targeted specifically at the 0-5 age range, and 422 grants totalling £5,240,021 have been targeted at the Under 18s.

9.52.6 Ministers want to build on the contribution that the lottery has already made to the quality of life of children. A leaflet, which heightens the availability of lottery funding for children's play, was published by the Department for Culture, Media and Sport (DCMS) in June 1998[114]. This leaflet emphasises the role of lottery distribution in opening up opportunities for children and young people. It also emphasises the importance of the lottery for reducing economic and social deprivation, which will help children living in areas of deprivation.

9.52.7 This Government and its predecessor have made clear that money raised by the National Lottery must be additional to any money which would have been spent by local or national government. There are strict conditions about young people buying lottery tickets – no one under 16 years old may purchase a National Lottery ticket, and the Government requires the lottery organiser vigorously to enforce this provision, with retailers being refused permission to sell National Lottery tickets if they breach this requirement.

9.53 The New Opportunities Fund

Article 31

9.53.1 The National Lottery Act, which received Royal Assent on 2 July 1998, established a new distributor, the New Opportunities Fund, financed by the extra £1 billion which the lottery is generating. The Fund will support one-off initiatives in health, education and the environment. The first of

114 Published by DCMS May 1998, ISBN DCMSJO298NJ.May 1998.

these will be training and support in the use of information and communications technology for serving teachers and librarians; out of school hours activities, including child care; and a network of healthy living centres.

9.53.2   Education initiatives will be wide-ranging and will include training and the provision of activities for children. The New Opportunities Fund will receive 13% of lottery proceeds for good causes. This will increase to 20% from October 1999.

9.53.3   The New Opportunities Fund is considering with the Welsh Office, the Scottish Office, the Department of Education in Northern Ireland, and other bodies, how best to manage the grant regimes in those parts of the United Kingdom. The impact of the initiatives for children and young people will be of significant and wide-ranging benefit.

9.54 Children and the arts: funding

Article 31

9.54.1   The Government believes that the performing and visual arts have a vital role to play in the development of children and young people. They have the power to initiate and sustain an awareness of creative potential and a sense of self, and enable young people to develop analytical and cognitive skills. The arts not only help to broaden understanding of artistic practice, but can also make an integral contribution to the development of a child's all-round education. The Government seeks to raise awareness of the importance of, and contribution the arts can make to, childrens' lives. Departments with responsibilities in this area work in close co-operation, and continue dialogue with other key players in the arts and education field.

9.54.2   Creating access to the arts is a cornerstone of the Government's arts policy. The 1998 National Lottery Act established the New Opportunities Fund, a sixth good cause to be supported by the Lottery. NOF will channel £205 million into out of schools hours education activities designed to raise educational standards. These activities may include projects in areas such as music, dance, drama, film and the full range of the arts. In addition, the New Audiences programme, administered by the Arts Council of England, provides up to £5 million per annum for pilot projects aimed at broadening audiences and at finding new ways of encouraging young people to participate in the arts.

9.54.3   Since the publication of Leading Though Learning (1997) – the Arts Council of England's Education and Training Policy document, the Arts Council continues to lead on a number of key initiatives in relation to developing high quality arts learning opportunities for young people. These include an Education Action Zone research initiative investigating the impact of the arts as a means of combating social exclusion and enhancing personal growth and learning development; and careers information for the arts sector aimed at helping young people make informed decisions about career opportunities within the cultural industries.

9.54.4   The National Lottery is an important funding opportunity for arts education activities. Awards under the capital programme have provided resources and improved facilities for schools and colleges, arts organisations and venues. The Arts Council recognises in its Lottery Strategy Plan (June 1999) that education is often the way in which people come to the arts for the first time, through activities at school and colleges.

9.54.5   On 24 June 1999 the Prime Minister launched the National Foundation for Youth Music, a new independent body, to give every child the opportunity to access music-making. Drawing on £30 million of Arts Council Lottery funds over three years, and working to complement the DFEE's £150 million Music Standards Funds measures, it will seek to increase and improve access, breadth, coverage and the quality of music making. It will deliver its objectives by: attracting and distributing funds; providing strategic advice and guidance; as the National advocate, raising the profile of the debate on music education.

9.54.6   The Arts Council's Arts for Everyone (A4E) programme continues to fund opportunities for innovative and experimental initiatives in arts education across a spectrum of youth groups, community groups and the voluntary sector. A total of £50 million was awarded to 425 organisations as a result of the four rounds of A4E applications. Significant awards include:

   a £350,000 to CAPE, an organisation which promotes and develops creative arts learning in schools or other educational establishments for pupils, teachers and others involved in education;

   b £31,000 to First Movement, which develops drama, dance, music and visual arts projects for people with severe and profound learning disabilities;

   c £93,500 to Get Art, a collaboration between the special schools in the London Borough of Tower Hamlets and Chisenhale Gallery which will enable the pupils and teachers from schools to work with professional artists and participate in a three-year programme of gallery visits, art workshops, discussions and exhibitions of their own work at Chisenhale Gallery;

   d £88,000 to Education Extra, additional funds to enable the organisation, which already works in partnership with schools to extend and enhance the curriculum by providing out of hours activities, to develop and deliver a programme of extra-curricular arts learning opportunities;

   e £69,000 to Play Train, a leading playwork training agency which uses Article 31 as its guiding principle to develop and implement policy in relation to young people and opportunities to experience fully and participate in the arts and culture.

9.54.7   There are no further A4E application rounds. A cross-distributor programme, Awards for All, is being launched during Summer 1999, and the new Regional Lottery Programme will provide funding for new arts education projects via the ten Regional Arts Boards.

9.55 Provision of broadcast programmes for children

Article 31

9.55.1   Currently the main United Kingdom terrestrial television channels are all required to provide a proportion of high quality children's programming in their schedules, and they all include readily identifiable children's programme strands, including "Children's BBC" and "Children's ITV". Programmes cater for a range of age groups from pre-school to teenagers and cover various genres including drama, factual and knowledge-building programmes, news and current affairs for children. Additionally, the BBC, Channel 4 and S4C provide a range of schools programming to complement the national curriculum.

9.55.2   The BBC has produced a Children's Television Charter and its Statement of Promises to Listeners and Viewers promises to maintain the range of children's programmes.

9.55.3   The proliferation of cable and satellite services in recent years has allowed specialist channels to address themselves to particular audiences and the Independent Television Commission has issued licences for several channels aimed at children, such as The Children's Channel (TCC). As new digital services develop there will be further scope for and interest in developing more choices for children.

9.56 Protection of children from unsuitable broadcast material

Article 17, 19

9.56.1   All broadcasters are required to ensure that they do not broadcast material which "offends against good taste or decency or is likely to encourage or incite to crime or lead to disorder or to be offensive to public feeling". There are specific arrangements to ensure the protection of minors, including the operation of a watershed which requires that programmes suitable only for adult viewing cannot be shown before a certain time.

9.57 Advertising and children

Article 17, 19

9.57.1   Commercial broadcasters have specific guidelines which they must observe in advertising to children. At times when children are likely to be viewing no product or service may be advertised, and no method of advertising may be used, which might result in harm to them physically, mentally or morally, and no method of advertising may be employed which takes advantage of the natural credulity and sense of loyalty of children.

9.58 Broadcasting for minorities

Article 31

9.58.1   The Radio Authority licenses 10 local radio services licences which provide programmes catering for the tastes and interests of ethnic minority audiences. Additionally, cable and satellite licenses have been granted to 16 Asian and 7 Afro-Caribbean broadcasters.

9.58.2   The Welsh Fourth Channel (S4C) caters for the estimated 500,000 speakers of the Welsh language. S4C transmits an average of 30 hours of Welsh language programming a week. The Gaelic Television Fund provides for approximately 350 hours of television programmes in Gaelic in Scotland each year.

9.59 The National Endowment for Science, Technology and the Arts (NESTA)

Article 31

9.59.1   The National Lottery Act 1998 established a new United Kingdom-wide Non Departmental Public Body, the National Endowment for Science, Technology and the Arts (NESTA). NESTA will help to promote educational and cultural opportunities for children, young people and adults. It will have three broad objectives: to help talented individuals in the fields of science, technology and the arts to achieve their full potential, to help turn inventions or ideas into products or services and to help promote public knowledge and appreciation of science, technology and the arts. It will receive an endowment of £200 million from the National Lottery and it will use the income generated by the endowment to fund its programmes.

9.60 Libraries

Article 31

9.60.1   There are 4,500 branch libraries around the United Kingdom providing an essentially free service. Under the Public Libraries and Museums Act 1964, local authorities have a duty to provide books and other material to satisfy the recreational, educational, cultural and information needs of all members of the population, including children and young people. Public libraries also provide access for children after school as well as during the day, homework space, trained specialist staff and activities designed to encourage them to use the library and to read regularly. The development of a public libraries IT network, which the Government announced in April 1998, will enable the wealth of public libraries' resources to be brought to an even wider audience in new and exciting ways.

9.61 Museums and galleries

Article 31

9.61.1   Education is a central activity for museums and galleries and one of the prime reasons for the establishment of many. They have much to offer schools in reinforcing classroom lessons and helping children to learn in attractive and enjoyable ways. Being able to see and handle real objects provides a much greater degree of understanding. The Government is particularly keen to encourage museums and galleries to develop their educational role. Hundreds of thousands of school children visit museums every year for study which supports and enriches the National Curriculum. Almost a third of the 76 million visitors to the United Kingdom's 2,500 museums are children either in school visits or independently.

9.61.2   In January 1997 the Department for Culture, Media and Sport (DCMS) published a report on museum education A Common Wealth: Museums and Learning in the United Kingdom[115] written by David Anderson of the Victoria and Albert Museum (one of central government's sponsored museums). The report has been widely distributed free of charge to encourage museums and other relevant bodies to consider afresh their educational role.

9.61.3   Many museums and galleries operate generous concessions for children offering discounts for school-age children and families, and free admission periods. All pre-booked educational groups are free to the national institutions and many others also offer concessions for children who

115 By David Anderson, published by the Department for National Heritage, reference no DNHJ0178NJ.

are not members of school groups, either as part of a family ticket or if they visit alone. Admissions is free for all children at all national museums and galleries in England. The Heritage Lottery Fund has recently set up a Museums and Galleries Access Fund of £7 million, to help museums and galleries to promote access to their collections. This might be through major touring exhibitions, or might mean more selective work i.e. funding transport costs or attracting wider audiences to museums. This should include work with school children or with socially disadvantaged groups.

9.61.4 In July 1997 the Museums and Galleries Commission published a report *Children as an Audience*[116] for museums and galleries aimed at increasing informal visits by children. It included the views of children aged 7 to 11. This suggested ways in which exhibitions and marketing could be developed to attract children. The findings have been widely disseminated.

9.61.5 The National Museums and Galleries of Wales (NMGW) help to enhance the education process through the relevance and scope of their collections and through the environment they present. Handling real objects is a vital element in the learning process and NMGW operate a loan service to schools which can call on a loan collection of some 15,000 objects. Their service to Wales and Welsh schools is significant in its size and scope and adds value to learning in schools. Around 120,000 pupils a year in Wales have access to objects in their schools via the loans service. School visits are also important. The proportion of these varies in the different locations of NMGW, but across the organisation some 20% of visitors are pre-booked school groups. When this figure is added to family and ad hoc visits, then over a third of visitor figures are accounted for by children. NMGW do not, at present, operate free admission for pre-booked educational groups.

9.61.6 As a result of the report *A Common Wealth: Museums and Learning in the United Kingdom* NMGW co-operated with the Campaign for Learning in Museums in running a conference for educationalists and education authority officers. Additionally, NMGW hosted the Group for Education in Museums Conference which considered the report and its implications.

9.61.7 As well as working to attract young people, NMGW subscribe to the support of lifelong learning. A particular aspect of their work is supporting the learning and use of the Welsh language through their bilingual annotation and explanation practice.

9.62 Cadw: Welsh Historic Monuments

9.62.1 Cadw: Welsh Historic Monuments is the Agency within the Welsh Office responsible for the conservation, protection and promotion of the built heritage of Wales. One of Cadw's roles is to educate the public about the built heritage and to encourage their participation in advancing the understanding and enjoyment of it.

---

116 *Children as an audience of Museums and Galleries*, by Harris Qualitative, on behalf of the Arts Council and the Museum and Galleries Commission. Published by Harris Qualitative on 17 July 1997.

9.62.2 Schools and educational establishments are encouraged to make full use of the 130 monuments in state care in Wales. Cadw encourages this through the provision of free visits for organised educational groups in term time; provision of education rooms at some sites; the funding of an Education Officer jointly with the National Museums and Galleries of Wales at Roman Caerleon; and the provision of resource materials such as Teachers' Packs, worksheets and videos.

9.62.3 Cadw attracts around 120,000 educational visitors a year to staffed sites with almost one fifth of that number making a visit to the Roman sites at Caerleon and Caerwent.

9.63 Heritage

Article 31

9.63.1 English Heritage (the Historic Buildings and Monuments Commission) is a non-departmental public body whose Chairman and Board of Trustees are appointed by the Secretary of State for Culture, Media and Sport. It has an income of about £130 million a year. A statutory role of English Heritage is to educate the public about the nation's historic environment and encourage their participation in advancing the understanding and enjoyment of it.

9.63.2 The English Heritage Education Service encourages schools and other educational establishments to make full use of the historic environment. This is accomplished at both national and regional levels. Regional work is led by locally-based education officers who work with schools, colleges and local education authorities to give help and advice on the educational use of sites in the custody of English Heritage and of the wider historic environment. The *History at Home* programme seeks to encourage and help parents educate their children about their local surroundings and English Heritage actively supports broader initiatives such as the European Union's *Schools Adopt a Monument* scheme. Nationally English Heritage offers a support service to teachers through a wide range of resources whilst collaborating with agencies such as the Qualifications and Curriculum Authority to formulate educational policy in the teaching of history and the use of the historic environment across the curriculum and at all levels of education.

9.63.3 In 1997-98 staffed properties in the custody of English Heritage received 494,000 educational visitors, 1 in 12 of all the visitors to English Heritage properties, and they aim to increase this to 525,000 in 1998-99. Free admission is granted to educational groups on the condition that the visit is properly organised and is part of planned curriculum work based around the study of the site. A growing number of properties have Education Centres specifically designed to meet the needs of these groups and to encourage other visitors to spend time considering the fun and formal educational aspects of their visit.

9.63.4 English Heritage education officers run a varied programme of courses for teachers and events for children to encourage the use of the historic environment as an educational resource. In 1996 English Heritage launched a membership scheme for teachers, *Windows on the Past,* which allows teachers unlimited access to sites to plan their school visits.

9.63.5 English Heritage produces a wide range of publications, audio-visual materials, posters and CD ROMs, including:

    a individual teachers' handbooks to guide teachers in maximising the benefits of visits to major sites;

    b an *Education on Site* series which includes national curriculum titles (such as *Geography and the Historic Environment, Mathematics*), and generic themes (such as *Using Castles*);

    c over 50 videos whose subject matters include training for teachers in the use of sites for National Curriculum work, a *History Trail* series aimed directly at the classroom, and awareness raising videos such as *Archaeology at work;*

    d *Heritage Learning,* a free magazine sent to schools on a termly basis;

    e free information sheets at each site;

    f *Visiting Historic Sites*, a free gazetteer of sites and advice on how to use them.

9.64 Scottish Natural Heritage

9.64.1 Scottish Natural Heritage is a non-departmental public body whose Chairman and Board are appointed by the First Minister of the Scottish Parliament. It has an income of about £40 million a year of which some £38 million is grant aided by The Scottish Executive. The primary purposes of SNH are to secure the conservation and enhancement of Scotland's wildlife and landscape, to foster understanding and facilitate enjoyment of the natural heritage, and to promote its sustainable use.

9.64.2 SNH considers that environmental education is fundamental to improving people's sense of responsibility for, as well as awareness and enjoyment of, the natural heritage. SNH has an educational programme targeted on key groups. The main effort has been directed at schools with advice on changes to the curriculum, changes to teacher training programmes, the provision of resource packs for use in the classroom and a very successful grant-aid scheme for wildlife in school grounds (Grounds for Learning). In addition, resources have been targeted on improving the awareness and practice of professionals and volunteers working in education and the environment, through our 'Getting to Grips with Learning' programme which offers opportunities to share good practice and develop new ideas.

9.64.3 However, the major effort, in resource terms, is through the sponsorship and financial support for some 90 ranger services in Scotland, employing approximately 300 Rangers. Their primary task is environmental education at key sites such as country parks and in the wider countryside, including liaison with local communities and with schools. More than £2 million per annum is provided by SNH to this activity. Rangers can be employed by local authorities, voluntary organisations and private estates. In order to ensure high standards and consistency of approach, SNH also supports the co-ordination and delivery of a national Ranger Training Course programme.

9.64.4   SNH owns and manages a number of key nature conservation sites within Scotland as National Nature Reserves (NNR). While their primary purpose is nature conservation, they offer opportunities to increase public understanding and enjoyment. Most NNRs have interpretative material on site, and a number also have visitor centres. Those near to population centres receive regular educational visits from schools and colleges, but no records of numbers are kept.

9.64.5   Scottish Natural Heritage produces a wide range of publications, audio-visual materials and posters, including a range of education & Teachers' Resources:

a collections of the best environmental education resource material in the form of "community chests", "sea chests" and "tree trunks";

b a pack of learning resources, 'Investigating the Environment - a Practical Guide', including a teachers' guide and students' handbook;

c several poster series on topics such as sustainability, biodiversity, geology, weathering processes and land cover in Scotland;

d factsheets and posters on Scotland's best loved species;

e the Pine and the Eagle, a video of a musical drama to help youth leaders and teachers explore the value of the natural heritage to contemporary life.

9.65 Play and sport

Article 31

9.65.1   The Government recognises the value of play in children's development and sees play opportunities as an important area of work. The Department for Culture, Media and Sport has lead responsibility for children's play in England. Since 1996 this has been channelled through a contract with the National Playing Fields Association (NPFA) which carries out a programme of work in the areas of information dissemination, playwork education and training and play safety on behalf of the Department.

9.65.2   As a part of the remit for education and training the NPFA grant funds four National Centres for Playwork Education. These are based in Birmingham, Cheltenham, London and Newcastle. Each Centre develops high quality training programmes for playworkers which support the principle that play is the province of the child and the child must have autonomy over it. Inherent in this child-centred playwork training is the child's right to take part in freely chosen play activities. All participants in training developed by the Centres are aware that the child must be at the centre of the play process.

9.65.3   In addition, all playwork training programmes are underpinned by the principles of equal opportunities and support the right of the disabled child to play in inclusive play settings.

9.65.4   Under the information dissemination remit of the work, the NPFA manages the National Play Information Centre (NPIC), the world's largest specialist resource on children's play. The Centre runs a variety of information service covering a range of aspects of children's play. Recent research undertaken by the NPFA about the difficulties playworkers have in locating information has shown that the information services provided are highly valued. The underpinning value of the centre's work is based in the child's right to play.

9.65.5   Under the safety remit of the work, the NPFA established a Play Safety Forum, consisting of key national organisations which deal with the provision of children's services and/or their safety. The Forum recognises the child's right to play and that a degree of risk is necessary for children in their play. Risk in play promotes the child's ability to analyse danger and, as a consequence, keep themselves and their peer group safe. The Forum is investigating a definition of the balance between safety, and risk to advise service providers. The NPFA has disseminated information about safety aspects of fixed equipment playgrounds. It has also revised 'Playground Safety Guidelines', the country's leading publication on playground safety.

9.65.6   The NPFA launched *Play Today*, a free bi-monthly newspaper to cover all aspects of its Agreement with the DCMS. It has received acclaim from all parts of the play sector and a recent reader survey has indicated that the majority of readers feel it has improved their practice.

9.65.7   The new Government established a Youth Sports Unit within the Department for Culture, Media and Sport in May 1997. The Unit works closely with the Department for Education and Employment and Sport England (formerly the English Sports Council), which undertakes a number of initiatives which aim to raise the profile and quality of physical education (PE) and sport in schools and for young people. A number of these come under the umbrella of Sport England's Active Schools Programme.

9.65.8   This major programme was launched in March 1996 and provides a framework within which schools, local authorities, governing bodies of sport, sports clubs and youth organisations can work together to provide quality sporting opportunities for 4 to 18 year olds in a planned and co-ordinated way. Developments within the programme include the production of curriculum resources and in-service training for teachers and a series of nationally produced resources to be delivered locally.

9.65.9   Initiatives include the TOP programme. TOP Play, BT TOP Sport and TOP Club have been developed and delivered jointly by the English Sports Council and the Youth Sport Trust. TOP Play involves teaching core skills and fun sport to 4-9 year olds, while BT TOP Sport introduces sport and games to 7-11 year olds. TOP Club is a sport-specific initiative, allowing governing bodies to customise sports to suit and promote particular club structures and needs. TOP Play and BT TOP Sport have also been recognised as a valuable resource to enhance the games element of the physical education curriculum.

9.65.10 Developments of the TOP programmes have included the introduction of training for individuals to work with children with disabilities and the establishment of a framework to extend the application of TOP Play and BT TOP sport into after-school clubs and wider community activities involving local authorities and governing bodies. There are currently 78 schemes being delivered in the community covering nine sports.

9.65.11 Champion Coaching aims to improve performance and develop coaching for 11-14 year olds. After an initial five-year commitment from the English Sports Council and the National Coaching Foundation, local authorities' involvement in Champion Coaching is recognised by an established accreditation scheme. The scheme offers benefits such as scholarships for coaches, assistance in coach development strategies and links with sports development networks.

9.65.12 Champion Coaching is now fully integrated within the National Junior Sport Programme. The scheme had been delivered to 126 local authorities by the end of 1996-97. Over 3,000 coaches are deployed within the programme with plans to cover over 20 sports.

9.66.13 Sports Fair promotes sporting activity in youth groups. Developed jointly with Youth Clubs UK, it includes Sports Train education and training materials for youth workers.

9.65.14 The Sportsmark and Sportsmark Gold awards were developed to recognise quality physical education and school sport. The secondary school scheme was launched in October 1996 and over 600 applications for the schemes were received. Schools were required to test their eligibility for the awards against a number of basic criteria. Of the 412 successful schools, 30 achieved special recognition by gaining the Sportsmark Gold award, a mark of special distinction for schools whose sports policies exceeded the basic criteria across a number of important requirements. Applications for the next round of awards have now been received. The English Sports Council (ESC) are now working up proposals for an Activity award for primary schools.

9.65.15 The Foundation for Sport and the Arts (FSA), which is funded by a reduction in Pool Betting Duty, is grant aiding a variety of sports projects for young people across the country as is the Government's Business Sponsorship Incentive Scheme for Sport, Sportsmatch, which operates in England, Wales and Scotland.

9.65.16 The Government announced in January 1998 how it will control the disposal and change of use of school playing fields in England, which schools and their local communities need. Two key measures were announced in a co-ordinated Departmental approach: the introduction of new legislation requiring the prior consent of the Secretary of State before the disposal, or change of use, of state school playing fields; and tighter planning controls over the development of playing fields owned by local authorities and other playing fields used by educational institutions. Together, these measures will ensure that schools' own needs, and those of the wider community, are taken into account. The Government will review the effectiveness of these measures after the first 12 months of their operation.

9.66 Sport in Wales

Article 31

9.66.1   The Welsh Office has responsibility for sports policy in Wales. One of the main aims of the Department is to increase participation in sports and physical activity in Wales, particularly among young people. This is pursued mainly through the work of the Sports Council for Wales.

9.66.2   Much of the Council's work has been towards providing a range of sporting opportunities for young people at all levels of ability, from recreationally-based extra-curricular activity in local communities, to the development of excellence at national level. This has involved working with partners to set up strong community networks and a national action programme.

9.67 Sport in Scotland

Article 31

9.67.1   Within the Scottish Office responsibility for sports policy rests with the Sports Policy Unit of the Education and Industry Department. One of the main objectives of the Department is to increase participation in sports and physical activity in Scotland, particularly among young people. This is pursued mainly through the work of the Scottish Sports Council (SSC).

9.67.2   The SSC is the Government's main advisory body on sport in Scotland. Youth sport is one of its main priorities and in May 1996 it launched the National Youth Sport Strategy. The key elements of the Strategy are coaching, clubs, equality, physical activity and school sports. While this strategy will benefit children of all ages, it also includes a framework for physical activity which focuses particularly on young children through the Start Young Stay Active programme.

9.67.3   The SSC is also involved in promoting the Top Play scheme in primary schools. The scheme aims to provide physical activities, including tuition for teachers, within the framework of the 5-14 national curriculum guidelines. Top Play is aimed at younger primary school pupils between the ages of four and nine.

9.67.4   In January 1998 the Government announced that School Sports Co-ordinators would be provided in every Scottish secondary school with the help of National Lottery Funding. The scheme has been developed by the SSC and builds on a number of pilot projects currently under way throughout Scotland. The programme is designed to promote sport to young people as an intrinsic part of their school life, to encourage them to build an active lifestyle into every day. Local authorities will be able to apply for funding in support of Co-ordinator appointments in all Scottish secondary schools. National Lottery Funding is also supporting the activities of junior sports groups.

9.68 The Sporting Ambassadors Scheme

Article 31

9.68.1 The Sporting Ambassadors Scheme is a new scheme established by the English Sports Council, which was successfully piloted during 1997-98 in four English Sports Council regions. The scheme will provide opportunities for successful sports men and women of all ages to visit schools to enthuse young people about the benefits of physical activity and a healthy lifestyle.

9.68.2 The objectives of the scheme are: –

    a to encourage and provide opportunities for sporting ambassadors to visit schools to make pupils, teachers, parents and governors aware of the benefits of a wide range of sport and physical activities;

    b to encourage positive and continuing links between schools and local sports clubs and centres;

    c to promote the value of sport and physical activity as essential element of every young person's lifestyle;

    d to promoting the concept of fair play and good sporting behaviour; to help motivate young people to realise their full potential in competitive sport;

    e to involve, in particular, women ambassadors to motivate girls to participate in sport; and

    f to offer role models to young people from a range of ethnic backgrounds, and to those with disabilities.

9.69 Sport and regeneration

Article 31

9.69.1 The Department of the Environment, Transport and the Regions supports local play and sporting provision for young people as part of its regeneration policy. Projects of this sort in England's deprived areas are supported through the Department's Single Regeneration Budget and New Deal for Communities.

9.69.2 In 1998 the Social Exclusion Unit published a report on neighbourhood renewal which showed that in the 44 local authority districts with the highest concentration of deprivation in England almost a third of children were growing up in families on Income Support, against less than a quarter in the rest of England. Following the report, 18 inter-departmental neighbourhood renewal Policy Action Teams were set up to look at complementary aspects of neighbourhood renewal.

9.69.3 Policy Action Team 10 reported to the Social Exclusion Unit in April 1998 on the contribution arts and sport could make to neighbourhood renewal. The team found that arts and sport can contribute to action to reduce crime and unemployment, improve health and increase educational attainment. The Government has welcomed the report of PAT 10 and intends to implement many of its recommendations.

10 SPECIAL PROTECTION MEASURES

This chapter covers articles: –

10.1 Drug misuse

Article 33

10.1.1 United Kingdom drugs legislation is based on the United Nations Single Convention on Narcotic Drugs 1961 (as amended by the 1972 Protocol), the Convention on Psychotropic Substances 1971 and the Convention against the Illicit Traffic in Narcotic Drugs and Psychotropic Substances 1988.

10.1.2 In May 1995 the Government introduced as a White Paper, *Tackling Drugs Together*[117],a strategy for the period 1995-98 to tackle drug misuse in England. Separate strategies were developed for Scotland, Wales and Northern Ireland.

10.1.3 Focusing on crime, young people and public health, *Tackling Drugs Together* recognised the need for stronger action on reducing the demand for illegal drugs whilst maintaining the emphasis on law enforcement and reducing supply. Co-ordination between Government departments was improved at national level and 106 Drug Action Teams, made up of senior representatives from health and local authorities and criminal justice agencies, were established across England to co-ordinate action in delivering the strategy at the local level. Each Team also set up a Drug Reference Group or Groups to provide a source of local expertise and to harness local

---

117 Cm 2846: ISBN 0 10 128462 4, published by HMSO.

communities in action to tackle drug misuse. Membership includes voluntary and statutory service providers, community groups, doctors, school governors and local business interests.

10.1.4   One of the three main aims driving the strategy was to reduce the acceptability and availability of drugs to young people. Overall it was recognised that the strategy was a step in the right direction but that a fresh long term approach was needed.

10.1.5   A United Kingdom Anti-Drugs Co-ordinator was appointed by the Government as a special adviser on drugs issues with effect from 5 January 1998.

10.1.6   In April 1998 the United Kingdom Government published a new ten year national strategy to tackle the problems of drug misuse. *Tackling Drugs To Build A Better Britain*[118] focuses on England but is relevant to Scotland, Wales and Northern Ireland and highlights the United Kingdom's international responsibilities. Local Drug Action Teams continue to be the mechanism by which the national objectives are delivered at local level and for involving communities.

10.1.7   The Government's vision is of a healthy and confident society, increasingly free from the harm caused by the misuse of drugs. The new strategy is long-term, evidence-based and positive in its approach. It sets out four overarching aims:

> a **young people:** to help young people resist drug misuse in order to achieve their full potential in society;
>
> b **communities:** to protect communities from drug related anti-social and criminal behaviour;
>
> c **treatment:** to enable people with drug problems to overcome them and live healthy and crime-free lives;
>
> d **availability:** to stifle the availability of drugs to young people (under 25).

10.1.8   Challenging targets have been set in respect of the strategy's key objectives. It is hoped to put a comprehensive survey in place to provide drug misuse data on young people from age 5 upwards.

10.1.9   Some children are involved with their peers in supplying small quantities of drugs to each other for their own use, but there is very limited evidence of their active participation in the wide-scale production or trafficking of drugs. The occasional case is reported of young people being involved in the carrying of small quantities of drugs for delivery across a city, but these reports are sporadic.

---

119 Cm 3495: ISBN 0 10 139452 7, published by the Stationery Office.

10.1.10 The United Kingdom Government recognises that the drug problem cannot be tackled in isolation. It is linked to other socio-economic issues and needs to be tackled in conjunction with social exclusion and regeneration initiatives. Drugs affect individuals and communities. The strategy aims to tackle both the supply of, and demand for, drugs through a detailed programme of action, supported by research.

10.1.11 Research is revealing a great deal about the relationship between drugs and young people. Many never take drugs at all, many who do experiment grow out of it quickly, but a small hard core develop very serious problems. The strategy sets out a programme of action involving young people which includes:

a informing young people, parents, and those who advise them or work with them about the risks and consequences of drug misuse;

b teaching young people from the age of five upwards both in and out of formal education settings the skills needed to resist pressure to misuse drugs;

c helping make the misuse of drugs less culturally acceptable to young people, including the use of effective and targeted national and local publicity and information;

d promoting healthy lifestyles and positive activities not involving drugs and other substance misuse;

e ensuring that the groups of young people most at risk of developing serious drugs problems receive appropriate and specific interventions;

f ensuring that young people from all backgrounds, whatever their culture, gender or race, have access to appropriate programmes; and

g building on and disseminating good practice in identifying what works best in prevention and education activity.

10.2 Drugs and health

Article 33

10.2.1 The Department of Health and the Health Education Authority began a national drug prevention campaign in 1995. The campaign has been based on the provision of accurate information for young people about the risks of drug misuse. The principal elements of the campaign are:

a A programme of research into the use of the media to help drug prevention;

b Radio and magazine advertisements about the risks of drug misuse;

c Written information materials provided free for young people and their parents;

d Use of new media including CD-ROM and the internet;

e Providing information to young people in clubs and at events, such as major music festivals;

f Partnership with major 'blue chip' companies to encourage them to participate in drug prevention activity and to help them channel their efforts.

10.2.2 In addition, since 1995 the Health Departments of England, Northern Ireland, Scotland and Wales have invested in a National Drugs Helpline. This is a freephone information service for anyone who is concerned about drugs. It is now used by hundreds of thousands of people each year.

10.3 Drugs: education and employment

Article 33

10.3.1 The Department for Education issued Circular 4/95 as guidance to all schools in England in May 1995. The Circular sets out the statutory position of drug education in schools, and offers guidance to help schools develop and implement programmes of drug education and deal effectively and consistently with drug-related incidents. To support and underpin the Government's strategy, in Autumn 1998 the DfEE issued further guidance to teachers, youth workers and other professionals which built on the messages within the DfEE's earlier circular. The guidance encouraged Local Education Authorities and individual schools to take note of best practice in drug education.

10.4 Home Office drugs prevention work

Article 33

10.4.1 The Home Office Drugs Prevention Initiative (DPI) has continued to test a wide range of community-based approaches to the prevention of drug misuse by young people. Following the United Kingdom's First Report in 1994, the DPI was reorganised to give a sharper focus to its work. Twelve larger drugs prevention teams were created in 1995, covering larger areas in England. The DPI managed a programme of over 70 local projects in partnership with bodies such as schools, local authorities, criminal justice agencies and the voluntary sector. This work had aimed to find out which approaches had a positive impact on young people, their families, and the wider community in which they lived. Much of the work was developed in consultation with the young people themselves. It included not only programmes aimed at the majority of young people, but also schemes which targeted those who might be at higher risk of drug misuse, such as children who had been excluded from school, those who were being looked after by local authorities, and young offenders.

10.4.2 The DPI's work was underpinned by a robust body of research harnessed to a national programme of learning. A key aim of the DPI was to spread good practice to policy makers and practitioners nationwide. In particular, guidance disseminated by the DPI helped the national network of Drug Action Teams to plan and implement effective local drugs prevention strategies aimed at young people and others as part of the national drugs strategy.

10.4.3 From April 1999, the Drugs Prevention Initiative was replaced by a new body, the Drugs Prevention Advisory Service (DPAS), established on an England-wide basis. Its support for work with young people includes:

a helping Drug Action Teams to develop prevention strategies locally and regionally, based on good practice findings

b development of demonstration programmes to provide further evidence of effective prevention c ensuring that prevention programmes are linked with relevant government policies such as action to tackle social exclusion

d contributing to consistent and coherent prevention policy across government.

10.4.4 DPAS will publish the remaining research findings from the DPI programme and further information about its own developing programme of work.[119]

10.5 Legislative measures related to drug and alcohol misuse

Article 33

10.5.1 Measures to prevent harm to young people caused by drug and alcohol misuse include :

- The Public Entertainments Licences (Drugs Misuse) Act 1997[120], which came into effect on 1 May 1998. The provisions of the Act give local authorities the power to close with immediate effect those clubs found to have a serious problem relating to the supply or use of controlled drugs at the premises, or at any place nearby which is controlled by the holder of the public entertainments licence.

- Under the Intoxicating Substances (Supply) Act 1985[121] it is an offence to supply any substance to someone under 18 knowing or believing that the substance is, or its fumes are, likely to be inhaled for the purpose of intoxication. As an additional measure, the Government is considering the introduction of a minimum age limit on the sales of butane lighter fuels, in view of their implication in a high proportion of volatile substance abuse deaths.

- The Confiscation of Alcohol (Young Persons) Act 1997[122] allows the police to confiscate alcohol from drinkers under the age of 18 in a public place, or from someone whom the police suspect is likely to pass alcohol to a person under the age of 18 for consumption in a public place. The police are able to use these powers in conjunction with other initiatives to combat underage drinking, including notifying the parents of those who have come to the police's attention in these circumstances.

- The Crime and Disorder Act 1998 introduced a new community sentence, the Drug Treatment and Testing Order. This is designed for seriously addicted offenders aged 16 or over with the aim of breaking the link between their drug addiction and acquisitive crime. Offenders must be susceptible to treatment and consent to the Order. The progress of the offender is

119 A list of publications produced by the *DPI and DPAS* is available from *DPAS HQ*, Home Office, Horseferry House, Dean Ryle Street, London SWIP 2AW. Or visit the DPAS web site at *http // www.homeoffice.gov.uk/dpas/dpas.htm.*

120 ISBN 0 10 544997 0 published by the Stationery Office.

121 ISBN 0 10 542685 7 published by the Stationery Office.

122 ISBN 0 10 543397 7 published by the Stationery Office.

reviewed periodically by the court and regular and random drug testing is used to check that the offender is staying off drugs. Breach of the Order could result in revocation of the Order and re-sentencing. However sentencers will have several options. Pilots began in October 1998 in three probation service areas in England, with a view to implementation nation-wide from April 2000. The Action Plan Order, also introduced in the Crime and Disorder Act 1998, could be available for younger offenders and include treatment for those with drug misuse problems.

Young people cautioned, prosecuted at Youth Courts and convicted at all courts for indictable drug offences by age and offence, 1994-1997

England and Wales

Offence & Disposal	Age	1994		1995		1996		1997	
		10-13	14-17	10-13	14-17	10-13	14-17	10-13	14-17
Drug Trafficking									
	Cautions	74	504	38	508	38	407	43	371
	Prosecutions	4	417	2	533	8	589	11	585
of which	Convictions	2	261	-	328	3	362	2	380
Unlawful importation/exportation of a controlled drug									
	Cautions	-	2	-	1	-	2	-	1
	Prosecutions	-	16	-	14	-	10	-	15
	Convictions	-	7	-	4	-	8	-	8
Production or being concerned in the production of a controlled drug									
	Cautions	7	128	4	165	8	106	6	79
	Prosecutions	-	52	-	70	2	49	-	39
	Convictions	-	39	-	55	1	37	-	29
Supplying or offering to supply a controlled drug									
	Cautions	48	238	21	203	19	164	25	173
	Prosecutions	1	154	-	199	4	237	7	249
	Convictions	1	107	-	119	1	124	2	146
Having possession of a controlled drug with intent to supply									
	Cautions	19	136	13	139	11	135	12	118
	Prosecutions	3	195	2	250	2	293	4	282
	Convictions	1	108	-	150	1	193	-	197

FIGURE 7: DRUGS OFFENCES BY CHILDREN IN ENGLAND AND WALES

10.6 Combating drug and alcohol misuse in Wales

Article 33

10.6.1 The current 5-year Welsh drug and alcohol strategy *Forward Together*[123] was launched in May 1996 with an emphasis on preventing the misuse of drugs and alcohol, particularly among young people; and providing treatment, support and rehabilitation for those misusing drugs and alcohol. At a national level the Welsh Drug and Alcohol Unit has been established to provide practical and administrative support to those involved in combating drug and alcohol misuse. A Welsh Advisory Committee on Drug and Alcohol Misuse, whose members were chosen to reflect the wide spectrum of those who tackle misuse, has also been established. At a local level the strategy is implemented by Drug and Alcohol Action Teams.

10.6.2 Action is in hand to review *Forward Together* in the light of the new United Kingdom strategy and to provide a report to the United Kingdom Anti-Drugs Co-ordinator on relevant developments.

10.7 Drug education in Scotland

Article 33

10.7.1 It is the policy of the Government to encourage education authorities in Scotland to address health education, including drug education, within a comprehensive programme of personal and social education. This approach is designed to ensure that information about drugs is given, not in isolation, but as part of a programme that considers a number of issues relating to sound moral choices and healthy living. Guidelines on health education have been issued by the Scottish Office as part of the 5 - 14 programme on Environmental Studies. This gives health education a firm place in the curriculum and highlights drugs education as a key feature.

10.7.2 In 1995, a curriculum framework for health education was jointly developed by the Scottish Office Education and Industry Department (SOEID) and Strathclyde Region. The framework is called the Health Education for Living Project (HELP) and it was offered free of charge to all schools in Scotland. HELP covers the span from pre-5 to S5/S6 and although it covers the full range of health education it gives particular focus to drug education. HELP is currently being updated to take account of recent developments in drug and nutrition education and will be available in its revised form in Summer 1998.

10.7.3 In addition, good quality health education resources are available for schools both for use with pupils and for staff development purposes. The Scottish Office Department of Health has funded the development of three support packages in drug education for schools. Two of these packages are aimed at secondary pupils; *Drugwise Too* for pupils aged 10-14 and *Drugwise Drug Free* for older pupils. *Drugwise First* was for primary pupils. These packages were offered free of charge to all schools in Scotland. The Health Education Board for Scotland (HEBS) has also produced a range of helpful resources.

---

123 *Forward Together: A Strategy to combat Drug and Alcohol Misuse in Wales.* Published 1996 by Welsh Office, Cathays Park, Cardiff CF1 3NQ.

| | | 1994 | | 1995 | | 1996 | | 1997 | |
Age of accused		10-13	14-17	10-13	14-17	10-13	14-17	10-13	14-17
Offence									
Production, manufacture or cultivation									
	Prosecuted	0	3	0	1	0	4	0	1
	Charge proved	0	3	0	1	0	4	0	1
Supply, possession with intent to supply									
	Prosecuted	0	52	1	51	0	4	0	72
	Charge proved	0	42	0	29	0	55	0	56
Possession of drugs									
	Prosecuted	0	268	0	293	0	285	0	276
	Charge proved	0	252	0	273	0	250	0	248

FIGURE 8: DRUGS OFFENCES BY CHILDREN IN SCOTLAND

10.7.4   The table above summarises statistics relating to drug offences by children in Scotland.

10.8 Increase in asylum applications

Article 22

10.8.1   Since the previous report was published, the number of asylum applications overall has risen dramatically, stretching further the resources of the Home Office Immigration and Nationality Directorate as well as other government and non-government bodies dealing with asylum seekers.

10.8.2   The number of unaccompanied children seeking asylum in the United Kingdom has also risen dramatically from 400 in 1994 to over 2800 in 1998.

10.8.3   In the light of the increase in asylum applications, an inter-departmental study of the asylum process was undertaken. The results of that review contributed to the White Paper referred to in section 10.16. An Immigration and Asylum Bill which will deliver key elements of the strategy set out in the White Paper is now before Parliament.

10.9 Refugee children

10.9.1   The Asylum and Immigration Appeals Act 1993, the Asylum and Immigration Act 1996 and HC 395[124] (as amended) now regulate the handling of all asylum applications including those made by children. When considering asylum applications from children, whether accompanied or not, close attention is given to the welfare of the child at all times.

10.9.2   Under the Immigration Rules applications from unaccompanied children receive priority and because of their potential vulnerability particular care is given to their cases. As an additional safeguard, the Government has made a commitment that no unaccompanied children under the age of 18 will be removed from the United Kingdom unless there are adequate reception and care arrangements for them in their country of origin. The Home Office passes details of every unaccompanied child who claims asylum to The British Red Cross which has established a register of unaccompanied children who are in the United Kingdom. The purpose of this register is to facilitate the restoration of family contacts and the tracing of parents.

124 Statement of Changes in Immigration Rules ISBN 0-10-239594-2, 23 May 1994, HMSO.

10.9.3   All asylum-seeking children and all asylum seekers who claim to be minors are referred as a matter of routine to the Children's Panel of the Refugee Council.

10.10   Panel of advisers for unaccompanied refugee children

Article 22

10.10.1   The United Kingdom's First Report under the Convention, in 1994, outlined the decision to fund the establishment of a non-statutory Panel of Advisers to assist unaccompanied children who are seeking asylum. The Refugee Council were subsequently asked to set up what became known as the Panel of Advisers for Unaccompanied Refugee Children. A Memorandum of Understanding has been established between the Home Office and the Refugee Council setting out the purpose of the Panel, the services provided by the Panel, the performance indicators to be used and monitoring and reporting procedures. The service to be provided by the Panel is consistent with Article 3(4) of the EU Council Resolution on unaccompanied minors who are nationals of third countries, agreed at the Justice and Home Affairs Council in May 1997, which states that Member States should provide "necessary representation" for minors.

10.11   Welfare of refugee children

Article 22

10.11.1   The Immigration and Nationality Directorate Public Caller Units based in Croydon have established a close working relationship with the Social Services Department of Croydon Borough Council. A meeting took place in Autumn 1997 to set out the relationship between the two departments in order that an efficient safety net was in place to care for unaccompanied minors or those considered to be vulnerable. Similar arrangements, modified dependent on the area, have been put in place with most local authorities in the vicinity of the major sea and air ports. Unaccompanied minors of compulsory school age have access to education on the same basis as other children. Additional English language teaching is provided for children whose first language is not English

10.11.2   A list has now been prepared, by the Department of Health, of child mental health professionals who can be contacted in situations where there is particular concern for a refugee child or adolescent. This list has been passed to the Refugee Council.

10.12   Family reunion for refugees

10.12.1   Those people recognised as refugees are immediately eligible to be joined by their pre-existing spouse and minor dependant children. The maintenance and accommodation criteria which are applied under the Rules to other immigration cases are waived for refugees.

10.12.2   Those refused refugee status may be granted exceptional leave to remain (ELR) if it is considered that there are compelling reasons why they should not be expected to return to the country of origin. This is a discretionary and temporary status and family reunion is not normally permitted until the sponsor has completed 4 years' exceptional leave to remain in the UK, by which time it has usually become clear that the sponsor's stay in the UK will be permanent. Sponsors with ELR must show that they are able to support and accommodate their dependants in the UK.

10.12.3 Family reunion does not apply to applicants who marry after leaving their country of nationality to seek asylum. In such cases, applicants must satisfy the normal requirements of the Immigration Rules.

10.13 Immigration staff training for work involving refugee children

Article 22

10.13.1 All caseworkers dealing with applications from unaccompanied children receive special training which broadly follows the guidelines set by UNHCR and the Red Cross. In accordance with the Immigration Rules, a child will not be interviewed about the substance of his or her claim if it is possible to obtain from written enquiries the information needed to consider the application fully. However, where an interview is necessary it must be conducted by a specially trained officer, in a language the child understands, and in the presence of a parent, guardian, representative or other adult who, for the time being, takes responsibility for the child. In practice, it is rarely necessary for an interview of this kind to be conducted. Most children are interviewed only briefly, for the purpose of establishing their identity.

10.14 The integrated casework programme for immigration

10.14.1 During 1999, a computerised caseworking system will be introduced within the Immigration and Nationality Directorate. It will increase caseworking performance to benefit all applicants. Within the Integrated Casework Directorate, two Casework Management Units (CMU) have been set up to take over the work formerly undertaken by the Unaccompanied Children's Module (UCM). The number of caseworkers within these new units will increase from 6 caseworkers to 32, and while they may not deal solely with applications from unaccompanied children, such applications will continue to be dealt with as a matter of priority by staff who have received special training.

10.15 Detention under immigration procedures

Article 37

10.15.1 In the majority of borderline cases where an applicant claims to be under 18, and the documentary or other evidence is not conclusive, he or she is usually given the benefit of the doubt.

10.15.2 There are circumstances, however, where a short period of detention in such cases is inevitable, usually when an unaccompanied child arrives at a port in the United Kingdom, often late at night, in circumstances where the local Social Services are unable to make an immediate response to the Immigration Service's request for assistance. Such cases are rare and the child is usually released the following day. Accompanied children are detained very much as a last resort, where there are compelling reasons for keeping a family together or where such detention would facilitate arrangements for the removal of a family unit from the United Kingdom.

10.15.3 The detention of a minor is notified as a matter of course to the official Visiting Committees, and exceptional risk status may be afforded to any vulnerable immigration detainee, whatever the cause of concern may be. Exceptional risk status requires the provision of one or more chaperons and frequent monitoring by contractor staff.

10.15.4 In the majority of cases where an applicant claims to be under 18, he or she is usually given the benefit of the doubt. However, there are circumstances where there is no conclusive evidence to show that a particular applicant is a minor. Whilst medical reports provided by the individual or his representatives can be a helpful indicator, they are not necessarily conclusive. Whenever someone claims to be under 18 the case is referred to the panel of advisors of the Refugee Council at the earliest opportunity. The Immigration Service also has leaflets which provide details of how to contact this organisation and these are available in 15 different languages.

10.15.5 On occasions children not liable to be detained are housed in detention accommodation with a detained parent or parents. However, this is done only with the agreement of the parents and in order to avoid separating family members. Such detention is normally for only a very short period prior to removal.

10.16 Benefits for asylum seekers

Article 22, 24, 26

10.16.1 Under the Social Security (Persons from Abroad) Miscellaneous Amendment Regulations 1996, which were subsequently confirmed by the Asylum and Immigration Act 1996 after a court judgement, social security benefits for asylum seekers have been restricted to those who claim asylum at the port of entry. The Act also confirmed that no persons from abroad, irrespective of whether they claim asylum, can claim child benefit. Under the Children Act 1989 however, where a child is found to be in need of care and support, Local Authorities are bound to provide all that is necessary to preserve the welfare of that child and any relative or carer who looks after the child.

10.16.2 Under new proposals set out in the White Paper on immigration and asylum (see below) responsibility for supporting families with children will be removed from local authorities and passed to a new central body, which will be responsible for providing accommodation and support for asylum seekers, except unaccompanied children, the responsibility for whom will remain with local authorities.

10.16.3 The Government published a White Paper on 27 July 1998 entitled *Fairer, faster, firmer – a modern approach to immigration and asylum*[125] which proposes new arrangements for supporting asylum seekers. These arrangements will ensure that the needs of children are fully respected and their welfare and rights safeguarded. Appropriate access to education will continue to be afforded to the children of asylum seekers. Provision will continue to be made under the Children Act 1989 and the Children (Scotland) Act 1995 for unaccompanied children claiming asylum, but local authority social services departments will no longer be expected to provide for asylum seeking families in the absence of needs requiring a social services

---

124 Cm 4018: ISBN 0-10-140182-5, published by the Stationery Office.

response. Where the need can be demonstrated, families will be provided with support under the same arrangements as for other asylum seekers. The Government is fully aware of the need to ensure that accommodation and support must be suitable to meet the needs of families in order to comply fully with Article 8 of the European Convention on Human Rights and Section 20(1) of the Children Act 1989.

10.17 Immigration and the treatment of refugees – views of NGOs

Article 22

10.17.1 This is a sensitive area which presents great problems for the Government in dealing fairly with those who seek to come to the United Kingdom, consistently with our international obligations. The Government must take account of economic pressures and the need to avoid the unfairness which would result if those who have abided by the controls were to see others obtaining advantage by ignoring the controls.

10.17.2 This is a difficult balance to strike, and not surprisingly the Government's efforts to do so are closely scrutinised. The Churches' Commission for Racial Justice, for example, have expressed concern about children of families where either or both of the parents face deportation, especially where the children have been born in the United Kingdom or lived a substantial proportion of their lives here. They also express concern about the children of asylum seekers, who face difficulties resulting from the more limited social security benefits now available to such families; and about the separation of families which may result when asylum-seekers may have to wait many years for a decision, during which time they cannot be reunited with their families. This latter point is supported by the Medical Foundation for Victims of Torture, who urge that cases involving children need speedy consideration, within a time limit of, say, 12 weeks, so that the period of uncertainty would be short, the stress on the child would be reduced, and the statutory authorities would have a better basis for discharging their responsibilities to the child whether its future was abroad (in which case consideration would need to be given to reception facilities) or in the United Kingdom.

10.18 Child witnesses: England and Wales

Article 34, 39, 40

10.18.1 The United Kingdom's First Report set out (in paragraphs 1.29 to 1.32) the existing measures available to protect child witnesses in court proceedings. Those included abolition of the presumption that children are incompetent witnesses; the transfer of child witness cases direct to the Crown Court; in the case of sexual offences and offences of violence, cruelty and neglect, the use of live TV links in courts; video recorded interviews; and a ban on a defendant himself cross-examining a child witness. That report indicated that the effect of these reforms was being monitored with a view to assessing the need for further reform, and a number of developments have taken place since 1994.

10.18.2 The Steering Group on Child Evidence (SGCE), comprising representatives from relevant Government Departments and the police, monitors and evaluates the implementation of the child evidence provisions and takes forward and resolves any issues arising. Since the end of 1997 the group has included a number of associate members from non government organisations such as the NSPCC and Childline. Developments in which the SGCE has been involved include a video, *A Case for Balance*, produced by the NSPCC in January 1997 as a result of co-operation between and funding by both government and non government organisations. This provides guidance on good practice for the judiciary and lawyers in cases involving child witnesses. The video has been endorsed by the Judicial Studies Board, and has been well received by its target audience of judges and advocates who deal with children's cases and Crown Court staff.

10.18.3 Revision of the child witness pack has also been completed – it was re-issued as *The Young Witness Pack*[126] produced by the NSPCC in conjunction with the Government in June 1998. The thrust of this initiative, which consists of a range of age-related booklets and leaflets for children, their parents and carers, is the belief that careful familiarisation with the court process can improve the quality of evidence given by children, without prejudicing the rights of the defendant. A Handbook has been produced to accompany the Pack, designed as a reference and training resource for child witness supporters.

10.18.4 Other issues which are being taken forward include fast tracking of child abuse cases in the criminal justice system; preparation of the child for court; and the development of guidance on pre-trial therapy by a multi-disciplinary group co-ordinated by the Crown Prosecution Service.

10.18.5 All Crown Courts have Child Witness Officers who are responsible for ensuring the smooth running of the arrangements for child witnesses, including pre-trial familiarisation visits. There is a Crown Court Witness Service (CCWS) run by Victim Support in every Crown Court, providing help to all victims and witnesses attending court including children. Arrangements made in 1997 with the Crown Prosecution Service enable the CCWS to receive advance copies of the lists of witnesses attending court so that children can be identified and arrangements made for their reception.

10.18.6 On 10 June 1998 the Government published *Speaking Up for Justice*, the report of a Government Working Group[127]. This makes over 70 recommendations to improve the treatment of vulnerable or intimidated witnesses – including children – in the criminal justice system. Approximately 26 of these will require legislation. Those recommendations relating specifically to child witnesses include:

    a the existing child evidence measures (video recorded statements and live TV links) should be available for all witnesses under 17 years;

---

126 June 1998: ISBN 0 902498 74 6, ISBN 0 902498 51 7, ISBN 0 902498 73 8, ISBN 0 902498 71 1, ISBN 0 902498 72 X, ISBN 0 902498 50 9, ISBN 0 902498 49 5 published by NSPCC and Childline,

127 *Report of the Working Group on Vulnerable or Intimidated Witnesses*, London, The Home Office, June 1998.

b the new special measures should be available to all witnesses under 17 years, regardless of the nature of the offence; these special measures include

- video-recorded pre-trial cross-examination

- assistance with communication where necessary, including the use of an intermediary

- power for the judge to clear the public gallery in cases involving sexual offences or intimidation so the witness can give evidence in private

- screening the witness from the defendant

- removal of formal court dress;

c there should be a presumption that child witnesses giving live evidence to the courts should do so by live TV link;

d all measures should be available in the magistrates' courts, youth courts and the Crown Court;

e the scope of the ban on defendants cross-examining child witnesses in person should be increased by extending the categories of offences to include false imprisonment, kidnapping and child abduction.

10.18.7 The Government has indicated its broad support for these recommendations and is consulting on the detail before reaching any final conclusions. The consultation exercise ended on 31 August 1998.

10.18.8 The Government has included legislative provision in the Youth Justice and Criminal Evidence Bill, currently before Parliament, to extend reporting restrictions over the identification of young people alleged to have committed criminal offences back to the point when the official investigation of the offence begins.

10.18.9 Concerns have been addressed about the confidentiality and security of record and privacy rights of children who have been the victims of sexual exploitation, particularly where the child's evidence is given on video. Under the Sexual Offences (Amendment) Act 1976, where an allegation has been made that a person has been the victim of a rape offence, neither the name nor the address of that person nor a photograph of them can be published or broadcast during their lifetime if it is likely to lead to members of the public identifying that person as an alleged victim of such an offence. The Sexual Offences (Amendment) Act 1992 also extended the anonymity of the alleged victim to certain other sexual offences, for example incest. The *Memorandum of Good Practice*[128] contains practical guidance on the storage, custody and destruction of such video tapes and all police

---

128 ISBN 0-11-341040-9, London, HMSO 1992.

records are confidential. There is, however, an obligation to disclose a copy to the defence.

10.19 Child witnesses in Northern Ireland

Article 34, 39, 40

10.19.1 The Children's Evidence (Northern Ireland) Order 1995 allowed video evidence to be admitted in the Crown Court and juvenile court to help reduce the trauma of children who are victims of, or witness to, violent or sexual offences. Provision was made in the Criminal Justice (Children) (NI) Order 1998 to amend the Police and Criminal Evidence (NI) Order 1989 to allow magistrates' courts to admit children's evidence in chief by video recording.

10.19.2 The Vulnerable or Intimidated Witnesses (NI) Working Group was established in April 1998 to examine the proposals for England and Wales in the Northern Ireland context. The group held two consultation exercises and plans to submit its final report to Ministers by the end of June 1999. It has already been agreed that the provisions in the Youth Justice and Criminal Evidence Bill relating to vulnerable or intimidated witnesses will be extended to Northern Ireland by Order in Council.

10.20 Child Witnesses: Scotland

Article 34, 39, 40

10.20.1 In Scotland arrangements were brought into effect in 1993 whereby children could give evidence by live television link through closed circuit television, by the use of pre-trial commission evidence sometimes recorded on video, or shielded from the accused person by a screen in the court. Those arrangements have been developed and are now more widely available in all parts of the country. In civil cases these special arrangements can apply where there is a referral to the children's hearing and the matter is then taken to the sheriff and a child has to give evidence. Other changes to the law of evidence in Scotland have meant that certain hearsay statements are admissible in both civil and criminal cases although there has been a limited use of these provisions and their use may be further curtailed by the incorporation of the European Convention on Human Rights into domestic legislation.

10.20.2 There has been published recently a Report and Consultation Document – *Towards a Just Conclusion*[129] – in which the Government makes further proposals with regard to the way in which all witnesses and in particular children should be supported and protected. In addition a Working Group dealing with support for child witnesses published its report and research findings in April 1999, detailing arrangements which have been in place in the Scottish courts and amongst the participants in the Scottish criminal justice system to make the giving of evidence by children a less daunting experience. The recommendations from both these reports will form the foundation for further developments in this area.

---

129 Scottish Office Police Division File Number JMCO5510

10.20.3 Furthermore, the Government has consulted on the proposal to remove the test of competency for child witnesses in Scotland in both criminal and civil proceedings and is likely to bring forward proposals to this effect along with other proposals to extend the use of closed circuit television, commission and screens to other types of civil proceedings. All these developments reinforce the support which children can expect from the Court Service, from the Procurators Fiscal Service and the Crown Office, and from other participants in the criminal and civil justice systems.

10.20.4 The Crown Office has also undertaken a thematic review of how prosecutors view and deal with sexual offenders.

10.21 Police procedures for child witnesses in England and Wales

Article 34, 39, 40

10.21.1 Improvements to the way child victims are treated by the police include the following: –

a Police forces have specialist units of fully trained officers to undertake child protection investigations and deal with related issues. The police have stringent powers to protect children which include powers to take pre-emptive action for the welfare of the child under the Children Act 1989. These include powers to take into protective custody children who are at risk of significant harm. The underlying principle of the Act is that the welfare of the child must come first.

b The Home Office have issued guidance to chief officers of police on joint training for police officers and social workers and the importance of inter-agency working. In addition to training by their employers, police officers and social worker now receive joint training known as the CAMAT course (Child Abuse Management and Training). Advice on interviewing child witnesses and victims is now incorporated in mainstream police training.

10.22 Privacy: identification of children in court proceedings

10.22.1 In the Access to Justice Bill, currently before Parliament, the Government has introduced an amendment to the Children Act 1989 so as to extend the prohibition on publishing material intended or likely to identify a child involved in proceedings under or related to the Children Act 1989 to proceedings in the High Court and county court. The prohibition already applies in the magistrates' court.

10.23 Juvenile offenders: summary of developments in England and Wales since 1994

Article 40

10.23.1 This section summarises the substantial changes which have been made in this area since the United Kingdom's First Report. These changes, and further developments which are in progress, are set out in more detail in section 10.27 .

10.23.2 Following the General Election in May 1997, the new administration began to put into effect its plans for a radical overhaul of the youth justice system. The Crime and Disorder Act 1998 was enacted on 31 July 1998 and governs the first phase of these reforms. The far reaching changes which seek to reduce offending and reoffending by young people are being piloted from 30 September 1998, for 18 months, with full implementation likely from April 2000.

10.23.3 The reform programme aims to provide:

a a clear strategy to prevent offending and reoffending;

b that offenders, and their parents or guardians, face up to their offending behaviour and take responsibility for it;

c earlier, more effective intervention when young people first offend;

d faster, more efficient procedures from arrest to sentence;

e partnership between all youth justice agencies to deliver a better, faster system.

10.23.4 The Government also sees a need for more fundamental reform to change the culture of the youth court, making it more open and accessible and engaging offenders and their families more closely.

10.23.5 There is a clear focus on preventing offending by children and young people, and this has been established in statute as the aim of the youth justice system in England and Wales. There is a statutory duty on agencies and individuals working in the youth justice system to have regard to that aim.

10.24 New legislation on young offenders in England and Wales

Article 40

10.24.1 Legislation in the Crime and Disorder Act has:

a abolished the rebuttable presumption of *doli incapax*, thereby ensuring that courts will be able to address offending behaviour by children between the ages of 10 and 14 at the earliest possible opportunity, and so nip that offending behaviour in the bud;

b allowed courts to draw inferences from the failure of an accused child to give evidence or answer questions at trial, thereby ensuring that all juveniles are treated in the same way in court;

c introduced a new reparation order, which will allow young offenders to understand the consequences of what they have done and make reparation to their victims;

d acknowledged the crucial role of parents and guardians in shaping and influencing a child or young person's development, and helped them to fulfil that role successfully by means of a parenting order;

e enabled local authorities, the police and the courts to protect young children from being drawn into criminal and anti-social behaviour by introducing the child safety order and the local child curfew;

f replaced the old system of cautioning young offenders with a new final warning, which initiates community intervention programmes for young offenders designed to address offending behaviour and turn young people away from crime before they end up in court;

g   introduced a new community sentence, the action plan order, which combines punishment with rehabilitation and reparation;

h   introduced a new detention and training order which will combine custody and community supervision to rehabilitate youngsters whose crimes require secure detention;

i   introduced new measures to speed up youth justice;

j   established a new Youth Justice Board for England and Wales, which advises Ministers on standards for service delivery and promotes and monitors good practice among local agencies involved with young offenders and young people at risk;

k   placed a new duty on local authorities to ensure the provision of inter-agency youth offending teams in their areas, in partnership with police, probation services and health authorities.

10.24.2 Proposals for a further element of reform of the youth court are contained in the Youth Justice and Criminal Evidence Bill, currently before Parliament. The Bill contains provision for a new style of disposal for first time defendants pleading guilty. The young offender will be sentenced to referral to a youth offending panel which will consider, with the young offender, his or her parent or guardian and others, a programme of activity to include some reparation to the victim or to the community at large, and to address the causes of the offending behaviour. The length of the referral will be set by the court. The young offender will meet the panel, without legal representation, to participate in a group conference and to agree a contract which will set out a programme of activity for the duration of the order. Where a contract cannot be agreed, or is breached, the young offender may be returned to court for re-sentencing. This will ensure a positive response to offending by young people, helping to encourage positive discussion and action by youth justice practitioners, the young person and his or her family.

10.25 Reforming the youth court in England and Wales

Article 40

10.25.1 The Government is in the process of a programme of reform of the youth court, following proposals set out in the White Paper *No More Excuses: a new approach to tackling youth crime in England and Wales*[130]. This includes both legislative and non-legislative measures to achieve long-term improvements. New legislative measures will streamline the way in which those appearing before the court for the first time are dealt with by introducing a new disposal in the form of a referral to a youth offending panel. The panel will work with the young offender and his or her parent or guardian – and other influential adults as appropriate – to draw up a contract to cover a package of measures designed to address his or her offending behaviour. The contract will also normally include an element of reparation. At the same time, non-legislative measures will encourage a system which is more open and accessible, and develop processes which engage young offenders and their parent or guardian more effectively, to help them to focus on their offending behaviour and how to change it.

---

130 Cm 3809 November 1997: The Stationery Office ISBN 0-10-138092-5.

| **10.26** | **Statutory time limits in England and Wales** | 10.26.1   The Government is introducing a range of legislative measures, including statutory time limits for all cases involving young offenders. Statutory time limits will cover the whole youth justice process from arrest to sentence, save for the trial itself. A number of other practical measures have been introduced, or are currently being piloted, to enable the courts to deal more speedily with young offenders. |

10.27   The Government's programme for young offenders in England and Wales

10.27.1   The new measures summarised above will be effective in further implementing the UN Convention on the Rights of the Child. They will make the juvenile justice process swifter, better co-ordinated and less stressful for all those involved with it. They will also ensure that all juveniles in England and Wales have equal access to an efficient court system, and programmes of intervention designed to address their offending behaviour and prevent reoffending.

Article 40

10.28   Youth Justice Board for England and Wales

10.28.1   The Crime and Disorder Act 1998 provides a clearer national framework for local action to deal with youth offending. It establishes a Youth Justice Board for England and Wales, which will promote good practice and monitor the performance of the youth justice system as a whole and advise the Secretary of State on this and on national standards for work with young offenders.

Article 40

10.29   Youth offending teams

10.29.1   The Government wishes to improve inter-agency working between those agencies most closely involved in work with young offenders in the community. The Crime and Disorder Act places a duty on local authorities with education and social services responsibilities, in partnership with the police, probation service and health authorities, to establish a multi-agency youth offending team or teams for their area.

Article 40

10.29.2   Youth offending teams will include social workers, probation officers, police officers and education and health staff. They may also include individuals from other agencies and organisations, including in the voluntary sector. Youth offending teams will plan and undertake the supervision of young offenders under community sentences and following release from custody. They will also carry out assessment and intervention work in support of a new final warning scheme, which will replace police cautions. The teams will be able to draw on programmes and services, such as bail support and intervention programmes, provided outside the team by relevant local agencies themselves and the voluntary sector.

10.29.3   The focus of the work of youth offending teams will be on preventing offending by children and young people. This will involve tackling offending behaviour and addressing problems which may underlie that behaviour, such as truancy or exclusion from school; poor behaviour or performance at school; or drug or alcohol misuse.

10.30 *Doli incapax* and the drawing of inferences at trial

10.30.1 The abolition of the presumption of *doli incapax* and the decision to allow courts to draw inferences from the failure of an accused child to give evidence or answer questions at trial both have the same purpose, namely, to ensure that, if a child has begun to offend, he or she is entitled to the earliest possible intervention to address that offending behaviour and eliminate its causes. The changes will also have the result of putting all juveniles on the same footing as far as courts are concerned, and will contribute to the right of children appearing there to develop responsibility for themselves.

10.30.2 In today's sophisticated society, it is not unjust or unreasonable to assume that a child aged 10 or older can understand the difference between serious wrong and simple naughtiness, and is therefore able to respond to intervention designed to tackle offending behaviour. If for some reason a child is lacking in this most basic moral understanding, it is all the more imperative that appropriate intervention and rehabilitation should begin as soon as possible. Similarly, it is common sense to expect a child who has an innocent explanation for his or her conduct to provide that explanation, rather than to deprive him or her of that responsibility. Children will continue to be protected by the court's discretion not to draw inferences from silence if it considers that the child's mental or physical state makes this undesirable.

10.30.3 It is important to stress that these changes will not have the effect of treating children in the same way as adults as far as the criminal justice system is concerned. The emphasis is firmly placed not on criminalising children, but on helping them to recognise and accept responsibility for their actions where this is appropriate, and on enabling them to receive help to change their offending behaviour. The criminal justice system provides for an entirely different set of sentences, graduated by age, for juvenile offenders. A court is therefore able appropriately to reflect a young offender's age and level of maturity at the point of sentence. There is no intention that children or young people will be treated as if they are adults.

10.30.4 It is also important to emphasise that the abolition of the presumption of *doli incapax* does not affect the age of criminal responsibility in England and Wales, which remains at 10 years. The Government considers that this is an appropriate level, reflecting the need to protect the welfare of the youngest. However if children aged 10 or older start to behave in a criminal or anti-social way, the Government considers that we do them no favours to overlook this behaviour. It is in the interests of children and young people themselves to recognise and accept responsibility, and to receive assistance in tackling criminal behaviour.

10.31 Pilot projects for new developments in England and Wales

Article 40

10.31.1 Pilots of youth offending teams and the new powers for the police and courts contained in the Crime and Disorder Act – the final warning scheme, the reparation order, the action plan order, the parenting order and the child safety order – began on 30 September 1998 and will run for 18 months in total. The purpose of the pilots is to help to identify good practice in the operation of the youth offending teams, the delivery of youth justice services, and the effectiveness of the new orders; this good practice will then inform guidelines which will be issued prior to nationwide roll-out. The pilots will also allow the costs and savings involved in nationwide implementation to be assessed. The pilots to introduce statutory time limits in the youth justice system will run for 18 months from November 1999.

10.32 Reparation orders

Article 40

10.32.1 The reparation order is a new court disposal which requires the young person to make specific reparation either to the individual victim of his crime, where the victim desires that, or to the community which he has harmed. The intention is that the reparation should be in kind rather than financial, as courts may use the compensation order if they wish the offender to make financial recompense. Reparation activities might include writing a letter of apology or apologising to the victim in person, weeding a garden, collecting litter, or doing other work to help the community. The purpose of this new order is to enable the young person to understand the consequences of what he has done and the effect of his actions upon his victim, and to enhance his right to develop responsibility for himself. By giving him a chance to apologise and make amends, the young offender will be better able to reintegrate into society.

10.33 Child safety orders

Article 40, 39

10.33.1 The child safety order is an early intervention measure designed to prevent children being drawn into crime. The order provides an early opportunity to intervene positively in an appropriate and proportionate way to protect the welfare of the child. The order supplements the existing welfare provisions currently available under the Children Act 1989. Child safety orders may be made in respect of children under the age of 10, and can be made by a family proceedings court following an application by the local authority social services department. Such an order may be applied for when a child below the age of criminal responsibility appears to be at risk of becoming involved in crime, or has already started to behave in an anti-social or criminal manner. Under a child safety order, a Family Proceedings Court will be able to require a child, for example, to be at home at specified times or to stay away from certain people or places. The court could also prohibit certain conduct, such as playing truant from school. If the requirements of an order are not complied with, it will be open to the local authority to commence care proceedings.

10.34 Parenting Orders

Article 5, 40

10.34.1 The parenting order is designed specifically to help and support the parent or guardian in addressing a child's offending behaviour. Parent is taken to mean the child's or young person's biological parent. Guardian is defined as a person who in the opinion of the court has for the time being the care of the child (section 107 of the Children and Young Persons Act 1933).

10.34.2 At the centre of the parenting order is the need to restore a proper relationship between the child and its parent or guardian. The main element of the order will be a requirement for the parent or guardian to attend counselling or guidance sessions to learn, for example, how to set and enforce acceptable standards of behaviour. It is, therefore, consistent with the aims of the Government's overall policy on supporting families and should be seen in that context. In the area of youth justice reform, it is not the only measure where there is parental involvement. The parent or guardian could, in appropriate cases, be required to exercise a measure of control over their child. This might include ensuring that the child attends school regularly or that the child avoids certain places or certain individuals who might have exerted a disruptive influence on the child. Failure to comply with requirements of an order without reasonable excuse will be a criminal offence. If convicted, the parent or guardian could be liable to a fine of up to £1,000.

10.35   Local child curfews

10.35.1   Problems can often be caused by unsupervised young children gathered in public places at night, who are too young to be out alone at night, and who can cause alarm and misery to local communities and encourage one another into anti-social and criminal habits. To protect both the young people themselves and their local communities, the Government is giving powers to local authorities, after consultation with the police and local community, to impose local child curfews on children under the age of 10. These provide local authorities with another option in addressing community safety problems, and they should be seen within the context of existing community safety practices and future developments.

10.35.2   The power to impose a local child curfew will be a permissive one. The decision as to whether or not a local child curfew is appropriate will be one which must be made locally following appropriate discussion with the police, the local community and other such bodies as the local authority considers it appropriate to consult. The support of the police and the local community will be crucial to the success of the scheme.

10.35.3   Once the local authority has established that there is a consensus for a local child curfew scheme, it will be required to draw up an outline scheme and submit its proposals to the Home Secretary for his agreement. The scheme will need to specify arrangements for consulting the police and local residents in the area to which the curfew is to be applied, and arrangements for making local residents and others aware of the curfew notice when it is brought into force. Each curfew notice under the scheme may last for up to 90 days. If the authority seeks an extension beyond that, it will have to consult the police and local community again. As part of its application for confirmation by the Home Secretary, the authority will need to signify how it proposes to do this.

10.35.4   Local child curfew schemes will be enforced by the police. Because of the child welfare issues involved, the social services will also have an important role to play. Although enforcement of the curfew will be carried out as part of normal duties, the police and social services may well decide that this will be best achieved as part of a multi-agency response to the problem involving a number of other agencies.

10.35.5   Similar schemes, under their different legislation, are under way in Scotland – see section 10.44.

10.36 Final warning scheme

Article 40

10.36.1 The current arrangements for the cautioning of young offenders in England and Wales have resulted in inconsistencies across the country in the way in which young people are dealt with by the police. Whilst some areas operate "caution plus" schemes designed to turn young people away from crime, in other areas young people may be cautioned repeatedly with no follow up action to address their offending behaviour. These arrangements are being replaced with a new Final Warning scheme, which will prevent repeat cautions and will be operated consistently across the country. The issue of a final warning to a young offender will trigger referral to a rehabilitation programme which will be aimed at encouraging young offenders to face up to the effects of their behaviour, and will work with them on the factors which influence the offending behaviour. Intervention programmes will be prepared by the new local Youth offending Teams, described in section 10.29.

10.37 Action plan orders

Article 40

10.37.1 The action plan order is a new community sentence available for a child or young person convicted of an offence other than one for which the sentence is fixed by law, where the court considers that it will help to prevent further offending. A child for this purpose is a person under the age of 14; a young person is a person who has attained the age of 14, and is under the age of 18. It is a highly focused three-month order which will involve the young offender in an intensively supervised programme of education and activities, and ensure that his parent or guardian are fully involved. The action plan order comprises a series of requirements specifically tailored to the circumstances of each individual offender. Before making such an order, the court will look at the circumstances which have contributed to the young person's offending behaviour, and will ensure that the subsequent action plan addresses those circumstances with a view to preventing re-offending. Where the young offender is under the age of 16, the court is also specifically required to take into account information about his family circumstances and the likely effect of the order on those circumstances, in order to ensure that no requirements of the order will cause stress or difficulty in the family situation. If abuse of drugs has contributed to the offending, the action plan may include an element to assist the young person in dealing with this problem; if truanting has been a contributory factor, the action plan may require the young person to comply with educational requirements. These action plans will be supervised by members of the new youth offending teams, and provide an individual response to the needs of each young offender.

10.38 Secure training orders

Article 40

10.38.1 A new sentence of detention, the Secure Training Order, came into effect on 1 March 1998. The legislation which introduced the Secure Training Order was contained in the Criminal Justice and Public Order Act 1994, and was referred to by the committee in their observations on the first United Kingdom Report. The Secure Training Order is for children aged 12 to 14 who persistently offend and who have failed to respond to community sentences. Before passing this sentence, the court must also be satisfied that the offence is so serious that only a custodial sentence is appropriate. The sentence may last from 6 months to 2 years, with half spent in custody and half under close supervision within the community. The custodial part of the sentence is served in a secure training centre, the first of which opened on 17 April 1998 at Medway in Kent. Plans are proceeding for provision of several further centres elsewhere in England and Wales.

10.38.2 It seems possible, from comments in the Committee's observations on the United Kingdom's First Report, made some time before the first STC opened, that the committee may have misunderstood the purpose and ethos of these institutions, and the circumstances in which young people might be sent there.

10.38.3 The primary purpose of STCs is not penal. STCs provide a positive regime with training programmes geared to individual needs. They also provide a high standard of education, and structured programmes designed to encourage the young people to address their offending behaviour, and to face up to the consequences of their crimes. Although the centres are privately managed, they operate under contract to the Government, it determines their regime and there are statutory rules governing their operation. The management of the centres is closely monitored by a Home Office official based at the STC, and staff recruitment, vetting and training have to comply with the recommendations made in the Warner and Utting reports.[131] The underlying principles of the Children Act apply. There is provision for the appointment of independent persons to whom representation may be made by young offenders detained in secure training centres. An organisation with experience in representing young people in secure accommodation has been appointed to provide the Independent Person Service at Medway. An Independent Person visits within 24 hours of a request and assists formal representation or complaint. Family links are encouraged, and an assisted visits scheme is funded by the Home Office.

10.38.4 The centres are subject to inspection by independent inspectors. A supervising officer from the young person's home area is closely involved in designing his or her training programme during custody and on release to ensure a consistent and positive approach.

10.39 Detention and training orders

Article 40

10.39.1 The Crime and Disorder Act introduces a Detention and Training Order to replace the Secure Training Order and the sentence of Detention in a Young Offender Institution for 15-17 year olds. The Detention and Training Order will meet the requirement that the ..."arrest, detention or imprisonment of a child...shall be used only as a measure of last resort", as the offence or offences in question must be of such a level of seriousness that

---

131 Warner: *Choosing with care* - the report of the Committee of Inquiry into the selection, development and management of staff in Children's Homes. ISBN 0-11-321559-2, published 1992 by HMSO.

Utting: *People like us:* The Report of the review of the safeguards for children living away from home, by Sir William Utting. Published by the Stationery Office on behalf of the Department of Health and the Welsh Office. ISBN 0-11-322101-0.

only custody is justified. If the young person is under 15 years of age, then it must be shown that he is a persistent offender.

10.39.2 There exists a provision to extend the detention and training order to 10 and 11 year olds, but there are no current plans to use it.

10.39.3 The Order itself will last for 4, 6, 8, 10, 12, 18 or 24 months. Half of it will be served in custody, and half under supervision in the community. The young offender will be supervised by a probation officer, social worker or a member of the youth offending team. They will help the young offender to build on the progress made in detention, and facilitate reintegration into society. The Order is due to be implemented in April 2000 for juveniles. It will replace the present sentences of Detention in a Young Offender Institution and the Secure Training Order.

10.40 Arrest and detention by the police in England and Wales

Article 40, 37

10.40.1 Paragraph 8.41 of the United Kingdom's First Report may have given rise to misunderstanding. A juvenile should not be placed in police cells unless

    a no other secure accommodation is available and

    b the custody officer considers that it is not practicable to supervise him if he is not placed in a cell, or

    c a custody officer considers that a cell provides more comfortable accommodation than other secure accommodation in the police station.

10.40.2 A child may not be placed in a police cell with a detained adult.

10.40.3 An intimate or a strip search of a juvenile may only take place in the presence of an appropriate adult of the same sex, subject to the wishes of the juvenile. An intimate search is one involving the physical examination of body orifices; a strip search is one involving a visual examination of intimate parts of the body.

10.41 Minor changes in secure accommodation arrangements in England and Wales

Article 40, 37

10.41.1 Since the United Kingdom's First Report, there has been one minor change in relation to the provision of secure accommodation for children in care. The Children (Secure Accommodation) Amendment Regulations 1995[132] extended the provision of secure accommodation, to permit such accommodation to be made available by the private and voluntary sectors. Secure accommodation can now be provided by community homes, voluntary homes and registered children's homes to restrict the freedom, when necessary, of children looked after by a local authority. This category may include children remanded by the courts to local authority care, or following criminal proceedings.

---

132 SI 1995/1398.

10.42 Secure accommodation in Scotland

10.42.1 In Scotland, there are now two main routes into secure accommodation. If the child is waiting to go to court or has been convicted of a serious offence, he/she may be sent to a secure unit under the Criminal Procedure (Scotland) Act 1995. The more common route, however, following the Children (Scotland) Act 1995, is through the Children's Hearing system under the Social Work (Scotland) Act 1968. There are also emergency procedures. No child can be kept in secure accommodation for more than seven days in a row or for seven days in a month, without the authority of a Children's Hearing or a Sheriff.

10.43 Administration of juvenile justice in Northern Ireland

Article 40

10.43.1 The Criminal Justice (Children) (NI) Order 1998[133] provides that where a court makes a juvenile justice centre order, half the sentence will be served in custody and half under supervision in the community. The aim of the order is to plan from the first day for successful rehabilitation and to that end an individual plan should be drawn up for each child. The objective of the disposal is to reduce offending behaviour and to re-integrate the child successfully into the community.

10.43.2 The principles underpinning the Government's juvenile justice strategy for Northern Ireland are as follows: –

a The key aim for any juvenile justice system must be to prevent children from committing offences in the first place.

b Statutory and other agencies with relevant responsibilities should focus on diverting children away from criminal behaviour and on reducing the need to bring criminal proceedings against children.

c Effective inter-agency co-operation and co-ordination, on a partnership basis, is an essential part of an effective strategy for diverting children away from crime and from the criminal justice process, and for addressing the needs of those who come into contact with it.

10.43.3 In setting out the guiding principles to be observed by all courts in dealing with children in relation to criminal proceedings, Article 4 of the Criminal Justice (Children) (NI) Order 1998 requires courts to have regard to the welfare of the child brought before it and of any delay. Articles 12 and 13 include a presumption of bail, and require a court to give its reasons openly if it decides not to release a child on bail, and if it extends beyond three months the total time for which the child has been remanded in custody.

10.43.4 Schedule 1 to the Criminal Justice (NI) Order 1996[134] provides for offenders, including those who are children, who are dependent on or misuse drugs or alcohol where this is associated with the offending

---

133 SI 1998/1504 (NI 9).

134 SI 1996/3160 (NI 24)

behaviour, to be required to undergo treatment for their condition as an additional requirement of a probation order.

10.43.5 Under Article 33 of the Criminal Justice (Children) (NI) Order 1998 a court has power where a child is acquitted, or is found guilty but is not given a custodial sentence or a community sentence, and the court considers that the child's welfare requires it, to notify social services of such matters as it thinks fit. The relevant Health and Social Services Trust will be able to consider whether it should exercise any of its powers and duties, for example to provide accommodation, or to provide various forms of family support, or to seek a care or supervision order through the Family Proceedings Court.

10.43.6 The range of programmes to which children can be sent has been developed and extended. Furthermore, there are now multi-agency arrangements for diverting young people from the criminal justice system and interventions of a restorative nature are being actively explored and evaluated. The emphasis, supported by the two-part custodial/supervision order, is now very much on maintaining young people in the community and using custody, in particular, as a measure of last resort and for the minimum period commensurate with the offence.

10.43.7 The Government's juvenile justice strategy is underpinned by principles to prevent children from committing offences in the first place. Health and Social Services Trusts are now required under the Children (NI) Order 1995 to take reasonable steps to encourage children not to commit offences and to reduce the need to bring criminal proceedings against them.

10.43.8 Health and Social Services Boards are now required to develop Children's Services Plans which will demonstrate how Health and Social Services Boards and other agencies in the voluntary and statutory sectors plan to provide services for children in need, including children who are at risk of offending. The first plans to cover the period 1 April 1999 to 31 March 2002 have been completed.

10.43.9 Work is in hand to develop and extend the Juvenile Liaison Bureaux. This will enable education, social services and other bodies, including those in the voluntary sector, to have an input into police cautioning decisions, and to develop, with others, programmes which tackle offending behaviour more effectively. Relevant agencies are already co-operating to develop schemes which support cautioning by an appropriate intervention, which may well be of a restorative nature in which the offender faces the consequences of his actions. It is expected that Juvenile Liaison Bureaux will be available throughout Northern Ireland by June 1999.

10.43.10 The Government believed that there was no reason for the law on *doli incapax* to be any different in Northern Ireland from that in England and Wales, and the rebuttable presumption of *doli incapax* was abolished in Northern Ireland in December 1998.

10.43.11 Until commencement of the Criminal Justice (Children) (NI) Order on 31 January 1999 arrangements for the detention of the small number of serious or persistent young offenders were made by a training school order under the Children and Young Persons Act (NI) 1968. A training school order was authority for the detention for up to 2 years in custody followed by 2 years after-care in the community. The period of detention was determined not by the courts but by management of the training schools. No account was taken of the time a young person may have spent on remand. The period of detention may not have been proportionate to the offence for which it was given.

10.43.12 Those arrangements have been changed. Under the Criminal Justice (Children) (NI) Order 1998, custodial orders are limited to the most serious or persistent offenders and if such an order is imposed the court determines the length of sentence taking account only of the seriousness of the offence. The period of the sentence is reduced by the time spent on remand. The maximum period of detention is one year, but a standard three month period is stated to be appropriate in all but the most serious cases.

10.43.13 Because of the serious nature of the offending for which this sentence will be reserved, the accommodation needs to be secure in most cases. But the regime is positive with increasing emphasis on education and training, with the supervision period of the sentence being used to support the child for a period after release to help him reintegrate back into society.

10.43.14 The Criminal Justice (Children) (NI) Order 1998 provides that where a court makes a juvenile justice centre order, half the sentence will be served in custody and half in the community. The aim of the order is to plan from the first day for successful rehabilitation and to that end an individual plan should be drawn up for each child. The objective of the disposal is to reduce offending behaviour and to reintegrate the child successfully into the community. The new provisions are strictly limited to exceptional cases.

10.43.15 The original proposal for a draft Criminal Justice (Children) Order would have removed the provisions in the Children and Young Persons Act (NI) 1968 allowing the court to transfer children aged 15 or over held in a training school to the young offenders centre. However, as there is no secure accommodation for girls in Northern Ireland it became apparent that exceptional cases could arise where a 15 year old could not be held safely, or could be a danger to others, in a training school. It was therefore decided not to remove the power to transfer such children to the young offenders centre. The new provisions are strictly limited to exceptional cases.

10.44 The child safety initiative in Scotland

Article 40

10.44.1 The Child Safety Initiative was launched in Scotland by Strathclyde Police and South Lanarkshire Council in October 1997 to protect the safety of young people, cut down youth disorder, and reduce crime concerns following pressure from local communities for action to tackle in dealing with groups of youngsters disturbing the peace, and frightening residents.

10.44.2 A key element of the Initiative is high-profile, weekend and evening street patrols, undertaken by a pool of community police officers selected for their experience, skill and empathy in dealing with young people. The police patrol the streets of the housing estates and approach young people who are considered to be causing a nuisance or are unsupervised and in vulnerable situations. Their task is to ensure that unsupervised children in the street at an inappropriately late hour, and thought to be at risk, are returned home to their parents. If there is no adult supervision at home, the children are taken to a safe room at a police office until their parents or carers collect them.

10.44.3 The pilot is being evaluated by the Scottish Office and Strathclyde Police Research and Development Unit.

10.45 Prisons – separation of young offenders

Article 40

10.45.1 The United Kingdom has previously entered a reservation relating to Article 37(c) because of its policy of mixing certain young offenders with adults. The United Kingdom must retain this reservation for the present time to permit the mixing of young offenders and adults where there is, at any time, a lack of suitable accommodation or adequate facilities for a particular individual in any institution.

10.45.2 The United Kingdom has determined its plans for the initial composition of an under 18 estate. The new estate will comprise juvenile-only establishments and juvenile units in other establishments. This is supplemented by a strategy for securing further improvements to the estate over the next three years. A major programme of capital development work, totalling £15 million, is now under way to deliver the estate by April 2000. There may continue to be a small number of juvenile prisoners whose particular circumstances mean that they are best temporarily held in local prisons, for example because of distance from court or for medical reasons. New regime standards for boys under 18 have also been developed. The standards are founded upon research into "what works" with offenders and draw upon good practices in young offender institutions as well as other settings.

10.45.3 The UK has decided that 15 and 16 year old girls should be placed in non-Prison Service accommodation with the introduction of the Detention and Training Order (DTO) in April 2000. As spaces become available, 17 year old girls will also be placed outside the Prison Service. In the interim they will be held with other young women under 21 in enhanced Young Offender Units.

10.46 Separation of young offenders – views of NGOs

Article 40

10.46.1 The National Children's Bureau, and some other NGOs, have supported the Review of the Juvenile Secure Estate. They hope that it may result in changes in the practice of mixed placement of young offenders and children with welfare needs in local authority secure accommodation – though they acknowledge that all such children may require welfare provision. The same issues apply to young people on remand in adult prisons.

10.46.2 It is Government policy to move to a position where no 15 and 16 year olds have to be remanded to Prison Service custody, but there is currently insufficient provision elsewhere. However, under the Crime and Disorder Act 1998, from 1 June 1999 all girls of that age, and vulnerable boys for whom a place is available, who need custody can be remanded to local authority secure accommodation.

10.47 Treatment of young offenders while in custody

Article 40, 37

10.47.1 It is the duty of the Prison Service to hold in custody those young offenders sentenced into their care by the courts. While in custody, it is the Prison Service's duty to look after such young offenders with humanity and help them lead constructive lives while in custody and prepare them for a law abiding life on release. The Youth Justice Board, which came into operation on 30 September 1998, will monitor the operation of the youth justice system as a whole and will help set and monitor standards for secure accommodation for children and young people on remand or under sentence. The United Kingdom has also decided, in principle, that the Board will from April 2000 become the commissioning and purchasing body for all forms of juvenile secure accommodation – central government, local authority and private sector. This will help to ensure that juveniles in custody are held in accommodation appropriate to their needs.

10.47.2 It is the duty of the Prison Service to hold in custody those young offenders sentenced into their care by the courts. While in custody, it is the Prison Service's duty to look after such young offenders with humanity and help them lead constructive lives while in custody and prepare them for a law abiding life on release.

10.47.3 Education is compulsory for young people under school leaving age in Prison Service custody. Prison education focuses on the core curriculum of basic educational skills, life and social skills, and IT skills. The Prison Service is also developing a broader educational curriculum for those under 18, which can be tailored to individual needs. This will include an action plan and timetable for each juvenile, based on an in-depth assessment.

10.47.4 The Prison Service is very aware of the importance of sustaining prisoners' relationships with close relatives, partners and friends, and is committed to promoting close and meaningful family ties between prisoners and their families. It is currently working on improving regimes for those under 18 in its care, and developing regime standards for juveniles which will highlight the need to involve families in sentence planning and review, where appropriate.

10.47.5 Young offenders have a right of access to a request and complaints procedure and may also communicate with whomever they wish in the outside community, including legal advisers and Parliamentarians. Health Care is also available on a regular basis and it is intended to meet the standards of the heath service in the community. A periodic review of each young offender takes place as part of each person's individual sentence plan, which charts the subject's progress through the system and highlights areas of need for each young offender.

10.47.6 The Trust for the Study of Adolescence began in May 1998 an 18 month evaluation of the effectiveness of the parenthood courses running in young offender institutions (currently such courses run in half of the young offender institutions).

10.47.7 The Prison Service has initiated an extensive programme designed to secure improvements in the accommodation and regimes available for juveniles in its care. Principal features of this work include:

a the development of new regimes standards for juveniles, which focus on the specific needs of this group;

b proposals for the creation of a distinct juvenile estate for male 15-17 year olds remanded or sentenced to custody;

c the establishment of 3 enhanced regime units for those under 18 sentenced under section 53 of the Children and Young Persons Act 1933;

d the investment, in this financial year, of additional funds in two establishments holding juveniles to establish enhanced regimes.

10.48 Detention as a last resort – Scotland

Article 40, 37

10.48.1 In view of the Committee's comment on the United Kingdom's First Report regarding detention as a last resort, the Government points out that sections 207 and 208 of the Criminal Procedure (Scotland) Act 1995 prevent detention being imposed on a person aged under 21 years unless the court is of the opinion that no other method of dealing with the defendant is appropriate.

10.48.2 Underpinning the legislation affecting children in Scotland is the principle that the state should intervene in the life of the child only where such action is in the best interests of the child. Before making a supervision requirement, a children's hearing must be satisfied that compulsory measures of supervision are necessary (section 70(1) of the 1995 Act). Section 73 stipulates that no child shall continue to be subject to a supervision requirement for any period longer than is necessary in the interests of promoting or safeguarding his welfare. Any child sent to residential or secure care from the children's hearings system is subject to a supervision requirement, which may last for a period of no more than 1 year and the child or his parents have the right to apply for a review after 3 months. In certain circumstances a review may be held earlier than 3 months.

10.48.3 Where a child is to be brought to a hearing or the hearing is unable to reach a decision, a warrant may be issued for the detention of the child in certain circumstances and for maximum periods of time, set out in sections 66 and 67 of the 1995 Act. No child may be kept in a place of safety for more than 22 days after the grant of the warrant. The warrant may be extended subject to an overall limit of 66 days.

10.49 Custody as a last resort in Northern Ireland

Article 40, 37

10.49.1 The Criminal Justice (Children) (Northern Ireland) Order 1998 introduced a number of important changes relating to the administration of juvenile justice in Northern Ireland which meet the Convention's recommendations that custody should be used only as a method of last resort and for the minimum period necessary. The Order replaced the semi-determinate 2-year training school order with a more focused, determinate disposal known as a juvenile justice centre order. Article 39 of the Order puts beyond doubt the requirement on the courts that a custodial sentence should be imposed only where the seriousness of the offence, or the failure of non-custodial sentences in cases of persistent offenders, makes a non-custodial sentence wholly inappropriate. The juvenile justice centre order lasts between 6 months and 2 years. Where a court makes a juvenile justice centre order for a period longer than 6 months it is required to state in open court its reasons for doing so. Half the sentence will be served in custody and half under supervision in the community.

10.49.2 Another important change, which should reduce the average period of detention in a juvenile justice centre, is that time spent on remand in custody will count in full to reduce the custodial element of the sentence.

10.49.3 The Order also seeks to reduce to a minimum the number of children remanded in custody. It provides for the child's release unless the offence with which the child is charged is of a violent or sexual nature, or is one which in the case of an adult is punishable with imprisonment for a term of 14 years or more, or is an arrestable offence alleged to have been while the defendant was on bail or within 2 years of having previously been convicted of an arrestable offence. This Article is subject to section 3 of the Northern Ireland (Emergency Provisions) Act 1996 which provides for a limitation of the power to grant bail in the case of offences specified in Part I or Part III of Schedule 1 to that Act.

10.50 Sexual exploitation and sexual abuse – further developments in law and practice

Article 34

10.50.1 The Government of the United Kingdom regards the protection of children as one of its highest priorities. The Government utterly condemns all forms of coercion and sexual exploitation and is committed to achieving measures to make children safe from exploitation and abuse.

10.50.2 The United Kingdom's First Report set out the wide range of measures then in force to prevent sexual exploitation and to deal with offenders. (It should be noted that Part II of the Sex Offenders Act extended the jurisdiction of UK courts to cover certain offences committed abroad). This report is confined to the additional measures which have since been taken to add to the network of measures in force.

10.50.3 Part I of the Sex Offenders Act 1997 obliges offenders who have been convicted of sex offences against children and other serious sex offences to notify the police of their name and address. Offenders have to notify the police of any changes of name, and address if they are living there for 14 days or more. Failure to notify the police is a criminal offence subject to a fine of up to £5,000, and or imprisonment of up to six months.

10.50.4 Offenders who have been sentenced to 30 months or more imprisonment for a specified offence will have to register for life – shorter periods of registration apply to those awarded shorter sentences. Using information about registered persons, the police can be made aware when a sex offender moves into their area, and can use this information to identify potential suspects in any future offence. It is hoped that the obligation to register will act as a deterrent to potential re-offenders.

10.50.5 The register established under Part 1 of the Sex Offenders Act is a valuable tool which enables the police to keep track of convicted sex offenders. The police attach a very high priority to maintaining it. Recent information suggests that almost 96% of offenders who are required to register have done so. Where an offender fails to register this is followed up by the police.

10.50.6 The UK Government understands the concern about sex offenders being able to go abroad without notifying the authorities and that British citizens who have a conviction for a sex offence abroad do not have to register. However, simply imposing a requirement to register in such circumstances would not be effective unless there were practical solutions to the problem of tracking offenders once they leave the UK.

10.50.7 The UK Government considers that significant benefits in protecting children in the UK and across the world would be achieved by the effective exchange of information between police forces on the movement of known sex offenders who pose a continuing risk. There are already systems in place via Interpol and work is being carried out to improve the exchange of information. A review of the effectiveness of the Sex Offenders Act is currently under way to assess how it is achieving its aims and whether changes are necessary. It is expected to report later in 1999.

10.50.8 In England and Wales all sex offenders sentenced to at least a year in custody, and those under 21, are subject to a period of statutory supervision by the probation service since 1992. In Scotland 1993 legislation allows courts to impose additional supervision on offenders where necessary to protect the public. In both jurisdictions, prisoners serving over 4 years in custody are automatically supervised on release. An additional period of supervision is provided in the Crime and Disorder Act which will enable courts to extend the existing period of supervision by up to 10 years when sentencing an offender.

10.50.9 Articles 26 to 28 of the Criminal Justice (NI) Order 1996, which came into operation on 1 January 1998, introduced arrangements which gave courts the option of requiring sex offenders to be supervised on licence from the date of release until expiry of their full sentence. An offender who breaches the terms of his licence or commits a further imprisonable offence while on licence could face a fine or a return to prison.

10.51 Penalties for offences against children

10.51.1 The Crime (Sentences) Act 1997 provides for a mandatory life sentence for a second serious sexual or violent offence, including offences against children. The Act also increased the maximum penalty for indecent conduct towards a child under 14 from two years to 10 years. Similar legislation in Scotland increased the maximum penalty for unlawful sexual intercourse with girls under 16 and indecent behaviour towards a girl between 12 and 16, to 10 years.

10.52 Role of the criminal law and the police service in preventing the exploitative use of children in prostitution or other unlawful sexual practices

10.52.1 Prostitution is not in itself an illegal activity in the United Kingdom but if the prostitute concerned is below the legal age of consent (16 for girls) then an adult who engages in sexual activity with her will be guilty of an offence.

10.52.2 There is a range of offences to deal with those who abuse children involved in prostitution. However, the UK Government recognises the widespread concern that children involved in prostitution have been inappropriately regarded as consenting adults by the police and others. The United Kingdom Government's aim is to prevent and deter children from entering or staying in prostitution and the Government believes that the best way forward is a multi agency approach with children's welfare as the prime concern. It is a tragedy for any child to become involved in prostitution.

10.52.3 In December 1998 the Home Office and the Department of Health issued joint draft guidance for consultation on children involved in prostitution. The consultation period closed on 29 March 1999. This guidance was prepared within the existing criminal law: it does not decriminalise soliciting, loitering and importuning by children but emphasises that children in prostitution are primarily the victims of coercion and abuse and that therefore the emphasis should be on the care and protection of young people. Those adults who exploit them, whether by pimping them or as clients, are child abusers. The draft guidance encourages the use of the full range of criminal offences against those who corrupt and abuse children.

10.52.4 The guidance should be a practical guide, the purpose of which is to enable all agencies to develop effective local arrangements to work together to

    a recognise the problem;

    b treat the child primarily as a victim of abuse;

    c safeguard children and promote their welfare; and

    d work together to provide children with strategies to exit prostitution.

10.52.5 The draft guidance was drawn up by officials and representatives from across government and the others such as the police, the Association of Directors of Social Services (ADSS) and the Local Government Association. It builds on guidelines developed by the Association of Chief Police Officers, with the help of the ADSS, the children's charities and government departments, for the police, social services and voluntary agencies to work together to treat the children as victims of abuse and the pimps and abusers as the real criminals.

10.52.6 These guidelines were piloted in Wolverhampton and Nottingham where they have worked well. Police and social services have worked closely together and with other services to help children found to be in prostitution leave that way of life. Many pimps and abusers have been charged with serious crimes in the pilot areas. ACPO have adopted the guidelines as national policy.

10.52.7 The Government's draft guidance works within the existing legal framework. The UK Government is not convinced that decriminalising prostitution for children is the best way to protect children who are at risk. The Government believes that the criminal law can play an important role in combating the commercial sexual exploitation of children. The Government is therefore opposed to decriminalisation because :

    a the existence of the criminal offence sends out a clear message –that society does not condone child prostitution;

    b decriminalisation would send all the wrong signals – it might appear that society was condoning child prostitution rather than condemning it;

    c the offence may act as a deterrent;

    d the police can use the offence as a lever to help divert girls from staying in prostitution; and

    e restricting the offence of soliciting to those of 18 or over would put those of 16 and 17, who could legally solicit, at greater risk of coercion into prostitution, so putting more, not fewer, girls at risk from pimps and exploitation.

10.52.8 The United Kingdom Government has also recognised that the criminal law on sexual offences, while comprehensive, may not offer children the best possible protection from abuse. The Government is undertaking a comprehensive review of the sexual offences and penalties in which the protection of children is a major theme. The terms of reference of this review were announced in January 1999. These include requirements to provide coherent and clear sex offences which protect individuals, particularly children and the more vulnerable, from abuse and exploitation, and enable abusers to be appropriately punished.

10.52.9 The review has published a leaflet seeking views on how the criminal law should apply in this area to protect people, especially children and the more vulnerable, from abuse and exploitation. Initial consultation will inform the work of the review which is being led by a Steering Group, advised by a separate External Reference Group of individuals and organisations with strong interests and views on issues relating to sex offences. Their conclusions are expected at the end of 1999 and will form the basis of a consultation document.

10.52.10 The principle of extra-territoriality has been incorporated in Part II of the Sex Offenders Act 1997 which makes it an offence in England, Wales and Northern Ireland to commit specified sexual offences (including rape, sexual intercourse with a girl under the age of 16, buggery and indecent assault on a child) in a country or territory outside the United Kingdom. In addition, child pornography offences will also be covered. The Act makes equivalent provision for Scotland.

10.52.11 The jurisdiction of the courts will be extended in this way only where the conduct concerned would be a criminal offence both in the United Kingdom's jurisdiction and in the territory of the state where it was committed. This is the so-called dual-criminality test. These provisions will not alter the United Kingdom's existing ability to extradite a person for trial to the country in which he is alleged to have committed an offence. In fact, extradition will always be the preferred option. However, where that is not possible for any reason, there is the alternative of prosecution here. Mounting a prosecution in this country will not be easy, but the United Kingdom will not be deterred where it is right and proper to do so.

10.52.12 Legislation has also been passed to extend the jurisdiction of our courts over conspiracies entered into in this country to commit crimes abroad. Under the Criminal Justice (Terrorism and Conspiracy) Act 1998 it is an offence for a person to conspire to commit an offence outside the United Kingdom, provided the substantive offence constitutes an offence both under the law in the United Kingdom and under the law of the country in which the act is to be committed. This enables courts in the United Kingdom to deal with conspiracies in this country to commit sexual offences against children abroad. Tour operators who knowingly organise travel abroad for paedophiles for the purpose of engaging in sexual acts against children, or groups of individuals who might organise a trip for that purpose, can therefore be prosecuted, with the consent of the Attorney General, for such activities. This replaces section 1 of the Sexual Offences (Conspiracy and Incitement) Act 1996. Under the remaining parts of the 1996 Act it is still an offence to incite people to commit certain sexual offences against children abroad.

10.53 Reducing child prostitution – views of NGOs

Article 34

10.53.1 Barnardo's drew attention, while this report was being prepared, to their particular concern for children who are abused by involvement in prostitution. Barnardo's has been working with young women so abused for some years now. On the basis of their experience they would like to see changes in the law to result in the conviction of men who abuse, and provide more appropriate support to the young people who are victims of such abuse. This point was echoed by others who contributed: they would like to see the law ensuring that it is the client of the child prostitute who is seen and treated as the offender, with the child prostitute being treated as the victim.

10.54 The exploitative use of children in pornographic performances and materials

Article 34

10.54.1 The United Kingdom has an absolute prohibition on the production, circulation, and possession of child pornography, carrying a sentence of 3 years' imprisonment. The Obscene Publications Act 1959 applies to material published via the Internet. The criminal law also applies to child pornography on the Internet: under the Protection of Children Act 1978, it is an offence to take, permit to take, distribute, show or possess with a view to distribution or showing an indecent photograph, film or video of a child under 16 – the maximum penalty is three years imprisonment and an unlimited fine. It is also an offence under Section 160 of the Criminal Justice Act 1988 for a person to have an indecent photograph or film or video of a child under 16 in their possession — this offence attracts a maximum penalty of six months imprisonment and a £5000 fine.

10.54.2 Under English law all are responsible for their own conscious acts or omissions. Thus service and access providers and telecommunications companies are responsible for material to the extent that they are aware of it. It follows that they are not responsible until they are aware of it. This situation provides a strong incentive for service providers to act to remove potentially illegal material from their servers. This element of enlightened self-interest underpins the success of the Internet Watch Foundation (see section 10.55).

10.54.3 The Criminal Justice and Public Order Act 1994 amended the definition of 'photograph' to include data stored on a computer disc or by other electronic means which is capable of conversion into a photograph. The 1994 Act amended the law to introduce the concept of 'pseudo-photograph' which means an image, whether generated by computer graphics or otherwise, which appears to be a photograph. It also increased the penalty under section 160 of the Criminal Justice Act 1988 to include a term of imprisonment.

10.55 Co-operation with NGOs to counter exploitation of children – the Internet Watch Foundation

Article 34

10.55.1 In response to concerns about the availability of child pornography and other potentially illegal material on the Internet, the Internet Watch Foundation (IWF) was established in September 1996. It is a self-regulatory organisation, financed by voluntary contributions from the United Kingdom Internet industry. It was set up by the Internet Service Providers (ISPs) following discussions between service providers, the Metropolitan Police, and officials from the Home Office and the Department of Trade and Industry. The aims of the Foundation are to determine whether particular newsgroups carry potentially illegal material, to trace the originator and to ask Internet Service Providers to remove it from their servers, and to send details of child pornography to the police, or to the enforcement agency concerned via the National Criminal Intelligence Service (NCIS) if the originator is abroad. Attention is now being given to ways of improving the operational interface between the police and ISPs across the country.

10.55.2 In December 1996, the Foundation established a 'hotline' to enable users to report the presence of potentially illegal material in a newsgroup or web-site. The Foundation determines whether the reported newsgroup or web-site carries illegal material and takes steps to have access denied to that site. Statistics for the first year of operation of the hotline show that 781 reports were received referring to over 4,300 items. Reports on which action was taken were predominantly about child pornography (85%) mostly from news groups. Only a small proportion of reported items originated from the United Kingdom (6%); the majority were from the USA (63%) and Japan (19%).

10.55.3 In March 1998, the Government announced a review of the work of the Foundation which will look at the structure of the IWF, progress on the removal of illegal material, and the possibility of extending its remit to focus on other types of illegal pornography. The intention is to report in Spring 1999.

10.55.4 Building on the work of the Recreational Software Advisory Council (RSAC), which produced a rating system for Internet sites — self-rated by the content provider — which covers nudity, violence, sex and language, the IWF has been looking to devise a rating system for legal material and also to apply the ratings to news groups. This will be compatible with filtering software packages which have been developed to enable schools and parents to restrict the types of websites to which children have access. A Working Group of representatives of ISPs and the Foundation has been devising a common ratings system suitable for United Kingdom Internet users.

10.55.5 In Scotland, the Scottish Office has set up a working group including representatives from local authorities, police and NGOs to prepare advice for parents and agencies on child safety and use of the Internet.

10.56 United Kingdom participation in international agreements

Article 34, 35

10.56.1 The United Kingdom has played a crucial role in relevant international agreements to prevent all forms of sexual abuse and exploitation of children. It took a leading role in the *Stockholm World Congress Against the Commercial Sexual Exploitation of Children* and has reported on progress under the agreed agenda for action. The United Kingdom is also active in taking forward measures referred to in international instruments such as the Joint Action on Combating Child Sex Exploitation and the Sexual Trafficking of Persons (the STOP programme).

10.56.2 In August 1997 the Government of the United Kingdom and the Philippines Government signed a memorandum of understanding to co-operate to combat the sexual exploitation of children. This was followed by a major new ASEM child welfare initiative to share good practice and develop dialogue between Europe and Asia in combating the commercial sexual exploitation of children. This initiative is co-sponsored by the United Kingdom Government and the Government of the Philippines and was announced at the Asia - Europe Summit (ASEM 2) in April 1998. A preliminary meeting was held in Manila in June 1998 to prepare for a meeting of experts from Governments and NGOs from ASEM countries in London in October 1998.

10.56.3 The National Criminal Intelligence Service (NCIS) has developed a database of people involved in or connected with paedophilia and child pornography. They provide assistance to a variety of national and international agencies, and have contributed to the work of the Interpol Standing Working Party on Offences Against Minors, which co-ordinates action to combat sex tourism.

10.56.4 The police have had a number of successful operations against child pornography including those using the Internet. *Operation Starburst* involved co-operation with police in six countries and 40 individuals were arrested.

10.56.5 Several United Kingdom police forces have run training courses in the Philippines, Thailand and Sri Lanka to develop expertise and share good practice.

10.57 Statistics on sexual abuse of children

Article 34

10.57.1 Statistics relating to sexual offences in England and Wales against children of 16 years and under are at Annex B.

10.58 Sale, trafficking and abduction of children

Article 34, 35

10.58.1 The United Kingdom is fully committed to opposing the sale, trafficking and abduction of children and associated activities.

10.58.2 The United Kingdom has comprehensive laws to deal with those who engage in activities associated with trafficking. It is also possible for the courts to confiscate the assets of those found guilty of trafficking. The most serious of offences attract severe penalties of up to life imprisonment (see section 10.52). In particular under section 22 of the Sexual Offences Act 1956 it is an offence in England and Wales to procure a woman to become a prostitute in any part of the world, and the courts have held that the English courts have jurisdiction to try if any part of the offence occurs in England and Wales[135]. Under section 23 of the same Act, it is an offence for a person to procure a girl under the age of 21 to have unlawful sexual intercourse in any part of the world with a third person. It is also an offence to detain a woman in a brothel under section 24. The maximum penalty for these offences is 2 years' imprisonment. Living on immoral earnings is an offence that carries a maximum penalty of 7 years. Anyone who takes a child from those who have lawful control of that child commits an offence under the Child Abduction Act 1984. Those who traffic women may also be liable to other charges relating to illegal immigration as well as procuration and prostitution offences.

10.58.3 Kidnapping is a common law offence defined as "the taking away of one person by another by force or fraud without the consent of the person

---

135 In Scotland, similar offences are to be found in the Criminal Law (Consolidation) (Scotland) Act 1995.

so taken or carried away and without lawful excuse". There is no limit to the penalty which can be imposed by the higher courts on conviction for this offence.

10.58.4 Under United Kingdom immigration legislation a child or adult who wishes to enter the United Kingdom needs to qualify for entry in the same way as an adult. Particular care is taken with applications from unaccompanied minors. Where it is considered that a person's purpose for entry does not qualify for leave to enter under the Immigration Rules, such as prostitution, the application would be refused. The rules requires that consideration be given to the removal of those found to be in the United Kingdom illegally but the United Kingdom will not seek to remove a child under the age of 18 unless it is possible to put in place acceptable reception and welfare arrangements in the country of origin.

10.58.5 The measures described under Article 34 on the sexual exploitation of children and sexual abuse of children also apply to the sale, trafficking and abduction of children, as the sexual exploitation of children is one of the main reasons why children are sold or trafficked.

10.58.6 Social services provide facilities for the protection and assistance of the victims of trafficking.

10.59 Individuals unsuitable to work with children

Article 36

10.59.1 The Protection of Children Act – July 1999 – requires regulated organisations to refer for inclusion on a new Department of Health list of names of individuals considered unsuitable to work with children, and not to offer work for any posts involving regular contact with children in a childcare capacity - to anyone so listed. It also introduces rights of appeal to an independent tribunal against inclusion on both this list and a similar Department of Education and Employment list. Finally, it paves the way for the introduction of a Criminal Records Bureau to act as a single point of access for information from criminal records and both the Departmental lists on those wanting to work with children.

10.60 Passport policy and child abduction

Article 11

10.60.1 The Government changed its passport policy in October 1998 so that all children not already on the passport of one of their parents must have a separate passport for travel abroad. Children already on a parent's passport will remain on it only until the passport expires, or the validity of the entry relating to the child require amendment, or the child becomes 16. Thereafter the child will need a separate passport. This change should reduce the risk of international parental child abduction, forgery and impersonation, thus providing additional safeguards for vulnerable children.

10.61 Current action to prevent sexual exploitation and sexual abuse of children in England and Wales

Article 34

10.61.1 In addition to the extensive changes which are already in force, further new measures are being introduced. Sex Offender orders, introduced in the Crime and Disorder Act, enable the civil courts to make an order against someone previously convicted of a sex offence against a child and whose subsequent behaviour causes concern such that an order is necessary to protect the public from serious harm from him. The orders will ban specific acts, such as loitering near school playgrounds. Breach of an order is a criminal offence carrying a serious penalty.

10.61.2 The Police Act 1997 will enable the creation of a new system of access to criminal records. When the new arrangements are introduced all organisations working with children will be able to obtain information on criminal records of employees and volunteers if they will regularly care for, train, supervise or be in sole charge of children.

10.61.3 The Government has also set up an interdepartmental working group on preventing sex offenders from working with children. Its main report was made public on 25 January 1999 and copies were placed in the libraries of both Houses of Parliament and are on the Internet[136]. It examined a range of issues and made recommendations on:

    a the establishment of a new integrated system for identifying those unsuitable to work with children, building on and drawing together existing safeguards;

    b a possible new criminal offence for a person identified under the new system as unsuitable, to apply for work, accept work or continue work with children;

    c the establishment of a central access point to the integrated system, or "one stop shop", to check who might be unsuitable to work with children.

10.61.4 The Group also made recommendations in its interim report in November 1998 that a new criminal offence should be created where a person aged 18 or over has sexual intercourse or engages in any other sexual activity with or directed towards a person under that age, if the person aged 18 or over is in a position of trust in relation to the younger person in specified circumstances.

10.61.5 New initiatives are being taken to ensure that cases of child abuse come to court quickly, including fast-tracking schemes for such cases. A national monitoring scheme of child witness cases is currently underway.

10.62 Research into the abuse of children

Article 34

10.62.1 An extensive programme of research into a wide range of issues involving children who are physically and sexually abused is under way. Issues

---

136 Placed in the libraries of both Houses of Parliament January 1999. Internet reference
    www.homeoffice.gov.uk\cpd\sou\sou.htm

include evidential matters; police training and procedures; repeat victimisation of children; the links between domestic violence and sex abuse; and assessing the risks posed by sex offenders.

10.62.2 Research projects on the way in which boys who have been abused may go on to be abusers, on therapeutic treatment for children who have been sexually abused, and on "What works in child sexual abuse" are also under way.

10.62.3 Her Majesty's Inspectorate of Constabulary has completed a thematic inspection of child protection issues. It is an examination of the wide range of responsibilities which the police service has in safeguarding the welfare and rights of children. The report was published in January 1999.[137]

10.63 Social care initiatives relevant to sexual abuse of children

Article 34

10.63.1 In addition to the Utting report (see section 7.8 above) the Government is building on experience gained in inter-agency working since the Children Act 1989 and is consulting on a revision of the key guidance on inter-agency co-operation in child protection work. The joint Department of Health and Welsh Office consultation paper *Working Together to Safeguard Children: new proposals for inter-agency co-operation* includes a section on the commercial sexual exploitation of children, inviting views on how best to address the problem. Corresponding guidance is being issued in Scotland.

10.63.2 In Scotland the Chief Inspector of Social Work has completed the first part of a major review of the supervision of sex offenders in the community. The recommendations of his report *A Commitment to Protect*[138] which was published in December 1997 have been accepted by Scottish Office Ministers and are being taken forward by a high level multi-agency group chaired by a High Court judge. The second phase of the review deals with empowering and involving communities in reducing risk from sex offenders, and accommodation of sex offenders, to improve community safety. The review is due to be completed *later this year.*

10.63.3 The ASEM2 child welfare initiative (described in section 10.56) will promote good practice examples from European and Asian countries in all the 4 areas of action identified in the Stockholm World Congress: prevention, protection, recovery and rehabilitation and co-operation, as well as encouraging dialogue and information sharing on all aspects of combating the commercial sexual exploitation of children.

10.64 Protection against sexual exploitation and abuse in Scotland

Article 34

10.64.1 The Sex Offenders Act 1997, discussed at section 10.50, applies in Scotland. Higher penalties for various sexual offences against children were included in the Crime and Punishment (Scotland) Act 1997. Under the Sexual Offences (Conspiracy and Incitement) Act 1996, it is now an offence in Scotland to conspire in or incite the commission of a sexual offence abroad. The Crime and Disorder Act 1998 also contains provision for Sex

137 ISBN 1-84082-217-1.

138 Published by The Stationery Office, December 1997: ISBN 0 11 495869 6.

Offender Orders to control the behaviour of sex offenders on release and for extended post-release supervision of sex and violent offenders.

10.64.2 As a means of further improving safeguards for children in Scotland, the Government is developing a fully comprehensive approach to information held about those unsuitable to work with children and young people. As part of that strategy it is intended that a statutory Consultancy Services Index will be introduced for Scotland. The Consultancy Services Index will hold, within carefully prescribed parameters, information provided by employers about staff (including volunteers) whom they consider unsuitable to work with children and young people."

10.65 Young people in the armed services

Article 38

10.65.1 The United Kingdom's policies on the recruitment and deployment of those under the age of 18 remain substantially unchanged from those set out in the First Report. However, personnel aged under 17 are no longer deployed by the Naval Service. Those policies are in accordance with the provisions of international humanitarian law, namely Article 77 of the First Additional Protocol to the Geneva Conventions 1949.

10.65.2 The Armed Forces policies on recruitment, deployment and terms of service for those under the age of 18 were addressed by the Armed Forces Bill Select Committee in 1991. It recommended, among other things, that the Ministry of Defence should examine the terms of enlistment of those under 18. The Ministry considered those findings, and decided not to make any changes. In 1996 the Armed Forces Bill Select Committee concluded that, on balance, it believed that it would be impractical, and unpopular with all concerned to place further restrictions on the ability of those under 18 to serve on active duty. It again recommended that careful consideration be given to requiring minors to commit themselves to a period of service no longer than that of adults.

10.65.3 As a result, a Working Group was set up to examine how this anomaly might be removed, and to see whether common terms of service might be introduced across the three services – the Royal Navy, the Army and the Royal Air Force. Work is now under way to draft revised terms of service for personnel under 18.

10.66 Health and safety of children at work

Article 32, 36

10.66.1 The United Kingdom has comprehensive health and safety legislation which generally is not age specific and is enforced irrespective of the age of the employee. However, in implementing the EC Directive on the protection of young people at work, regulations were introduced requiring employers when conducting any assessment of health and safety risks to young people (under 18 years) to have particular regard to possible inexperience, immaturity, and lack of awareness of risks. There are some specific health risks, for instance from toxic substances such as lead, where young people under the age of 18 are prohibited from doing the activity. In addition, regulations implementing the EU Directive on the organisation of working time contain requirements relating to working hours of young workers, entitlements to periods of rest and annual leave, and health and capacities assessments for work at night.

10.67 Prevention of the economic exploitation of children, and control of child labour

Article 32, 36

10.67.1 The Convention defines a child as a person below 18 years of age (except where relevant legislation provides for an earlier age of majority). In the United Kingdom, in common with adult workers, those aged above the minimum school leaving age (around the child's 16th birthday) were generally free to negotiate their hours and other conditions of employment with the employer. This aspect of our legal provision for young people between the ages of 16 to 18 made it necessary for the United Kingdom, when acceding to the Convention, to enter a reservation on this point.

10.67.2 However, since the first report, the United Kingdom has implemented the EC Directives on the protection of young people at work and on the Organisation of Working Time. These Directives required EC Member States to bring their domestic law into compliance with certain standards in relation to the employment of young people. These standards include restrictions on the working conditions and hours of work of all young people under age 18. Those changes to our law have now been made.

10.68 Withdrawal of the United Kingdom reservation relating to Article 32

Article 32, 36

10.68.1 As a consequence of the developments reported above, the United Kingdom is now able to lift the reservation previously entered on this Article.

10.68.2 The law on children's employment, that is those under the minimum school leaving age, can now be outlined as follows.

10.68.3 Children between age 13 and the minimum school leaving age may work

- a for a maximum of 2 hours on schooldays
- b for a maximum of 2 hours on Sundays
- c for a maximum of 5 hours (if aged under 15) or 8 hours (if 15 or over) on Saturdays and weekdays during the school holidays, subject to an overall limit of 25 hours (under 15) or 35 hours (15 and over) a week in the school holidays.

10.68.4 Children may not:

- a do anything other than light work
- b work before they are 13 years of age
- c work for more than one hour before the start of school
- d work during school hours
- e work before 7.00 am or after 7.00 pm
- f work for more than four hours without a break of at least one hour
- g work throughout the Summer holidays; they must have a break of at least two weeks
- h work without an employment card issued by the local authority
- i work in any industrial undertaking, e.g. factory, building site etc.
- j work in many occupations prohibited by local bylaws or in other legislation, e.g. in pubs or betting shops, or in any work which is likely to be harmful to their health, well being or education

k take part in certain theatrical or other performances or in professional sport or modelling without a licence issued by the local authority.

10.68.5 These restrictions are enforced by local authorities, in general through the education welfare service.

10.68.6 In the case of adolescents (ie those over the minimum school leaving age but under 18) there is a limit of 48 hours on the average number of weekly working hours that they can work and an average limit of 8 hours per 24 hour period when working at night. These limits are enforced through the health and safety enforcing authorities.

10.68.7 Adolescents are also entitled to two days off per week, 12 hours rest between each working day and a minimum of 30 minutes rest if they work for longer than 4 hours per day. They are also entitled to minimum periods of paid annual leave. These entitlements are enforced through the Employment Tribunals.

ANNEX A: Text of the UN Committee's Observations on the first UK Report

UNITED NATIONS CRC

Convention on the
Rights of the Child

GENERAL
CRC/C/15/Add.34
15 February 1995
Original: ENGLISH

COMMITTEE ON THE RIGHTS OF THE CHILD
Eighth session
CONSIDERATION OF REPORTS SUBMITTED BY STATES PARTIES
UNDER ARTICLE 44 OF THE CONVENTION
Concluding observations of the Committee on the Rights of the Child:
United Kingdom of Great Britain and Northern Ireland

1.   The Committee considered the initial report of the United Kingdom of Great Britain and Northern Ireland (CRC/C/11/Add.1) at its 204th, 205th and 206th meetings (CRC/C/SR.204—206), held on 24 and 25 January 1995, and adopted* the following concluding observations.

A.   Introduction
2.   The Committee appreciates the opportunity to engage in a constructive dialogue with the State party and welcomes the timely submission by the Government of the written responses to the Committee's list of issues (see CRC/C.7/WP.1). The Committee welcomes the additional oral information provided by the delegation of the State party which greatly assisted in clarifying many of the issues raised by the Committee. The additional oral information was particularly useful, in view of the Committee's observation that the initial report of the State party lacked sufficient information on the factors and difficulties impeding the implementation of various rights provided for in the Convention.

B   Positive aspects
3.   The Committee takes note of the adoption by the State party of a Children's Act applicable to England and Wales. The Committee also

* At the 208th meeting, held on 26 January 1995.

---

observes that the State party has extended the application of the Convention to many of its dependent territories. The Committee welcomes the intention of the State party to consider withdrawing the reservation it made to article 37 of the Convention as it relates to the procedures governing Children's hearings in Scotland.

4.   Moreover, the Committee welcomes the initiatives being taken by the State party to reduce the incidence of Sudden Infant Death Syndrome and to combat the problem of bullying in school. In addition, the Committee is encouraged by the steps taken to address the issue of the sexual abuse of children, including through the development of the "Working Together" initiative which advocates and promotes an interdisciplinary approach to addressing this serious problem.

5.   The Committee welcomes the information it received concerning the commitment of the Government to review its legislation in the area of the employment of children and to present new legislation in matters relating to the family, domestic violence and disability. Likewise, the Committee welcomes the measures being taken to pass further legislation in the area of adoption, including the intention of the Government to ratify the 1993 Hague Convention on Protection of Children and Co-operation in Respect of Intercountry Adoption. The Committee takes note of the Code of Practice for Children with Special Educational Needs which has statutory force and has been developed within the framework of the 1993 Education Act.

6.   The Committee takes note of the Government's commitment to extend the provision of pre-school education. The Committee is equally appreciative of the recent initiative taken by the State party to require local authorities, in conjunction with health authorities and non-governmental organisations, to draw up Children's Service Plans.

C.   Principal subjects of concern

7.   The Committee is concerned about the broad nature of the reservations made to the Convention by the State party which raise concern as to their compatibility with the object and purpose of the Convention. In particular, the reservation relating to the application of the Nationality and Immigration Act does not appear to be compatible with the principles and provisions of the Convention, including those of its articles 2, 3, 9 and 10.

8.   The Committee remains unclear about the extent to which an effective co-ordinating mechanism exists for the implementation of the Convention on the Rights of the Child. It is concerned whether sufficient consideration has been given to the establishment of mechanisms, including of an independent nature, to co-ordinate and monitor the implementation of the rights of the child.

9.   With respect to article 4 of the Convention, the Committee is concerned about the adequacy of measures taken to ensure the implementation of economic, social and cultural rights to the maximum

extent of available resources. It appears to the Committee that insufficient expenditure is allocated to the social sector both within the State party and within the context of international development aid; the Committee wonders whether sufficient consideration has been given to the enjoyment of fundamental rights by children belonging to the most vulnerable groups in society.

10. The Committee notes that the initial report of the State party contains little information on the difficulties experienced by children living in Northern Ireland and the effect on children of the operation of emergency legislation there. The Committee is concerned about the absence of effective safeguards to prevent the ill-treatment of children under the emergency legislation. In this connection, the Committee observes that under the same legislation it is possible to hold children as young as 10 for 7 days without charge. It is also noted that the emergency legislation which gives the police and the army the power to stop, question and search people on the street has led to complaints of children being badly treated. The Committee is concerned about this situation which may lead to a lack of confidence in the system of investigation and action on such complaints.

11. The Committee is concerned about the apparent insufficiency of measures taken to ensure the implementation of the general principles of the Convention, namely the provisions of its articles 2, 3, 6 and 12. In this connection, the Committee observes in particular that the principle of the best interests of the child appears not to be reflected in legislation in such areas as health, education and social security which have a bearing on the respect for the rights of the child.

12. With regard to article 2 of the Convention relating to non-discrimination, the Committee expresses its concern at the insufficient measures undertaken to ensure its implementation. In particular, it is concerned about the possible adverse effects on children of the restrictions applied to unmarried fathers in transmitting citizenship to their children, in contradiction of the provisions of articles 7 and 8 of the Convention. In addition, the Committee is concerned that children of certain ethnic minorities appear to be more likely to be placed in care.

13. Furthermore, in the light of article 6 of the Convention, the Committee expresses its concern at the health status of children of different socio-economic groups and those belonging to ethnic minorities.

14. In relation to the implementation of article 12, the Committee is concerned that insufficient attention has been given to the right of the child to express his/her opinion, including in cases where parents in England and Wales have the possibility of withdrawing their children from parts of the sex education programmes in schools. In this as in other decisions, including exclusion from school, the child is not systematically invited to express his/her opinion and those opinions may not be given due weight, as required under article 12 of the Convention.

15. The Committee notes with concern the increasing number of children living in poverty. The Committee is aware that the phenomenon of children begging and sleeping on the streets has become more visible. The Committee is concerned that the changed regulations regarding benefit entitlements to young people may have contributed to the increase in the number of young homeless people. The rate of divorce and the number of single-parent families and teenage pregnancies in the State party are noted with concern. These phenomena raise a number of issues, including as regards the adequacy of benefit allowances and the availability and effectiveness of family education.

16. The Committee is disturbed about the reports it has received on the physical and sexual abuse of children. In this connection, the Committee is worried about the national legal provisions dealing with reasonable chastisement within the family. The imprecise nature of the expression of reasonable chastisement as contained in these legal provisions may pave the way for it to be interpreted in a subjective and arbitrary manner. Thus, the Committee is concerned that legislative and other measures relating to the physical integrity of children do not appear to be compatible with the provisions and principles of the Convention, including those of its articles 3, 19 and 37. The Committee is equally concerned that privately funded and managed schools are still permitted to administer corporal punishment to children in attendance there which does not appear to be compatible with the provisions of the Convention, including those of its article 28, paragraph 2.

17. The administration of the juvenile justice system in the State party is a matter of general concern to the Committee. The low age of criminal responsibility and the national legislation relating to the administration of juvenile justice seem not to be compatible with the provisions of the Convention, namely articles 37 and 40.

18. The Committee remains concerned about certain of the provisions of the Criminal Justice and Public Order Act 1994. The Committee notes that its provisions provide, *inter alia,* for the possibility of applying "secure training orders" on children aged 12 to 14 in England and Wales. The Committee is concerned about the compatibility of the application of such secure training orders on young children with the principles and provisions of the Convention in relation to the administration of juvenile justice, particularly its articles 3, 37, 39 and 40. In particular, the Committee is concerned that the ethos of the guidelines for the administration and establishment of Secure Training Centres in England and Wales and the Training Schools in Northern Ireland appears to lay emphasis on imprisonment and punishment.

19. The Committee is equally concerned that children placed in care under the social welfare system may be held in Training Schools in Northern Ireland and may be placed in the future in Secure Training Centres in England and Wales.

20.   The Committee is also concerned that the Criminal Evidence (N.I.) Order 1988 appears to be incompatible with article 40 of the Convention, in particular with the right to presumption of innocence and the right not to be compelled to give testimony or confess guilt. It is noted that silence in response to police questioning can be used to support a finding of guilt against a child over 10 years of age in Northern Ireland. Silence at trial can be similarly used against children over 14 years of age.

21.   The situation of Gypsy and Traveller children is a matter of concern to the Committee, especially with regard to their access to basic services and the provision of caravan sites.

D.   Suggestions and recommendations

22.   The Committee wishes to encourage the State party to consider reviewing its reservations to the Convention with a view to withdrawing them, particularly in light of the agreements made in this regard at the World Conference on Human Rights and incorporated in the Vienna Declaration and Programme of Action.

23.   The Committee would like to suggest that the State party consider establishing a national mechanism for the purpose of co-ordinating the implementation of the Convention, including between governmental departments and between central and local governmental authorities. Furthermore, the Committee suggests that the State party establish a permanent mechanism for the monitoring of the Children's Act and the Convention on the Rights of the Child throughout the United Kingdom. It is further suggested that ways and means be established to facilitate regular and closer co-operation between the Government and the non-governmental community, particularly with those non-governmental organizations closely involved in monitoring the respect for the rights of the child in the State party.

24.   With regard to the implementation of article 4 of the Convention, the Committee would like to suggest that the general principles of the Convention, particularly the provisions of its article 3, relating to the best interests of the child, should guide the determination of policy-making at both the central and local levels of government. This approach is of relevance to decisions taken about the allocation of resources to the social sector at the central and local governmental levels, including with regard to the allocation of benefits to children who have completed compulsory schooling and have no full-time employment. The Committee notes the importance of additional efforts to overcome the problems of growing social and economic inequality and increased poverty.

25.   With regard to matters relating to the health, welfare and standard of living of children in the United Kingdom, the Committee recommends additional measures to address, as a matter of priority, problems affecting the health status of children of different socio-economic groups and of children belonging to ethnic minorities and to the problems of homelessness affecting children and their families.

26. The Committee recommends that in line with the provisions of article 42 of the Convention, the State party should undertake measures to make the provisions and principles of the Convention widely known to adults and children alike. It is also suggested that teaching about children's rights should be incorporated into the training curricula of professionals working with or for children, such as teachers, the police, judges, social workers, health workers and personnel in care and detention institutions.

27. The Committee would like to suggest that greater priority be given to incorporating the general principles of the Convention, especially the provisions of its article 3, relating to the best interests of the child, and article 12, concerning the child's right to make their views known and to have these views given due weight, in the legislative and administrative measures and in policies undertaken to implement the rights of the child. It is suggested that the State party consider the possibility of establishing further mechanisms to facilitate the participation of children in decisions affecting them, including within the family and the community.

28. The Committee recommends that race relations legislation be introduced in Northern Ireland as a matter of urgency and is encouraged by the information presented by the delegation of the State party regarding the Government's intention to follow up on this matter.

29. The Committee would also like to suggest that a review be undertaken of the nationality and immigration laws and procedures to ensure their conformity with the principles and provisions of the Convention.

30. The Committee recommends that further measures be undertaken to educate parents about their responsibilities towards their children, including through the provision of family education which should emphasize the equal responsibilities of both parents. While recognising that the Government views the problem of teenage pregnancies as a serious one, the Committee suggests that additional efforts, in the form of prevention-oriented programmes which could be part of an educational campaign, are required to reduce the number of teenage pregnancies.

31. The Committee is also of the opinion that additional efforts are required to overcome the problem of violence in society. The Committee recommends that physical punishment of children in families be prohibited in the light of the provisions set out in articles 3 and 19 of the Convention. In connection with the child's right to physical integrity, as recognised by the Convention, namely in its articles 19, 28, 29 and 37, and in the light of the best interests of the child, the Committee suggests that the State party consider the possibility of undertaking additional education campaigns. Such measures would help to change societal attitudes towards the use of physical punishment in the family and foster the acceptance of the legal prohibition of the physical punishment of children.

32. With regard to matters relating to education, the Committee suggests

that children's right to appeal against expulsion from school be effectively ensured. It is also suggested that procedures be introduced to ensure that children are provided with the opportunity to express their views on the running of the schools in matters of concern to them. Further, the Committee recommends that the training curricula of teachers should incorporate education about the Convention on the Rights of the Child. It is recommended that teaching methods should be inspired by and reflect the spirit and philosophy of the Convention, in the light of the general principles of the Convention and the provisions of its article 29. The Committee would also like to suggest that the State party consider the possibility of introducing education about the Convention on the Rights of the Child into school curricula. Legislative measures are recommended to prohibit the use of corporal punishment in privately funded and managed schools.

33.   The Committee also suggests that the State party provide further support to the teaching of the Irish language in schools in Northern Ireland and to integrated education schooling.

34.   The Committee recommends that the emergency and other legislation, including in relation to the system of administration of juvenile justice, at present in operation in Northern Ireland should be reviewed to ensure its consistency with the principles and provisions of the Convention.

35.   The Committee recommends that law reform be pursued in order to ensure that the system of the administration of juvenile justice is child-oriented. The Committee also wishes to recommend that the State party take the necessary measures to prevent juvenile delinquency as set down in the Convention and complemented by the Riyadh Guidelines.

36.   More specifically, the Committee recommends that serious consideration be given to raising the age of criminal responsibility throughout the areas of the United Kingdom. The Committee also recommends the introduction of careful monitoring of the new Criminal Justice and Public Order Act 1994 with a view to ensuring full respect for the Convention on the Rights of the Child. In particular, the provisions of the Act which allow for, <u>inter alia</u>, placement of secure training orders on children aged between 12 and 14, indeterminate detention, and the doubling of sentences which may be imposed on 15- to 17-year-old children should be reviewed with respect to their compatibility with the principles and provisions of the Convention.

37.   Within the context of the law reform being considered with regard to matters relating to the employment of children, the Committee expresses the hope that the State party will consider reviewing its reservation with a view to its withdrawal. Similarly, the Committee expresses the hope that the Government may consider the possibility of becoming a party to ILO Convention No. 138.

38.   The issues of sexual exploitation and drug abuse as they affect children

ANNEX B

Offences against children of 16 years and under 1994 – 1996

Offenders cautioned and defendants prosecuted at magistrates' courts and convicted[1] at all courts for sexual offences against children aged 16 years and under, 1994 – 1996

England and Wales

Offences	Cautions			Prosecutions			Convictions[1]		
	1994	1995	1996	1994	1995	1996	1994	1995	1996
Buggery with a boy under the age of 16 or with a woman or an animal	41	8	5	345	125	16	135	86	5
Attempt to commit buggery with a boy under the age of 16[2] or with a woman or an animal	6	1	1	21	6	3	16	14	2
Buggery by a male of a male under 16[2]	-	2	5	-	48	66	-	29	66
Buggery by a male aged 21 or over with a male aged 16 or 17[2]	-	1	-	-	1	2	-	2	3
Buggery by a male aged 18-20 with a male aged 16 or 17[2]	-		-	-	-	-	-	-	-
Buggery by a male with a female under 16[2]	-	1	1	-	25	26	-	7	17
Buggery by a male aged over 21 or over with a female aged 16 or 17[2]	-	-	-	-	2	-	-	2	2
Buggery by a male aged 18-20 with a female aged 16 or 17[2]	-	-	-	-	-	-	-	1	-
Indecent assault on male person under 16 years	176	137	120	449	400	325	324	339	355
Gross indecency by a male aged 21 or over with male aged under 18[3]	-	-	-	-	-	1	-	-	-
Rape of a female aged under 16[4]	-	5	11	-	336	477	-	113	210
Rape of a male aged under 16[4]	-	-	-	-	18	20	-	2	13

FIGURE 9: OFFENCES AGAINST CHILDREN IN ENGLAND AND WALES (PART 1)

Offences	Cautions(number of persons)								
	1994	1995	1996	1994	1995	1996	1994	1995	1996
Attempted rape of a female aged under 16[4]	-	2	4	-	32	44	-	21	35
Attempted rape of a male aged under 16[4]	-	-	-	-	-	4	-	2	2
Indecent assault on a female under 16	849	670	664	2,036	1,797	1,604	1,355	1,446	1,597
Unlawful sexual intercourse with girl under 13	45	41	40	88	77	40	64	81	54
Unlawful sexual intercourse with girl under 16	500	400	369	202	165	164	205	203	207
Incest with a girl under 13	11	8	4	41	22	26	35	21	19
Inciting girl under 16 to have incestuous sexual intercourse	-	-	1	5	3	2	4	5	-
Housholder permitting unlawful sexual intercourse with girl under 16	2	-	-	-	4	4	2	3	-
Person responsible for girl under 16 causing or encouraging her prostitution etc.	-	1	-	1	-	2	-	3	1
Male aged 21 or over procuring or attempting to procure a male under 18 of gross indecency with another male[3]	-	-	3	-	1	-	-	2	3
Abduction of unmarried girl under 16	5	2	2	27	11	9	9	6	3
Gross indecency with boys aged 14 and under	49	28	21	87	62	61	77	56	53
Gross indecency with girls aged 14 and under	36	30	33	129	109	97	112	99	109

1 Includes persons proceeded against in earlier years or for other offences.
2 Buggery and attempted buggery offences under the Sexual Offences Act 1956, Section 12 as amended by the Criminal Justice and public order Act 1994, Section 143.
3 Indecency between males offences under the Sexual Offences Act 1956, Section 12 as amended by the Criminal Justice and public order Act 1994, Section 144.
4 Rape and attempted rape offences under the Sexual Offences Act 1956, Section 12 as amended by the Criminal Justice and public order Act 1994, Section 142.

Source: Criminal statistics England and Wales

FIGURE 10: OFFENCES AGAINST CHILDREN IN ENGLAND AND WALES (PART 2)

C | ANNEX C: Consultation with children in Scotland

'Our Lives – Chidren's Rights in Scotland'

In recognition of the importance of taking the views of children, The Children's Issues Unit of The Scottish Office commissioned the *Our Lives* Project. This was a Scotland wide consultation exercise which gathered the views of young people in relation to children's rights. The project was carried out by Save the Children Scotland and was jointly funded by both parties. The *Our Lives* consultation process reflected the principle of Article 12 - the right of young people to be listened to in matters which affect them.

Over a three month period Save the Children consulted 43 groups of children and young people (326 in total), between the ages of 12 and 18, from 20 local authorities, representing schools and youth groups from urban and rural Scotland and a wide spectrum of interest groups. The groups of young people were invited to discuss one of five themes: education, family life, health, protection from harm and participation; and their views were sought on how successful the implementation of the UN Convention on the Rights of the Child has been so far in Scotland. Findings were gathered from audio recordings of structured and facilitated discussions and group exercises.

The consultation process was taken forward with the *Our Lives* young people's conference on 29 January 1999. Representatives of each group consulted were invited to discuss the main issues which emerged from the consultation process and to explore further how their views can be listened to and acted on when addressing the issues which are of greatest concern to young people in Scotland. The Minister for children's issues addressed the conference and took the opportunity, through a question and answer session, to hear at first hand the views of young people in Scotland.

Save the Children Scotland produced a summary report of the "Our Lives" consultation in November 1998. They aim to publish an extended report in June 1999 which will present an in depth and comprehensive analysis of the views of young people as well as an evaluation of the whole process of consulting young people.

Of the 326 young people consulted, 271 completed questionnaires on the UN Convention on the Rights of the Child. Of those who completed the exercise 66% said that they had never heard of the UNCRC before the *Our Lives* Consultation'. In his address to the *Our Lives* conference, the Minister for Children's issues highlighted the lack of awareness of the UN Convention among young people as a gap in the Government's implementation of the Convention and announced that a leaflet for young people would be produced to tackle this deficiency.

The leaflet for young people on the UN Convention was produced by the Scottish Child Law Centre and funded by the Children's Issues Unit. It describes in easily understandable terms what the Convention is, what it says, and what that means for young people in Scotland. The text and design of the leaflet were prepared, with the target audience having a reading age of about 11-13 years. The leaflet has been positively received by young people involved in the production process and has been designed so that it can also be used as a poster on a young person's or classroom wall. To ensure that the leaflet reached its target audience, sufficient copies of the leaflet have been made available to schools throughout Scotland.

D | ANNEX D: Inequalities in conception rates below age 16

by Health Authority 1994-96

20 Highest and 20 Lowest
rated HA's

Conception rate per 1,000 females aged 13-15 years	20 Highest
17.6	Lambeth, Southwark & Lewisham
15.9	Sunderland
15.9	Sandwell
15.4	Wolverhampton
14.5	Manchester
14.3	Barnsley
14.3	South Humber
13.9	Tees
13.6	Doncaster
13.3	Walsall
12.5	County Durham
12.2	Dudley
12.1	North Staffordshire
11.9	Nottingham
11.7	Newcastle & North Tyneside
11.7	Wakefield
11.7	Rotherham
11.4	West Pennine
11.2	East London & the City
11.0	Bury & Rochdale

>
>
>
>
> 8.8 **ENGLAND**
>
>
> **20 Lowest**
>

6.5	North & East Devon
6.5	North Yorkshire
6.4	Sefton
6.3	Cornwall & Isles of Scilly
6.2	Suffolk
6.1	Buckinghamshire
6.0	Kensington, Chelsea & Westminster
5.9	Dorset
5.9	North Essex
5.7	Oxfordshire
5.5	West Sussex
5.5	West Hertfordshire
5.2	Kingston & Richmond
5.2	Bromley
5.1	East & North Hertfordshire
4.7	North & Mid Hampshire
4.7	Cambridge & Huntingdon
4.4	Barnet
4.1	West Surrey
3.5	East Surrey

Source: ONS

E | ANNEX E: Glossary of abbreviations

Abbreviation	Explanation
ABCD	Access for Black Children with Disabilities
ACE	Advisory Centre for Education
ACPC	Area Child Protection Committee
ACPO	Association of Chief Police Officers
ACTIONAID	A British based overseas development charity
ADSS	Association of Directors of Social Services
AHC	After housing costs - a statistical measure of poverty
AIDS	Acquired Immuno Deficiency Syndrome
ASEM	Asia Europe Summit Meeting
BAAF	British Association for Adoption and Fostering
BBC	British Broadcasting Corporation
BFI	UNICEF's Baby Friendly Initiative
BHC	Before housing costs - see AHC
BT	British Telecom
CAMHS	Child and Adolescent Mental Health Services
CCS	Regional Commissions for Care Standards
CCWS	Crown Court Witness Service
CD	Compact Disc
CESDI	Confidential Enquiry into Stillbirths and Deaths in Infancy
CMU	Casework Management Unit

COMA	Committee on Medical Aspects of Food and Nutrition Policy
COSLA	Convention of Scottish Local Authorities
CTC	Childcare Tax Credit
DCMS	Department for Culture, Media and Sport
DETR	Department of the Environment, transport and the Regions
DfEE	Department for Education and Employment
DFID	Department for International Development
DH	Department of Health
DHSS	Department of Health and Social Services (in Northern Ireland)
DPAS	Drugs Prevention Advisory Service
DRTF	Disability Rights Task Force
EC	European Community
ECCO	Extra-Curricular Creative Opportunities
ECHR	European Convention on Human Rights
EEC	European Economic Community (now the EU)
ELR	Exceptional leave to remain
ENHPS	European Network of Health Promoting Schools
ESC	English Sports Council
EU	The European Union
EYDP	Early Years Development plans
FE	Further Education
FSA	Foundation for Sport and the Arts
GCSE	General Certificate of Secondary Education
GEST	Grants for Education, Support and training
HA	Health Authority
HC	House Of Commons
HEA	The Health Education Agency
HEBS	Health Education Board for Scotland
HIV	Human Immunodeficiency Virus
HMSO	HM Stationery Office (former publisher of UK Government documents – now see SO)
HO	Home Office
HPW	Health Promotion Wales
ICRC	International Committee of the Red Cross
IS	Income Support
ISBN	International Standard Book Number
ISP	Internet Service Provider
IT	Information Technology
ITV	Independent Television
IWF	Internet Watch Foundation

JRF	Joseph Rowntree Foundation - a charitable trust which funds academic research	
JSA & JSA(IB)	Jobseeker's Allowance & JSA (income based)	
LAC	Looking After Children (specialist material published by DH)	
LCD	The Lord Chancellor's Department	
LEA	Local Education Authority	
LSA	Learning Support Assistant	
LTI	Life threatening and life limiting illness	
MAP	Management Action Plan	
MP	Member of Parliament	
NCB	National Children's Bureau	
NCIS	National Criminal Intelligence Service	
NDNS	National Diet and Nutrition Survey	
NESTA	National Endowment for Science, Technology and the Arts	
NGO	Non-Government Organisation	
NHS	National Health Service	
NI	Northern Ireland	
NJSP	National Junior Sports Programme	
NLCB	National Lotteries Charities Board	
NMGW	National Museums and Galleries of Wales	
NNBC	National Network of Breastfeeding Coordinators	
NPFA	National Playing Fields Association	
NPIC	National Play Information Centre	
NSPCC	National Society for the Prevention of Cruelty to Children	
NVQ	National Vocational Qualification	
NWCAT	North Wales Child Abuse Tribunal	
NWCCET	North Wales Child Care Examination Team	
OFSTED	Office for Standards in Education (the school inspection authority for England and Wales	
OHCHR	Office of the UN High Commissioner for Refugees	
OSCI	Out of School Childcare Initiative	
PACE	The Police and Criminal Evidence Act	
PAFT	Policy Appraisal and Fair Treatment	
PE	Physical education	
PEAG	Pre-School Education Advisory Group	
PPG	Planning Policy Guidance	
PSI	Promoting Social Inclusion	
QCA	Qualifications and Curriculum Authority	
ROM	Read only memory	
RSAC	Recreational Software Advisory Council	
SACHR	The Standing Advisory Commission for Human Rights (in NI)	
SCEC	Scottish Community Education Council	

SEN		Special educational needs
SGCE		Steering Group on Child Evidence
SIAAA		Scottish Initiative on Attendance, Absence and Attainment
SID		Sudden Infant death (also known as cot death)
SO		Stationery Office, publisher of UK Government documents
SOEID		Scottish Office Education and Industry Department
SOHD		Scottish Office Home Department
SSC		Scottish Sports Council
SSD		Social services departments (of local authorities)
SSI		The Social Services Inspectorate (in England)
SSIW		The Social Services Inspectorate for Wales
STC		Secure Training Centre
STEP		Scottish traveller Education Programme
STOP		Joint Action on Combating Child Sex Exploitation and the Sexual Trafficking of Persons - the STOP programme
TCC		The Children's Channel
TEC		Training and Education Council
TSA		Trust for the Study of Adolescence
TSN		Targeting Social Need
UCM		Unaccompanied Children's Module
UK		United Kingdom
UN		United Nations
UNCRC		United Nations Convention on the Rights of the Child
UNECE		United Nations Economic Commission for Europe
UNHCR		UN High Commissioner for Refugees
UNICEF		United Nations Children's Fund
USA		United States of America
WFTC		Working Families Tax Credit
WHO		World Health Organisation
WLGA		Welsh Local Government Association
WO		Welsh Office
YPHN		Young People's Health Network

E **GLOSSARY**